mCommerce Security: A Beginner's Guide

KAPIL RAINA
ANURAG HARSH

McGraw-Hill/Osborne

New York   Chicago   San Francisco
Lisbon   London   Madrid   Mexico City
Milan   New Delhi   San Juan
Seoul   Singapore   Sydney   Toronto

McGraw-Hill/Osborne
2600 Tenth Street
Berkeley, California 94710
U.S.A.

To arrange bulk purchase discounts for sales promotions, premiums, or fund-raisers, please contact McGraw-Hill/Osborne at the above address. For information on translations or book distributors outside the U.S.A., please see the International Contact Information page immediately following the index of this book.

mCommerce Security: A Beginner's Guide

1234567890 CUS CUS 01987654321

ISBN 0-07-219460-X

Publisher
   Brandon A. Nordin
Vice President & Associate Publisher
   Scott Rogers
Acquisitions Editor
   Jane K. Brownlow
Project Editor
   LeeAnn Pickrell
Acquisitions Coordinator
   Emma Acker
Technical Editor
   Gus Rashid
Copy Editor
   Bart Reed

Proofreader
   Susie Elkind
Indexer
   David Heiret
Computer Designers
   Jean Butterfield, Lauren McCarthy
Illustrators
   Michael Mueller, Lyssa Wald
Series Design
   Peter F. Hancik
Cover Series Design
   Amparo Del Rio

This book was composed with Corel VENTURA™ Publisher.

To Amrita, for her patience and support throughout the long hours spent on this project and without whom I would have not been able to undertake such a feat. To my parents, who have always encouraged and supported me to write. To Priya, who has always helped me keep things in perspective and who has already started a brilliant career with her own publications. And to Papa-ji, with whom I wish could have shared this milestone.

—*Kapil Raina*

To my dear wife Malvika, who put up with a lot of long hours and lost time and who remained a pillar of strength for me throughout this project. Her love, support, and encouragement keep me going. To my parents, who made me the person I am by setting goals for me and making me learn from their mistakes, others' mistakes, and my own mistakes. To Siddarth, Ravi-Papa, Tirthy-Ma, Badi Mummy and Daddy, who have always shown a sense of pride in all my endeavors. To dada-ji and dadi, who continue to be a source of spiritual support for me. To Cider, Dox, King, and Jojo. And lastly, but most importantly, to my Guru-ji, Shri Chandrakant Apte, under whose tutelage, I learned the value of perseverance, discipline, and practice.

—*Anurag Harsh*

About the Authors

Kapil Raina, CISSP   Kapil Raina, a security technologies expert, has years of experience in architecting and implementing complex security projects for multinational corporations. At VeriSign, Inc., he is responsible for strategic partner solutions. In this position, Mr. Raina identifies key emerging technologies and develops them into marketable solutions. In previous positions for such globally recognized companies such as Lucent Technologies and Applied Materials, Mr. Raina developed various Internet technologies and consulted on a range of computer and physical security issues. A renowned speaker, Mr. Raina has spoken at companies and conferences around the world, including the Vanguard IT Security Conference, the Frost and Sullivan IT Conference, British Telecom (U.K.), and KPN Telecom (Netherlands), among others. Mr. Raina holds the prestigious CISSP certification from the ISC2, an internationally recognized organization for security professionals. Mr. Raina can be reached via email at **krprojects@hotmail.com**.

Anurag Harsh   Anurag Harsh has been quoted by IBM as having implemented "one of the largest and most technologically sophisticated commerce sites in India." With over a decade of global experience in technology management and implementation with top-tier companies in Europe and the U.S., Mr. Harsh is currently the Chief Technology Officer of FrequencyM, a boutique San Francisco–based consultancy firm through which he has done cutting-edge work implementing many niche technology solutions. Previously, Mr. Harsh headed the West Coast consulting and professional services division for Plaut-AG, an international management-consulting firm with a global presence of 34 subsidiaries in 18 countries. In this position, Mr. Harsh managed large-scale mobile and ebusiness projects and also led panel discussions at leading technology conferences. He holds degrees and certificates from the University of Sheffield in England and has six certificates of excellence from Microsoft Corporation. Mr. Harsh has also been a technology broadcaster for the BBC in London and performs Indian vocal classical music. He now lives in the San Francisco Bay Area and can be reached via email at **ahprojects@yahoo.com**.

CONTENTS

FOREWORD

m*Commerce Security: A Beginner's Guide* is the first and currently only book of its kind that addresses a key factor governing all mobile commerce transactions—security. The book discusses those aspects of mobile commerce in which security plays a key role. It is very well written in terms of covering all aspects of security within the mCommerce space, including PKI and digital signatures. *mCommerce Security: A Beginner's Guide* offers the readers a thorough discussion of most major industries and verticals touched by mCommerce and highlights specific security issues concerning each. Many chapters contain a "Message for the IT Manager" section that adds focus to the content, educating the technical manager on cutting-edge techniques to use to secure their mCommerce implementations. The case studies provide real-life examples of the security behind complex mCommerce architectures, both from a technical as well as a business point of view.

All in all, a very enjoyable read for all mobile enthusiasts!"

Naveen Dhar
Vice-President of Marketing and Business Development
Mobility Network Systems
www.mobilitynetworks.com

ACKNOWLEDGMENTS

When we look back over the time spent writing this book, we realize the importance of our colleagues, contacts, and friends—without whom this book would simply not have been possible. Our sincere thanks go to

- Aroop Zutshi, Senior Partner and President Asia-Pacific at Frost and Sullivan, for providing valuable guidance in the design and implementation of the book.

- Gus Rashid, Co-Founder and Chief Technology Officer of Salsa Systems, for reviewing each chapter page-by-page and providing valuable comments and direction at all stages.

- Ken Beames, VP of Information Security at Chase/JP Morgan, for his help with quotations and executive review.

- Michael Picard, VP of Solutions at BitGroup (Ex-VP of eBusiness at Plaut-AG), for helping us with cutting-edge research material for the project.

- Naveen Dhar, VP of Marketing and Business Development at Mobility Networks, for providing us an insight into next-generation wireless networking technologies.

- McGraw-Hill/Osborne: Jane Brownlow for overseeing the project and giving us crucial executive feedback; Emma Acker for being an absolute delight to work with; Bart Reed for being the fastest copy editor on the West Coast, and a special thanks to LeeAnn Pickrell for being the most conscientious project editor on the West Coast and without whose help this book would simply not have been published! We realize that there are many more at McGraw-Hill/ Osborne whose efforts have made this book possible, and we thank each one of them.

- Philippe Erwin, VP of Interactive Entertainment at Warner Brothers, for helping us define new business models within interactive commerce and for being a source of inspiration.

- Rajeev Tipnis, Co-Founder and Chief Scientist of Netmorf for providing very good insight into the latest mCommerce technologies and their underlying security principles, especially in terms of his product Sitemorfer.

- Ravi Tickoo, Principal Engineer at Avici Systems, for his direction.

- Rik Brar, CTO of Xavient Technologies, for giving us the opportunity to implement world-class hands-on solutions.

INTRODUCTION

In a meeting a few months back with some executives in Asia, we were told that there is no need to worry about security in mobile applications. Let the mobile infrastructure be rolled out first, and then worry about security, they said. This remark eerily reminded us of how the WWW (a.k.a. Web Wild West) was embraced by network professionals with no thought to security. After a number of highly visible attacks, everyone came out as a proponent of strong Internet security. By then, of course, billions of dollars of real and potential revenue had been lost; reputations had been tarnished; and, perhaps fortunate for those of us in the field, demand for computer security professionals soared.

Morgan Stanley Dean Witter has called the mobile Internet the most radical development since Marconi invented wireless telegraphic radio communication in 1894. Indeed, it has been predicted the mobile commerce, or mCommerce, world will grow by 2004 to a whopping $20 billion in the U.S. alone, with each user spending an average of $75 per month on mCommerce transactions, and wireless carriers earning anywhere between $624 million to $1 billion in mCommerce service revenues. In line with these estimates are the promises of security threats. Whether you spend your time fighting off the rumors and bad press or focusing on your core business of making money through mCommerce will largely depend on how prepared you are. By addressing some of the security issues in mCommerce early on, most organizations can build into their mCommerce plans a good security model and protect themselves from a lot of pain later on. It is with this in mind that we started to write this book.

One tricky aspect about writing a technology book, especially one centered on the cutting-edge area of mobile commerce, is that by the time the ink is dry, the information is old. It is with this perspective that we have designed this book to highlight the issues and create action plans that could serve as a reference point even as the technologies evolve or change. The focus on applications and industries versus technology components allows this book to become a blueprint for creating a secure mCommerce strategy.

The difficult aspect of writing about mobile technology is that the subject matter is very broad. Keeping this in mind, we centered our discussions around the topic of mobile commerce, or mCommerce. Broadly defined, mCommerce involves transactions that have financial or other intangible values over a mobile device. We focused on mobile devices in general, rather than just on mobile phones, since the adoption rates for various types of mobile devices vary greatly throughout the world.

WHO SHOULD READ THIS BOOK

We have designed this book to address two main audiences: IT managers or business professionals who need this information to make critical business decisions; and IT professionals who need to understand some level of detail about security. Other audiences, such as university students and researchers, nontechnology professionals, and consultants, will all benefit as the information has been given in an educational manner with plenty of case studies and pointers to leverage best practices in the field.

WHAT THIS BOOK COVERS

Although this book could be used to design hacking strategies for mobile devices, the intent was to create an awareness for businesses and individuals to create a secure mCommerce infrastructure plan. The book has specific implementation instructions where readers can learn to recognize the time-and cost-saving benefits of secured mCommerce applications through comprehensive real-life case studies. It also boasts a special "Message for the IT Manager" section that highlights the key points to remember when implementing or thinking about security for any mobile implementation. The book discusses how security comes into play when implementing and administering short-range mobile networks, such as Wi-fi and Bluetooth, and highlights aspects of these networks as has not been done before. It also previews the security of future mobile applications—such as 3G/4G networks and wearable computers.

The Basics

The first five chapters lay the foundation for the book, discussing mCommerce transactions, their building blocks, the technology landscape, and the cutting-edge technical knowledge required to understand and address security threats within each of these building blocks. The reader is also introduced to the differences and similarities between mobile and wired security. The security concepts introduced in this part of the book form the supporting layer for all applications and industries discussed in the later chapters.

Chapter 1

Everything must start at the beginning. In order to understand mCommerce security, it is necessary to have a good understanding of the way people fulfill their needs in a commerce-enabled, mobile, pervasive-computing world and how businesses create new and effective services to generate revenue and add value to people's lives. This chapter discusses the market, scope, and definition of mCommerce as related to security. The opportunities afforded by mCommerce are enabled through mobile security in terms of new and upcoming business models as well as new revenue streams and the growing competition over customer ownership. The chapter then goes on to discuss the functional foundation that supports all mCommerce applications and, therefore, creates a need for securing mobile transactions.

Chapter 2

mCommerce data services exist in two primary market segments: vertical and horizontal. Vertical markets refer to industry-specific services and applications customized for those particular industries. Horizontal markets refer to applications and services with a common utility across many industries with the purpose of serving the mass consumer market. This chapter discusses within the context of these markets, the basic building blocks for understanding mCommerce applications as well as their value propositions and services landscape.

Chapter 3

Just as you need to understand the fundamentals of mCommerce applications, you will need to learn about the basics of mobile security as well. This chapter focuses on establishing some basic building blocks for mobile security for the purposes of understanding the impact of security on mCommerce.

Chapter 4

The extra challenge mobile devices add to the security mix is that the usual tools to mitigate threats in the security world cannot necessarily be applied to the mobile world. Because the wireless industry is fairly old relative to the world of the commercial Internet, there are many legacy items to struggle with. Furthermore, the nature of the mobile devices themselves require that they be portable and yet power efficient. Thus, we must deal with many physical constraints on the devices. All of these concerns push us to come up with new and innovative solutions for mobile device security. This chapter compares some of the high-level, general differences between wired world security and the mobile world, so that we can use the lessons we have learned from the wired world and, to the extent possible, apply them to the wireless world.

Chapter 5

Before diving into the security aspects of each application, service, and vertical from Chapter 6 onwards, it is important to gain an understanding of the types of mobile networks and the infrastructure that supports the world of mobile applications. If you are entering the world of mobile networks for the first time, you might find it full of discrepancies in the legacy terminology used to describe the networks. However, all you really have to understand is how the architectures, technologies, devices, and networks stand with respect to each other and what the underlying concepts behind mobile communications really are. Therefore, this chapter talks about the current and future wireless networks, their evolution, their specialties, and the types of applications and devices they support.

Application Categories

Chapters 6 to 8 discuss all aspects of security within key mCommerce horizontals, such as commerce (including payment mechanisms), communications, and information delivery applications. These chapters discuss security risks and loopholes from the business as well as consumer point of view. After reading these chapters, businesses should be able to improve and secure the commerce, information, and communications services they offer to their customers.

Chapter 6

This chapter discusses the security behind advertising, trading, and banking applications, as well as the credit card industry. This chapter covers the basic areas of security for these applications, such as privacy, integrity, secrecy, and nonrepudiation. We discuss how privacy for mobile advertising, trading, and banking generally centers on the physical movements and activities of individuals; integrity ensures that the data has not been modified in transit; secrecy involves ensuring transactions are not seen by malicious parties; and nonrepudiation is similar to the wired or physical world in that we must prove with reasonable effort that a particular party has willfully conducted a particular transaction.

Chapter 7

This chapter discusses the security behind information delivery applications. By examining service provider, content-based, and WASP-based information delivery models and critiquing how security comes into play within each and by noting some key areas of security concern, including viruses and administrator access, you can avoid being "stung" by WASPs. We also discuss the security flaws in common mobile information servers, such as IBM and Oracle. The chapter then examines the security behind some common examples of applications in the information space, such as stock quotes, news headlines, navigation and traffic updates, and location-based technologies. The case study at the end of the chapter discusses how security can be configured while implementing a mobile information delivery portal using IBM and Tivoli technologies.

Chapter 8

Customer Relationship Management (CRM) and Sales Force Automation (SFA) are two of the hottest areas in the mCommerce space. Both these applications allow organizations quicker and easier access to data as the sales and support forces interact with the customers. This chapter discusses the challenges of opening up confidential customer data to the mobile sales force and shuttling this data around the wireless airwaves without compromising security. Because communication is a key aspect of the CRM process, this chapter discusses Instant Messaging (IM) and Short Messaging System (SMS) applications, both of which, when used in conjunction with CRM and SFA applications, greatly enhance the end user's experience. It highlights the security issues concerning both IM and SMS applications, especially since they can circumvent well-designed and guarded firewalls as well as other wired security infrastructure.

Vertical Industries

Chapters 9 to 11 discuss the security risks, threats, and the solutions for mobile transactions within key industry verticals, such as retail, banking and finance; travel, manufacturing, and distribution; healthcare, public services, and hospitality; as well as in entertainment, defense and the military.

Chapter 9

Given the magnitude of mistakes in IT architecture, the financial industry has had some of the most stringent backup and security requirements. The mobile sector of the financial industry has led to an additional set of security issues. This chapter highlights the various areas of security risk within this industry and recommends strategies to mitigate such risks. This chapter also discusses other key verticals, namely the retail, travel, manufacturing, and distribution industries. The security within most of these verticals is addressed in terms of middleware security, data-level security, and data-storage security. The case study at the end of the chapter provides a detailed discussion of the procedures a large online bookstore followed to extend its reach to mobile consumers. The case study highlights the various layers of security within the architecture, namely front-end, back-end, server-level, and application-level security.

Chapter 10

This chapter covers security within the healthcare, public services, and hospitality industries. The Health Insurance Portability and Accountability Act mandates the integrity, availability, and confidentiality of medical records and information to protect patients' rights and privacy. Biometric devices, which authenticate an individual's identity based on something physically unique about a person, have helped healthcare companies comply with HIPAA regulations for privacy and security. Other healthcare applications are discussed along with their security implications. The public sector uses mobile technology to protect police officers by providing them with sufficient information in real-time at the point of conflict. Police departments and other law enforcement agencies have been using mobile technology to check up on criminals and suspects in the field, issue electronic citations, query multiple databases, such as those of the state and federal governments, automatically run license plate checks through motor vehicle databases straight from their handheld devices, and perform many other functions that greatly improve performance and speed. Each of these functions' security implications are discussed in this chapter. We also highlight the privacy and security issues concerning mCommerce use within the hospitality and gambling industry, mainly for using wireless services to generate revenue and make gambling easier. The chapter ends with a real-life case study of a Rochester, New York–based health insurance company that has implemented a secure mobile solution to provide its authorized physicians with detailed medical information and HMO guidelines.

Chapter 11

This chapter discusses the security issues within the final two verticals: entertainment and the military. According to a study released by the consulting firm Strategic Analytics, the mobile gaming experience is expected to be worth $5 billion, with over 100 million players by 2006. The entire mobile entertainment industry is based on a fundamentally secure infrastructure because many of the revenue opportunities are based on reoccurring revenue from gaming. This chapter discusses the security issues involved with the use of mobile platforms for gaming, the privacy guideline boundaries, and legal issues concerning the use of mobile devices by underage consumers. We also talk about the major security issues behind the burgeoning adult mobile commerce industry, an industry already well known for fraud violations in the wired web sector. This chapter also discusses how to implement a secure mobile game using Nokia's Mobile Entertainment Platform. Following the September 11th terrorist attacks on New York City and Washington DC, security has become one of the most important issues to national defense officials and along with that a growing concern about cyberterrorism. Because much defense technology is mobile, this raises some serious questions regarding the nature of mobile technologies being used in our military and government security agencies. In this chapter, we discuss the security behind the use of mobile technologies for information analysis and/or cost savings. These security principles can also extend to agencies of countries outside of the United States such as England and the European Union.

Other Applications and Bluetooth

Chapters 12 and 13 highlight the security implictions of 802.11 networks, discuss how security comes into play within environmental and remote device monitoring scenarios, such as those involved in vending management and usage, and give a detailed overview of the cutting-edge security aspects of Bluetooth.

Chapter 12

The latest fad in the mobile world is 802.11x wireless technology. This new set of standards allows for the creation of a wireless LAN. We will address, at a high level, how these networks work and some key issues surrounding them. The chapter also covers mCommerce applications for environmental and energy management, which can result in lower costs and improved efficiencies. Traditional technologies, such as vending machines, can use new wireless capabilities to conduct mCommerce transactions and/or maintain inventory and distribution. You will see that some of these applications have more security uses than others. The fundamental principal in security is that damage to an application due to a security breach is proportional to the value of the data/ platform being attacked. This chapter discusses all such security concepts within these applications.

Chapter 13

Bluetooth can be viewed as a technology and as an application. The idea of Bluetooth freeing us from cables and wires and yet keeping all our electronic devices in perfect synchronization is indeed inspiring. New applications can be developed because a device no longer has to be everything to everyone. The beginning stages of this concept will be influenced quite heavily by specific technology implementations. We explain Bluetooth basics and then drill down into its security implications. If you are building Bluetooth into your strategy, then this chapter is essential.

The Future of mCommerce Security

The final chapter highlights and discusses the future of mCommerce security.

Chapter 14

This chapter addresses some of the key trends in next generation mCommerce technologies and applications and their possible security implications. By keeping abreast of future technologies, you are better suited to address security implications as they arise. We discuss the security behind the "always-on" mobile networks, new and potential viruses and worms for mCommerce applications, the possibility of every future mobile device having a personal proxy, the security behind roaming data, and also the management of digital rights. We take you into the dream world of 4G networks that promise mind-boggling speeds of 20Mbps. These networks promise virtual mobile navigation, uses within tele-medicine and also in tele-geoprocessing. Each of these sectors involves a high level of security for them to function at all. We also discuss wearable computers running on wireless personal area networks. From a corporate security and risk-management perspective, wearable computing is a complex issue to manage. The future of wireless LANs, WASPs, biometrics, PKI, mobile payment strategies, smartcard roles, barcode transactions, use of mini-mobile servers (such as the WebCamSIM designed by Microsoft to run on a GSM card), intrusion detection systems, and next-generation mobile security infrastructures are discussed in detail in this chapter.

CHAPTER 1

mCommerce Overview

"Pervasive computing is a billion people interacting with a million e-businesses with a trillion intelligent devices interconnected."

—*Lou Gerstner, CEO, IBM*

The world is in everyone's pocket. The major inhibitor of mCommerce is the perception that it is not safe. However, once consumers buy something using their mobile devices, in all likelihood, they will do it again, thus expanding the mobile market. To attract consumers, vendors must make it more secure to make a purchase over a mobile device. This will require cooperation from various software providers, merchants, and carriers. Security concerns about payment processing may also deter a consumer from entering credit card numbers on a mobile phone. Instead, an existing mobile security feature might offer more comfort by holding information about the end user such as name, address, preferred billing address, shipping address, and credit card number.

Current lack of consumer confidence in mobile network security poses one of the greatest challenges to the growth of mCommerce. The carriers, hardware and software providers, security providers, and merchants must ensure data confidentiality—only the company and the end users must have access to the information being exchanged—and secure authentication, to ensure that the consumers they are dealing with are actually who they claim to be and vice versa.

In order to understand mCommerce security, it is necessary to have a good understanding of the way people fulfill their needs in a commerce-enabled, mobile, pervasive-computing world and how businesses create new and effective services to generate revenue and add value to people's lives. This chapter discusses the market, scope, and definition of mCommerce as related to security. The opportunities afforded by mCommerce are enabled through mobile security in terms of new and upcoming business models as well as new revenue streams and the growing competition over customer ownership. The chapter then goes on to discuss the functional foundation that supports all mCommerce applications and, therefore, creates a need for securing mobile transactions. It is necessary to understand what this foundation is, why it is the way it is, and how almost all mCommerce applications can be categorized within the various functional blocks of the foundation. The discussion on security that follows in the proceeding chapters can be better understood after gaining an understanding of the functional world of mCommerce applications and their supporting parameters.

mCommerce is an enabling technology for delivering greater business volume, customer loyalty, and support for urgent transactions such as travel changes and stock transactions. mCommerce applications won't work if they simply mirror the e-commerce applications that are available on web sites. They must offer the correct format for a specific device, plus secure access and intuitive navigation.

> "The mobile Internet is the most radical development since Marconi invented wireless telegraphic radio communication in 1894. A confluence of technical leaps in devices, networks, and applications is setting the stage for wireless to become the ultimate media."
>
> *—Morgan Stanley Dean Witter, The Mobile Internet Report,*
> *October 2000*

Imagine being able to make last-minute flight changes from your mobile phone as you race through an airport terminal. Or using your pager to sell a stock the instant it reaches a certain price. Or stepping out into the hallway during a meeting break and using your personal digital assistant (PDA) to order a book your customer said he'd like to read.

Many of us already use mobile devices to transact business, work more efficiently, and make our lives easier. GartnerGroup predicts that by the year 2003, there will be more wireless devices than Internet-connected PCs.[1]

While the wireless web market is in its infancy, these figures indicate that mobile commerce—mCommerce—is about to explode.

---

[1]   S. Hayward et al. "Beyond the Internet: The 'Supranet.'" GartnerGroup. 11 September 2000.

To paraphrase Woody Allen, in the early days of the Web, 90 percent of success was just showing up. Web sites were static, transaction-free "publishing" sites that simply offered information. Then e-commerce emerged, expectations rose, and a web site's user experience became a competitive differentiator. Customers wanted reliable web site content that met their personal needs with convenience and simplicity.

Today's successful e-commerce companies have met those challenges with rich web sites that feature comprehensive offerings, fast transactions, and compelling value. Now the challenge is to bring that same formula for success to the world of mCommerce, leveraging new generations of wireless devices such as web phones, connected PDAs, and pagers.

mCommerce offers an immediate business value for corporations that want to leverage investments in back-end e-business integration through the one-to-one connection of wireless devices. However, to provide true business value, companies need to ensure that their mCommerce strategies go far beyond simply scraping content from a web site meant to be viewed and used on a laptop or PC monitor screen.

NOTE: Mobile strategies must reflect the unique size and space requirements of specific wireless devices to provide greater business value to mobile workers, partners, and customers.

There are many reasons why enterprises are looking toward taking their business offerings to the next level—mCommerce:

▼ To increase their number of transactions and their rate of customer retention

■ To increase their service offering to customers

■ To help justify their subscription rates

■ To maintain their competitive edge

■ To build a one-to-one relationship with their customers

▲ To provide customers with an "always-on" application

SCOPE AND DEFINITION OF mCOMMERCE

An mCommerce user is anyone who accesses information from a mobile or wireless device or synchronizes information onto a mobile or wireless device thereby initiating a transaction from the mobile or wireless device across a wireless network (such as GSM, GPRS, TDMA, CDMA, PDC, PHS, Mobitex, Reflex, or UMTS). mCommerce users may view and interact with information that appears through SMS (Short Message Service), WAP (Wireless Application Protocol), or a standard HTML browser on a PDA, web-enabled mobile phone, or laptop computer connected to a mobile phone on a wireless network. The user must have some level of user-initiated interactivity with the information—that is, a transaction of some sort must take place. The scope of mCommerce includes transactions of products, services, and payments that occur across a wireless data platform, such as GPRS, SMS, HSCSD, UMTS, or just the basic 9.6 Kbps wireless network, as a result of some interaction with the subscriber. The definition includes voice-recognition services that interact with the user on the handset or with the Internet on the network in order to initiate or complete the transaction.

Some examples of mCommerce included in this definition are

▼ Paying a bill using a mobile phone or handheld device

■ Purchasing of products and services using a mobile phone or handheld device, such as:

    ■ Buying a drink from a vending machine using a mobile phone and charging it to the mobile phone bill

    ■ Using voice recognition on a mobile phone to buy a movie ticket (voice recognition to initiate the transaction on a wireless data network)

    ■ Buying an airline ticket using a handheld device and being invoiced by a travel agent

    ■ Paying for an MP3 file downloaded through a mobile phone or handheld device

    ■ Buying stocks using a mobile phone or handheld device and initiating a request to have the money transferred from a preconfigured bank account

- Browsing through books from an online bookstore on the PDA and then buying one

- Initiating and placing a purchase order on a handheld device or laptop computer over a wireless network linked to a supplier's intranet

▲ Completing mobile interactions, such as:

- A user's receiving a short message stating that he or she can get $10 off a product, or seeing a sign in a mall stating that he or she can get $10 off a product, with the user then proceeding to the store and purchasing the product using a mobile phone or the store's wireless point of sale terminal. (Short messaging service, or SMS, is generally limited to around 150 characters and is available in one-way form to the device from most digital cellular operators. Two-way SMS, which allows the handset itself to compose and send a message, is also available on some networks.)

- A user's receiving an alert notification from an online travel company, such as Travelocity or Expedia, about a new lower fare. The user has the option of responding to the alert by reserving and purchasing the advertised fare over the handset.

- A user's browsing through movie listings and other directory services and even buying a movie ticket and paying by credit card using the mobile phone.

OPPORTUNITIES

Is mCommerce the next vehicle to a brighter business future? This section discusses the various opportunities that have come up as a result of the sudden spike in mobile device usage.

Categories

mCommerce opportunities for companies can be divided into three main categories: those that allow companies to reach existing consumers through new and extended channels, such as mobile and wireless channels; those that allow companies to reach new consumers in new markets through new as well as existing channels; and those that allow companies to offer new and enhanced mCommerce applications and services that are unique to the wireless world.

Reaching Existing Consumers Through New and Extended Channels

Traditionally on the wired Web, most companies reach their customers by allowing them access through their personal computers. However, mobile commerce and wireless technology offers a new way for companies to reach existing consumers by allowing these users the ability to configure applications such as SMS messages, news clips, stock quote alerts, and weather forecasts on their PC-based portals for use on their mobile handsets. This results in multifold use of a given portal network. mCommerce also allows companies the opportunity to offer their existing customers the ability to purchase items and check product availability, prices, and delivery times directly from their handheld PDAs.

Reaching New Consumers in Recently Opened Markets Through New and Existing Channels

In many Scandinavian countries as well as in the rest of Europe, the penetration of mobile phones, as compared to that in the U.S., is higher than that of wired PCs (see Figure 1-1). This, therefore, opens up a new market for companies to exploit because they can now offer mCommerce services in addition to wired services to potential consumers they could not otherwise reach while their business model was purely PC-based (PCs implying personal computers and laptops that are not using a wireless link to access information).

Offering New and Enhanced mCommerce Applications and Services

As we discuss in Chapter 7, many mCommerce services being offered today are simply reformatted from the PC environment (for example, stock quotes and news clips), a concept known as *screen-scraping*. We

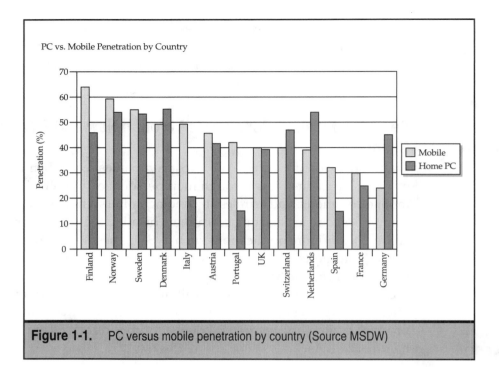

Figure 1-1.   PC versus mobile penetration by country (Source MSDW)

also discuss why screen-scraping is not the right solution for a robust mCommerce architecture, thus requiring companies to invent novel methods for conducting wireless business. mCommerce has, therefore, opened up a whole new era of new wireless application development in areas such as *location-based services*. For example, a street retailer could offer anyone walking past its retail outlet a flash-alert mobile coupon on the consumer's PDA or WAP phone. The key success factors of a new mCommerce application include the application's sensitivity to time (for applications such as online auction updates, stock quotes, priority e-mail), its sensitivity to location (for applications that provide access to directory listings from a PDA or mobile coupons that flash on a consumer's PDA when the person comes within a certain distance of a retail outlet), and its ability to offer quick and easy transaction query services. Applications that force a user to initiate long product searches or other complex inquiries on a WAP phone screen are inconvenient. However, simple transactions involving a yes or no answer, a voice command, or a number-key entry for tasks such as booking a cinema or flight ticket or checking seat availability are very suitable for the mobile consumer. An example of this type of application is the American Airlines Flight Information System, which can be accessed over a mobile phone and is mostly voice activated.

Sources of mCommerce Revenue

mCommerce revenue could ultimately come from multiple channels such as eCommerce portals, short messaging services (SMS), customer introduction fees, advertising based revenue, subscription based fees, and revenue sharing between wireless network operators. Each of these revenue channels are highlighted next.

Revenue from eCommerce Portals

Many eCommerce portals use mCommerce companies and Wireless Application Service Providers (WASPs) that charge them a hosting fee and commission for each customer sent. In exchange for this premium, the mCommerce companies provide wireless services to the eCommerce portal or wired company. This is analogous to the arrangement on wired portals.

Revenue from Short Messaging Services (SMS)

SMS is a major revenue source for wired portals, enabling them to capitalize on the mCommerce market through a reward model, whereby a portal receives a share of the usage revenue it generates for the network operator.

Revenue Accrued from Introducing New Customers

In the early years of wired eCommerce, providers such as Amazon and Buy.com paid introduction fees to its portal distribution partners for every customer that came to their site through their affiliate partners. In fact, most online retailers now offer such an affiliate incentive to their referring partners. It is expected that this process will be repeated in the mCommerce industry where mobile retailers and mCommerce portals may be able to generate some revenue by negotiating a "customer introduction fee" for each new customer they introduce to their offline and online commerce partners.

Revenue from Wireless Advertising

We discuss the various avenues of wireless advertising along with the underlying security implications in Chapter 6. Because of real-estate constraints of a small WAP-phone or PDA screen, wireless advertising may not offer the same level of revenue opportunity that some optimists think it will. One possible exception could be directory listing services, where an mCommerce portal could charge additional fees to its advertisers if it promotes their services to its mobile customers. Other revenue generation models, such as wireless affiliate advertising, are also discussed in Chapter 6.

Revenue from Subscription-Based Services

Currently, most mobile content accessible from handheld devices is of a trivial nature, offering news alerts, stock quotes, weather forecasts, directory listings, and other minor user-initiated transactions. However, new killer applications are being developed that offer valuable services for which users may want to pay. Chapters 6, 7, and 8 discuss value-added applications that open the door to possible recurring revenue generation.

Revenue-Sharing Between Wireless Network Operators

In the wired world, Internet Service Providers (ISPs) negotiate revenue-sharing agreements with network operators and carriers to receive a portion of the revenue generated through the use of the network. In a similar manner, WASPs could also generate revenue for themselves by working out deals with the carriers.

The Battle for Customer Ownership?

For now, the customer gateway controllers are the network operators and carriers such as AT&T and Sprint. While on the one hand, these network operators and carriers have a fighting chance of keeping their customers due to their historical market position, it is possible, on the other hand, that they may not win if they go it alone. To maintain their consumer advantage, the carriers will have to transform themselves from network-centered companies into consumer-centered service companies. This can be accomplished through mergers, equity investments, joint ventures, partnerships, alliances, and spin-offs with more customer-centric companies. The most important element to winning and keeping customers is to keep them enthused. Thus, although the customer acquisition war will be waged on many fronts, the most important strategy will be to sell consumers and corporations services that are useful to them and those that they enjoy using and even paying for. For example, by controlling location information, carriers can maintain control of customer access. The carrier can then create value by providing companies with their customers' location information.

It is also worth noting a major difference between the dial-up Wireless Application Protocol (WAP) connection of today and the always-on WAP gateway that comes with General Packet Radio Services (GPRSs), which are discussed in Chapter 5. Unlike with a WAP dial-up connection, carriers can be positioned to tie the GPRS packet network to the phone within a subscriber's home country, in a manner similar to that for voice services, thus forcing the subscriber through a carrier's gateway without giving the subscriber the option of using another service provider unless the subscriber dialed out using a circuit-switched call, which would not be cheap. When it comes to circuit-switched dial-up connections (the way to get WAP access today), in most cases the carriers are providing the gateway services to their customers mainly because they are the first to market with value-added services. There are other ways for carriers to win customers, such as by allowing customers to dial into their gateway at a reduced rate (or for points, discounts on land lines, and so on) or even by hard-coding the gateway configuration into the handset.

Always-on connectivity enabled by the rollout of GPRS (discussed further in Chapter 5) should boost the operator's position as service provider and "customer owner" significantly. Most subscribers commit to an annual contract when purchasing a new phone, and with GPRS, the mobile device will be always on, defaulting to the carrier's gateway. This gateway is generally controlled by the carrier, which also ends up controlling most customer-specific information such as the sites to which the user is going. This provides a lot of intelligence to the carrier as it tries to build its own service offerings (an AOL-style advantage of being both an ISP and a content provider). Moreover, as most WAP phones today do not support cookies, content providers are therefore unable to provide any personalization. Because carriers control the gateway and unique user information such as the mobile number and phone ID, they are best positioned to customize and personalize content. At least until the next generation of phones that support cookies show up, the carriers can use this to their advantage to maintain their handle on the mobile customer. However, with the rapidly changing business models of today, the tension between the existing ISPs and portals and the mobile network operators and carriers will gradually increase.

The Emerging mCommerce Lifestyle

Vincent has a graph of his investment portfolio on his PDA. He can conduct trades simply by changing the graph's shape with his stylus. A simple change triggers a bunch of transactions within a disparate set of remote servers run by network operators, brokers, banks, and retailers. Mary has set an invisible software agent that is on the lookout for that 1960 Mustang convertible she so desires. She is also bidding on a piece of land in San Antonio, where she plans to build a house.

Vincent is contained, yet mobile, living a life governed by time, location, and goal—that is, mCommerce. There are many such Vincents in Japan where users of NTT DoCoMo's i-Mode wireless Internet service have access to shopping, trading, banking, and airline reservations in addition to information services such as listings as well as entertainment. Another good, real-life example of location-based mCommerce advertising is a mall where subscribers can receive special offers from shops as they pass them. One such company is Spotcast, which has leased its technology to SmartTone and PeoplesTel in Singapore to allow users to get free "call minutes" in exchange for listening to a few seconds of advertising. Many new wireless affiliate networks have been set up through which wireless portals, service providers, and operators can drive merchant traffic to their wireless sites on a pay-for-results basis. Advertisers are trying to tie in geophysical information to determine how best to position sales strategies. For example, if a large number of Starbucks customers go to a bagel shop after buying their coffee, then perhaps Starbucks may consider selling bagels. The possibility of tapping into mCommerce to generate advertising revenue has created new and distinct mobile advertising models.

In the United States, PDAs are frequently being used for conducting trades and logging on to wireless brokerage services. Wireless banking is rapidly becoming a significant market worldwide for mobile consumers. In most cases, customers are now able to log in to their web banking accounts and register for wireless banking. For people to be able to see their own money instantly offers them an emotional, intimate relationship with their bank, thus serving as a good example of personalized mCommerce at play. IDC has forecast the growth of the mobile banking and finance market to reach $1311.1 million by 2005. In Europe, the situation is expected to be even more dramatic, attracting one-third of the European population into the wireless user-base. Special financial exchanges have been developed for the purpose of enabling mobile banking. Chapter 6 discusses the aforementioned areas of mobile banking and trading as well as wireless advertising and their security implications in further detail.

Most current news sites, such as CNN, Reuters, and BBC, have started offering services whereby users can configure their mobile device to receive news and information content from online news providers. The use of in-car location-based information services, such as On-Star and Mercedes Benz SOS Service, have increased. Here, the use of a Global Positing System (GPS) along with location-based mobile technology allows the service provider to assist customers by providing directions, maps, traffic information, and emergency roadside assistance services. These topics are further discussed in Chapter 7 along with the underlying security.

Messaging is perhaps the most widely used mobile technology. In Europe, for example, the short messaging system (SMS) has become quite popular with young people, who use their mobile phones to send messages to each other. Both instant messaging (IM) and SMS are now being used in conjunction with Customer Relationship

Management (CRM) and Sales force Automation (SFA) applications to greatly enhance the end user's experience. IDC estimates that by 2004 there will be 43 million wireless IM users. Companies are rapidly seizing the wireless Internet opportunity to elevate their sales force from lone representatives to powerful team players. If you are a business traveler, you will notice many salespeople nowadays depending on their PDAs for scheduling and contact management. These topics are all discussed in Chapter 8.

Shopping has already gained tremendous popularity on the wired Internet, and despite security issues and concerns from wireless end users, it is believed by analysts such as IDC that retail mCommerce over the wireless web will also be equally, if not more, popular, reaching a market size of $491.7 million dollars by 2005. However, the goods and services bought over the mobile Internet will be somewhat different from those purchased on the wired Internet. It is also likely that consumers might shop differently on the mobile Internet than over a wired connection. For example, the typical mobile consumer will not browse the mobile Internet looking for the ideal gift to buy; however, if they know exactly what they want, do not have access to a wired connection, and know they can make their purchases over their mobile device, then they might actually go ahead and do so. It is expected that time-sensitive, threshold purchases may also become a popular feature of mCommerce. For example, when a stock or airline ticket reaches a specific price, a notification is sent to a consumer's mobile device. The consumer can then have the option of buying the stock or ticket over that mobile device. In Japan, a user can receive an SMS displaying a discount coupon for a pair of jeans and then proceed to the store to purchase the jeans using his/her i-Mode phone. Department stores are increasingly using mobile devices for price management and inventory tracking. Wireless technologies are also ideal in the online food and grocery delivery business. These topics are discussed in detail in Chapter 9.

Given that travel has traditionally been a large area of consumer spending, another key area of growth is in the travel industry. Sabre Holdings, one of the most comprehensive travel processing systems in the U.S., now offers wireless services where customers can create, access, and change flight, car, and hotel reservations using WAP-enabled handheld devices. The company also makes its consumer Web site **www.travelocity.com** viewable on mobile devices. Most leading airline sites and online travel providers, such as Expedia, Worldspan, and Getthere.com, now offer wireless services (see Chapter 9).

Mobile technologies are also playing a key role in streamlining the processes and functions governing manufacturing and distribution. The task of automating part or all of a company's route sales process, making key information available anytime, anywhere—throughout the sales flow from the initial order through the load creation to delivery and adjustments at the customer site—has become a major driver of mCommerce technology use (see Chapter 9).

Wireless technology is also becoming an integral part of the healthcare field, enabling caregivers to review patient records and test results, access charge captures, enter diagnostic information during patient visits, and consult drug formularies, all without having to resort to a wired network connection. IDC has forecast the U.S. based mobile healthcare market to grow to $1966.6 million by 2005. Mobile technologies have also been instrumental in improving the efficiency of public service agencies especially within law enforcement and safety services. Police departments and other law enforcement agencies have been using mobile technology to check up on criminals and suspects in the field, issue electronic citations, query multiple databases, such as those at the state and federal level, automatically run license plate checks through DMV databases, and perform many other functions that greatly improve performance and speed. For a discussion of mCommerce usage and security within the healthcare and public services arenas, please refer to Chapter 10.

Mobile entertainment and gaming is also rapidly expanding into the mobile arena. Datamonitor recently estimated that four out of five mobile phone users will be playing mobile games by 2005. The advantage of mobile gaming is the market reach of mobile technology. Analysts estimate it took Nintendo 10 years to sell 100 million GameBoys, whereas four times as many mobiles phones are estimated to sell each year, forming a potential worldwide market of 950 million mobile subscribers. The mobile gaming experience is expected to be worth $5 billion with over 100 million players by 2006, according to a study released by consulting firm Strategic Analytics (see Chapter 11).

Short-range mobile networks such as Wi-fi and Bluetooth are increasingly penetrating our daily lives. Many airports, hotels, and restaurants are installing Wi-Fi access throughout their facilities. Starbucks has announced that each of its coffeehouses will provide Wi-Fi access for its customers. Wi-Fi is also working its way from the office into the home with Wi-Fi wireless home networks (for details see Chapters 12 and 13).

mCommerce is driven by distinct consumer forces. The consumer-payment model of mobile services is one such driving force. In the United States, both the user making calls and the one receiving calls pay for the communication; in Europe, however, only the call-making user pays for the charges incurred. The receiver does not pay anything, thus making this user more inclined to keep the cell phone on all the time. Prepaid cellular phones have also become very popular among young people, thus creating a personal mobile channel to a huge consumer market, many of whom may not be fixed Internet users.

eCommerce itself has become very popular, with all successful businesses migrating to the e-channel; mobile commerce simply extends that channel. mCommerce also becomes a logical brand-value-enhancement channel for the pure net players, such as Amazon.com, Yahoo, and Buy.com. France Telecom introduced dual-slot phones that accept smartcards (note that almost all credit cards in France are smartcards); hence, phones can process payments, thus becoming fully mCommerce-enabled, point-of-sale terminals.

Note that mCommerce is not just an extension of the Web to a PDA or cell phone. It has characteristics that differ from the traditional Internet models and thus demands a new look at the business-to-consumer (B2C) and business-to-business (B2B) models. mCommerce behavior is derived from cell phone use rather than from fixed-PC use, and cell phone systems follow neither B2C nor B2B models. Instead, they really are person-to-person systems.

THE FUNDAMENTAL FUNCTIONAL PLATFORM OF mCOMMERCE APPLICATIONS

Most mCommerce services are enabled for a five-pronged fundamental functional platform consisting of wireless messaging services, wireless web access services, voice-activated services, location-based services, and digital content services. We start by exploring how each of these services is used. In Chapter 2, we will go into detail about the many applications that are based on this functional platform.

Messaging Services

In the wired world, e-mail and messaging have become part and parcel of our daily lives. Some analysts believe that such messaging service offerings extended to mobile devices make them a candidate for being so-called killer apps. In the current corporate world, to be away from e-mail really means being out of the loop. Most sales personnel on the road connect their laptops to the Web primarily for one main purpose: to check e-mail. Mobile-to-mobile messaging is also popular in Europe (SMS for GSM phones) as well as in the United States (paging). SMS appeared on the wireless scene in 1991 in Europe. The European standard for digital wireless, now known as the Global System for Mobile Communications (GSM), included short messaging services from the outset. In Europe, for example, all e-mail sent to *<username>@service provider.co.uk>* is forwarded to the user's cell phone as a text message. The user's mobile mailbox can also pick up e-mail from other POP accounts. In North America, SMS was made available initially on digital wireless networks built by early pioneers such as BellSouth Mobility, PrimeCo, and Nextel, among others. Now Palm PDA users in the U.S. can send and receive e-mail using a wireless modem and can also run Yahoo! Instant Messenger (IM). In fact, it is not even necessary to have a wireless modem. For example, Palm PDAs fitted with PocketMail's Backflip device (which translates modem control characters into audio signals) act as modems that the user can hold against a telephone to access e-mail. SMS also provides a wide variety of information services, including weather reports, traffic information, entertainment information (for example, cinema, theater, and concerts), financial information (for example, stock quotes, exchange rates, banking, and brokerage services), and directory assistance.

There are some feature enhancements that would give a boost to current mobile e-mail systems:

▼ Improving the e-mail reply mechanism from the current cumbersome numeric key (even with predictive text entry) or letter-clicking method to perhaps a voice-recognition mechanism that converts spoken words to text.

■ Improving the means of handling attachments so that mobile e-mail doesn't resemble old-fashioned telegrams. Mobile e-mail, especially on cell phones, should provide the ability to view images and document attachments. On PDAs, the installed reader software does the job of opening a variety of file types. Perhaps cell phone manufacturers should preinstall similar readers in their phones, making them more intelligent, especially in receiving and reading popular file types.

▲ Offering the ability to forward mobile e-mail or propagate mobile content among user groups and individuals.

Web Access Services

IDC expects the wireless web access space to grow quickly in 2002 and to total $732 million in revenue by 2004. There are many players in this category. Typically, most are Wireless Application Service Providers or WASPs, analogous to wired ISPs. One such provider is GoAmerica whose wireless Internet service provides wireless access to virtually any Internet site, as well as branded content grouped into useful channels. The company also allows businesses and consumers to access wireless e-mail and information on corporate intranets. GoAmerica's web access services go through its network operations center (NOC). The NOC forms a bridge between Internet/intranet content and the wireless networks and the mobile handheld devices. Each handheld device comes with GoAmerica's browser (client) embedded in it. There are other web access providers similar to GoAmerica, such as OmniSky, Aether Systems, Outercurve Technologies, Openwave (previously Phone.com), Wireless Knowledge, InfoSpace and AvantGo. AvantGo, for example, offers a popular web access service that can format any web site for display on a mobile device screen. Content channels or sites can be added to the user's personal web site portfolio by selecting from the list of sites on AvantGo's menus, which include stock prices, news, flight information, and directory listings. In the PDA market, this service helps synchronize the user's desktop and PDA, keeping both devices updated. Users can automatically transfer their latest and greatest web sites, working files, contacts, and calendar events into their PDAs before leaving the office. On the corporate side, AvantGo goes directly to the database for user-specific data rather than targeting web sites. Microsoft's PocketPC ships with AvantGo's web browser in addition to Microsoft's own native Pocket Internet Explorer browser, the latter offering superior color and graphics content on mobile web pages, rescaling them to the PocketPC's device specifications. Palm.Net, on the other hand, offers web-clipping services for the entire Palm family of devices (supporting Palm OS 3.5 and higher). Although AvantGo reformats existing HTML resources to send information to web browsers, content can be sent to a mobile browser using a variety of other technologies, such as Wireless Markup Language (WML).

Voice Activated Services

The strength of a good mCommerce implementation lies in how well it deals with natural human behavior. Hence, AT&T, Lucent, Motorola, and IBM founded the VoiceXML standard with the intention of bringing voice control to web sites, enabling voice response paradigms to navigate web sites and general speech recognition interfaces. Voice-enabled mCommerce sites instantly target the mass market, expecting no special equipment or skills from the cell phone or PDA user. The Kelsey Group estimates that by 2005, in North America alone, about 45 million cell phone users will be using voice portals.

An example of a voice portal is etrieve, an mCommerce company that offers a monthly service whereby a corporate user can dial into a server and have their e-mail read over a phone. Mapquest.com also offers spoken driving directions as an added accompaniment to its graphic maps.

Limitations of Current Voice-Enabled mCommerce Methodologies

Currently, customers dialing into an automated voice-menu-driven phone system have to go through a series of complex commands and inputs to get to their goal. The "Please press 1 for…, 2 for…" approach is not the easiest one to follow, forcing the customer to remember the required option after listening to all of the options on the voice menu or more often than not repeating the menu choices. This system is not expected to work well for mCommerce.

A possible solution is a voice interface driven by predefined questions and comments. In such a system, mobile users might ask mCommerce services questions such as "What is my account balance?" or "When is the next showing of <*Moviename*> at <*Theatername*>?" mCommerce services can then recognize common voice inputs and respond to them accordingly. American Airlines's flight booking system offers such a voice-command option for basic services such as flight arrival and departure timings and other inquiries.

Location-Based Services

A key difference between regular eCommerce using a PC on a fixed line and mCommerce is that with mCommerce, vendors may have access to users' locations because the FCC issued a mandate requiring cellular, PCS, and SMR carriers to be able to locate their subscribers within 50 meters 67 percent of the time for emergency situations. The carriers could leverage this location information, providing it to mCommerce vendors and application service providers (ASPs). This could lead to a suite of valuable location-based applications and services such as for driving directions, finding and purchasing air tickets, booking a restaurant, or even making hotel reservations based on the location of the user.

The Risk to Privacy

It is possible using modern tracking technology to determine the precise location of a wireless handset whenever it is operational. It is also possible that such information may have to be made available to law enforcement agencies and emergency services organizations by the carriers. WASPs may also be able to receive location information from the carriers to enable them to target and enhance their products. Such types of data consolidation will undoubtedly present a serious risk to individual privacy, since its consolidation will provide hitherto unavailable specific information about the movements of a cell phone and hence its user. A handset's location information can be calculated using various methods, a few of which are described next.

Handset-Based Location   Handset-based location solutions incorporate a global positioning system receiver into the handset. The U.S. Government funds and operates a constellation of satellites known as GPS that transmit coded radio signals to the earth. At least three such satellites can be used to send information signals to a GPS receiver from which it can calculate a unit's position. A disadvantage of this system is that the receiver has to be in the line-of sight of the satellites and hence may not function properly in major city blocks or inside a building. A GPS-based solution may also involve a major upgrade of users' mobile handsets, which may possibly deter users from adopting this type of location tracking.

Network-Based Solution   In the case of network-based solutions, the handset's location information is calculated based on triangulation and other sophisticated calculations, similar to GPS. The solution makes use of the existing cellular infrastructure (towers, switching, and so on) and spectrum to calculate the location. However, because it is difficult to receive a good cellular signal from one tower, let alone three, the adoption of network-based solutions for location determination is slow. Some companies, such as U.S. Wireless, do base their calculations on just one cell site, however.

Future Solutions   Up until now, location information has been the monopoly of the carriers and network operators themselves. In the future, however, this may not be the case. Bluetooth, for example, can contribute to location determination in that a network of fixed devices may constantly communicate with mobile devices over a Bluetooth network or Wireless LAN. Using such a solution, a mobile device can request its own location relative to that of the fixed device because the fixed device already knows its location; the mobile device's location information can then be submitted by the fixed device either to the device itself or back to the carrier over a land-line connection. There are many other examples of location determination algorithms that are independent of carriers or network operators. The above is only one of them.

Figure 1-2 shows how the various location mechanisms interact to determine a handset's location-ID.

Digital Content Services

Just as Amazon.com was the torch bearer of online commerce with its book business, e-books is a key factor influencing the development of mCommerce. The ease of use of an electronic book, which can be read anywhere that a portable device can go, clearly helped create a market for e-books. The concept also offers the facility of being able to delete the completed e-book from the portable device as opposed to having to recycle an unwanted paper book through second-hand or charity book shops. E-books also paved a path for the sale of digital music to mobile consumers; where e-books go, e-music follows. Although

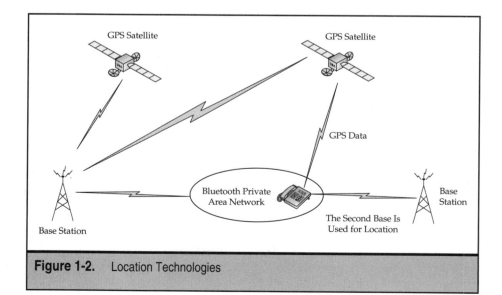

Figure 1-2.   Location Technologies

e-books are confined to the publishing industry, their effect is profound because they have persuaded many consumers to buy PDAs. Despite the low-bandwidth limitations of wireless networks, several technologies are in development that aim to offer video to the PDA consumer, enabling users to, for example, install ActiveSky's player on a PocketPC or Palm device or play content from Atom Films, a film publisher currently focusing on short animated features. Atom Films, which is now merged with shockwave.com, may create an additional market for PDAs, provided that the PDA consumer is persuaded to consume video content on a mobile device.

Case Study: Cable-Modem Company Field Services

Aim To show cost and time savings of mCommerce.

Scenario A cable modem company's field services department ensures that the infrastructure (modems, routers, networks, gateways, and so on) required to support cable Internet connection in its customers' homes is up and running.

Actors Field service technicians who ensure that the infrastructure is in place, expert engineers who solve problems, and supervisors who manage personnel and cases.

Workflow

1. Field service technicians in the field investigate problems (as reported by the customers or otherwise) and take notes on paper forms.

2. Technicians return to their offices and do one of two things: enter their paper-based information into a computer or fill out additional paper-based forms that are later entered into the computer databases.

3. Supervisor reviews database reports and analyses and groups the problems by geographic region.

4. Depending on employee availability, the supervisor assigns experts to look into the problems.

5. Experts take the paper reports, go to the problem sites, and fix the problems.

6. Experts return to the office and enter the paper report status into the computer database.

7. Supervisor reviews the problem status and closes each case.

The preceding process appears to be inefficient and tedious, involving days or months to resolve each problem.

Bottleneck　The process-tracking mechanism that gets in the way of solving problems in a cost-effective and timely manner.

Solution　To arm the field-technicians, experts, and supervisors with global positioning system (GPS) enabled mobile PDAs with task-specific applications.

▼ Field technicians file their reports on their PDAs while at the job site.

■ Supervisors assign tasks to field experts in real time based on preprogrammed business rules in the PDAs.

■ Field experts get instant messages (IMs) on their PDAs regarding assignments based on their locations and expertise levels.

▲ After solving the problems, field experts enter the status information on their PDAs, which automatically populates the office database servers.

Result

▼ Time spent on problem solving is reduced from months and days to hours and minutes.

■ No paperwork confusion or paper trail.

▲ The cable modem company saves money.

WHAT'S NEXT?

In this chapter, we discussed the fundamental functional platform that supports all mCommerce applications. In the next chapter, we will venture into a brief discussion of some key mCommerce applications within the various horizontals and vertical industries. Each of these applications and industry verticals require different security solutions and it is, therefore, necessary to address them individually.

CHAPTER 2

mCommerce Applications and Services Landscape

In order to understand how to establish security for mCommerce, you need to understand the business drivers and the value of the various applications. Security solutions are chosen based on the value and business drivers of an application. For example, we buy monitoring and alarm services for our homes because the value of the contents is relatively high. On the other hand, we generally secure a bicycle with no more than a simple steel lock—we do not pursue alarms and monitoring services because the cost of these advanced security solutions may outweigh the cost of the bicycle itself! The security solution must be appropriate based on value and business need. As the mobile Internet evolves, many new services are seen unfolding around existing and wireless-specific content. mCommerce data services exist in two primary market segments: *vertical* and *horizontal*. Vertical markets refer to industry-specific services and applications customized for those particular industries. Horizontal markets refer to applications and services with a common utility across many industries with the purpose of serving the mass consumer market. This chapter discusses the mCommerce applications and services landscape within the context of these markets. The applications and industries introduced here will be further discussed in the context of security in the forthcoming chapters.

THE VALUE CHAIN SUPPORTING mCOMMERCE TRANSACTIONS

Imagine the world of mobile commerce as a motor car that requires a number of moving parts as well as gasoline to run smoothly. The failure of any of these parts could cause the car to stop functioning. This analogy of a running car can be extended to an mCommerce transaction cycle, which would not occur if all its supporting parts are not working together as a value chain (see Table 2-1 for a bird's eye view). This chain includes parts such as radio data networks, operator infrastructures, portals, horizontal and vertical applications, and the operating systems they run on, the handset and terminal devices used by the consumers, and, most importantly, the security that supports them all. Each of these parts have its own rate of innovation. Each of the terms in Table 2-1 are explained and discussed in detail in future chapters.

Data Networks Radio	Network/ Operator Infrastructure	Security	Horizontal Applications	Vertical Applications	Operating Systems	Handset and Terminal Devices	Portal
GSM	Base stations	RSA	Calendar	Field sales	PalmOS	Display	Content development
GPRS	MSCs	DES	Sync	Field support	Symbian EPOCH	Embedded systems	Interface design
EDGE	SMSCs	Kerberos	E-mail	Telemetry	Microsoft CE	RTOS	Usability services
					Sun Microsystems		User access and control
UMTS	Prepaid	PKI	Messaging	Banking	Linux	SIM toolkit	Personalization
CDPD	Billing/Rating	W-PKI	Contact management	Trading		DSP	Content Management
Bluetooth	IP billing	Encryption	Unified messaging	Healthcare			
DECT	Mediation	Digital signatures	Location	Shopping			
HomeRF	Web servers	CA	Voice Recognition				
IP	WAP gateways	Triple-DES					
VO/IP	Over-the-air provisioning						
Mixers	Location						
Amplifiers	RDBMS						
Transmitters	Middleware						
	Jini Technology						

Table 2-1. mCommerce Transactions Value Chain

Key Challenges Facing the mCommerce World

There is more to providing mCommerce solutions than simply implementing a technology and rolling out the transaction and billing capability. Different applications will have different technology and hosting needs in order to reach a multitude of mobile devices. Relationships will need to be managed with different content and service providers. End-to-end security issues will also need to be addressed. The key is to create an integrated and compelling end user experience and control the implementation costs.

NOTE: Integration between disparate technical platforms and with legacy appliances and applications will perhaps be the greatest challenge facing the mCommerce world.

It is difficult to bring together the different technologies present in phones, pagers, personal digital assistants, and Internet networks with a multitude of competing wireless standards that have created confusion in the marketplace. Within the crowd of standards, communication protocols, and various functional components as well as high network latency, low bandwidth, and relatively thin clients lies the real test of getting mobile applications to perform to acceptable performance levels.

NOTE: The ability of the mCommerce server to recognize different client types and serve appropriate content to them is proving to be a tough challenge.

This book will talk about a great many mCommerce applications that rely upon the successful adoption and implementation of high-speed wireless networks. Topics such as how fast these networks will get, when they will actually come into the market, and the pricepoint that will influence the service adoption rates are all issues that need to be ironed out.

It is also worth noting that according to the National Highway Traffic Safety Administration, a significant number of car crashes occur as a result of drivers being distracted by cell phones and other in-car devices. In addition, reports of possible complications arising from radiation levels emitted from cell phone handsets have also led to many lawmakers calling for limited or restricted use of mobile devices. In New York City (Manhattan), for example, drivers are not allowed to use a cell phone while driving.

Another challenge concerns the security of payment transactions, which has been one of the key topics of discussion among mCommerce panels. The acceptance of mobile payment use is one that is not just an acceptance of the underlying security technologies, but also one that will involve changing perceptions of users and their habits.

In addition, the "always-on" handset is not something every mobile user is enthused about. Why? Because it is quite easy for corporations to track the whereabouts of a mobile device when it is "on" and thus keep tabs on where you are! Most consumers believe that privacy protection levels will have to be enhanced from what they are at the moment to prove sufficient in an mCommerce world.

Another issue that we take for granted in the United States is that of mobile bill payment. In other words, who pays the bill? In Europe, particularly in Scandinavian countries where mCommerce has been adopted in mainstream usage, only the caller pays for the phone call. In the U.S., both the caller and recipient pay, which means consumers in the U.S. leave their cell phones off unless they want to place a call. It is, therefore, more difficult to stream information and services to a user's mobile phone in the U.S. than it is in Europe. This difficulty leaves us with a big question—will mCommerce really kick off in the U.S. if billing policies remain the way they currently are?

Lastly, there are many constraints within the mobile devices themselves, such as their screen size, ease of use, the size and weight of the devices, which are the real limitations of handhelds. On top of this, the mobile consumer's characteristics also present challenges that will revise the shape of mCommerce business models from time to time. Limited screen size, low bandwidth, and user attention span, for example, may suggest a shift away from advertising-driven economic models.

Building Blocks for mCommerce Applications

The building blocks for basic mCommerce services include software components and setup process for the devices, the network, and the corporate servers. Figure 2-1 illustrates this further, and a description of each is provided in the following subsections.

Client Software

The mobile browser can be downloaded for most types of PDAs. Mobile browsers are manufactured by many companies, such as Nokia, Openwave, and Ericsson. These browsers are downloadable from the Web onto PDAs and have different GUIs. Other popular browsers include the Palm mobile browser (Clipper app that runs PQAs), PocketIE on PocketPC, and AvantGo on RIM. Most of these browsers support only simple bitmaps (WBMP).

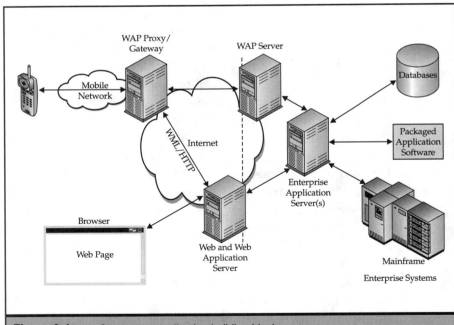

Figure 2-1.   mCommerce application building blocks

Client Service Setup

One of the reasons for mCommerce consumer adoption being slow has been the rather cumbersome and long setup process for a new Wireless Access Protocol (WAP) phone. Users have to specify numerous parameters before they can connect to a WAP gateway. Moreover, generally after taking about half a minute to establish a wireless connection, the user needs to follow a pattern of entering a number of parameters as the phone handshakes with the server and establishes a connection. The General Packet Radio Service (GPRS) should alleviate the need to dial up every time a user wants to access services, and over-the-air (OTA) provisioning servers can be used to automatically configure phones to reach a particular site. However, modern networks such as Palm.Net and PocketPCs integrated with Cellular Digital Packet Data (CDPD) modems are alleviating the connectivity situation and increasingly finding their way into the enterprise and corporate marketplace.

Network

Over the Web, mCommerce data passes from the content server to the Global System for Mobile Communications (GSM) network, which then carries the data to the mobile device. The service provider does not have to worry about the wireless network as long as there is web connectivity. Sometimes the service provider will need to use a short messaging service (SMS) gateway for network access if the data is carried by an SMS bearer. The components that are called up during this interaction are generally the Base Stations (BSs); the Home Location Register (HLR), which is the main database of permanent subscriber information for a mobile network; the Mobile Switching Centers (MSCs), which are switches used for call control and processing and which also serve as a point-of-access to the Public Switched Telephone Network (PSTN); the Visiting Location Register (VLR); which maintains temporary user information (such as current location) to manage requests from subscribers who are out of the area covered by their home system, as well as a rating and billing system. The GSM system is big in Europe; however, in the United States, networks such as CDPD, Mobitex, CDMA, and DataTAC are more common. Chapter 5 provides a detailed overview of each of the networks and the types of applications they can support.

Server Software Components

Mobile software servers generally rely either on a version of the Hypertext Markup Language (HTML) or on the Extensible Markup Language (XML). HTML only deals with data presentation and not the substance of the data itself—in other words, it merely arranges text, images, and buttons in a graphic environment. This has given rise to XML, the popular standard that can interpret information beyond the display parameters, allowing information providers to define not only the appearance of the information but also its "functional attributes." For example, if the information is going to a wireless screen, it can be stripped of any graphics and so on.

NOTE: Content coming from the content server is encoded into a compressed binary format by the wireless gateway for transport over the mobile network to the WAP-enabled device.

Gateways are generally able to read and write common standards, common e-mail protocols, and popular corporate operating systems such as Windows NT/2000, Unix, and Linux. A service provider or company's application server will need to recognize different client types in order to serve appropriate content to them.

SERVICES AND APPLICATIONS IN HORIZONTAL AND VERTICAL MARKETS

mCommerce data services exist in two primary market segments: vertical and horizontal. Vertical markets refer to industry-specific services and applications customized for particular industries. Horizontal markets refer to applications and services with a common utility across many industries with the purpose of serving the mass consumer market. Generally, all mobile professionals and mCommerce consumers fall within the horizontal applications sector. Horizontal markets can be further segmented into basic communications (voice and messaging), accessing or sharing data and information (personal and business), media and entertainment (video and audio), and engaging in commercial transactions (purchases and sales). Figure 2-2 illustrates the segmentation of different vertical and horizontal markets and applications.

mCommerce solutions for vertical markets move information quickly between a mobile user (employee or customer) and an enterprise. Such solutions help companies increase productivity, profitability, and customer satisfaction. Examples of mCommerce vertical markets are transportation, field services, field sales, financial services, real estate, travel, asset tracking, telematics, healthcare, telecommunications, public sector, and retail.

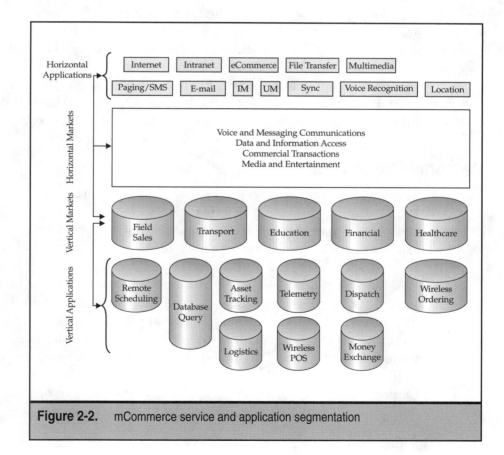

Figure 2-2. mCommerce service and application segmentation

An ideal vertical market has generally involved heavy spending on both IT and wireless—for example, every UPS driver carries a portable device to track, in real time, the logistics of the company's delivery network. Historically, the productivity gains suggest only businesses are able to justify an mCommerce investment. Also, most enterprises deploying vertical mCommerce solutions for employees (B2E) or vendors (B2B) may also simultaneously deploy solutions for customers (B2C). The combining of vertical applications with horizontal applications also further enhances their utility, making an mCommerce service sometimes indispensable to an end user.

In horizontal markets, on the other hand, a single mCommerce service applies across many different industries—for example, wireless e-mail can be accessed by any person regardless of industry, thus making it a horizontal application. The same holds true for services built around personal information management, Internet/intranet access, mobile e-commerce, and multimedia. Figure 2-3 illustrates the different horizontal applications and the technologies that enable them.

The following sections discuss horizontal and vertical mCommerce services and applications in further detail. These applications have been discussed individually in the later chapters of this book with in-depth analysis of the security considerations involving each.

Personal Organizers

Many wireless ASPs (or WASPs) have sprung up in the last couple of years, offering employees mobile services that connect them to their corporate e-mail accounts, calendars, intranet content, and contact information. Consumers can use their savvy personal digital assistants (PDAs), such as the Palm VII, Pocket PC, Compaq iPAQ, HP Jornada, RIM Blackberry, and many other leading PDAs available in the market, to access the services of a Wireless Application Service Provider (WASP). The WASP hosts personal organization applications and offers each consumer a "slice" of the pie with his or her own private space within the application. Most modern PDAs also come preinstalled with software applications that work similar to mini Microsoft Outlooks running on tiny PDA-size databases. Any personal data

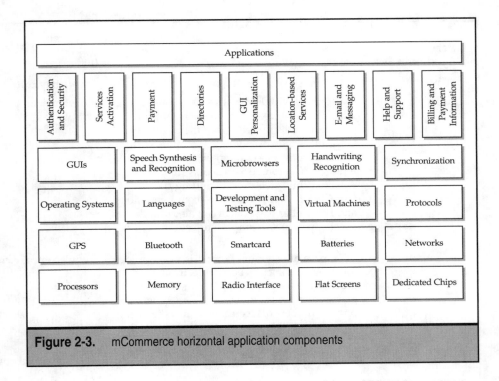

Figure 2-3.   mCommerce horizontal application components

recorded on these PDAs can generally be easily synchronized with their desktop equivalents at the touch of a button.

E-commerce Applications

These are applications that enable the buying and selling of products and services over mobile networks and devices.

NOTE: Auctions and retail are two industries that have been key to mobile e-commerce.

Mobile auction sites offer their users the ability to buy and sell products anywhere, anytime. Table 2-2 shows examples of such mobile e-commerce sites and application providers.

Mobile E-commerce Sites	Description	URL
eBay	Offers person-to-person online auctions.	www.ebay.com
Amazon	Subscribers with Internet-ready handsets who are registered with Amazon.com can purchase items directly from their handsets. Customers who do not have accounts with Amazon.com can set them up from their handsets. Customers can access some of Amazon.com's features, including the Gift-Click feature, Personal Recommendations, and Best Seller lists. Users can also search for specific products, compare prices, and check on orders.	www.amazon.com
eCompare	eCompare offers online comparison shopping for categories such as books, electronics, music, videos/movies, auctions, software, games, appliances, wines, and cars. When phone numbers of electronic retailers (etailers) are available, eCompare offers users an option to initiate a voice call to buy a product.	www.ecompare.com
InterAuct	Singapore-based auction site.	www.interauct.com

Table 2-2.   Sample Mobile E-commerce Sites and Application Providers

Location-Based Services and Applications

Using some approximate location-pointing techniques, many vendors are offering location services based on zip code and cell-side location. Basically, location-based services developed or under development today allow the user to find content relevant to a specified location by entering details such as a street name. The system returns a list that matches the user's request and, with it, directions from the present location to the destination. Estimated duration, progress, and step-by-step route instructions are also provided. Other types of location-based consumer applications are also being developed. Figure 2-4 shows the value chain for location-based services.

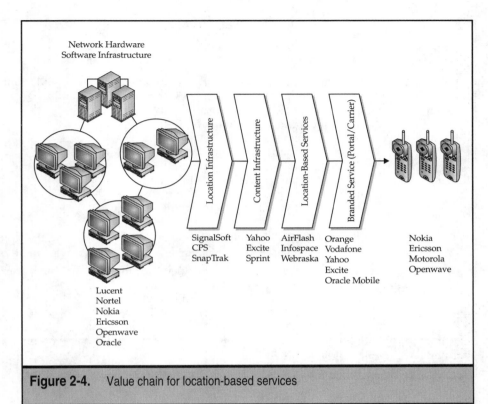

Network Hardware
Software Infrastructure

Location Infrastructure

Content Infrastructure

Location-Based Services

Branded Service (Portal/Carrier)

SignalSoft
CPS
SnapTrak

Yahoo
Excite
Sprint

AirFlash
Infospace
Webraska

Orange
Vodafone
Yahoo
Excite
Oracle Mobile

Nokia
Ericsson
Motorola
Openwave

Lucent
Nortel
Nokia
Ericsson
Openwave
Oracle

Figure 2-4.   Value chain for location-based services

TIP: Sending alerts to users within three blocks of a grocery store around closing time announcing a sale on specific goods could help stimulate purchases.

Location-based applications are also beginning to serve in telecom fraud detection. Although complicated techniques have been developed to monitor usage patterns in order to detect fraud and identify cloned telephone numbers, this leaves out the most important step—actually locating the perpetrator. Therefore, location technology closes up that gap by offering the location of the perpetrator, which may then be passed on to the law enforcement authorities. The same applies to an emergency caller using a mobile device. Table 2-3 provides a list of some location-based applications and service providers.

Location-Based Applications	Description	URL
WAP 411	WAP 411 is a personalized travel information service. You can choose your favorite cities, restaurants, hotels, and more as well as rate the quality of each place and event—from one star to four stars. WAP 411 gives you information for hundreds of cities across the United States. If you find yourself stranded in Burbank, ask WAP 411 for a hotel recommendation and the best place for a hot meal. If you are on a street corner in Charlotte searching for a taxi, WAP 411 will find you the number and dial it for you.	**www.wap411.com**
WhoWhere	Search for e-mails and phone numbers.	**www.whowhere.com**
Vicinity	Location-based information provider. Vicinity StationFinder allows users who visit Shell or Texaco Web sites and Vicinity's MapBlast! to enter a zip code and find the Shell and Texaco stations nearest them.	**www.vicinity.com**

Table 2-3.   Sample Location-Based Applications and Service Sites

NOTE: One of the most important applications to support today is location-based billing. For instance, given the length of usage and time of day, carriers may offer different rates for using mobile devices at home, at the office, on the road, or even in a shopping mall (zone tariffing).

mCommerce Portals

There are different types of wireless mCommerce portals depending on the type of company providing the service, the three main ones being the pervasive wired-to-wireless mCommerce portals, the wireless network operator or carrier run mCommerce portals, and the independent mCommerce portals. The pervasive portals aim to provide a range of services offering access from both wired as well as wireless devices with increased security and convenient self-registration and service selection. A pervasive mCommerce portal must also be able to deliver access to new and third party applications rapidly. A user's profile should be able to travel from the wired to the wireless site, and back, and still be accessible by the user from anyplace, anytime.

NOTE: The reality is that because users constantly seek out the best experience, a portal that lets either their wired or wireless services fall behind the competition is going to lose its user base to the competitor.

Wired-to-Wireless mCommerce Portals

Another kind of portal is the wired-to-wireless type. AOL, Yahoo!, MSN, Excite, and Lycos have quickly established their mCommerce portal presence, enabling their users to receive service from their mobile devices. Among the mCommerce services offered by these portals are messaging, chat, content, and bulletin boards, among others. Table 2-4 shows a list of portals and their associated applications and services (extrapolated from various MSDW and Gartner reports).

Portal	Mobile Applications	Mobile Services
Yahoo! Everywhere	Yahoo! Mail, Calendar, Address Book, Finance for phones, Palm, and pager alerts	Active on OmniSky, Sprint, and Palm.Net
MSN Mobile	Hotmail and alerts for phones	Active on Nextel and AirTouch
Lycos Anywhere	Paging alerts and access for Palm phones	WAP site available for phones with web access
AOL Anywhere	AOL Mail for Palm, PocketPC, WinCE devices and phones, and IM for pagers	Active on SprintPCS and AT&T. AOL-branded devices and e-mail/applications with RIM, Motorola, Nokia, and OmniSky
Excite Mobile	Excite eMail, Phonebooks, Planner for Palm, WinCE, PocketPC, Symbian, and Phones	Active on AT&T and OmniSky

Table 2-4.   Wired-to-Wireless mCommerce Portals

NOTE: Although many companies are working on them, the most popular portal applications (chat, bulletin boards, instant messaging, and other community features) are yet to be extended wirelessly in commercial form.

Currently, most users sign up with a wireless version of a wired portal to access e-mail and other easy-to-use features, such as stock portfolio tracking.

Wireless Network Operator–Run mCommerce Portals

Wireless network operators are also launching mCommerce portals because two main sources of mobile access are evolving: the mobile ISPs (such as OmniSky and GoAmerica) and the virtual private network operators. Generally, from the user's viewpoint, a wireless carrier is simply a mobile transportation provider.

NOTE: Wireless network operators control the key aspects of mobile service today: activation, airtime, handsets, fulfillment, customer service and support, promotions, location, and billing.

Table 2-5 shows a list of network operator–run wireless portals and their associated content providers and services (extrapolated from various MSDW and Gartner reports).

Independent mCommerce Portals

The emergence of the mobile Internet has also given rise to many new independent portals. The viability of these stand-alone wireless portals comes from many factors. The following subsections detail some of these factors.

Content Adapts to Win Its Consumer Base   Most mCommerce service providers provide content that offers little latitude for personalization because it can generally only be viewed on the providers' limited channels. Independent wireless portals differ from this norm by allowing their subscribers to create individualized content channels

Portal/Carrier	Content Provider	Content
Verizon MobileWeb	InfoSpace and InfoSpace/direct relationships	Customer Care, eMail, Calendar, Contacts, ToDo, Alerts, General News, and Entertainment
AT&T PocketNet	InfoSpace/direct relationships	Customer Care, eMail, Calendar, Contacts, ToDo, Alerts, Bookmarks, General News, and Entertainment
SprintPCS Wireless Web	None/direct relationships	Message Center and Alerts
Nextel Online	Openwave, MSN, and MSN/direct relationships	Hotmail, MSNBC.com, MSN MoneyCentral, Expedia, Yellow Pages, General News, and Entertainment

Table 2-5.   Network Operator–Run mCommerce Portals

for themselves. It is for reasons such as this that portal giants like AOL have partnered with other providers, such as AT&T, SprintPCS, and OmniSky, to expand their pool of services.

Bookmarking   The ability to add a "bookmark" or "favorite place" on a portal is an important aspect of a pervasive portal. The importance of bookmarks is this: A particular portal might only satisfy 70 percent of a user's basic needs, with the other 30 percent taken care of by other sites that are bookmarked on the user's mobile device to enhance the quality of their wireless web experience.

 TIP: Users can bookmark their favorite URLs from across the Internet and thus have the option of easily going to another portal if the one they are on is not serving their needs.

Uniqueness of mCommerce Content   The new portals leverage a mobile web user's wireless connectivity, short browsing time, and need for personalization and location-based services.

Table 2-6 shows a list of independent wireless portals and their associated products and services (extrapolated from various MSDW and Gartner reports).

Communications and Messaging

Mobile communications at the basic level is simply one-way numeric paging that includes text messaging. Certain digital wireless phones also have short messaging service (SMS) capabilities. SMS has been very popular in Europe given the common GSM digital systems.

E-mail

A level above SMS can be e-mail, which can be classified in the neighborhood of 1,000 characters, something that can only be received with some convenience if split into multiple SMS messages. However, lengthy e-mails can now be delivered to interactive pagers and Palm devices through mobile e-mail services from Research in Motion (Blackberry), OmniSky, and Go-America. These services also allow true "one address" sending and delivery.

Company	Product	Mobile Service
Shadowpack	Personalization, enhanced navigation, e-commerce information, and content translation	Any interactive wireless device through any wireless service provider
Yodlee2Go	Online personal account access and synchronization with general Internet content partners for mobile e-commerce	Any interactive wireless device through any wireless service provider
Spyonit Mobile	Search engine and wireless alerts for user-specified content	PalmOS through wireless service provider
OmniSky	Branded Internet content, open Internet access, and e-mail	Palm V with modem
GoAmerica	Branded Internet content, open Internet access, and e-mail	A variety of Palm, RIM, Windows CE and laptop devices
Palm.Net	Branded Internet content and e-mail	Palm VII

Table 2-6. Independent Wireless Portals

Instant messaging (IM) allows two users on the same network to send IMs to one another. Since this is a network-specific "closed" system, it eliminates most bottlenecks and delay normally caused during internetwork hops. Leading service and content providers, such as AOL, ICQ, and Yahoo!, have cashed in on the growing popularity of IM, seeing as it is particularly suited for wireless communications:

▼   Wireless IM allows a user to reach people at anytime, which is an enhancement to the wired version.

■   The short length of IM messages coupled with closed communications on the same network allows for IM communities to be successfully deployed on a wireless network.

■   The text-based nature of IM makes it appropriate for today's narrowband wireless networks.

■   New enhancements to user-friendly text-entry modes on modern handheld devices facilitate mobile wireless messaging, making it quicker and more feasible.

▲   Coupled with alert-notifications, wired IM buddy lists can extend to the wireless world as well; mobile users receive an alert on their handhelds or on their PC screens when their friends are available.

Unified Messaging

The proliferation of SMS, mobile e-mail, IM, voice mail, and fax has in many ways complicated communications. The delivery of a single message across all wired and wireless formats irrespective of the physical location of the user, in the form of a unified messaging application, has become more and more critical, especially in recent times where mobility has become almost part of doing a job.

Because Unified Messaging aims to be device, network, or location independent, the development of an intelligent unified messaging platform that dynamically synchronizes between wired and wireless devices and that possesses the ability to route an incoming message to the most appropriate device, depending on a user's current location and reception capability, has become increasingly crucial in recent times. Key players in the IM scene include Critical Path, Comverse, and Lucent.

mCommerce Data Synchronization

In the previous section, we discussed how crucial dynamic synchronization of data, such as e-mails, calendars, to-do lists, contacts, and other personal content, has become in the wireless world, especially when it comes to keeping our data updated in both the wireless as well as wired environments. This, therefore, leads us into a stage beyond Unified Messaging—that of mCommerce data synchronization across a variety of devices and networks. Although proprietary synchronization solutions exist in the marketplace, companies such as Ericsson, IBM, Lotus, Matsushita, Motorola, Nokia, Openwave, Starfish Software, and Symbian have developed a common data synchronization framework protocol called SyncML, which is an open industry standard that leverages XML to enable users of a device supported by one synchronization solution to be able to share data with another device or service supported by a different synchronization solution across multiple networks, platforms, and devices. Further information on SyncML can be found at **www.syncml.org/technology.html**.

mCommerce Voice Portals

Because the majority of wireless users today use simple voice-only analog or digital phones and are reluctant to switch over to more complex and expensive wireless devices, companies are coming out with new business models centered around voice-recognition technology. This has led to the development of many "voice portals" and service providers such as TellMe Networks, ViaFone, BeVocal, HeyAnita, iNetNow, SpeechWorks, Microsoft's Airstream, and Quack.com. New voice portals are being implemented to offer toll-free mCommerce services that can answer customer inquiries, such as questions about restaurants, movies, news, stocks, and sports.

Digital Secretaries

Beyond simple voice portals are voice-controlled smart agents that can act as a personal filter for unified messaging, personal information management, and web access. Ananova and Wildfire are two such companies in this space (now part of Orange in the United Kingdom). Ananova is a virtual digital newscaster (video and audio) that can be configured by a user to provide information on specific Internet topics. Wildfire (**www.wildfire.com**) is a voice-controlled e-secretary that manages phone, fax, and e-mail. Motorola's Mya is a combination of both Ananova and Wildfire. An interactive agent that reads relevant web content as well as performs other tasks is a powerful model, especially as voice telephony prices are on the decline.

NOTE: This has resulted in several firms (AT&T, IBM, Lucent, and Motorola) backing a standardized language for voice Internet services called VoiceXML.

Travel

One of the areas in which mCommerce is becoming increasingly popular is travel. In most cases, the mCommerce services are extensions of the wired Internet sites or traditional travel guides such as Citysearch and Fodor's. When in a new city, mobile travelers can access the city guides from their handheld devices and do basic searches on information such as restaurants and theaters. Most of these guide services are provided as part of a portal's content-channel by companies, such as AvantGo, that offer wireless access to dining, movie, and walking guides among other travel-related services. mCommerce is not limited only to static travel guides, but has been used in many sectors of the travel industry to increase speed, efficiency, customer service, and value.

Airlines, Rail, and Road

Many airlines have developed mCommerce applications and programs. These devices can be used by gate agents and maintenance floor personnel for accessing the ticketing system, scheduling information, accessing and updating maintenance records, handling baggage as well as tracking lost items. For example, field engineers at KLM use handheld terminals to input status information, order parts, and schedule routine or emergency repairs. One of the most important real-life uses of mobile technology in the airline industry is that of accurate baggage handling: For instance, Scandinavian Airlines uses handheld scanners and terminals to match individual bags with passengers in real time; Frankfurt Airport baggage handlers use handheld terminals with radio modems and readers for scanning baggage tags. Delta Airlines also uses mobile scanners to scan barcoded information from the baggage tags directly into a database. Such wireless technology is now being enhanced and implemented even more since the September 11th terrorist attacks on the United States. Quick and accurate baggage reconciliation with passengers helps reduce the probability of terrorist attacks.

Mobile commerce and wireless access is not limited just to the airlines, but has also pervaded the railway industry. Conrail An has implemented a wireless work-order application embedded into pen computers that runs on a RAM Mobile Data network. The RAM network is also being used along with a GPS system in a U.K. based research project to test highway toll-collection technology. The project is based on the Road Billing Network (Robin) system, with the objective of keeping traffic disruption to a minimum.

For a detailed discussion of the mobile travel industry and its security implications, please refer to Chapter 9.

Financial

Financial services have found an eager marketplace for wireless services. From stock quotes to options and commodity trading, major brokerage firms now offer wireless mCommerce services to their customers either for a fee, or for free. Customers of high street banks are able to access their accounts over a wireless network for balance transfers, billing, and other mCommerce transactions. Two of the leading proponents of financial mobile technology are 724 Solutions and Aether Systems, which also provide wireless financial service hosting to companies. Wireless trading devices have proliferated in the B2B finance space, integrating and interacting with existing and legacy trading systems.

As you will see in the "Retail" section, wireless POS terminals are being used by some retailers to do on-the-spot credit checks and card authorizations. Many banks now support such systems. Another good example of innovation in this area is the New York Stock Exchange that has done away with its manual paper-based process and replaced it with wireless technology across the board allowing its on-floor brokers to collect orders, check stock values, and enter trades directly from their handheld terminals. The brokers' PDAs are connected to NYSE's financial servers over a wireless network for data access.

NOTE: Wireless financial applications offer significant market potential for two major reasons. The first reason is the need for consumers to constantly manage their money, and the second reason is the numerical nature of financial data, rendering it perfect for optimized wireless display.

Retail

A major growth area for mCommerce is in retail. Such technology allows a supermarket chain or high-street retailer to use wireless POS terminals over a wireless data network and to accept mobile credit card payments. The Food Fair supermarket chain of North Carolina uses one such system comprising a POS terminal with a radio modem that processes credit cards over the wireless network by interfacing with MasterCard's Automated POS Program (MAPP). Another company, DataWave, uses wireless vending technology to dispense single-use cameras and film. The system runs a merchandiser software in Kodak vending machines that are run over a Mobitex network to register and verify credit card transactions. Handheld terminals can be used to download sales and inventory information for stock replenishment over a wireless network. Thresholds can be set such that if a vending machine malfunctions, or a particular sales target is reached by a vending zone, an alert notification is immediately triggered. Please see Chapter 9 for more discussion on retail.

TIP: During high-volume sales periods (such as Christmas) and special discount events, retailers could increase the number of wireless POS terminals. Wireless devices can also be used to perform on-the-spot markdowns and inventory counts.

Education

There are many uses of mCommerce technologies in the Education sector such as for managing and accessing homework, attendance, grading, communication with parents, event and test planning, managing extracurricular activities, accessing reference materials on campus, accessing wireless e-mail and demonstrating science applications. A real-life example of an mCommerce education application is Mindsurf Networks **(www.mindsurfnetworks.com)**, a joint effort by Sylvan Learning Systems and Aether Systems that offers a wireless computing environment for classrooms. Such a mobile learning environment comprises at its underlying core, a wireless network such as a Symbol Spectrum24 wireless LAN. Many universities use such technologies to interconnect with each other's wireless campuses. Symbol Technologies is playing a leading role in bringing high-speed wireless networking to colleges. Symbol's Spectrum24 wireless LAN solution connects the campuses of universities such as Wake Forest, New York Polytechnic University, Shenandoah University, Suffolk Community College, and Sacred Heart University.

NOTE: Some Universities have started to install wireless local area networks on their campuses. Using a laptop equipped with a wireless LAN card, students can sign up for classes, download and upload assignments, access campus libraries, collaborate on study projects, contact professors, conduct research, and basically connect to the Web from anywhere on campus.

Other benefits of mCommerce technologies in education include the following:

▼ **Library Access**   Allow college staff and students to instantly access library databases and other online resources using a handheld computer or laptop with a WLAN card.

■ **Research**   Allow researchers to access and monitor the results of computer experiments or tests over a wireless network using a handheld device.

■ **Collaboration**   Allow staff, students, and researchers to exchange documents and mutually collaborate over wireless workgroups.

▲ **Information Exchange**   Allow instant exchange of critical laboratory data between research centers and laboratories and also to monitor experiments remotely.

There are many examples of educational institutions using mCommerce technologies on campus. For instance, a leading North Carolina–based university has implemented a wireless infrastructure maintained by Symbol's Wireless Network Management System. The system allows access to the University's networks, databases, libraries, and student services, using a laptop with a WLAN card. Another New York–based university has also installed wireless technology across some of its buildings and plans to equip its student base with notebook computers that are wireless compliant. For more information on the security implications of using wireless LANs, please refer to Chapter 12.

Case Study: A Day in the Life of a Wireless Student

Malvika is a student who has been using a lot of mobile technology lately. She boots up her notebook computer to send a quick message to her dad to pay her tuition for next semester. "It's due tomorrow, Dad," she writes.

Half an hour later, she's on the Boston University campus, computer in her backpack. When she reaches the library, Malvika takes out her notebook and accesses the campus box office, managing to book the last two tickets for the forthcoming Madonna concert. She takes time to e-mail her boyfriend: "I have booked two tickets for the Madonna concert. Hope you are coming!" She also checks her college account. Dad hasn't paid the tuition yet, so she sends another quick note to him.

Malvika also checks enrollment in Biochemistry 101 and finds that a place has opened up. She quickly e-mails the instructor and enrolls on the spot. However, she's now a week behind on the homework, so she visits the professor's campus web site to wirelessly download the assigned reading list. She then reserves the textbooks from the online campus bookstore.

Malvika's first class is a biology lab, where she uses her wireless computer to take notes on the experiment. As the lab instructor recommends a biology lab guide, Malvika sends a quick query to the library's online catalog verifying that the book is available for checkout.

Over lunch at the cafeteria, she visits the chat room for Organic Chem 1. The moderating professor is explaining some complex formula. Malvika joins in with some questions of her own and copies the explanations into memory for further study.

Another check of her e-mail a few hours later finds an announcement that her study group is already meeting over a pizza. She's off to join them, although she quickly sends out another message: "Dad?"

As Malvika heads off-campus, she notices that a rowdy argument has been quickly broken up by campus police, who are using PDAs and wireless phones to manage the incident.

She has heard that the new security cameras and phones are all tied into the same campus wireless system. At dinner, the study group focuses on its new project. Several members are joining in online, sending materials and comments in real time.

After a hard day's work, Malvika returns to her dorm. From her room, she finishes the homework assignments and uploads them to the class web site for grading. Just before turning in, she checks her campus account one more time to find that her account is up to date; Dad has paid the tuition.

Defense and Military

Mobile and wireless technology has been an integral part of defense and military systems ever since radio technology was invented. In light of the recent terrorist attacks on New York City and the growing concern with cyberterrorism focused around the vulnerability of U.S. defense networks, security has undoubtedly become the single most important issue of discussion among national defense officials. The National Security Council, the Department of Defense, the CIA, and the FBI all believe that terrorists may look at online technologies as a means for causing future economic destruction. The General Accounting Office (**www.gao.gov**), which is the investigative arm of the U.S. Congress, says that the U.S. Department of Defense itself has a sprawling computer infrastructure spreading across some 2.5 million unclassified computer systems, 10,000 local area networks, and hundreds of long-distance networks. The GAO has further revealed that there have been nearly 1,400 combined attacks against the computer systems of the U.S. Army, Navy, and Air Force in 1999 and 2000 alone. Many U.S. intelligence services use mobile technologies and wireless networks for communications and commerce. Advanced security technologies are being developed that will allow intelligence services to track down mobile network crackers, computer vandals, and possibly even international terrorists. For a detailed discussion on the security behind the U.S. mobile defense networks, refer to Chapter 11.

Automotive

When we think of wireless technologies and the automotive industry, the first thing that comes to mind is in-car assistance services such as OnStar (offered by General Motors) and Wingcast (offered by Ford). Such systems use GPS and the location of the vehicle is automatically sent over to the assistance center the moment a button is pressed in the car. When a representative comes online, a variety of in-car services can be requested via a conversation, such as traffic and weather information, directions and maps, vehicle tracking, remote vehicle operation, roadside and emergency assistance. Most services are connected to the airbag system of the car and are triggered if any of the airbags get deployed. It is expected that with increasing network speeds, such assistance programs will be able to offer enhanced services such as in-car mobile entertainment (the ability to download a video or game over the wireless network straight to your in-car visual console for your kids to watch or play!) as well as in-car shopping services and Internet access. Government safety concerns about communication services in the automobile have given rise to stricter laws, however. In fact. in many cities, such as New York, the law prohibits the use of cell phones while driving. Another wireless in-car gadget that's becoming popular is the AutoPC , a Microsoft Windows CE-powered car computer that offers navigation, information, and entertainment services, and most importantly, it follows your verbal commands!

mCommerce Gaming Services

The proliferation of video game consoles, online gaming, and hand-held game devices among the youth cannot be overlooked as a potential market for mCommerce gaming services. Online gaming has many benefits. It connects people in different locations, allowing them to play head to head, post scores, and download characters. For example, a person playing a tennis video game in Boston can play against someone in San Francisco. It would be very appealing to have the functionality of a Nintendo Game Boy by extending a mobile device. Sega, Nintendo, Activision, Sony, Electronic Arts, and Microsoft have all started implementing wireless extensions to their gaming devices. Table 2-7 shows a list of wireless gaming portals and the

mCommerce Gaming Portals	Service Description	URL
Digital Bridges	Provides entertainment and gaming content for use by WAP-enabled mobile phones and wireless PDAs as well as for the growing market for portable, wireless game consoles. The marketing channel, **www.wirelessgames.com**, offers a selection of games, from simple quiz and puzzle games to multiuser game experiences.	**www.wirelessgames.com** and **www.digitalbridges.com**
Friendly Giants	Friendly Giants develops games, desktop toys, and Web-aware applications for the Internet, mobile phones, Digital TV, and hand-held devices. Game titles include *BattleCards* (a cross between *Cross Trump* and *Pokemon*, for WAP), *CrazyGolf*, *Arcade Grand Prix*, and *Arcade 5-a-Side* (available at **www.sportsmad.com**) as well as *Blastian*, *Moon Defender*, and *Demon Invaders* (available at **Freeloader.com**).	**www.friendlygiants.com**
Handy Games	Handy Games offers embedded games for mobile phones, WAP games for the mobile Internet, and online games on conventional systems. Their titles include *Mice, WAP Fighters, WAP Kings, WAP Dungeons, WAP ChemCorp, WAP Crates, WAP Golf,* and *WAP Escape*.	**www.handygames.com**
In-fusio	In-fusio offers a number of products, ranging from simple card games to sophisticated video games. Titles include *Adventure Land, BlackJack, Football Plus, Crazypet, In Spirit, Jackpot, Push, Quizz,* and *Reshape*. All games are either SMS or WAP supported.	**www.in-fusio.com**
Picofun	*Picofun Football* was the first multiuser game for WAP and has now been modified to also run on GPRS. The game is a strategic "football manager–type" game, where users can buy and sell players to set up individual teams, challenging each other in tournaments. *Picofun Football* has been tested and verified in Ericsson's Mobile Applications Initiative (MAI) labs in Sweden.	**www.picofun.com**

Table 2-7.   mCommerce Gaming Portals

mCommerce Gaming Portals	Service Description	URL
Riot-E	Riot-E creates, publishes, and distributes entertainment games and leisure services to be used globally in any mobile device. The products are based on SMS, WAP, and other emerging technologies. In May 2000, Riot-E announced a cooperation with 20th Century Fox to develop a mobile phone game as a spin-off of the movie *Titan A.E.*	**www.riot-e.com**
Springtoys	Springtoys focuses on mobile games. The key persons from Housemarque, a company producing PC games, established the company. Springtoys creates entertainment content, games, and related e-commerce to be deployed by wireless terminal equipment.	**www.springtoys.com**
Indiqu	Indiqu is a wireless programming company specializing in wireless entertainment. The products include quTribe (games, content, chat and polls for Generation Y), quEden (services and entertainment especially designed for women), quVox ("extreme" game challenges for the mobile gamer), and quVertical (mobile information for the winter sports enthusiast).	**www.indiqu.com**

Table 2-7. mCommerce Gaming Portals *(continued)*

games they have developed (as extrapolated from various MSDW and Gartner reports).

NOTE: Before gaming becomes popular on wireless platforms, the network speeds and bandwidth must increase to handle action-oriented graphic-intensive games offering an experience similar to the one on a console or CD-ROM.

Despite potential obstacles, Nintendo released its Game Boy Advanced, which will be Internet-enabled through a PCS phone connection. Among other things, this will allow players to download new versions of Nintendo's *Pokemon* characters and exchange them online with friends. Sega and Motorola are developing software that will allow PCS phones to transfer information at high speeds. Also, Sony announced its wirelessly enabled PSone, which is a portable version of the PlayStation. Many narrowband games are now being offered in the marketplace by companies such as wireless-games.com, In-fusio, Digital Bridges, and Red Jade. Games such as trivia, adventure, puzzles, word games, board games (chess and backgammon), cards (bridge, hearts, and solitaire) and casino games are suited to the narrowband environment.

Games of chance are an extremely logical application for wireless devices. The ability to play a few hands of Blackjack on a PDA while waiting at a train station or sitting in a taxi could be very compelling for some. Also, most casino games are very simple in design and require little bandwidth. Therefore, it would not be difficult to see mobile devices tied to live gaming servers and consumers' bank accounts.

NOTE: The wired online gaming industry has seen more than $1 billion being wagered online annually.

In the international countries where wagering is legal, wireless gaming applications are beginning to make a commercial appearance. Betmart is a European wireless gaming application for WAP phones. It enables players to compete against each other as opposed to a bookmaker.

Distribution

Distribution is perhaps one industry where mobile technologies have played a key role. Take, for example, the trucking industry where it becomes difficult and expensive to manage long haul delivery and pick up trucks. Mobile terminals can be used to access key information such as emergency drop shipments and in-route pickups. The industry is known for using satellite-based communications for sending and receiving messages to and from long-haul trucks on the highway. Other uses include remote monitoring of on-board sensors that record data such as temperature of the items in the vehicle, performance statistics of the vehicle itself (tire pressure, number of miles traveled, engine oil level, amount of gasoline in the truck) and other vital statistics that can be sent to the central dispatcher who can troubleshoot problems. For instance, a time threshold can be set such that if the goods are not picked up or delivered within a preset time period, an automatic alarm is triggered and sent to the vehicle along with an alert note to the driver's pager and his/her supervisor.

Another example of mCommerce use in this industry is in the rental car business. In this case, GPS navigation technology allows the renter to press a button on an on-dash monitor, enter a few destination parameters, and then watch (and hear) a color map of the area change on a regular basis until the destination is reached!

Route accounting and warehouse inventory management is another area of the distribution industry where mobile technologies are used. Warehouse managers can read inventory information by scanning barcodes of the products from the shelves and beaming the information straight to the corporate servers. Alternatively, they can also synchronize the data with a desktop PC and then transfer it over a wired connection to the corporate databases. This process facilitates inventory management and product replenishment.

The courier delivery sector has also been using mobile technology for quite some time to optimize its business process. For example, UPS and FedEx delivery personnel are often seen with handheld devices on which people sign off to acknowledge receipt of a package. This data can be instantly beamed to the couriers' corporate servers and linked to the company's web site tracking mechanism should the sender later wish to go online to see whether the package reached its destination or not.

NOTE: Distribution is perhaps one industry where mobile technologies have played a defining role, mainly for the reason that radio communication has, for quite some time, been critical to this industry.

Public Sector

mCommerce applications embedded within handheld terminals have been widely used in the public sector. Lets take law-enforcement.

Many police and traffic patrol agencies have implemented mobile technologies with pen-based terminals accessing state and law-enforcement databases over a CDPD, ARDIS, or RAM network. Law-enforcement personnel have also been using handheld devices to issue citations, query the DMV, and also to check up on potential suspects by requesting instant information on them from the crime databases. The fire department has also implemented different versions of mobile technologies for tracking and fighting fires and recording fire damage.

There are other areas of the public sector where mobile technologies have been helpful. For instance, many agencies have developed accident data collection programs that are embedded in handheld devices enabling them to record information and data at the scene of accident. The collision information can then be uploaded to the insurance company and law enforcement agency's servers for analysis. Many public agencies have also been using wireless networks to access state/provincial transport systems databases for real-time vehicle and driver information. Such use of mobile technology has been around for quite some time with companies like Motorola and MDI initially developing systems and applications that run on mini-computers and mainframes.

Mobile devices have also been used in environmental monitoring for collection of data, such as irrigation statistics, viscosity and soil density, using sensors placed in the field that send data to the environmental agency servers for analysis. This topic is further discussed in Chapter 12.

NOTE: Public welfare and law-enforcement agencies, such as police, fire safety, and ambulance services have been making use of mCommerce applications over wireless radio networks long before they could be cost-justified in the private sector.

Agriculture

There are many real-life applications of mobile technologies in the agriculture industry. For instance, some timber and logging companies use handheld terminals with modems and WLAN cards mounted on their tree harvesters. The terminals provide a wireless link between the sawmills and the harvesters recording crosscut measurements and other data on timber production within a preset time period. At the end of the felling time period, the terminals send the collected data from the harvesters straight to the head office and sawmills. This way, the timber companies come to know of the amount of timber being delivered to them in advance and do not have to worry about rising inventory levels in their warehouses.

Manufacturing and Mining

The utility of mobile technologies in the mining and manufacturing sector becomes clear when you think of the complexities involved in laying a communications cable inside a mine or factory floor, or the expenses involved in leasing a WAN. To resolve LAN extension problems, especially in remote areas, companies are installing wireless bridges to extend the LAN. It is important to note that these bridges require a clear line of sight and work well only for communications over relatively short distances—up to 10 miles (or 16 kilometers). Portable computers can also be used in vehicles, mines, and on shop floors. Real-life examples of mobile technology installations include companies such as Placerdome Canada Ltd., which has connected three of its mining sites with wireless bridges, and John Deere, which uses mobile notebooks with WLAN cards mounted onto indoor vehicles.

Utilities

One of the areas where mobile technologies are being used in the utility industry is for gathering inventory data about field assets such as transmission towers and transformers (in the case of an electric company) and then transmitting this information to the company's servers for analysis. Wireless devices are also mounted on the transformers and towers to monitor statistics within set thresholds. The system keeps synced up with the local tower-house desktop computer keeping it updated at all times. Before wireless technology started getting implemented by the utility companies, such field data was recorded and brought back from field trips on sheets of paper and then manually entered into computers. Now mCommerce has reached a point where gas, electric, cable TV, and most other utility companies are able to send real-time service requests to their field technicians who carry pen-based handheld computers that allow them to receive real-time information on customer orders, repair requests, and even customer addresses and photos of the area. Once a job is completed, the technicians can enter the completion details into their handheld terminal and beam it up to their head office databases. A case study on this subject was discussed toward the end of Chapter 1.

Healthcare

mCommerce technology in healthcare can be used for many purposes, such as ordering prescriptions, retrieving patient data, and researching a disease from the hospital or at home. With ever-tightening healthcare budgets, particularly in the U.S., the use of technology to reduce costs has been given a tremendous boost. An example is MobileNurse, a handheld software that enables mobile nurses to remotely access over a Mobitex RAM network the hospital inventory, to query patient records and insurance information, and even to order medicines on behalf of the home-care patients. Many hospitals are experimenting with mobile technologies by implementing wireless LANs and using IR or RF technologies to access data remotely from anywhere on the hospital premises. Handheld devices connected to hospital LANs through wireless PCMCIA cards (which are the Personal Computer Memory Card International Association's standard for computer plug-in, credit card-sized cards that provide about 90 percent compatibility across various platforms, BIOS, and application software) are increasingly being used to carry out a variety of functions, a few of which are discussed in Chapter 10. This technology is expected to grow with improving handwriting-recognition software.

Wireless technology also plays an important role when critical patient data needs to be transmitted from an ambulance to a hospital or between two medical centers. A real-life example of this is the Remote Patient Monitoring System (RPMS), in which a patient's vital statistics, such as EKG waveform, pulse, heart rate and blood pressure, are captured at the scene or in route to a hospital and are immediately transmitted over a wireless network to a hospital emergency room (ER). The ER doctor can then monitor and analyze the received data and even transmit advice back to the ambulance. The system has been developed by Systems Guidance Ltd., a computer software and hardware supplier in the U.K. Quite often, when a patient is in a rehabilitation room after surgery, the medical worker treating the patient may need access to the medical records or a master computer, which is easily possible using a wireless device. An EMS wireless application has been developed that provides end-to-end support from the time an emergency call is dispatched to the arrival of the patient in the emergency room. The system has been developed by Westech Information Systems, Inc., a Vancouver, British Columbia company.

Electronic News Communication

A good example of mCommerce for news communications is being seen during the war in Afghanistan where field journalists record content onto their handhelds and then wirelessly sync it to their newsrooms in the U.S. Many reporters now carry wireless computers or handheld devices. Some even use mobile digital cameras to transmit photos over wireless networks. An example of a wireless editorial and communications tool is Copymaster that runs on an HP Omnibook notebook PC. The notebook uses a Mobidem AT modem to transmit information over a RAM network. For details on news communications please read Chapter 8.

Hospitality Industry

Since survival in the hospitality industry depends on customer satisfaction, hotels have started using mobile technologies to enhance their customers' experience. They are taking orders, processing credit cards, checking in guests and mini-bar items used, reordering supplies, and maintaining housekeeping ledgers, all using wireless devices. Further discussion on this topic is provided in Chapter 10.

WHAT'S NEXT?

This chapter has provided the basic building blocks for understanding mCommerce applications and their value propositions. The next chapter focuses on establishing some basic building blocks for security. Just as you need to understand the fundamentals of mCommerce applications, you will need to learn about the basics of mobile security, as detailed in Chapters 3 and 4. Most of the security solutions for the various mCommerce applications are based on the fundamentals described in these chapters.

CHAPTER 3

Mobile Security Overview

The previous chapter detailed examples of mCommerce applications as building blocks for future topics. This chapter explores the basics of security for the purposes of understanding the impact of security on mCommerce. Security in mCommerce is based on the main concepts introduced in this chapter and Chapter 4. Let's look at the world of mobile security...

In the world of security, we never talk about absolute security, but rather acceptable risk. In the physical world, the entire insurance industry has been built around estimating levels of risk and providing financial protection. Likewise, in the wireless world, we cannot guarantee 100 percent security, but we can make the security so strong that if it is compromised, the data is no longer useful. Thus, it is always important, in any security evaluation, to determine the length of time a piece of data needs to be protected. For example, a product design specification for a company may need to be protected only until the product is retired; however, national defense secrets may need to be protected years after a particular threat has expired.

Currently, carriers of mobile device services do provide some security through the use of encryption protocols (more on this in Chapter 5). However, without a solution to provide end-to-end security, mCommerce cannot grow to the lofty levels described by so many analyst reports. *End-to-end security* can be defined as maintaining authentication, confidentially, and integrity of a communication from sender to recipient. In mCommerce, the sender may be a person with a mobile phone executing a financial transaction, for example, with the recipient being the sender's bank's eCommerce server. Implemented properly, even the data carrier has no visibility into the data being carried over its networks.

The network/wireless professional will note that there are, in fact, various security provisions built into various mobile standards. We will briefly review these standards in Chapter 5 and will also review some of those security features. However, those standards perform only some level of authentication of the mobile device and encryption to and from the mobile device to the carrier. In the world of mCommerce, the transaction goes beyond the wire and into the wired world, so our solution to mitigate these security concerns must protect a transaction from its origin at the mobile device through when it reaches the mCommerce destination server.

There are many issues related to security for a mobile device and mCommerce. We can concisely describe these issues as follows:

▼ **Physical security**   Given that mobile devices are generally small, theft of the device, and thus access to valuable data and digital credentials, can easily compromise any mCommerce network.

■ **Carrier bearer**   Since many mobile devices receive service from a public carrier, traditional wireless issues related to interception of mid-air communication and replay-type attacks can hinder mCommerce (this is an increasingly alarming issue for certain wireless communications such as 802.11b, which is the latest wireless LAN standard).

■ **Transactional**   Since many mCommerce transactions eventually get routed over a public network, such as the Internet, it is important that security be maintained not only to the carrier, but all the way through to the mCommerce server.

▲ **Post-transaction**   Given that there is a need to provide digital receipts or some type of proof for problem resolution after a transaction has occurred, a system must be maintained to prove, securely, that a particular transaction occurred.

The ideal solution encompasses all of the aforementioned issues. Practically, a mix of technology and solutions are needed to achieve those goals. The most complete solution to securing mCommerce applications has been the implementation of public key infrastructure (PKI) for the wireless world. PKI is perhaps the only technology that provides the key elements of *authentication, confidentiality, data integrity,* and *nonrepudiation.*

NOTE: According to *Datamonitor*, in a May 2001 report titled "Creating Trust: PKI and Authentication and Encryption Technologies," when 3G services (which provide large amounts of bandwidth) are available, 45 percent of PKI revenues will come from wireless applications.

Physical security is not addressed directly through PKI (although well-defined policy statements and insurance protection can help mitigate loss), but additional components, such as biometric devices and personal identification number (PIN) locking techniques, can minimize damage done when a mobile device is not physically secure.

WHAT IS PUBLIC KEY INFRASTRUCTURE (PKI)?

Every business and individual has the need for a certain element of confidence that business conducted electronically is safely completed with the expected parties. In the physical world, this is achieved through physical identification with identification cards, voice recognition, facial recognition, legal documents, and so on. However, in the electronic world, we cannot be certain who we are dealing with or who else may be privy to a conversation, and we may even be unsure whether the communication was altered in transit. Furthermore, in physical commerce, contracts or signatures bind a party to a legal transaction. Likewise, electronic transactions also need to be bound to particular parties. Imagine if someone were to purchase an automobile online, prompting a factory to produce that machine to specifications, and then the buyer refuted ever conducting that transaction. Financial losses from these types of events could wipe out businesses.

A simple, common way of protecting data is by using either proprietary methods or encryption using *symmetric keys*. Symmetric keys are a mathematical equivalent to physical locks and keys. For example, a single key (like a symmetric key) may unlock a house's door, and that same key may be used to lock that door. The strength of these symmetric keys is measured in the size of the key, or number of bits. Generally, the greater the number of bits used in a key, the more secure the transaction. The problem with such a method is that to conduct business over the Internet, not knowing or having physical access to the parties involved, how do we ensure that everyone has the keys required to communicate securely? Although we could e-mail such information, we run the risk of those keys' being intercepted and copied so that someone else could then also have the keys to unlock the secret communication. To resolve this problem, the concept of *public key technology* was developed in the 1970s to provide a method of exchanging these secret keys securely. This approach is somewhat analogous to the situation in which a postal carrier delivers your house key through a mail slot in an office. Only you, the intended recipient, can open the door to the office to access the contents of the mailbox and retrieve the key, but anyone can drop a key through the slot. Once you have retrieved the key, then you can enter your house. This example describes the core aspects of public key technology.

However, simply using this public key technology is insufficient for all security needs. After all, since anyone can drop a key into the mail slot, how do you know whether the key is the correct one for your house, whether someone else's key was substituted for your key, or even the identity of the person who mailed the key? For a complete solution, we turn to PKI.

One of the generally accepted methods for creating a secure connection on an open system, like the Internet or the wireless world, is PKI. A PKI is composed of a number of systems that include policies, legal practices, and technology to deliver a solution for providing essential features for secure mCommerce or eCommerce (also known as *meCommerce*).

One of the fundamental components of PKI is the concept of public and private keys. In basic terms, the public key (like the mail slot described earlier) is freely available to anyone to send a message securely. The corresponding private key (like the key to the office that accesses the mailbox) is used to decode the message. A characteristic of this mathematical relationship also allows the sender to provide his or her identity by digitally signing, or encoding, a message with the private key rather than the public key. Then, the corresponding public key is used to verify that message. In the mailbox analogy, using digital signatures is akin to someone's being able to describe the secret location of your house key, writing this on a piece of paper, and slipping the paper into your mail slot at the office. In this manner, you can be sure of the identity of the author of the note since only that person could have known the location of the secret house key.

To bundle or protect these public keys, digital certificates (often simply called certificates) are used. As shown in Figure 3-1, a certificate

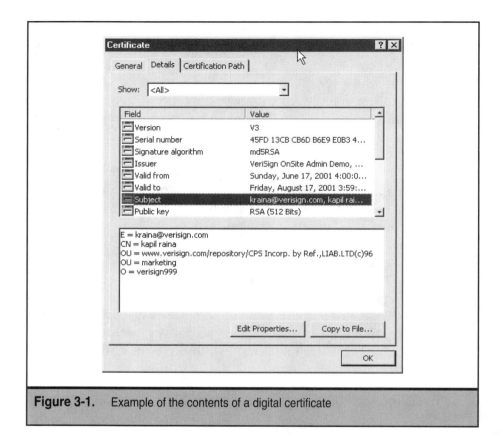

Figure 3-1. Example of the contents of a digital certificate

is simply a package with some unique data about an entity. This data is in the form of a predefined set of standards, known as X.509 (the latest version widely being used is version 3). To protect this bundle of information from being altered, an issuing authority (called the certificate authority, or CA), uses its private key to digitally sign this bundle, or certificate. This is similar to governments' use of special paper or holograms on paper currency to ensure that the currency has not been forged or altered in any way. In this manner, when the recipient receives the certificate, the recipient can verify that the certificate was not altered by using the CA's public key. Because the public and private keys are mathematically related in a unique way, the CA's signature can be verified with a high degree of confidence. To ensure that the CA's public key, which is used to detect tampering, is delivered without being tampered itself, the key is delivered through some type of secure mechanism. Usually the public key is installed in an application, such as a browser, at the time of the software's creation (otherwise, we may doubt that the CA's public key itself has not been faked).

NOTE: It may take two or more years for a CA's public key to appear in software like a browser because people use older software for quite some time.

The concept of verifying certificates is described through the use of a certificate hierarchy. This is similar to, for example, the hierarchy of some large nonprofit groups, which have an international organization, with various national chapters, each having its own state chapters, and each of those state chapters having local or city chapters. Membership in a local charity allows the member to gain some of the benefits and recognition from all of the other member chapters through the international organization. Each digital certificate, to have successful verification, must contain the highest-level authority (or root key) in the recipient's verifying device (for example, in the PDA, mobile phone, or PC). Thus, CAs such as Baltimore and VeriSign have worked with various mobile phone vendors and PDA manufacturers to ensure that root keys are embedded in the devices. Without such efforts, the recipient would not know whether a received digital certificate was issued as claimed or was altered or forged.

In a mobile environment, however, the chain is usually very small, due to the mobile device's constraints. Many CAs actually have a separate hierarchy for issuing certificates just for mobile devices. A different hierarchy allows a CA to create a separate, simpler chain of trust, as shown in Figure 3-2.

That is PKI in brief—not a simple conversation over coffee, but rather an entire industry (although the coffee chain Starbucks plans to have wireless computer connections in some of their cafes by 2001 or 2002, so in fact, PKI and mCommerce security may be a conversation over coffee!). The expansion into mCommerce is a natural extension of this technology.

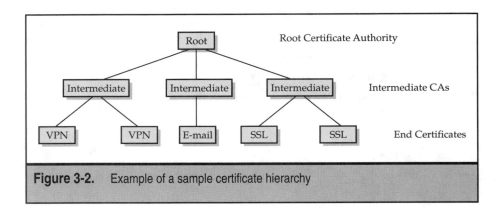

Figure 3-2. Example of a sample certificate hierarchy

NOTE: Public-area wireless access networks, such as the one Starbucks plans to roll out, require additional security measures, including personal, software-based firewalls.

How PKI Eases Consumers' Fears

According to a Datamonitor/Impact 2001 survey, the majority of Internet users say security is a major concern. To a large extent, this is justified, with a significant portion of all Internet-based transactions being claimed as false. Currently, in the United States, the most popular method of transaction is by credit card. Because the liability for credit card misuse lies with the merchant (that is, the merchant must prove that a transaction is valid), the merchant bears the cost of any forged or improperly used credit cards employed in transactions on the Internet.

Authentication Through PKI

Authentication is the ability to verify an individual or device's identity. Most PKI systems accomplish this by allowing the entity to be verified to sign something and then send that signed text or snippet for verification. The receiver then verifies that the signature of the sent information is still valid. The assumption is that only the sender knows the private key and that it has not been compromised. In most mobile devices, risk from loss of the device that may contain the private key can be mitigated by methods such as PIN-protecting access to the device or terminating mobile service.

Confidentiality and Integrity Through PKI

Almost all valuable transactions require some level of ability to ensure that only the intended parties are privy to the details of the transactions. Furthermore, for sensitive applications, such as financial applications, it is imperative that the recipient be aware of whether the message or data was altered. In a PKI-enabled transaction, only the recipient can decode the data; thus, there is a high degree of confidence that the message was not decoded in transit. Integrity is verified through the use of mathematically defined hashing algorithms both before the data is sent and when it is received. If the integrity parameters match, then the data can be said to have maintained integrity.

Nonrepudiation Through PKI

Because the assumption in PKI is that the private key is owned by and under the control of only the owner, then all transactions with this key, especially signing functions, prove that the owner has intended and conducted a transaction. This prevents the owner from later refuting that a transaction, for example, a bank withdrawal, has occurred. This level of nonrepudiation can be further enhanced through the use of devices such as fingerprint readers, which link the use of the private key to some physical attribute, such as the fingerprint of a person. Mobile devices, due to their form factor (in other words, the shape and size), generally do not take advantage of such technology.

STRATEGIES IN WIRELESS INTERNET SECURITY

The challenge in the mobile space centers on the fact that the use of PKI requires heavy (relatively) computational ability (this will be discussed in greater detail Chapter 4). Since most mobile devices are optimized for space and battery consumption, the use of standard PKI certificates, as found in the wired world, is not practical. For this reason, the concept of *Wireless Transport Layer Security* (WTLS) was developed. In addition, the use of the *Wireless Application Protocol* (WAP) to better address the small display size on a mobile device raises another set of security issues.

WAP Specifications and Security

WAP has become a global standard for presentation and delivery of information and telephony services to mobile devices. Its origin was the WAP Forum, the joint development effort of Ericsson, Nokia, Motorola, and (then) Phone.com. WAP addressed the issue of limited resources, especially the limited size of the display screen, in mobile devices. Web sites have become more and more sophisticated, and it is not possible to display many sites on a mobile device without some type of modification. *Wireless Markup Language* (WML), a language based on *eXtensible Markup Language* (XML), was developed to enable creation of WAP-compliant web sites. Much like HTML is used in the world of TCP/IP, WML is used in the world of WAP.

The initial specifications from the WAP Forum, the main body developing the WAP standard, did not include much security consideration. Later revisions (WAP 1.2) incorporated guidelines on how to address security concerns.

The most important protocol specification for security that the WAP Forum developed is WTLS. WTLS bears some similarity to *Transport Layer Security* (TLS), the wired world's security protocol specification that provides privacy between two communicating applications using the industry-standard TCP/IP networking protocol.

Wireless Transport Layer Security (WTLS)

WTLS is the security layer in the WAP protocol, similar to the TLS protocol in TCP/IP; however, WTLS has been modified to account for:

▼ Ability to support connection and datagram protocols

■ Long round-trip times in message communication (up to 10 seconds)

- Dynamic key refreshing
▲ Low bandwidth (as low as 100 bits per second), processing power, and storage space

Of course, you may ask, so if WAP truly can solve many of the problems of bringing web content to the handset, why haven't I seen it? The dirty little secret of WAP is that a device must be WAP enabled. Generally, this means having a microbrowser to handle WAP data. In addition, the mobile device should have a reasonable amount of visual screen space to make the use of WAP worthwhile.

In Europe, WAP has gotten much more traction than in North America. As a result, WAP has not yet had the reach that its creators would like. This layer was designed to address the constraints of memory, processing, storage, and slow bandwidth/response time in a mobile device. Many mobile carriers do provide some type of encryption of air traffic, but that type of security can vary from carrier to carrier and does not provide end-to-end (for example, mobile-phone-to-eCommerce-merchant) security.

WTLS server certificates, as shown in Figure 3-3, were originally defined in WAP 1.1 and are primarily used to validate the identity of a server and provide an encrypted tunnel for subsequent communication. Encrypted tunnels are point-to-point streams of encrypted data. Encrypted tunnels are formed through the use of the public key to encrypt a randomly generated session (symmetric) key that can be exchanged securely and then used for subsequent secure communication. This is something like writing a secret password in a code system, transmitting that coded password, and then having the receiving party decode that phrase to get the password. From that point on, the two parties can use the common password to access the same data. Public-private key technology is more computationally intensive than symmetric encryption. WTLS client certificates, as defined in WAP 1.2, are designed for the client to authenticate itself to the server.

Wireless Markup Language (WML) Script SignText

The mobile-world equivalent of HTML in the wired world is WML. To support digital signatures in the wireless worked, the WAP WML

```
                                                    analyze certificate

    certificate_version = 01
    signature_algorithm: rsa_sha

    Issuer {
     identifier_type: 01
     character_set: 0004
     name: "freecerts.com; keyon; CH; WTLS Test CA; Test Purposes Only. No Assurances"
    }

    Not valid before: Wed Jan  3 16:44:11 2001
    Not valid after: Sat Jan  1 16:44:11 2011

    Subject {
     identifier_type: 01
     character_set: 0004
     name: "freecerts.com; keyon; CH; WTLS Test CA; Test Purposes Only. No Assurances"
    }

    m_publicKeyType: rsa

    Lenght of the public exponent e = 3 bytes
    00000000   01 00 01

    Lenght of the public modulus n = 128 bytes
    00000000   B8 90 E4 DB 38 17 44 10 9C AE 13 F3 F2 76 0F 57
    00000010   BB 7B 5E 38 75 52 48 BC B7 20 6B F1 92 44 29 A2
    00000020   79 3F 4D 10 63 A1 59 0C 04 7A 6B 0D 24 E2 61 A9
    00000030   1B F2 39 EF CD 1C 8A 00 23 AF 62 C8 B6 43 C2 55
    00000040   1A DD 11 48 E6 33 59 BC 4C 8B 14 E8 B6 CC 74 F6
    00000050   E8 D8 5F 79 C5 F8 87 9E 86 10 44 4E 8B 13 D8 A7
    00000060   AE 5A 2B CC C0 0E A4 BF 4B CA D8 9E FF 83 82 AE
    00000070   C8 1B BA 38 B5 DF 88 82 15 2E 7E 47 A9 E2 EC EF
```

Figure 3-3.   Analysis of typical WTLS certificate contents

Script SignText function was developed. This function is part of the
WAP Forum–defined cryptographic library. The function defines
how a certificate is managed and used.

Wireless Gateways

Wireless gateways (*WAP gateways*) function as a method of translating
HTML to WML so that a feature-rich web site can be simplified for
a small display and footprint on a mobile phone. By using a WAP
gateway, content providers can write original content using HTTP
without worrying about who might access the data. The WAP gateway

is then installed to ensure proper, dynamic conversion of that HTTP traffic into WAP traffic. Table 3-1 details some of the available WAP gateways.

A wireless gateway is hosted by the network provider or, for high-end content, perhaps the merchant directly (as in some mCommerce-enabled bank sites). The choice of who hosts the gateway can influence security policy and controls. This whole concept has given rise to the *Wireless Application Service Provider* (WASP) market. WASPs provide mCommerce application solutions through a service model, maintaining security and updating software. Some WASPs can host a gateway as well. A typical mCommerce architecture example is shown in Figure 3-4.

The main difference between a wired device and a portable, mobile device lies in the processing and storage capacity of the mobile device. The main functions that are handled differently between wired and wireless systems include generation of keys, storage of keys, and revocation checking of certificates. Another major difference is that most mobile devices do not function with SSL and have to use WTLS (with the exception of the I-mode mobile telephone standard). This requires a PKI gateway to convert a transaction from WTLS to SSL and vice versa.

Vendor	Customer Adoption	Relative Cost	WAP Standards Compliance
CMG	Low	High	High
Ericsson	Medium	High	High
Materna	Low	Medium	High
Nokia	High	High	High
Openwave (previously Phone.com)	High	Medium	Low
Source: Mobile Lifestreams Limited			

Table 3-1.   Sample of Commercial WAP Gateways

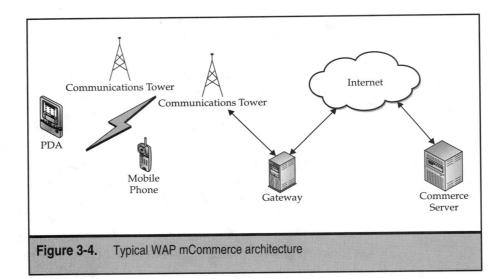

Figure 3-4. Typical WAP mCommerce architecture

SECURITY ISSUES IN WTLS

As with most protocols, WTLS does have a number of security issues. It is important to note that protocols are simply a roadmap for code developers to follow, and security flaws can occur in the implementation of a protocol. This occurred, for example, in Netscape's implementation of an earlier version of the SSL protocol. Netscape's initial attempts created an implementation flaw that made the Netscape web browser vulnerable to attacks. In later releases, the company fixed the implementation problem. Likewise, the flaws of a protocol may be mitigated or exacerbated depending on the quality of the implementation. We will not discuss all of the possible flaws in this book due to the technical nature and length of discussion; however, we will look at some of the best-known security issues in WTLS, including:

▼ Weak crypto ciphers

■ Null cipher acceptance

■ Sequence number weaknesses

▲ False alert messages

Weak Crypto Ciphers

Earlier versions of WTLS used a 40-bit cipher, which we know today to be very easily broken, thus invalidating any security provided against eavesdropping or sniffing. Later versions of WTLS specifications warn against the use of such a weak cipher; however, due to the need for backward compatibility, 40-bit ciphers on servers may still need to be supported (see WAP-261-WTLS-20010406-p, proposed version April 6, 2001).

Null Cipher Acceptance

If the implementation of the WTLS protocol accepts null cipher requests (that is, requests without any encryption) without having specifically asked for such requests, the transmission runs the risk of a man-in-the-middle attack. In this type of attack, the attacker poses as both the recipient and sender, without either party knowing. Both sender and recipient then believe that they are sending an encrypted message, yet all traffic is being deciphered and perhaps changed in transit. Later WTLS specifications warned against null cipher acceptance.

Sequence Number Weaknesses

The WTLS protocol uses sequence numbers to identify all data packets associated with a particular session. However, the protocol allows this number not to be used. If the implementation uses this option, then the transmission is subject to playback attacks. Playback attacks are attacks in which a sequence of events are recorded and played back to repeat the original result (for example, logging into a password-protected system). Although higher layers, such as application-level layers, may help mitigate this vulnerability, it is dangerous in a bandwidth- and CPU-constrained environment to rely on any other layer to perform this task.

False Alert Messages

System alert messages under WTLS can be divided into two types: critical and fatal. Whenever a process flags one of these types of errors, the connection between the mobile device and server is broken immediately. Fatal errors force a new session identification and renegotiation of a session. Critical errors may allow future sessions to continue using the same setup parameters. These alerts are meant to give feedback to running applications on the current status.

These alert messages are vulnerable to a denial-of-service attack, where the mobile device and server would not be able to communicate (thus preventing the execution of an mCommerce transaction). A denial-of-service attack is simply a barrage of fake or improper requests directed at the same server, thus tying up the server's resources and preventing legitimate queries from being serviced. An attacker could create false alert messages and, for unencrypted sessions, send alert messages to terminate connections.

WTLS FIXES

The recent version of the WTLS standard does offer a number of fixes over previous versions. However, as is the case with any emerging technology, flaws will be discovered and then addressed later.

Some of the major issues that WTLS addressed in the April 2001 WAP proposal include:

▼ Increased awareness, through warnings, of various types of attacks to which the protocol is susceptible

■ The removal of a particular weak algorithm (SHA_XOR_40)

■ Better support for X.509 standards

■ Inclusion of more features of *elliptical curve cryptographic* (ECC), a popular encryption algorithm for mobile devices

▲ Ability to support stronger RSA algorithms

WAP VERSUS SIM TOOLKIT

The *subscriber identity module* (SIM) *toolkit* (STK), used in GSM (*Global System for Mobile Communications*) networks, dominates in Europe and Asia. STK, using SIM, supports communication services, control of the human-machine interface, menu management and application control, and accessory management, among other features. SIM cards, through STK, enable the use of personalized menus that provide services offered by the carrier. At present, there is not extensive interoperability between SIM cards from carrier to carrier. Key security advantages of STK for mCommerce applications include the ability to handle public key technology.

Building on the popularity of WAP, WAP 1.2 defines a method for the WAP identity module (WIM). WIM allows authentication of a mobile client. WIM, combined with WTLS, provides strong authentication using WAP. WIM is a tamper-resistant electronic computer chip that can reside in the WAP device or in smartcards. Many devices have slots for such devices. WIM can store critical information such as private and public keys used in initiating and authenticating secure connections.

The use of WIM depends on the penetration of WAP-enabled handsets and mobile devices. Because STKs are available today, they are still popular. Going forward, there will be room for both SIM and WIM (also known as S/WIM) platforms for mobile applications. However, WAP-based technologies will become increasingly used since WAP describes a standard that works across different types of network standards.

COMPONENTS OF WIRELESS PKI

A traditional PKI system has components to determine the roles of various parties. The basic elements of a wireless PKI system, as shown in Figure 3-5, are slightly modified from those of a wired PKI system. They include:

▼ A *registration authority* (RA) that defines who gets a certificate

■ A *certification authority* (CA) that actually generates and issues the digital certificate

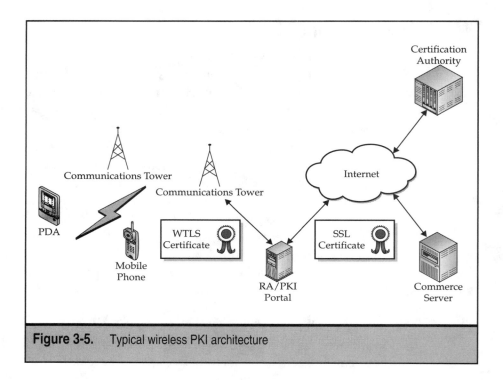

Figure 3-5. Typical wireless PKI architecture

- An end entity application (EA), which is the PKI-enabled application that runs in the WAP device on a WIM card

- A directory to store certificates so they can be accessed on demand

▲ PKI portal that typically acts as the RA and translates requests made by the WAP client to the RA portion and interacts with the CA over the wired network

The function of a registration authority (RA) is to provide a mechanism for validating an entity's credentials and approving or rejecting the request to receive a digital certificate.

The traditional PKI system relies on ASN.1 standards to service requests. These standards are too computationally intensive for mobile devices. Thus, mobile devices use WML and the WML Script SignText function.

The modern trend is to use the elliptical curve cryptographic (ECC) function, which can perform encryption and decryption with a smaller bit size (that is, using less computational power) without compromising security strength. Typically, 1,024 bits is considered strong security in the traditional PKI world, whereas equivalent security in ECC is accomplished using only 163 bits. To further increase mobile device efficiencies, *wireless PKI* (WPKI) certificates are a subset of X.509, with some reduced-length fields in the certificate to conserve resources.

CAUTION: Remember that strong algorithms such as ECC are designed to provide strong protection; however, these algorithms must be implemented properly to take advantage of security. Ensure that the products you use incorporate a good implementation as determined through third-party certification evaluation and testing.

CHALLENGES TO WIRELESS INTERNET PKI

Although PKI can provide a range of security benefits, limitations of mobile devices force some changes to the standard implementation. We will first discuss how to determine the validity of a certificate and then some of the issues related to the management of WPKI certificates over the Internet.

Control of Revocation of Certificates

One of the fundamental requirements of a well-designed PKI solution is the use of revocation and revocation checking. Imagine if the immigration office revoked a criminal's passport, but never bothered to seize the passport or update computers indicating denial of exit or admission into a particular country. Such lack of enforcement would not limit the movement of the criminal. Likewise, if certificates are issued without the ability to check for revoked certificates, a major security problem occurs. The traditional way to manage this checking in PKI is to use *certificate revocation lists* (CRLs). CRLs must list all of the revoked certificates for the period of time during which the certificates were originally valid (in most cases, this is up to one year). Obviously, these lists could become quite large, and in the context of mobile devices, even unusable. To address this issue in the world of mobile PKI, WTLS introduced the concept of short-lived certificates. This strategy avoids the use of CRLs.

These short-lived certificates work like this: A master certificate is issued that is valid for, say, a year. Then, based on verification at a wired server, a shorter-term certificate is issued that is valid for, say, a day. Thus, when the master certificate is revoked, no short-lived certificates could be issued, thus preventing the use of the certificate. So by limiting exposure to the use of a certificate for a day, we can avoid having to check the validity of the certificate on the mobile device. The validity of the master certificate, however, can be checked because it resides on a fixed or more powerful computer.

The Hand-off Between SSL and WTLS

Except for the I-mode mobile phone standard, used in Japan, most wireless PKI solutions must include the use of some type of gateway to translate the Internet communication to the wireless portion. The gateway then contains an SSL certificate to identify itself to the rest of the eCommerce servers on the Internet. The gateway also has the ability to issue the WTLS certificate, which is basically a short-term SSL certificate to accommodate mobile devices' various constraints.

The key concern in this architecture is that the gateway is vulnerable (this is sometimes referred to as "the gap in WAP"). In terms of uptime availability, the gateway must be available for the mCommerce service to function. In terms of security, the hand-off by the gateway from SSL to WTLS must be implemented correctly.

We know that the encryption from one side of the WAP gateway must be decrypted, only to be reencrypted for forwarding onto the Internet, and the opposite situation occurs for communication in the opposite direction. Why is this an issue? The gateway is simply a software program. This piece of software may write memory fragments to disk. Should the data being transmitted be written to disk, a hacker may try to obtain this fragment of memory from disk and read its contents. Ideally, such information should never be written to disk, and most gateway solutions take care to avoid such poor security implementations; however, that risk is still there.

To further add to potential risk, unless the mCommerce vendor hosts the gateway directly (as opposed to the mobile service carrier), WAP gateways are usually in an unprotected area of the (carrier's) network called the *demilitarized zone,* or DMZ. As the costs of gateways drop, more and more mCommerce vendors will host their own gateways in improved security networks.

There are several commercially available gateways on the market, as detailed in Table 3-2. Selection of a gateway should be based on not only feature set, but also the quality of implementation. No one knows when you have good security, but everyone knows when you do not.

	WAP	SIM	WPKI
Timeline	Used today	Used today	Used today
Benefits	Similar to known Internet standards	Hardware based (better security)	Compatible with all other standards
Providers	Openwave, Nokia, Motorola	Gemplus, Setec	VeriSign, Baltimore, Entrust
Issues	Requires WPKI rather than standard PKI	Most costly (price of toolkit)	Interoperability issues among different providers

Table 3-2.   Some Approaches to Mobile Security

MESSAGE FOR THE IT MANAGER

The ability to extend confidence through security for mobile devices can be accomplished through the use of public key infrastructure (PKI) technology such as certificates. With mobile versions of these certificates, an adequate solution can be presented to enable authentication, confidentiality, integration, and nonrepudiation.

NOTE: If you already have a PKI infrastructure and plan on extending it for the mobile environment, ensure that your vendor has a well-established product/service offering for the mobile space. Not all PKI vendors have good, mature mobile PKI strategies.

The use of PKI technology on mobile devices can enable users to conduct transactions with confidence. This allows applications such as financial or other confidential transactions to extend outside a typical enterprise. Furthermore, given that there is legal support for digital signatures in most parts of the world, mobile transactions can be legally binding.

Implementation Issues

Implementation of a PKI infrastructure, especially as a security solution for the mCommerce world, must be approached with careful planning. The key elements in planning include:

▼ Certificate use (vendor and contents of certificates)

■ PKI gateway/portal for translation between the wired and wireless worlds

■ Ensuring that the mobile device has the required embedded root certificates

■ Ensuring that the mobile device is compatible with the chosen gateway solution and certificate vendor

■ Costs, which are typically on a subscription basis for the certificates, but license fees may apply for the gateway and custom development

▲   Management of certificates for WPKI, which can be easy for low numbers, but will require a separate PKI management system for large numbers; some vendors, such as VeriSign, Baltimore, and Entrust, offer scalable solutions

Security Issues

The use of WAP and WTLS does bring up a number of security issues. We will take a look at some of the major issues and highlight some strategies to minimize this risk.

▼   **Risk**   WAP gateways do pose a small security risk that may be increased or decreased depending on the network architecture and who hosts the gateway.
Mitigation   Perform rigorous testing of the chosen gateway and understand from the vendor the architecture and method of dealing with the SSL/WTLS translation. *Hardening* (that is, removing as many known security holes as possible) the machine (UNIX or NT) on which the gateway resides should also mitigate risks.

■   **Risk**   Physical security of the gateway and other components.
Mitigation   Host the WAP gateway onsite, and house the gateway with the same level of security as other data processing systems.

▲   **Risk**   Physical security of the mobile device.
Mitigation   Use policy and procedures to ensure whatever protection the mobile device offers (PIN, password, physical locks, and so on). Ensure that backup is performed regularly, and that the user of the mobile device understands the importance of protecting the physical device.

CHAPTER 4

Mobile Versus Wired Security

L ife as a security professional is a never-ending game of cat and mouse. Just as new technologies or new techniques for computing are developed, new security threats are always emerging. Imagine leaving your house in the morning, locking your door, and returning to find that you have to replace the locks because in that brief time you were gone, someone has figured out how to break your lock. Such is the world of computing today.

The extra challenge mobile devices add to the security mix is that the usual tools to mitigate threats in the security world cannot necessarily be applied to the mobile world. Because the wireless industry is fairly old relative to the world of the commercial Internet, there are many legacy items to struggle with. Furthermore, the nature of the mobile devices require them to be portable and yet power efficient. Thus, we must deal with many physical constraints on the devices.

All of these concerns push us to come up with new and innovative solutions for mobile device security. This chapter compares some of the high-level, general differences between wired world security and the mobile world so that we can use the lessons we have learned from the wired world and, to the extent possible, apply them to the wireless world. The important point to remember in this chapter is that regardless of where a transaction occurs (mobile or fixed location), eventually all transactions are routed through the Internet and to a merchant somewhere on the Internet. This gives us a common set of security problems. In later chapters, we will take these basic concepts and explore how each mCommerce application uses these concepts in their own security solutions. For example, CRM (customer relationship management) applications have different security needs and solutions than, say, healthcare-specific applications.

We will not attempt to go through all of the security concerns in the wired world and relate them to the mobile world. Entire books have been written just on the wired-world security threats. However, we have selected some of the key threats that can have the most impact on an mCommerce deployment. As mCommerce becomes more prevalent, we shall see a clear divergence of security professionals and skills into specialization in either mobile or wired security. Perhaps specialists in mobile security will be called mSecurity professionals.

MOBILE DEVICE CONSTRAINTS

Perhaps the main reason why mobile security and wired security take slightly different approaches is because of the constraints of the client: the mobile device. Mobile devices, whether they are mobile phones, PDAs, palm top computers, or whatever, have certain limitations, including:

▼ Memory

■ Computational processing

■ Form factor

▲ Bandwidth

Memory

While it is common for PCs to have 128 MB or more of memory and many gigabytes of hard drive storage, such capacity on a mobile device, within a reasonable price and form factor, is nearly impossible. New and inventive ways of managing memory on mobile devices have had to be created. Certain devices, such as Pocket PCs, have scaled-down versions of applications that are normally found on regular PCs. In addition, it is more common for these mobile devices to have flash memory or smartcard storage capability.

Smartcards are quite common in Europe for mobile phones. Smartcards provide features that solve two problems: a place for storage of data such as digital certificates or subscriber identity and the ability to take data from phone to phone. Although smartcard technology can be used for wired devices such as traditional PCs, because the need for portability and extra storage is not so great, smartcard readers (required for smartcards to operate) are not prevalent in PCs.

NOTE: Smartcard technology adoption is much slower in North America than in Europe or Asia. National identity cards are driving much of the large scale use of smartcards.

So why haven't smartcards been the answer across the world for mobile devices? The main reason is that smartcard technologies and standards vary from manufacturer to manufacturer based on region. Certain standards for mobile phones, such as SIM or WIM (S/WIM) cards, have been developed. The SIM toolkit (STK), as described in the previous chapter, has been used for many years. Practical applications allow a user to take this card from phone to phone and still maintain proper identification and billing information. Without such a card, as is the case in most of North America, a new phone requires a new setup and configuration by the carrier. The advent of the WAP standard created another standard called WIM.

Computational Processing

Another area in which mobile devices have constraints is in the ability to process large amounts of mathematical functions. Although devices such as PDAs have increased computational abilities that rival those of some older PCs, in general, for cheaper devices and for mobile phones, there is a great gap between PCs and mobile devices. Table 4-1 shows the memory and processing power of a sample of mobile devices.

One method that has become a standard for reducing computational need for encryption, while still maintaining strong security, is elliptical curve cryptography (ECC). Most companies now have mobile devices that use ECC whenever processing power is an issue. ECC is based on a complex mathematical problem, making it difficult

Device	CPU (MHz)	Memory (MB)
Desktop PC	1,000 (1 GHz)	128
Compaq/HP PocketPC	133+	128+
Palm Vx	20	8
Handspring Platinum	33	8
Kyocera PDQ SmartPhone	16	2

Table 4-1. Sample Survey of Computational Speeds of Different Devices

to break the protection it provides for a set of data. The popularity of ECC rests on the fact that it requires fewer bits (relative to other algorithms such as those for RSA security, for example) for strong protection. Table 4-2 shows a comparison of these different algorithms. Fewer bits implies that the algorithm can be processed more quickly and with reduced requirements for computational speed. In addition, the bandwidth required is reduced because fewer bits need to be passed back and forth between sender and recipient.

Form Factor

Due to the small size of mobile devices, screen space is very limited. As a result, different methods of data entry and data delivery must be applied to mobile devices versus wired devices.

In Chapter 3, we discussed WAP, which is designed specifically to manage the display constraints on a mobile device. The use of a microbrowser, as required for WAP, allows a user to see and enter only the essentials of an mCommerce transaction.

In addition, in the design of a mobile device, creating a lighter, smaller device means giving up some battery life and some key functionality, such as memory storage.

Bandwidth

One of the biggest topics of conversation in the mobile phone industry is how to improve bandwidth. *3G networks* (3rd generation mobile phone networks) are slated as the next evolution of our current mobile phone network infrastructure with desktop-like

Type of Encryption Algorithm	Signature Size (in Bits)
RSA	1,024
DSA	320
ECC	320

Table 4-2. Sample Comparison of Signature Length of Long Messages (over 2000 Bits)

Internet speed. The nirvana of 3G networks will probably not arrive until late 2002 or later for most of the world. Among the unique aspects of mobile device communication are long round-trip times and periods where connections are broken. Short-range wireless devices, such as cordless phones or radios, can manage this more effectively; however, for mCommerce applications, invariably the transactions must take place some distance away and over different types of networks, including wired networks. Again, standards such as WAP allow mobile devices to minimize bandwidth use.

Wired devices generally have more tolerance as they can accommodate better connection states and reconnect much more quickly if a connection is broken. One place where mobile devices will outperform wired devices is in the area of always-on connections. Mobile devices, in the next-generation networks, will have the capability to always be connected, or at least to have that appearance. In this situation, mCommerce transactions can truly be conducted on the spur of the moment. Today, wired devices such as PCs incur large costs for high bandwidth (such as with DSL or cable modems). Most (consumer) devices still get a maximum of 56K on wired networks through traditional dial-up connections.

Security implications for always-on devices are more complex than for other types of systems. Mobile devices, if they are always connected to the Internet, increase their exposure to being discovered and hacked.

NOTE: The problems facing users of mobile, always-on connections are very similar to the problems faced by broadband users (using DSL or cable modems, for example). DSL or cable modems increase the likelihood of hacker penetration simply because the hacker has more time to attempt a break in. Always-on mobile phones or PDAs will face similar issues.

The use of always-on devices creates the need for mitigation techniques such as virus checkers and personal firewalls for mobile devices. In 2001, these issues and some solutions were raised, but this will become more of a concern in the years to come. As mobile devices perform more automated functionality, viruses will have much more potential impact. Examples of malicious virus behavior for mobile phones, for example, could include initiating 1-900–type pay-per-minute calls that incur a charge of $3 per minute or more.

SECURITY MODEL

Having a background on the specific constraints and issues of mobile devices, we can now approach the security issues created by these unique features. It is important to keep in mind that every mCommerce implementation will require a link back to the wired world. Thus, security issues for the traditional wired world still affect mCommerce.

There are many aspects to security since there are so many components in a typical meCommerce transaction. This section will note any similarities between wired and mobile worlds and then focus on the mCommerce security specifics. We will break down the discussion into these components (as shown in Figure 4-1):

▼   Client (originates transaction)

■   Client network (transaction starts transmission)

■   Internet (transaction flows over the public network)

■   Merchant network (receives transaction)

▲   Server (receives and terminates transaction)

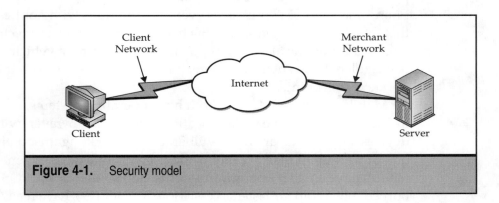

Figure 4-1.   Security model

Client

A *client* is basically defined as a device or terminal that initiates an meCommerce transaction. For the mobile world, that could be a PDA or a mobile phone, for example. For the wired world, that could be a PC or laptop computer.

This first component poses the first set of security threats. Considering that the physical device may be stolen, compromised, or left unattended, the easiest way to penetrate a strong security system is to get physical access to an unprotected client. There are several methods mobile device manufacturers have devised to mitigate damage due to the physical loss of a mobile device:

▼ **Encryption software**   Encodes information protected by a PIN code or password.

■ **Power lock codes**   PIN codes that are required as soon as power is turned on the device.

▲ **Physical cables**   Some PDAs, such as Palm Pilots, have steel cable cradles that can secure the device.

In general, these mechanisms are fairly weak against determined, deliberate attacks. Generally, we can assume loss of the physical device will eventually lead to the compromise of all data on the device.

One interesting method Dutch police have used in the theft of mobile phones is the SMS message bomb. Through some basic research, police can determine the unique number identifying the stolen mobile phone and send SMS messages every few minutes with notification that the phone has been stolen. Such a method is a defense mechanism akin to automobile alarms that go off during or after a vehicle has been stolen. With such a message, it is much harder to resell the phone at this point.

Mobile and wired devices both have operating systems, as shown in Table 4-3, that drive the applications they run. However, wired devices such as PCs are more vulnerable to attacks against their operating system than are mobile devices. Mobile devices generally tend to have smaller operating systems, and sometimes the OS is burned into a chip for faster access. More recent PDAs have read/write

Device	Type	Operating System
Palm	PDA	Palm OS
PocketPC	PDA	Win CE
Psion	PDA	Epoch/Symbian
Handspring	PDA	Palm OS
Ericsson (R380)	Mobile Phone	Epoc
Qualcomm pdQ™ 800	Smart Phone	Palm OS

Table 4-3. Some Mobile Devices and Their Operating Systems

operating systems to allow easier upgrades for functionality. Wired devices generally tend to have software-based operating systems or at least some type of read/write chip access.

TIP: Generally, there are fewer hacker problems with the Palm operating system than with the Win CE platform. This difference is mainly due to the very basic nature of the Palm OS relative to the Windows-like Win CE OS.

Attacks on the operating system of a device are common for wired devices. Generally, wired devices have full-featured operating systems and thus pose many security risks. For example, with desktop PCs, memory is heavily swapped to a disk medium to accommodate multiple application threads. In addition, many PCs create log files when the OS kernel crashes, leaving sensitive data from memory in readable disk format.

On the other hand, mobile devices generally do not suffer these problems because the OS does not get overwritten or replaced. In addition, mobile devices have stripped-down and very basic feature sets (to conserve space and increase speed).

Generally, most client applications in wired devices are based on Microsoft platforms (Windows 98, 2000, NT, XP). However, due to the complexity of such operating systems, there are many weaknesses that can be used to compromise a security system. Some common examples include gaining access to administrator accounts, forcing buffer flows in computer memory, and reading operating system kernel dumps. Generally, Microsoft provides patches to fix security holes as they are noted; however, there is always a significant gap between the noting of a security issue and the resolution of that issue.

The other most common operating system is the UNIX operating system, implemented in various forms by many companies such as Sun Microsystems and Hewlett-Packard (HP). Considering that UNIX has been around for so long, a large number of security holes exist, with patches widely available. Typically, the setup of a UNIX system is complex and so are efforts to improve the security of the system.

In a process called hardening, the operating system in use is stripped of unneeded features, debugging tools, and anything else not essential for the direct purpose of that function. By this means, security threats are minimized.

Next we move to the application layer of the client. The application layer handles programs such as the browser (Microsoft Internet Explorer, for example). Applications pose the greatest risk to security compromise, whether on a wired or a mobile device. Because applications share resources with each other on a computer system, all sorts of security threats can be exploited at this level. Some common threats on wired devices include:

▼ **Viruses** These come in many forms, but most replicate themselves and cause malicious data destruction or theft.

■ **Port attacks** Attacks that take advantage of certain parts of a program that are awaiting instructions from other programs.

▲ **Memory attacks** Attacks that take advantage of information in memory or data temporarily written to disk.

Mitigation of application threats can be achieved through additional programs such as virus checkers, restriction of program scope, and reduced application functionality. A fundamental principal of computer security says that if you do not need something on a device, then disable it.

Although not widespread today, the security risks discussed for wired applications are slowly becoming problems for mobile devices as well. Viruses on mobile phones started to appear in late 2000 and 2001. Hacks created through manipulation of applications can yield a hacker information such as the cell site, carrier, and diagnostic information, and possibly even the ability to read mobile traffic through a particular cell site. Table 4-4 shows some commercial answers to these new security risks on mobile devices.

NOTE: One of the first known viruses on a mobile phone was the timofonica virus, which originated in Spain. This virus used SMS messages to send random people messages and make random, computer-generated phone calls. In the future, with mCommerce transactions gaining in popularity, viruses such as this could move money from the victim's account to the hacker's account, for example. Several products on the market address some of these problems. According to Gartner Group's John Pescatore (Gartner Symposium/ITExpo, Florida, October 2000), phone viruses will not appear as a major threat until 2005. In the interim, care will have to be taken to avoid viruses at the server level.

Security Risk	Solution Type	Product	Manufacturer
Virus	Virus Scanner	F-Secure Anti-Virus for EPOC	F-Secure (Data Fellows)
Virus	Virus Scanner	McAfee VirusScan Handheld	McAfee (Network Associates)
Sniffing	VPN	OnRoad	RoamSecure
Virus	Virus Scanner	InoculateIT	Network Associates
Sniffing	VPN	Movian VPN	Certicom Corp

Table 4-4.   Sample of Mobile Device Protection Products

Client Network

Network security is another crucial aspect of meCommerce. Security issues depend on the design of the network that hosts the client. This area is where the biggest difference lies in the security of wired and mobile devices. We will first address wired networks and then discuss mobile networks.

Wired Client Network Security Issues

If the client is hosted inside a corporate network, for example, then most likely the client receives some type of protection against threats from the Internet. Such devices may include firewalls, proxy servers, and routers. Most studies show that compromise in a corporate environment generally is due to insiders. Network security threats to be aware of include:

▼ **Sniffing**   The ability for a hacker to monitor traffic as it crosses the wires (as shown in Figure 4-2)

■ **Port attacks**   The ability to access an idle process on a hardware or software system

▲ **DoS**   Denial of service for the network by sending garbage across the network or otherwise keeping servers busy with dummy requests

A particularly vulnerable setup includes a typical dial-up or remote-access user. In this scenario, a road warrior uses a regular modem or other means to connect to the corporate office. In the past, many companies maintained large banks of modems so that computers could dial into the network. Today most companies create a secure way in through their firewalls, such as the use of virtual private networks (VPNs). Attacks at this point, depending on the setup, could include:

▼ **Sniffing**   Same as defined previously except applied to dial-up lines

▲ **IP spoofing**   Going to a site believed to be the destination, but in fact ending up at an impostor's site

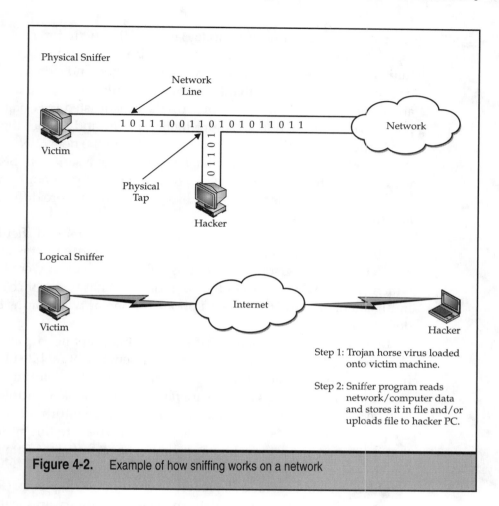

Figure 4-2.   Example of how sniffing works on a network

Mobile Network Issues

Generally, mobile security varies greatly among the types of mobile networks being used. For example, there are several standards for mobile phones, including GSM, I-mode, and CDMA. In Chapter 5, we will describe these standards in greater detail and discuss the unique security features and risks associated with each standard.

Wired devices are each assigned some type of IP address that identifies them; similarly, mobile devices are assigned some type of electronic serial number (ESN) that uniquely identifies that hardware device. In addition, a phone number (for mobile phones) may also be associated with the device (usually programmed at the time the service for the device is purchased).

In general, authentication (today) is very difficult to forge, especially for GSM (which will be discussed in greater detail in Chapter 5). Initially, when analog phones were common, theft and cloning of phones was common. At that time, thieves would simply use a scanner and listen on the airwaves and pick up the broadcasted ESN of a phone. Then, they would get a production phone and replace the production chip with another programmed with the new ESN. Advanced techniques included *tumbling,* in which a series of ESNs were used. In this manner, one ESN be could used for a phone and then another for the second call and so on, making it more difficult to identify stolen ESNs.

Today, with standards such as GSM, it is much more difficult to fake the authentication of a device. However, identity theft is on the rise. A thief steals personal data and uses that data to get real credentials, which can then be used to initiate a phone purchase or service setup. In this manner, a thief may use a phone for one or two months before detection.

In addition to using standards such as GSM, mobile carriers have also used profiling systems to detect fraudulent use of mobile phones. In this type of detection, the historical data of a caller is surveyed, and calls outside of this pattern are flagged as possible fraudulent calls. Automated profiling systems can immediately turn off access if a pattern of fraud is detected. The main drawback to this system is that it is based on historical data and must have sufficient data from which to draw.

Other systems of fraud detection, such as radio frequency (RF) fingerprinting, have been used extensively for military applications. In this method, the assumption is that most phones have a unique RF pattern and can be detected accordingly. The system relies on capturing an RF pattern and associating it with an EIN/MIN pair stored in a database. Subsequent use of that EIN/MIN pair would cause the system to verify the RF pattern against the version stored in the database. A problem with RF printing is false positive ratings of up to 2 percent. In addition, this technique does not work on all models of phones. Finally, the carrier is required to purchase and set up equipment to employ RF fingerprinting, and not every carrier has done so (although the majority of the top 100 *Metropolitan Service*

Areas (MSAs) do use RF fingerprinting today). In addition, several variations are implemented in the market, thus making roaming more difficult as RF fingerprinting solutions are not necessarily compatible.

One mechanism for protection of mobile network communication is the use of VPNs for mobile networks. The concept is similar to that of VPNs for traditional wired networks. VPN clients for mobile devices, initially PDAs with sufficient memory and processing power, have been developed by companies such as Certicom. Initial releases of Certicom's VPN client in 2000 did not include major functionality such as digital certificates (a fundamental part of the IPSec standard to which most VPN vendors conform). Their later solutions, such as Movian VPN, did include some rudimentary key exchanges; however, the connection time to set up a VPN session took from 10 seconds to a minute or more. Other solutions, such as Carrier VPN solutions from Ericsson that came out in June 2001, include a service provisioning concept that does not require specialized VPN equipment at the customer's site. VPNs on large mobile devices, such as laptop PCs, are what are most common in the VPN business. Because there are no storage and processing constraints to prohibit full-featured VPN clients, the best VPN clients are available for laptop PCs. Finally, another solution that was announced in May 2001 is the SafeNet/Texas Instruments joint effort to create a specialized chip to handle PDA VPN functions to increase speed. Because VPNs can slow bandwidth speed, a hardware-based solution could alleviate performance problems that may appear in a client-based (software) solution.

Internet

The next step in the meCommerce security model addresses transmission flow over the Internet. Given that the Internet is a shared, public medium, the last guarantee that anyone can make is for security on the Internet. All meCommerce transactions flow over the Internet. Therefore, the same security issues are common to both mCommerce and eCommerce applications. Although most sites seem credible and it does not appear that data can be compromised, the likelihood of unprotected data being stolen or altered is high.

Recall from the previous chapter that for mCommerce, a gateway or PKI portal is required to convert from the use of WTLS certificates to a regular SSL connection. This is the only unique aspect of mCommerce versus wired eCommerce for the Internet component. After the transaction flows past the gateway, it is then carried over the Internet just like any other transaction, including eCommerce transactions. This "gap in WAP," as we described it in the previous chapter, is one of the main areas of vulnerability in an mCommerce infrastructure.

We have chosen two main areas of vulnerability to discuss in more detail (there are many more areas, but we will focus on the ones most relevant to mCommerce):

▼ **Spoofing**   Setting up a fake site or set of data to look authentic

▲ **Sniffing**   Ability to read data that passes over the Internet

Spoofing

Spoofing can take many forms. At the simplest level, fake information can be circulated on the Internet as has happened with several news articles. One particular case involved a technology company in which a press release, written to appear authentic, was sent out by a hacker. The press release found its way to legitimate news wires, and they in turn published the information as authentic. As a result, the word got to the financial community that this company was having severe financial difficulties. The stock of that company nose-dived minutes after the press release was issued. On the Internet, how can you know that data that you are reading is legitimate?

A more complicated and sophisticated spoof involves tricking people into thinking they are going to a particular web site when, in fact, they are being lured to a fake one. This has been done by publishing the IP address of a site instead of a URL. People go to the site and it appears to look like the site they have seen before, but in fact it is not the real site. Alternatively, a web server or network device may be compromised so that even when the correct URL is typed, the client will be routed to the impostor's site. Such an attack may be used to trick users into entering valuable information such as passwords, bank account numbers, social security numbers, and other confidential data. The compromise of this data could allow an attacker to steal a person's identity and buy things on credit or take loans against the victim's assets. Direct compromise of credit card information can allow the attacker to buy goods on the Internet with the victim's line of credit.

NOTE: There are new technologies and services coming onto the market to provide protection against such attacks. Secure DNS services and web page signing tools seek to ensure that a user can trust a site's identity.

Both types of spoofing just described can be mitigated through the use of a web server security technology called Secure Sockets Layer (SSL). By obtaining a digital certificate from vendors such as VeriSign, SSL certificates can validate the site you are accessing and create an encrypted tunnel from the client to the merchant's web server. The certificate will identify the merchant and provide the validity period of that certificate. In the most popular web browsers, the use of SSL is usually indicated by a lock symbol or a key symbol at the bottom of the screen (see Figure 4-3). Other devices or browsers may use a different display to represent the use of SSL.

Spoofing in mCommerce can take a further spin through the use of new services offered by some companies. Due to the form-factor constraints of mobile phones, some companies have offered mapping services from a short address to a full, standard URL. This would allow, for example, someone to enter **411** and then connect to www.informationdirectorypages.com. Having to enter that URL on a mobile phone can take well over 5 minutes! Now we need to ensure that spoofing does not occur in this mapping process as well.

Sniffing

Sniffing, as previously described, is when a hacker intercepts data en route from the client and server and back. Sniffing on the Internet, however, is much easier than on a client network, due to the openness of the Internet. For some corporate networks, a hacker may need physical access to the network. For the Internet, there are myriad entry points to the data. Most sniffing can be done through simple

Figure 4-3.   Example of an SSL-enabled session (note the solid lock symbol)

software that grabs data over a particular machine or network segment and displays the data. For unencrypted data, a hacker can easily read data flowing over the Internet.

The only way to mitigate this risk of eavesdropping, or sniffing, is to encrypt data. There are many tools available to encrypt data. Microsoft Outlook, a popular mail package, allows for the use of digital certificates to encrypt mail in transit. SSL certificates, as described in the previous section, can protect data in transit during a web commerce session.

For mobile devices, the constraints of the devices do not allow encryption of all possible data. Therefore, most sites trim down what is necessary to conduct mCommerce. However, good security principles tell us to encrypt all data so that an eavesdropper will not know what is important data and what is useless. Consider this example from World War II, where cryptography was a major aspect of the war. Just before the Japanese bombing of Pearl Harbor, U.S. intelligence agencies noted a massive increase in coded traffic. This tipped the Allies off to a major activity; however, they were unable to decipher the messages in time to halt the bombing of Pearl Harbor. If they had been able to decode the messages in time, the surprise attack on Pearl Harbor might have been averted. Likewise, when conducting mCommerce transactions, it is important that the commerce site take care in deciding what to encrypt if it cannot, as it ideally should, encrypt all traffic. Most hackers have an easier time when all they have to focus on is a few transactions and how to break them instead of having a continuous stream of encrypted data to sift through.

TIP: If at all possible, encrypt all data. If resources do not allow such capability, then data blocks should be encrypted to hide the specific messages or data that is critical.

Other areas unique to mobile devices include launched sniffer attacks. It is common for hackers to break into an eCommerce server and then place a sniffer program on that server. From here, they arrange to get the sniffer data remotely. This technique allows them to capture data on networks they would not normally be able to access or break into. In the mobile world, with phones and PDAs being increasingly used to access corporate or private networks, it is possible to put a sniffer program onto a mobile device through some type of Trojan horse. From this, the sniffer program could capture account or personal information and perhaps even PIN codes used to access the device itself. The biggest risk of this is in the always-on mobile networks planned for the future.

Merchant Network

Although the client or initiator of an meCommerce transaction may have taken great lengths to ensure that security measures were taken, the receiver of that transaction, or the merchant, must also protect his or her network.

Risks similar to those posed for the client network face the merchant network. In addition, the merchant network faces additional risks. For example, the merchant most likely will be conducting some type of payment processing. This makes the merchant network a more likely target of an attack by hackers since the merchant is an aggregator of many transactions, as opposed to the client network, which may initiate only a few transactions. Risks include:

▼ Denial of service

■ Payment processing compromise

▲ Credit fraud

Denial of Service

Many news stories during 2000 and 2001 described commerce sites that went down due to *denial-of-service* (DoS) attacks. These attacks, as shown in Figure 4-4, consist of numerous dummy requests made to a site's servers every second to keep them so busy that legitimate transactions cannot get through. Eventually, the server becomes overloaded and crashes. The scenario is similar to what would occur if a million people called one company for a catalog with false addresses; legitimate customers wanting a catalog may not get through, and catalogs may run out. The nature of the Internet makes stopping denial-of-service attacks impossible. However, software and tools known as intrusion detection systems can observe traffic patterns and make guesses as to whether a denial-of-service attack is being performed; if it is, then the suspect data packets can be ignored.

Although DoS attacks have been well-documented for the wired Internet, the new mode of communication using mobile devices will feature a new breed of DoS. For example, a computer-generated set of SMS messages to GSM phones could fill up all memory and take up network traffic if done on a large scale. *Distributed DoS* attacks, in

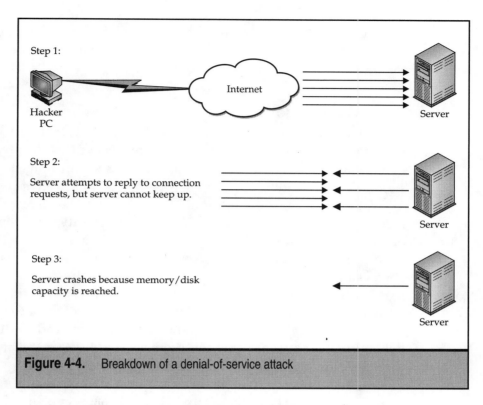

Step 1:

Hacker
PC

Internet

Server

Step 2:

Server attempts to reply to connection
requests, but server cannot keep up.

Server

Step 3:

Server crashes because memory/disk
capacity is reached.

Server

Figure 4-4.   Breakdown of a denial-of-service attack

which multiple sites take part in a DoS attack against the same target,
could easily cripple mobile traffic.

Payment Processing

Naturally, every meCommerce merchant wants to get paid. As a
result, there is a need for payment processing. Payment processing
may involve another network connection (private or public) to the
payment processor. Information that flows to the payment processor
may include credit card information and personal data of the buyer.
In addition, there are data services now that allow for real-time
validation of a buyer's identity, age, and credit history.

CAUTION: When using a data provider to perform real-time validation of
a user, ensure the provider is using strong security practices. Some data
providers simply transmit data such as social security numbers as extra data
with a URL in the clear—without any encryption.

Generally, secure communication through SSL can work. Some payment processors have private networks, making it more difficult for an outsider to get to the data in transit.

Credit Card Fraud

Most credit card companies consider an meCommerce transaction to be a person-not-present transaction. This means that the physical identity of the buyer has not been confirmed, lacking a physical signature, as would be required when a person physically presents a credit card. In these cases, should the transaction be disputed, the merchant bears the loss. This means that in a security compromise of credit card numbers, for example, a merchant may inadvertently accept a stolen credit card and then have to bear the cost of loss of goods shipped or services performed.

Most good payment processors provide some type of automatic fraud detection capability. Such detection consists of an automatic scoring system calculated based on the transactional and credit card holder buying pattern. Using this score as a basis, the merchant can then decide whether or not to proceed with the transaction.

One advantage mCommerce has in the area of payments is that mobile devices can easily be set up to handle micropayments. Because the device usually is physically with a person, micropayments (usually no more than US$50) can be an efficient means of paying for fuel, small amounts of goods, and tolls. Since micropayments usually work on either a debit or low-ceiling credit system, the damage from a compromise of a device with micropayment capability is very low. Although the wired world is also attempting to roll out micropayments, the main mode of payment, through credit cards, is not suited for this purpose because of credit cards' high transactions fees (2 to 3 percent of the transaction value).

Server

To highlight the importance of server security, let's take a simple example. Say that you are using your PC or mobile device to buy some movie tickets for tonight. You use the best virus-scanning software, connect to trusted sites only, use SSL protection, and ensure that the network you are sending from is secure. However, if the network that the movie theater uses to receive your request is weak and is hacked, the hackers can take the credit card number you gave to buy those tickets. So despite your best efforts, the transaction is compromised.

Thus, the server must be the strongest security component in the entire meCommerce chain. Techniques described previously, such as hardening the system and using SSL, can help. Good network defense devices, such as intrusion detection systems (IDSs) and firewalls, can also help. IDSs are monitors that detect a pattern of data traffic that appears to signal a hack. When a pattern is found, logs are generated and system administrators are alerted. In addition, some advanced IDSs can dupe the hacker by redirecting him or her to a fake area (called a honey pot) until administrators can track down the hacker. In the end, though, we can simply make it difficult for a hacker to get through, but never impossible.

In addition, we also have to be aware of insider threats with servers. The majority of data compromise risks are from internal employees. With the recent downturn in the economy, there will likely be more disgruntled employees. This situation—the ability to access privileged resources and instable work environments—can lead some to insider theft or vandalism. *Insider threats* are security risks from an employee or administrator of the server company who steals or manipulates data on the server. Insider risks can be mitigated through separation of duties (keeping one administrator from having access to all parts of the server), encryption of data, and regular third-party auditing (keeping the auditor role separate from the administrator role).

Database Security Issues

Protection of the server encompasses protection of applications such as databases. In any mCommerce transaction, a database is an essential application component. Transactions must be displayed, logged, and resolved. Generally, databases provide mechanisms for error recovery and data rollbacks to compensate for dropped connections. In a mobile environment, data connections are dropped frequently. Such erratic connection behavior is due to signal loss, cell site handovers, and operator disconnection.

NOTE: Many companies do not store information in an encrypted form in their databases. By not taking such action, insiders (such as database administrators) can easily see or modify the data they are maintaining. If at all possible, all data should be encrypted in a database.

Some specific issues related to mobile database security include:

▼ Limiting transparency operations

■ Proper state locking

■ Separate mobile context

▲ Replay attacks

Limiting Transparency Operations

Most applications perform standard operations in the background, transparently, to improve user experience. Due to the lack of ability to manage stateful connections in the mobile world, when connections are dropped, it is unclear whether that same user has reconnected, or whether another user forging authentication datajacked the session. *Datajacking* can be defined as stealing data and control from a previously authenticated session. It is much easier to datajack a session than to forge authentication to initiate a session. Limiting transparency by keeping the user informed of disconnects, reconnects, and data operations can keep users aware of the state of their data security.

Proper State Lock

If data is being read or written to, then it may be worthwhile to ensure that the database is automatically locked from changes when a disconnect occurs. Keeping a lock open can allow a datajacker to continue that session as if he or she were the legitimate user. Figure 4-5 shows how this might happen.

Separate Mobile Context

Normally, good database security principles demand separation of duties and information. Separation of duties prevents a single person

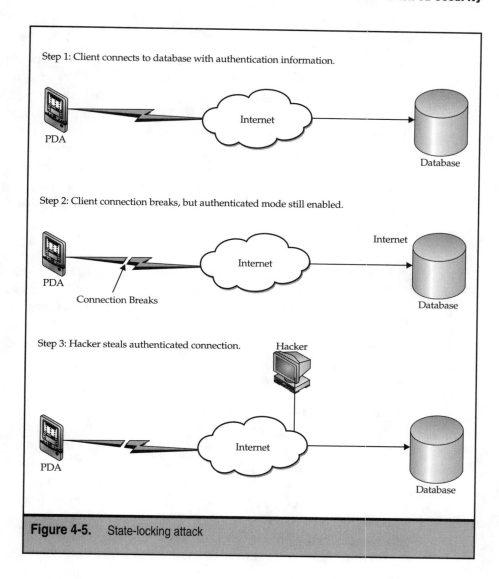

Step 1: Client connects to database with authentication information.

PDA

Internet

Database

Step 2: Client connection breaks, but authenticated mode still enabled.

PDA

Connection Breaks

Internet

Internet

Database

Step 3: Hacker steals authenticated connection.

Hacker

PDA

Internet

Database

Figure 4-5.   State-locking attack

from abusing data privacy and prevents data manipulation by spreading a particular task over two or more people. Likewise, in a mobile database context, it is important to separate data access or simply avoid the use of individual data record keeping. Furthermore, because a user's physical location may be tracked, it is important, if that data must be kept, to protect the user's identity.

Replay Attacks

It is possible for unauthorized parties to pick up sessions that have been dropped in mid session. This pickup could take place after authentication has occurred, allowing the hacker easy access to that user's database and other privileges. Although certain standards, such as GSM and PKI, make this sort of attack more difficult, depending on the implementation of the database, it is not impossible to implement. For example, an attacker might intercept session or authentication keys and reuse them over and over. A good implementation will not allow session or any temporary data or keys to be reused, but the risk still remains.

NOTE: The first public example of a replay attack was in the 1970s movie "War Games." In that movie, the main character records (on an audiotape) the key-coded entry to a locked room as a guard types the codes. Then the main character replays the tape recording of those keys and successfully opens the locked door. Today's attacks are much more sophisticated and are primarily data based.

Database Information Aggregation

A common technique for capturing data without tying the data back to an individual user is to aggregate the data points from many users and track statistics over multiple numbers of users. This abstraction allows data such as location to be tracked, but not necessarily tied to specific devices. Such methods are required when a mobile user leaves a home area and needs to roam. Roaming requires cooperation with cells not directly tied to the same privacy policies. In this case, data aggregation can be used to query the various cells and determine the pattern of movement and predict the future location of the roaming user. For example, if a person is using a mobile phone while driving, it would be easy to predict the person's location in the next minute based on his previous communications with mobile cell sites.

Backup/Data Recovery Issues

Most good information technology (IT) infrastructure processes include a process for backing up data to be recovered in the event of a security breach or other crises. Normally, most back-end systems can accommodate this as they are designed for fault-tolerant and automatic backups. In addition, client systems, such as PCs, are usually synchronized to a backup server (or at least some data is backed up automatically). With mobile devices, backup facilities are not centralized, nor are they automatic. Most PDAs, for example, can be synchronized with a PC, which, in turn, can be backed up, but this process requires manual intervention. Other fixed-purpose devices may have some type of read/write memory without any ability to back it up in an automatic fashion.

From the perspective of security, backing up data and creating clean copies is essential. In the event of a security incident, it is essential to be able to go back to a reliable copy. Many hackers leave a back door in systems they have hacked so that they may easily return. This necessitates reinstallation of the hacked system. A hacked or infected mobile device must have the ability to revert to a known, safe state.

PRIVACY ISSUES

One unique advantage and corresponding disadvantage of mobile devices is simply the fact that they are mobile. Analysts indicate new "killer applications" for mobile devices will be location-based services. Location-based services are information services that transmit data customized for a specific geographical region, based on knowledge of the mobile user's location. An example would be an online restaurant guide that, from a mobile phone, for example, would give a listing of all Indian restaurants within a 10-minute walk and then connect you to the one you select, or even perhaps the closest one. Other applications include targeted advertising and pass-by advertising based on proximity to a particular store. Yet other applications include automatic emergency-based location services, such as the laws the U.S. requires for 911 emergency calls. This would allow emergency workers to hone in on a mobile phone's location without the caller's assistance. This could also assist law enforcement agents in locating criminals.

Location-Based Technology Overview

There are several approaches to location-based technology:

- ▼ E-OTD
- ■ TOA
- ■ AOA
- ▲ GPS

These are summarized in Table 4-5.

E-OTD

Network-based location methods use mathematical triangulation and timing through a technique called *enhanced observed time difference* (E-OTD). The basic approach is to compare the relative timing of the arrival of signals from at least three different base sites, the handset, and a fixed receiver, called the *location measurement unit* (LMU). This method is not reliable all the time due to proximity to base stations in urban areas and natural barriers such as hills and buildings.

Technique	Accuracy	Disadvantage
E-OTD	50 to 150 meters	Requires carrier network and handset upgrades
TOA	125 to 150 meters	Slow location times of up to 10 seconds
AOA	Moderate	Requires large numbers of antennae and long transmission times to be accurate
GPS	Less than 50 meters	Requires modification of handset (increasing power drain and increasing size of phone)

Table 4-5.   Survey of Location Techniques

TOA

Handset-based location solutions use GPS to measure signal responses bounced off of GPS satellites through a technique called *time of arrival* (TOA). The use of GPS removes the need for determining the LMU, thereby reducing cost. Accuracy can be as fine as within 15 feet of the handset. Military applications can achieve even greater accuracy. The requirement for such a solution is having GPS capability within the handset (which can add weight and power burden to the handset).

AOA

A method commonly used in military applications is the *angle of arrival* (AOA) technique. In this technique, a base cell site uses a complex array of antennae to measure the origin of a signal from a handset. This method, however, has the drawbacks of reflection problems (say from large buildings in urban areas) and inaccuracy for short transmissions.

GPS

The United States Department of Defense has in orbit a series of satellites to help determine the location of objects or people anywhere in the world to an accuracy of a few meters. This system is called the global positioning system (GPS). Although this method is very accurate for outdoor (and line-of-sight-to-sky, which requires visual, direct access to the overhead GPS satellites) applications, it suffers from lack of accuracy inside buildings and wooded, foliage-covered areas. In addition, it requires a modification to the handset.

Risks of Location-Based Service

Location-based services pose the danger of compromised privacy. Using location-based technology, some critics would argue, the government or other agencies could not only listen in on data and voice communication (if they are not encrypted), but also track the physical location of people. In addition, hackers compromising such a system could also track citizens for malicious purposes. For example, knowing that you are with your mobile phone and not at home could allow a thief to rob your home. This same technology can also help law enforcement agencies, as was the case when the infamous hacker (or "cracker" in purist security terms) Kevin Mitnick, who was using a wireless modem, was captured by authorities using triangulation location methods.

Because of the important issues related to location-based privacy (also called *l-privacy*), a group called the Wireless Advertising Industry Association (WAIA; see **http://www.adforce.com/waia/**) was formed to promote awareness in the advertising industry. Many online marketers were sued for violating privacy rights of users in traditional Internet advertising. One notable example was the web community site GeoCities. In that case, the Federal Trade Commission (FTC) slammed GeoCities for its misuse and undeclared use of users' private information. Following the order, GeoCities was required to be explicit on how it collected data, for what purpose, and who could request it. (For more information, see **http://www.ftc.gov/os/1998/9808/geo-ord.htm**.)

L-privacy issues will also require some type of declarative statement by advertisers. The challenge, of course, is in how to allow advertisers to use location-based mCommerce with a push model (where data is pushed to the mobile device). Most likely, there would have to be some type of privacy statement with an opt-out clause.

Another major group in the telecommunications industry, the Location Interoperability Forum, was started in September 2000 by Motorola, Ericcson, and Nokia. Their goal is to improve location technology. In the near future, they will also need to address privacy issues as location technology becomes cheaper and more accurate.

POLICY CONTROL

One of the most difficult aspects of computer and electronic security (of any type) is security policy development and implementation. A key component of security threat mitigation is proper policies and procedures, outlined in Figure 4-6. People tend to view policy development and deployment as the least sexy part of the security business. After all, it's "cool" to follow the trail of a hacker until he or she is caught, but determining the roles and responsibilities of users

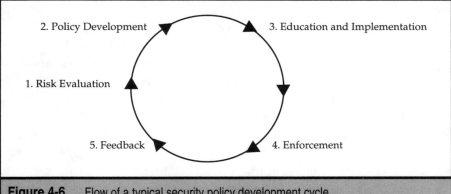

Figure 4-6. Flow of a typical security policy development cycle

and administrators in protecting the organization from security threats is not so exciting. However, the entire threat could have been avoided if the user, for example, had not downloaded an unknown document that contained a virus. The truth is that technology alone cannot stop security threats.

TIP: Hire a good consultant to write the first draft of your security policy. Many top consulting companies have created tried-and-tested templates based on various scenarios. Subsequent revisions could easily be made in-house.

Good policies and procedures are needed for good organizational protection. A good policy has to fit within the risk acceptance level of a business and yet mitigate the risks involved in that business. Individuals conducting mCommerce transactions must be aware of these key issues and how the merchant or service provider addresses them. After all, we do not take our money to a nongovernment-recognized and -regulated bank, so why buy something from an organization that does not have proper policies and regulations to ensure the security of transactions?

For the mobile world, security is somewhat more complicated. In a wired world, usually at least physical security and physical control over all devices is ensured. However, in a mobile world such as today's computing environment, it is increasingly difficult to keep track of all assets and all individuals in an organization. And for mass market mCommerce, it is even more difficult because the participants in a transaction are not easily tracked or regulated.

Although it would take another book to discuss good policy development and design for the mCommerce security infrastructure, we will mention some of the highlights, again building on the lessons learned in the wired world.

The key roles in a security policy are the user, the administrator, and the organization. The user is defined as a user of the mobile device within a specific domain of an organization. This user may be an employee or perhaps a trusted vendor or contractor. The administrator is a trusted individual who maintains and supports the infrastructure of an mCommerce environment. The organization is a collective of related users and administrators who work in a common system.

The goal of a security policy is to define the responsibilities and the consequences of ignoring these responsibilities for all of these parties. Policy gives guidance and provides legal recourse in enforcing these policies and procedures.

The main elements of an mCommerce policy include:[1]

▼ Roles and responsibilities

■ Access control methods

■ Network security methods

■ Business continuity planning

■ Risk management

■ Application control security

■ Computer operations security

▲ Physical security

---

1 Krause, Micki; Tipton Harold, Auuerbach. *Handbook of Information Security Management 1999.*

Roles and Responsibilities

Good security policies clearly define the roles and responsibilities of all individuals in a security policy. In the world of PKI, for example, these are concisely defined in a certification practice statement, referenced within the certificate itself. Because mobile commerce implies potentially more users then a traditional, wired network (since the ability to access the system is made easier and cheaper), more security levels than in a standard security policy need to be defined. For example, policies for these security levels may be defined:

▼ **General users**   These are unproven and minimally validated users. For example, these users may be able to access public areas of an organization's network. They are responsible for the data put on the network (for example, that it does not contain viruses).

■ **Semi-trusted users**   These are users who may access nonpublic systems, but not systems that are deemed confidential. For example, they may be able to access a company's travel policies or internal job transfer policies.

■ **Trusted users**   These are users who have access to confidential data and who are expected not to reveal this information and to secure their mobile devices.

▲ **Administrators**   These users have the highest level of access as they implement policies and procedures. It is important to have strict auditing and logging of these activities because they are trusted to such a large extent. Security policy is slightly more difficult to define in an mCommerce transaction since administrators at both the gateway (for a PKI gateway) and the merchant server must be trusted, but they may not be part of the same organization.

Access Control Methods

Access control methods are perhaps the weakest point in an mCommerce architecture from a security perspective (although from a functional perspective, access is what gives mCommerce the greatest benefit since users are not fixed to a single location). A good policy will address issues such as whether a VPN or one-time password scheme is required. The use of certificates is also covered in this policy. For mobile devices, this policy must explain how S/WIM cards are used and whether they are required for certain mobile devices. In addition, policing and enforcement of this policy can be difficult since the use of VPN and one-time passwords for mobile devices is still not widespread. Client authentication methods are also riddled with interoperability and technical difficulties (as described in the WTLS section in Chapter 2).

Network Security Methods

Protection of the network in a traditional wired world is simple because the organization owns most of that segment of the network. A mobile device, however, usually uses a carrier to transmit the mobile network signals. Thus, the security from the device to the actual back-end network, whether it is to a corporate environment or to a merchant network, is partially dependent on the carrier's security. In this case, security policy should incorporate some type of service-level agreement with the carrier that defines the security components of the carrier's network.

Business Continuity Planning (BCP)

In general, BCP concerns the merchant or corporate network and servers. However, if mobile devices are used as part of mission-critical applications, for example, in tracking shipping distribution network nodes, then BCP must include these devices as well. Security policy should define how the devices should be replaced or substituted. For example, if a mobile device is secured, but destroyed, can business function with wired access as a backup? If not, can the use of outsourced functions suffice until the business function is available via mobile access again? In addition, the specific steps to follow in the event of a security incident or a natural disaster need to be described. Depending on the value of information or operational costs, a maximum amount of time for recovery must be defined that will minimize risk.

Risk Management

A security policy should define the level of risk that is acceptable. Because it would take an infinite amount of money to guarantee total security, organizations must accept certain levels of risk based on time and budget constraints. Is it acceptable for mobile devices to be used in public areas, where other people can read confidential information? Is risk acceptable if, say, 20 percent of mobile phones are lost and must be replaced? Will the data on those devices need to be encrypted, or is it okay that the finder of the lost device can read its contents? Are biometric devices required (which are very expensive for mobile devices)?

Application Control Security

Both wired and wireless devices have the same application control issues:

▼   How are viruses prevented and managed?

■   Can applications fail into an insecure state (for example, in the middle of a database transaction, leaving the connection open and allowing a datajacker to steal the connection and the data)?

▲   Can the user add his or her own applications, or must all applications be defined by a central authority? Is the user liable for nonapproved applications? The height of this concern occurred in relation to the Year 2000 bug, with organizations requiring strict approval and review of applications and hardware and not allowing noncertified devices or applications to be used.

Computer Operations Security

Computer operations security concerns both wired and wireless security architectures. Computer operations have to do with the back-end administration of servers and other critical components. For mCommerce, this includes the gateways, which may or may not be controlled by a single organization.

Physical Security

Perhaps the biggest difference between wired and wireless devices is in the area of physical security. Because mobile devices tend to be smaller than desktop devices and yet relatively expensive, theft or loss of the device poses a big risk for organizations. Asset tracking systems are very important in managing mobile devices for an organization. Even for individual consumers, the loss of a mobile phone, for example, could mean that an unauthorized user may have access to a digital certificate or other vital information on the phone. Some security vendors have started issuing insurance policies for certain aspects of the security infrastructure (for example, some certificate authorities issue certificates with insurance coverage for certain liabilities).

BUILDING ON THE FUNDAMENTALS

In Chapters 1 and 2, we established the basic building blocks of mCommerce applications. In Chapter 3 and in this chapter, we explained the basic concepts of mCommerce security. With this foundation, we can now go on to explore security solutions for each type of mCommerce application. Because the security solutions may vary, it is important to look at each set of applications separately.

MESSAGE FOR THE IT MANAGER

The theory and techniques used to improve security in the wired world can, to a degree, be applied to the mCommerce world. Some key differences to be aware of when implementing mCommerce applications include the following:

▼ The location of the mobile device can pose privacy and security risks due to the ability of location technology to pinpoint the geographical location of a mobile device, and thus its user.

■ Loss of the mobile device can yield the easiest entry into an otherwise closed network.

- Use of mobile devices can increase potential access points to a network or system, increasing security exposure.

- Database and data transactions can be more easily compromised than in wired transactions due to mobile data's lack of reliable statefulness.

- Mitigation techniques for mobile device security threats in mCommerce include:

  - Use of removable S/WIM cards

  - Use of WTLS as a digital certificate method to ensure encryption and nonrepudiation

  - Use of mobile VPNs

  - Use of mobile virus scanners

- ▲ Selection of mobile devices based on strength of protection from known weaknesses of the operating system

In addition, it should be noted that costs for mobile security can incrementally (per device) be much greater than security for wired devices. This statement reflects the fact that there are so many mobile devices (PDAs, phones, and so on) in use, and security mitigation techniques are still in their infancy and thus expensive. The small form factor of these devices makes them easy to steal or lose, thus increasing potential asset loss. Further, a typical mobile device, such as a PDA, requires virus-scanning software, VPN software, cryptographic software for data protection, digital certificates (WTLS), and possibly smartcards.

Other key factors to consider are the incompatibility of various security methods, including:

- ▼ Not all PKI portals can be used with all phones and PDAs.

- Not all PDA and phones use ECC-based cryptography (because it must be licensed, and thus drives up the cost).

- Not all WTLS (short-lived) certificates are issued with the same level of trust, because the trust depends on the issuer and its ability to protect its infrastructure.

▲   When using a mobile device to interact with a traditional
    wired network, the levels of security will vary (since some
    mobile devices will not have dual- or tri-factor authentication
    as do some corporate, fixed-network devices).

Finally, the development of good security policies is essential; the
introduction of mobile devices creates security risks that cannot be
controlled just through technology. In the end, security policies are
the best measure of an organized security strategy.

CHAPTER 5

Overview of Wireless Networks

A t the beginning of Chapter 2, we discussed the supporting elements of the mCommerce value chain and over the course of Chapters 2 to 4, introduced its member parts, such as the portals, horizontal and vertical applications, the operating systems they run on, the handset and terminal devices used by consumers such as yourself, as well as the security basics that support them. You will recall that the value chain also comprised the data networks and operator infrastructure, both of which have not been discussed as yet. Therefore, before we dive into the security aspects of each application, service, and vertical from Chapter 6 onward, it is important to gain an understanding of the types of mobile networks and the infrastructure that support the world of mobile applications. If you are entering the world of mobile networks for the first time, you might find it full of discrepancies in the legacy terminologies used to describe the networks. However, all you really have to understand is how the architectures, technologies, devices, and networks stand with respect to each other and what the underlying concepts behind mobile communications really are. Therefore, in this chapter, we talk about current and future wireless networks, their evolution, their specialties, and the types of applications and devices they support.

HOW DOES A MOBILE SYSTEM WORK?

All application development, communication, and interaction in the world of mCommerce takes place on a mobile network, which is the underlying infrastructure that supports them all. It is therefore essential for managers and technical personnel alike to understand the components that comprise this mobile system to figure out how these networks function and how they affect the performance of an mCommerce application. Let's start with the sample mobile system shown in Figure 5-1. A very basic mobile system infrastructure consists of a *base station controller* (BSC), a *mobile switching center* (MSC), three *mobile stations* (MSs) and three *base transceiver stations* (BTSs). Base transceiver stations are also called *base stations* and *radio base stations*. There are thousands of these in the U.S., Europe, and other parts of the world.

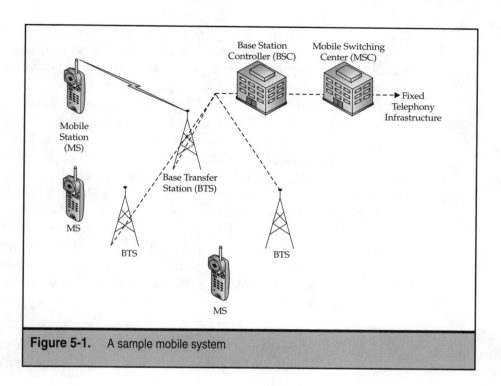

Figure 5-1.   A sample mobile system

The handset is used to make phone calls or access data services. Now let's look at a formula:

MS = TE + MT

Here, the *handset* (MS) consists of *terminal equipment* (TE), the device that hosts applications (such as a PDA), and a *mobile terminal* (MT), such as a cell phone that connects to a mobile network. This formula shows just one such basic configuration. More complicated configurations combine both parts into one physical device. In some systems, such as the *Global System for Mobile Communications* (GSM), *General Packet Radio Service* (GPRS), EDGE (part of the GSM Environment), and *Wideband Code Division Multiple Access* (WCDMA), which will be discussed in more detail later in this chapter, the subscriber data is stored separately on a *SIM card,* an extractable storage card popular in Europe, that is central not only to subscriber identification, but also for providing value added services such as customer location information, secure signing, transaction processing, customer relationships, customer data and customer identification. Simply changing the SIM card can change a phone's number, thus turning an office phone into a home phone, for example.

Signals from a handset are received by the antenna and transported to the mobile network. The antenna is generally connected to a base station that processes and routes the calls to the network. Each base station antenna system provides its own radio coverage area known as a *cell*. Each cell has a unique identity number; hence, a mobile system consists of a large number of these cells. When a user initiates a call, some resources such as power, transceiver, and so on are allocated to the user in the base station. Such resource allocation is more flexible in third-generation (3G) networks than it is in second-generation (2G) networks. In a GSM system, base stations are connected to a BSC, and in a WCDMA system, base stations are connected to a *radio network controller* (RNC).

NOTE: Business intelligence (BI), such as radio functions, cell-to-cell handoff, channel assignments, cell configurations, and service quality, mostly resides in the BSC/RNC.

The core network, which contains switches and subscriber-handling functionalities, routes the traffic entering from other networks to the appropriate base station. It also routes calls from a mobile station to the relevant destination network, which may be another mobile network, a phone network, or even the Internet. If this destination network is a mobile system, this route is repeated in reverse order.

In order to avoid collisions and catastrophic interference during communications, users in a mobile system use different channels. Three main methods are used to achieve collision-free traffic:

▼ **Frequency Division Multiple Access (FDMA)** Generally used by First-generation (1G) systems, this method basically gives each user a different frequency to communicate on.

■ **Time Division Multiple Access (TDMA)** This method assigns a timeslot for each channel. In GSM, a mobile system that uses TDMA, there are eight timeslots allowing each user to send every eighth timeslot. There are various mutually incompatible implementations of TDMA technologies in use worldwide but the one commonly known as TDMA is actually defined by the Telecommunication Industries Association (TIA) as TDMA (IS-136). An evolution of the older IS-54 (also known as Digital AMPS or D-AMPS) standard, TDMA IS-136 was first specified in 1994.

▲ **Code Division Multiple Access (CDMA)**   Used by most 3G systems as well as cdmaOne, this method separates different users by different codes. CDMA does not assign a specific frequency to each user like TDMA does. Instead, every channel uses the full available spectrum, encoding individual conversations with a pseudo-random digital sequence.

NOTE: CDMA was first used during World War II by the English allies to prevent Germans from jamming their transmissions. The allies managed to transmit over several frequencies, instead of one, making it difficult for the Germans to pick up the complete signal.

EVOLUTION AND MIGRATION OF MOBILE NETWORKS

The mobile network infrastructure was initially developed with the intention of providing as much geographical area to the subscribers as possible. Now that more advanced networking technologies are being developed, new networks and standards are evolving such that they can be layered on top of the older network systems for the sake of easy upgrades and some backward compatibility with the older handsets (although as we will see later on in this chapter, this does not hold well). There are four different 2G systems with different available frequencies; therefore, operators use different techniques to migrate to 3G systems. A migration path is shown in Figure 5-2. Note that there are other more creative methods for migration not discussed in this chapter.

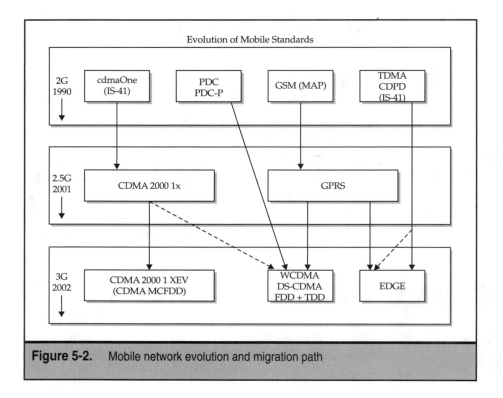

Figure 5-2. Mobile network evolution and migration path

Boasting an international roaming feature with one in ten people on the planet possessing a GSM phone, the Global System for Mobile Communications (GSM) is an open, nonproprietary, and constantly evolving mobile system that gives consumers a "one-number" contact capability in more than 170 countries. The transmission methods used by GSM are different from first-generation wireless systems in that they use digital technology and Time Division Multiple Access. 2G technologies bring with them the possibility of high bandwidth network access for which services are already becoming available. The upgrade path to 3G brings with it the possibilities of even higher data rates opening up doors for sophisticated data transfer and multimedia applications.

NOTE: The GSM standard will continue to evolve, offering greatly expanded services that include high data rates, multimedia applications, built-in support for parallel use of such services, and seamless integration with the Internet and wired networks.

MOBILE PACKET DATA STANDARDS

In this section, we talk about "packet based" mobile data standards such as GPRS, CDPD, Mobitex, DataTAC, and I-Mode.

General Packet Radio Services (GPRS)

Supplementing today's circuit switched data and Short Message Services (SMS), the General Packet Radio Services (GPRS) for GSM networks is an intermediate (2.5 generation) standard for digital mobile communication services that allows information to be transmitted across a wireless network.

Key Features of GPRS from a User's Perspective

With GPRS, a user may not need to pay by the minute but yet can maintain constant connectivity. This feature can be used with a *Digital Subscriber Line* (DSL), a Web access service popular in homes that offers a faster "always-on" Internet connection than a standard dial-up connection. We realize that one of the differing and perhaps most important features of all 3G networks, such as GPRS, is "constant connectivity." GPRS, in a way, is like using a broadband or DSL connection, instead of a traditional phone line to connect your home to the Internet. With a broadband connection you are always connected, and the network is always accessible.

GPRS is basically an upgrade that gives a boost to existing GSM systems. In other words, GPRS will at the very least give us the coverage that is possible on current GSM systems in addition to providing enhanced features and functionality. In most cases, GPRS can be layered as a simple, centralized software upgrade of the operator equipment at base stations (see Figure 5-3). Because the introduction of GPRS will create an urge for more speed, capacity, and bandwidth, it is expected that the eventual introduction of faster 3G systems, will be another simple upgrade from the GSM/GPRS networks.

GPRS transmission rates are about three times faster than today's wired communications networks and about ten times faster than current circuit switched data services on GSM networks. Such enhanced speeds are expected to require new handsets to deal with the new GPRS applications that may be implemented. These handsets fall within three classes:

- ▼ **Class A**   These devices can handle voice and packet data simultaneously.

- ■ **Class B**   These devices can handle both voice and packet data but not simultaneously.

- ▲ **Class C**   These devices can handle either packet or voice data.

NOTE: Class A GPRS devices are very expensive; therefore, most manufacturers have announced that their first handsets will be Class B devices.

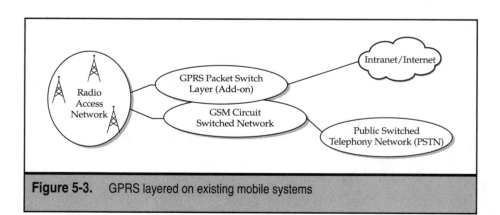

Figure 5-3.   GPRS layered on existing mobile systems

GPRS Applications   When considering a GPRS application implementation for a wireless network, you should realize that this may not be dissimilar from one built for a LAN.

NOTE: GPRS applications are really IP applications, and GPRS networks in a way are like corporate intranets with protected private IP addresses.

Like the Internet, client/server technology rules the GPRS applications world, where a user/client sends a request that the server processes and sends back to the client. In this context, transmitting information to the user (that is, pushing data from the network to the user's hand-held device) is done in two ways:

▼   The user configures their online profile on the web sites from which they will accept pushed information on their WAP-compliant device.

▲   A special client, such as AOL Instant Messenger, can be configured to link to a particular server.

Due to the low data rates of circuit switched networks (9.6 Kbps) and limited message length of SMS (160 characters), many mCommerce applications have not been developed to their full potential. GPRS opens new doors for these applications not previously available over GSM networks, by fully enabling the day-to-day Internet desktop applications we all use such as web browsing and Chat over the mobile network. GPRS also paves the path for the development of many new mCommerce applications, a few of which are discussed in later sections of this chapter. File transfer (FTP over wireless) and *home automation* (that is, the ability to remotely access and control home appliances) are among them.

GPRS User Requirements   To use GPRS, users specifically need the following items:

▼   A GPRS-compatible mobile device (existing GSM phones do not qualify).

■   A subscription to a GPRS-compliant mobile network.

- An enabled GPRS account for that user. Some networks may allow automatic GPRS network access but some operators may require a specific opt-in.

- Software and hardware configurations for the specific GPRS handset.

▲ A destination address, likely to be an Internet address since GPRS is designed to make the Internet fully available to mobile users.

Key Features of GPRS from a Network Perspective

GPRS is a packet data transmission system. A circuit switched connection to a site is basically analogous to a regular phone call in that the user connects to the Internet through an ISP and maintains a steady kilobits-per-second bit rate as long as he or she remains connected. If the bit rate is constant, this is a good solution, but because WAP-based sessions work in bursts, the system does not function satisfactorily. For example, suppose a user checks stock prices on a WAP phone and then disconnects. Five minutes later, if the user wants to check stock prices on the phone again, he or she will have to establish a new connection, which may take 20 to 40 seconds (or around 5 to 10 seconds if special routers are used). Packet data not only resolves these problems, but also allows subscribers to share bandwidth and other radio resources (that is, when no packets are being sent or received, there is no load on the network). GPRS takes this to the next level and allows more subscribers to be accommodated on the same network as well as secures higher network utilization.

The high data rates afforded by a GPRS system make it possible to extend existing fixed Internet applications, such as FTP, web browsing, Chat, e-mail, and so on, to also be available over the mobile GPRS network. Thus, GPRS allows inter-working between the existing Web and the new GPRS network.

GPRS is not only compliant with mobile networks based on the GSM digital mobile phone standard but also with the IS-136 *Time Division Multiple Access* (TDMA) standard, which is popular in North and South America.

Suggested Applications for GPRS

As mentioned earlier, the high data rates possible on a GPRS network open the door to a wide range of new and exciting mCommerce applications and services, a few of which are discussed next.

Chat   Similar to participating in chat groups on the wired Web, mCommerce users have started using wireless handheld devices as a means to chat and communicate. Because GPRS boasts the ability of extending the wired Internet, mobile users can participate fully in existing wired Web chat groups from their handheld devices, rather than having to set up their own new mobile chat communities.

NOTE: Since most current handheld devices are SMS compliant, it is expected that chat will still primarily take place via SMS, especially to maintain brevity and focus and keep people from inundating the Chat servers with spurious and irrelevant postings. However, experts have already started experimenting with the use of GPRS as a medium for wireless chat.

Visual Communication and Content Delivery   Most cell phones and PDAs currently receive content such as weather, flight information, news, stock prices, and traffic and location services in the form of textual data. With the advent of GPRS and its high data rates, such text-based content applications will be upgraded to include images such as maps, graphs, and other types of visual information, especially for information of a qualitative nature, such as horoscopes and news stories that are currently being delivered using SMS (a medium generally limited to a 160-character message). To save on GPRS bandwidth abuse, it may make sense to keep using SMS for the delivery of content that is quantitative (for example, scores or stock prices). Enhanced GPRS data speeds also allow consumers the ability to send a whole new type of content over wireless networks, such as pictures, postcards, greeting cards, and presentations as well as posting digital camera images through a GPRS handheld device directly to an Internet site. Such content is not limited to static information but also extends to dynamic or moving data such as video messages and movie previews that may be made possible by

GPRS to being downloaded via data streaming on a compliant handheld device. Many other dynamic applications come to mind, such as monitoring parking lots or building sites for intruders and wirelessly transmitting a patient's image from an ambulance to a hospital. Another example is remote videoconferencing for sales meetings.

Wireless Web Browsing   The low speed limitations of current circuit switched data networks make browsing a web site over a wireless link a rather painful experience, particularly if the data contains images. Most users opt for text-only versions or simply go straight to the information that they are actually seeking rather than browsing through the site as they would do over a wired high-speed connection. Many sites get muddled up when users opt for their text-only versions, delivering cryptic text layouts on the handheld screens. GPRS will allow users to "browse" the web sites rather than target them for specific information.

Document Sharing and Collaborative Work   GPRS bandwidth and speed facilitates document sharing and remote collaboration, where different people in different places can simultaneously work on the same document containing text, pictures, and even voice. Any type of work that allows people to comment on a visual depiction of a situation or matter that involves problem solving, such as firefighting (see Chapter 10), medical treatment (see Chapter 10), advertisements and copy setting (see Chapter 6), architecture, and journalism, can make use of such collaboration.

High Quality Audio Transfer   The quality of voice calls on mobile networks is still not broadcast quality. On-the-spot journalists, such as those who were recently broadcasting from the war trenches in Afghanistan, or undercover police officers with portable microphones and amplifiers for capturing interviews, can't send broadcast-quality data back to their radio, TV, or police stations in real time and expect the content to reach the public without some serious noise reduction. Although they can speak over their mobile or satellite phones as many war reporters do, or leave it on during an interrogation, as many police personnel do, it would simply not provide sufficient broadcast-standard voice quality, nor would it be adequate for the purposes of speech analysis, where the transmitted speech is matched against recorded speech in police records. In many cases, the sound bytes are received in broken bursts that are either incomplete or in a form requiring substantial rework. Because of the rather large file size of sound bytes, the only network that can do justice to such data transfer is a high-speed mobile data network system such as GPRS.

Job Dispatching   In Chapter 1, we discussed a case study scenario of a typical service-based call center or helpdesk, where the customers typically call a helpdesk staff member who then categorizes the complaint or problem and passes it on to a supervisor. The supervisor then uses a vehicle-positioning application to determine the nearest available field engineer who can be deployed to serve the calling customer. The field engineer or salesperson can keep the office informed of the work in progress—for example, by sending in a status message such as "Job 456 complete, proceeding to 947."

In this case study, we learned how the nonmobile paper-based system required a fair amount of paperwork at different levels between the office and its field personnel. While a 160-character SMS text message may be sufficient for communicating to the field engineer (or for communicating addresses for a sales, service, or some other job-dispatch application such as pizza delivery or courier service), the 160 characters do not leave much space for transmitting any information about the nature or depth of the problem logged on the customer's profile. In most cases, the supervisor also has to call the engineer and give them some more details on the problem, so the engineer can carry the right tools from the service van to the service address. This is where GPRS can help by allowing more information to be sent to the field engineer's handheld, such as providing assistance in finding and identifying a customer or even a photograph of the customer and their premises.

Corporate E-mail   Most corporate e-mail systems, such as Microsoft Mail, Outlook, Outlook Express, Microsoft Exchange, Lotus Notes, and Lotus cc:Mail, are LAN based, and because the corporate environment is where GPRS will predominantly be deployed, there are likely to be more corporate e-mail applications using GPRS.

Wireless Web Mail   Wireless Web-Mail services come in two forms:

▼ **Gateway services**   In this type of service, the messages are translated from the Simple Mail Transfer Protocol (SMTP) into SMS and sent to the SMS conter without being stored. *Simple Mail Transfer Protocol* (SMTP) is a protocol used for sending e-mail messages between a mail client (such as Microsoft Mail, Outlook, Outlook Express, Eudora, Lotus cc:Mail) and a mail server.

▲ **Mailbox services**   In this type of service, the messages are first stored and the user gets an alert-notification on their mobile phone. The user then dials in to retrieve the full e-mail. Smart applications allow the user to dial in straight from the alert itself.

Let's take the scenario of "wired" users who want to access their e-mail. Unless they are "always connected" (for example, through a cable modem, DSL line, or office LAN-based connection), they would not be notified of the fact that they have a new e-mail waiting for them in their inbox until they dial-in through their phone lines and check their mail boxes. Now let's extend this analogy to the "wireless" world where even now mobile phone users have to dial in periodically to check their mailbox contents. Had this wireless network been an "always-connected" mobile network system such as GPRS, then the wireless web mail could be linked to an alert mechanism, such as SMS, so that the mobile phone or handheld users could be notified when there was a new e-mail waiting in their mailboxes.

Location-Based Services   The U.S. Department of Defense runs a global network of 24 satellites, and anyone with a GPS receiver can obtain their satellite position and thus determine their location on the planet! The GPS receiver processes specially coded satellite signals provided by the satellites to compute the position, velocity, and time. Such location-based technologies are being used by law enforcement officials, as well as by car manufacturers in the form of emergency in-vehicle support systems (OnStar and WingCast) that provide services such as remote diagnosis of any problems with the vehicle and stolen vehicle tracking, among many other functions. Because the average GPS coordinates are about 60 characters in length, bearing position information such as longitude, latitude and altitude, the SMS and GPRS systems can both be used for data transmission.

Wireless LAN Access   Chapter 8 discusses the importance of offering anytime, anywhere wireless access to critical information to the field or mobile forces of a company so that they become extended team players instead of disconnected lone salespeople. Such applications include those that employees normally use while at their office desks—accessing the corporate intranet, database servers, and messaging and e-mail systems as well as inventory information. Remote access to such applications can be provided by running small client versions of applications embedded in the handheld devices that the field force uses to connect to their corporate servers over a mobile network. Of course, it all depends on the amount of data being transmitted, but the speed and latency of GPRS make such applications ideal.

Wireless File Transfer   Downloading any sizeable data across a mobile network is currently an almost impossible feat. PowerPoint slides for sales meetings while on the road, manuals for field engineers, and even a common software tool such as Microsoft Word for reading documents are all examples of information and applications that are needed especially when one is mobile. Moreover such data could come from any source—*File Transfer Protocol* (FTP), Telnet, HTTP, Java, or even a database. Regardless of the type of file being transmitted and the source it may be coming from, downloading such files over a wireless network (and a wired network, for that matter) tends to be bandwidth intensive and therefore requires a high-speed system such as GPRS, EDGE, or 3GSM to run satisfactorily. 3GSM is the enhanced version of 3G, involving an evolved, extended, and enhanced network to include an additional radio air interface, better suited for high speed and multimedia data services. 3G is the generic term we use to describe the next generation of mobile communications systems.

Home Networking and Automation   Imagine being able to monitor your home from anywhere! If your car or home burglar alarm goes off, you not only get alerted but also get to see who the burglars are and perhaps even lock them in. You can remotely administer your home, too. For example, you can program your VCR to record your favorite show and preheat your oven by the time you arrive home—in other words, you can treat your GPRS phone like a remote control device that's useable from anywhere! All home appliances and devices will soon have their own IP addresses and therefore be able to be programmed. The Bluetooth system will be a key enabler for home automation applications; it allows disparate devices to communicate with each other. A detailed and focused discussion of Bluetooth is provided in Chapter 13.

Challenges Faced by GPRS

The rollout of GPRS will bring with it a new set of problems and challenges for both consumers as well as the operators. This section discusses the key challenges to be faced by GPRS such as billing, tariffing, and customer service.

Billing and Tariffing   As was mentioned previously in this section, GPRS differs from today's networks in that it is essentially a packet switched overlay on a circuit switched network. GPRS networks split the information that customers send and receive into volumes of packets; therefore, they need to be able to count these packets for the purpose of charging customers. This creates a large number of new variables for the circuit switched billing system to process, such as destination and source addresses, radio interface usage, external packet data network usage, packet data protocol address usage, usage of general GPRS resources, and location of the mobile station.

NOTE: Today's non-voice services that modern billing systems find rather difficult to accurately bill have limited variables compared with the large number that get created with GPRS. Is it therefore likely that the existing circuit switched billing systems will be able to process GPRS transactions accurately?

GPRS call records are generated in the service nodes that may not be able to store charging information for processing. Therefore, an intermediary charging platform might need to be used to perform billing mediation by collecting the charging information from the

GPRS nodes and preparing it for submission to the billing system. Most GPRS infrastructure vendors support charging functions as part of their GPRS solutions, which simplifies the challenge of being able to bill for GPRS and still earn a return on investment. Billing and charging functions are also part of other existing non-GSM packet data networks, such as X.25 and *Cellular Digital Packet Data* (CDPD). A per-packet charge may not be applicable since it is possible that the cost of measuring, counting, and tariffing the large number of packets may turn out to be more than the value of the packets themselves! In light of this, carriers and network operators are likely to tariff certain amounts of GPRS traffic at a flat rate, thus expecting a charging gateway to simply keep track of the thousands of packets per day being generated by a single traffic-monitoring application rather than individually charging each packet being sent or received.

The preceding does not imply that, analogous to wired ISP providers such as NetZero, the wireless carriers will initially begin offering free Internet connection services and rely only on advertising sales on mobile portal sites as their sole revenue model.

NOTE: Mobility comes at a premium, and because there is a shortage of mobile bandwidth, it cannot be viewed as a commodity. Reducing prices might possibly even devalue the perceived value of mobility given the billing complexities and additional customer care demanded by the mobile Internet.

Operators must decide whether to charge for GPRS services by packet or simply as a flat monthly fee. Different rates for different packets may deter some users and make billing more complicated, as explained earlier, whereas a flat monthly rate might favor users who utilize bandwidth heavily, even when it's not required or for purposes not entirely suitable for a mobile service, thus leading to bandwidth abuse. Therefore, billing analysts believe an optimal GPRS pricing model may possibly need to be based on both the time and packet variables. A model such as a nominal per-packet charge during peak times plus a flat rate and no per-packet charge during off-peak times may work. Such mixed charging may encourage applications such as remote monitoring, meter reading, and chatting to be used at night, when spare network capacity is available.

At the same time, bandwidth-heavy applications, such as file and image transfers, may be charged a nominal per-packet charge during the day that's more than applications that use less bandwidth. In other words, customer charging may be adjusted according to application usage.

Customer Service   Corporate customer service departments ought to be aware of the complex and unique customer problems and requirements that mobile GPRS services may generate, such as different configurations of phone types, data cards, handheld computers, subscriptions, operating systems, Internet Service Providers, and so on. They should then develop solutions and strategies so that their customer service representatives (CSRs) are able to tackle these problems when the customers call them. Customers may sometimes call up to request additional add-on services that may not be offered with core subscriptions, thus necessitating a customer service process.

As mobile devices and services become easier to use and as the services themselves are used more widely for customer service purposes, the need for dedicated CSRs may decrease in the future. However, as new and complex devices and mobile services are being launched into the marketplace, at least in the short-to-medium term, this would also increase the need for customer support for value-added services. (For more information, see *Data on GPRS* by Simon Buckingham, Mobile LifeStreams Limited, U.K., from which some of the information in this section was derived.)

NOTE: Perhaps a good approach is to keep initial customer support contact in-house and outsource the complex customer service problems arising from GPRS connectivity or compatibility issues.

Cellular Digital Packet Data (CDPD)

Cellular Digital Packet Data (CDPD) terminals are usually found inside PC cards meant for laptop computers, but lately they have also been built into *Advanced Mobile Phone Service* (AMPS) and *Digital Advanced Mobile Phone Service* (D-AMPS) phones as an overlay for sending small text messages. According to telecom analysts, AMPS is the most widely deployed cellular system in the United States and the rest of the world. D-AMPS is the 2G digital version of the 1G analog AMPS standard and is currently the most widely used digital wireless standard in the Americas and Asia. AMPS and D-AMPS are being phased out to be replaced with CDMA.

Since all users on a CDPD network share bandwidth during a call, it reduces the throughput available per user. CDPD can be accessed at speeds up to 19.2 Kbps using services provided by carriers and network operators.

NOTE: CDPD is compliant with the Open Systems Interconnection (OSI) model and therefore has potential to be extended.

Companies can use the CDPD network to do mass broadcasts to their field employees (known as a *one-to-many IP multicast*). Using the same system, news agencies can also broadcast issues to their user-base in real time as they are published. Although the data network and bandwidth is shared among its users, the correct packets intended for a user are recognized by their receiving modem and forwarded immediately to the user without a circuit connection having to be established. For heavy traffic use, a circuit switched version can be used that offers a dedicated connection.

Many mCommerce applications and services can be built for CDPD. For example, point of sale (POS) transactions, such as credit card authorizations over a CDPD network, may be a good fit, especially in areas where installing a wired telephone line is difficult. Let's look at an example. Say you live near Lake Tahoe in California and own a small home-based ski rental shop. You know the high cost of renting dock space on the lake, so you store your boats and skis in your garage at night. Because you don't have a formal shop by the lake, it's difficult to install a telephone line at the lakeside. You also know that most customers carry little cash and generally want to pay by credit card when on holiday. So you either take a big risk and accept your customer's cards, hoping they go through later on when you enter the numbers from your home or you have a CDPD terminal that you can use to conduct credit checks immediately at the scene.

This solution would also work for a remote taxi cab agency, flea market, or even concession stand. The following case studies discuss some more real life examples of how CDPD has been successfully used in various industries.

Case Studies: CDPD Within the Utility and Public Service Sector

The following case studies discuss real-life scenarios of the use of CDPD within the utility and public service sectors.

Public Safety and Law Enforcement Agencies Public safety agencies are quickly realizing CDPD's benefits. Some police departments have installed CDPD capability. CDPD can also cover a cellular area, and officers can perform various checks even when they're out of their jurisdiction. Public safety organizations also like the fact that CDPD automatically encrypts its data transmissions, making it a secure mobile data technology. When agencies use two-way radios, the communication may be heard by unwanted listeners. Officers using CDPD can send private e-mail to a dispatcher as well as from patrol car to patrol car, for example. Most law enforcement departments implement mobile data because they want in-the-field access to national and state databases, such as the National Crime Information Center (NCIC). In addition to using the NCIC, officers can tap into state databases to run license plate checks and determine whether someone is wanted. Many in-the-field applications have been developed to provide mobile access to a law enforcement agency's computer-aided dispatch (CAD) and record-management software to allow officers to write in-field reports, among other things. In the past, registration lookups tied up a lot of air time. Now, officers can enter in a vehicle's license, and the computer searches motor vehicle databases to check whether the vehicle is properly registered or stolen. They can also verify the registered owner's information, such as making sure his or her driver's license is valid or whether the owner is a wanted person—all in a five-second time frame. On an average, an officer with CDPD capability can run about 100 plates during one work shift. Before CDPD, when officers contacted a dispatcher for license plate information, an officer could make only three or four plate checks per shift.

The California Highway Patrol (CHP) uses an automatic vehicle location (AVL) system that communicates via CDPD in some counties in California. The systems provide vehicle location and tracking data. In an emergency situation, the headquarters can immediately identify the location of a police vehicle and coordinate response activity without waiting for an officer to transmit the location. This system uses GPS technology, and CDPD is used to transmit GPS location data from a car to the CHP dispatch center.

Electric Utility Service Companies   Some utility companies' electrical service business units use pen-based computers to send and receive real-time information on customer orders over the CDPD network, improving their efficiency and effectiveness. The automated system allows field personnel to directly receive real-time information on customer requests, maintenance orders, collection orders, and customer billing history. Once a job is completed, details are entered into a pen-based, portable computer and sent back in real time, via CDPD, to the appropriate databases. The wireless connection to the utility company's field service specialists improves overall response time to customers, reducing order-processing time, improving accuracy, increasing productivity, and lowering the number of recurring orders—all adding up to improved customer satisfaction and significant cost savings.

Wireless CDPD technology represents a new way for utilities to become more competitive, especially as deregulation approaches and more players enter the market. CDPD has proven itself in a range of applications, such as telemetry and field sales automation, providing organizations in both the public and private sectors with a solution for reengineering the way they work.

Several companies across the East Coast of the United States have selected the CDPD technology to improve the way they conduct business.

Mobitex

At the beginning of this chapter, we discussed the basics of a mobile network infrastructure, which consists of cells each served by a radio base station connected to other base stations, cells, and network nodes using fixed links. Developed by Ericsson, the *Mobitex* network also follows a similar basic infrastructure but is unique in that it is a narrowband data-only network communicating on a channel bandwidth of 12.5 KHz, uses packet switching, and is based on an open international standard administered by the Mobitex Operators Association. Mobitex is available on the 400, 800, and 900 MHz bands. Let's look at a few real life examples of Mobitex networks.

Case Studies

The following case studies discuss real-life scenarios of the use of Mobitex networks in the food delivery, communications, and defense industries.

Salad Delivery: Vehicle and Shipment Management   Ever wondered what it takes to deliver salads to supermarkets "fresh"? We all know full well the limited shelf life they have! Well, a U.K.-based chilled food manufacturer does over 3,000 miles a week of chilled-salad delivery shipments nationwide to superstores such as Sainsbury, Safeway, Asda, Boots, and Iceland. Each week, the company manages over a hundred refrigerated transport vehicles carrying temperature-sensitive chilled salads, some of which only have a shelf life of two days. The company's business almost entirely depends on the timely delivery of these salads while they are still fresh. In order to do this, it needs to accurately track vehicles, know the exact location of each customer as well as monitor the temperatures at which loads are carried while in transport. For this reason, Mobitex wireless data communications and a wireless system have been used to provide the solution.

The delivery vehicles are installed with GPS receivers and electronic sensors with microprocessor technology. A special software program is used to precisely monitor and record various parameters over a Mobitex network, such as trailer security, refrigeration system performance, load temperatures, relative humidity, pressures, door operation and security, defrosting, and even diesel coolant activity. The slightest variation in the threshold parameters triggers an alert-notification to the central dispatching office. For example, the system records temperatures every 15 minutes and sends out an alarm via the Mobitex network if temperatures deviate significantly from plus 2 degrees centigrade, which is the threshold. The satellite link via GPS provides logistics reports on vehicle locations over the Mobitex network. All onboard data can be reviewed at anytime using a standard desktop computer and the Mobitex link to the vehicles.

Communications During an Earthquake   Anybody who experienced the January 17, 1994, Los Angeles earthquake knows the severe disruptions it caused in many areas. Electricity was one of the basic services hit that affected the communication's system. However, the battery backups at the base stations kept the network running. The foundation for emergency communications was provided by the Mobitex network. As was explained at the beginning of this section, the Mobitex network has a hierarchical cell structure with each radio cell served by a base station. Because intelligence is distributed throughout the network, data is only forwarded to the lowest network node common to the sender and the receiver. The base station is thus able to handle all local traffic within the cell, which is how the Mobitex network was used to facilitate communications in the aftermath of the earthquake.

Swedish Armed Forces   Since 1991, the Swedish Armed Forces have been operating a Mobitex system for inventory and transportation management, as well as the monitoring of medical and other supplies. The system runs Mobilink software under Windows NT on over two thousand Mobitex terminals. Special encryption devices are used for data security. The system was first used at full scale during Operation North Wind, a major military exercise run in 1991. The system was used again two years later in Operation Hurricane. The system provides nationwide coverage, so the mobile users anywhere in Sweden are in continuous contact with the communication network.

DataTAC

Developed by IBM and Motorola, the *DataTAC* system sets up a connection during data transfer offering many possibilities for applications such as fleet dispatch and management, among many others. DataTAC can also support database inquiries from field personnel to obtain information from central computers as well as reporting and messaging. A sample DataTAC network is illustrated in Figure 5-4.

DataTAC network systems are suited for small mobile workgroups that need to stay in touch and collaborate while away from the office. The network is also suitable for information services such as allowing stockbrokers to access market data, real estate agents to access the latest listings, sales representatives to access central corporate databases regarding customer orders, product inventory levels, and availability. DataTAC uses an advanced Radio Data Link Access Procedure (RD-LAP) radio channel protocol to provide a high data transmission rate (up to 19.2 Kbps or 9.6 Kbps, depending on the country).

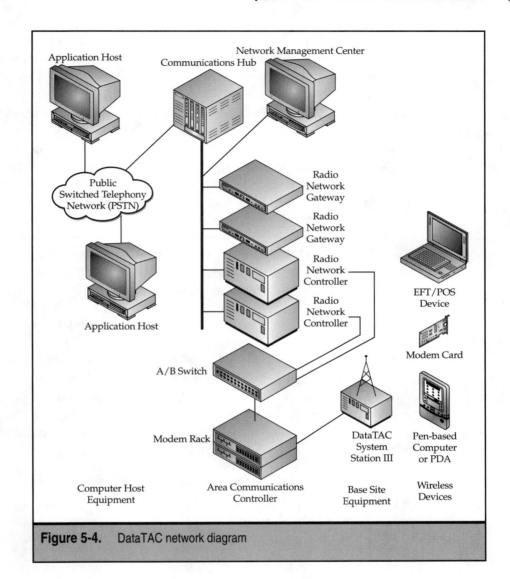

Figure 5-4. DataTAC network diagram

I-Mode

It's a pretty rare site in Japan to be sitting on a local commuter train and not see someone with their head pointed down constantly checking their mobile phone. That's because widespread mobile Internet access in the form of the I-Mode phone has penetrated the

Japanese consumer market, with its portable size making it the coolest way to stay current and in touch. I-Mode can be considered the gatekeeper to the future of the wireless Internet (the "I" in I-Mode stands for *Information*). A creation of NTT's DoCoMo mobile phone division, I-Mode is a mobile access system that allows its users to view specially formatted web sites and receive e-mail via their mobile phones. It uses a protocol known as the personal digital cellular-packet (PDC-P) for the interchange of data packets. The I-Mode service is based on a 3-channel TDMA model, allowing it to be shared by multiple random mobile terminals.

NOTE: With I-Mode, you are "always connected," unlike other Internet-enabled mobile phones that do not offer constant connectivity. I-Mode equals truly instantaneous instant messaging.

I-Mode is basically the wireless AOL service for Japan offering access to the wireless Web, e-mail, financial information such as stocks and online banking (see Chapter 9), as well as travel (Chapter 9), news (Chapter 7), and entertainment (Chapter 11). It also offers mobile gaming on a monthly subscription basis, generally ranging from ¥100 to ¥300 per month.

Some free wireless services accessible on the I-Mode phone are listed here:

▼ Most bank and charge card accounts in Japan

■ Flight information and bookings on JAL (Japan Airlines), ANA (Japan and Asia's largest airline,) and JAS (Japan Air System)

■ *Pia* (an entertainment magazine) guide to entertainment listings such as movies and shows

■ Online restaurant guides and recipes

■ Karaoke charts and locations

▲ Music charts and information

Some premium wireless services and content are available for the I-Mode phone:

▼ Asahi News

■ Nikkei News

■ Lawson's Ticket System

■ Mobile games from major software firms (Bandai, Konami, Nintendo, Sega, and so on)

▲ Cartoons, virtual pets, and Manga

I-Mode has a unique pricing system unlike the current typical Internet-access pricing model. I-Mode consumers are charged based on the number of data-packets sent per month, not at a fixed or timed rate. Basically, the more web pages you request and the more e-mail you send and receive, the higher your bill will be. I-Mode runs on a packet switched network at a slow 9.6 Kbps, but with the majority of content being text only, it suffices for today's constant connectivity needs.

3G WIRELESS STANDARDS

This section is derived from a variety of network manuals and encyclopedias, such as the *Yes to 3G Report* by Simon Buckingham, Mobile LifeStreams Limited, U.K. For an in-depth discussion of 3G, please refer to this report. There will be a significant change in the evolution of technology with the introduction of third-generation mobile systems as compared with the changes that took place when first and even second generations of mobile technologies were introduced. Some of the changes include the following:

▼ Not only will people hold their mobile phones close to their ears, they will also look at the phone screens for information access and transaction query initiation.

■ Mobile communications will reach a stage where many people only have a mobile phone for both their fixed and mobile communication needs.

▲ The mobile phone will become an integral part of people's lives and not just an accessory. People may even use it as a remote control device.

3G is also more topical for the following reasons:

▼ 3G is based on the Code Division Multiple Access (CDMA) technology platform, which is different from 2G networks and even GSM networks that use Time Division Multiple Access (TDMA) technology.

▲ 3G unifies the different mobile standards of the U.S., Europe, and Japan, thus challenging the separate wireless evolution paths taken by the various nations.

Highlights of 3G

The introduction of 3G wireless standards offers new avenues of service, enhanced capacity, increased bandwidth, and opportunities for a number of multimedia applications that were not possible before. Some highlights of 3G are

▼ 3G brings with it significantly more bandwidth and video-centric devices compared with GPRS terminals that have the same range of form factors as today's 2G phones.

■ 3G offers far greater call capacity than today's digital mobile networks allow.

■ Mobile multimedia applications such as mobile postcards, movies, and music will drive the development of new applications and services along with corporate applications, thus increasing the data traffic.

■ Provided the network operators adopt an open-to-all Internet traffic model, it appears that the business case for implementing a 3G network is compelling.

■ 3G technology is essential—think about the change from text-based SMS to moving video clips.

■ It is expected that corporate applications will be the first to adopt 3G, but due to the high-bandwidth capability of 3G and the transition of consumer-intensive applications, such as mobile multimedia games and entertainment from the web world to the wireless world, it is expected that 3G will be a consumer revolution more than a corporate one.

■ It is possible that with the high communication speeds offered by 3G, many people will not need a fixed phone at home. This has not happened until now because 2G and even 2.5G systems have not reached the speeds required to replace home phones yet.

■ It is expected that portable consumer electronics devices will have mobile communications (and short-range wireless communications) technology built in, thus causing a proliferation of mobile devices.

■ 3G terminals (which will be different from 2G and 2.5G devices) will offer enhanced video services, more storage, new software applications, a new set of interfaces, extended battery life, or even no battery. Thus, 3G devices will be significantly more complex and different than today's GSM phones.

▲ From a network architecture point of view, the layering of 3G over older systems such as GPRS will not be as big a jump as the move from circuit switched networks to GPRS, because GPRS was a first-time addition of packet capability to a circuit switched network, whereas 3G is the addition of more packets. However, from a consumer point of view, the move from GPRS to 3G is much more revolutionary than the move from 2G data services to GPRS, because GPRS brings mobile network data bandwidths to the same level as fixed telecommunications networks, whereas 3G enhances bandwidth to a level where new applications will need to be developed to use it.

Applications for 3G

The enhanced bandwidth provided by 3G will give rise to a plethora of new applications. These applications are discussed in the following subsections.

Audio Downloads

With the very high available bandwidth of 3G, MP3 and other audio files will be downloadable over the air directly to mobile phones from a server. In the next few years, this market should pick up to the extent that consumers will be able to retrieve voice, Internet, or music data—anytime and anyplace, through 3G-compliant mobile devices.

Making Calls over the Internet

Voice over IP (VoIP) provides the ability to make telephone calls over the Internet at local call rates to anywhere in the world. With 3G and higher rate 2.5G technologies such as EDGE, VoIP can be made possible on mobile phones as an alternative to regular service. However, because VoIP services are bandwidth demanding, they may not be a replacement for standard fixed voice services unless the switching rate on the IP backbone is very high, so as to minimize the high likelihood of delays and packets getting lost.

Static Image Transmission

For still images such as photographs, pictures, letters, postcards, greeting cards, presentations, and static web pages to be transmitted over mobile networks, a large amount of bandwidth is needed. Currently, such bandwidth is not available. However, with the introduction of mobile packet data networks such as GPRS, small images (such as 50KB to 100KB JPEGs) can be transmitted quickly using mobile packet data.

Dynamic Image Transmission

3G will make the Internet more of a multimedia environment, enabling the display and transmission of moving images and access to web services. But this has a long way to go. Currently, it is difficult to even conduct an online video conference using a 1MB PowerPoint demo on a wired phone connection link with Microsoft NetMeeting. The only way this can be accomplished is over a high-speed wired network such as a T1 line, DSL, or cable modem connection. Even on these networks, the video images appear slightly distorted. Research is being conducted to improve the compression techniques that should make the quality of video images acceptable for transmission over a 64 Kbps link. Eventually over 3G networks, corporations will be able to hold virtual remote meetings between several people with video-capable mobile phones.

Now, although still images such as pictures and postcards will be a significant application for GPRS, moving images may not be of high enough quality initially, at least for GPRS-class transmissions. This is where 3G can help, with its super-high transmission rates and ample bandwidth, to allow full-length movies to be downloadable from Internet sites.

Virtual Home Environment

The *Virtual Home Environment* (VHE) is a common 3G service that lets customers have seamless access to their services from wherever they are, as if they've never left their homes. However, this may not be a killer application for 3G because a lot of services have already migrated to the Internet and can therefore be accessed from any Internet browser or mobile device with or without a VHE module. Storing customer profiles onto mobile smartcards that can be inserted into a variety of mobile devices for virtual service access has also been a point of discussion among mobile enthusiasts. However, it should be noted that smartcards have very limited storage capability (64KB is top of the line) and are more useful in switching devices especially in the 3G world where users are likely to have multiple devices and smartcards, and for identification and security purposes for mobile banking and other such uses.

Mobile Agents

Mobile agents are programs that carry out searches and tasks on the Internet according to the instructions given to them and then report back to their senders. They provide an efficient way to get things done on the move.

It is anticipated that 3G will give consumers much more control over their lives with new tools such as mobile assistants, mobile secretaries, mobile advisors, and mobile administrators. These tools and services will be discussed further in the forthcoming application chapters.

Software Downloads

Instead of being purchased as a boxed product in stores, software will likely be downloaded over the 3G network to your 3G terminal. This method of procurement has advantages in that there is no packaging to throw away or store (hence, it's environmentally friendly), not to mention that the software will arrive within minutes with no shipping charges. Currently, many tools can be downloaded over the fixed Internet in this way; however, product suite downloads over a wireless medium will only be possible over 3G.

SHORT-RANGE MOBILE NETWORKS

In this section, we talk about popular short-range networks such as Bluetooth and Wireless LANs that enable devices and users to collaborate within closed wireless networks. Solutions such as infrared ports and web synchronization are employed to attempt to keep the devices and users connected. These topics are further discussed in Chapters 12, 13, and 14.

Bluetooth

Bluetooth eliminates the need for cable attachments for connecting computers, mobile phones, home appliances, and handheld devices. These devices can have a tiny Bluetooth chip containing a radio transceiver that makes a connection between the devices possible— without any cables and even when the devices are not within the line of sight.

NOTE: The radio frequency is globally available, so the devices can work anywhere in the world.

Bluetooth makes personal communications a breeze—for example, you can send and receive e-mails from the mobile computer using a mobile phone, which doesn't even have to be in the line of sight of the computer. Bluetooth-enabled devices can be set up to automatically exchange data and synchronize with one another—for example, an acceptance of an appointment on a PDA will automatically update the records on a PC as well, as soon as the two devices are within range of each other. Bluetooth is the achievement of nine leading global companies (3COM, Ericsson, Intel, IBM, Lucent, Microsoft, Motorola, Nokia, and Toshiba) and more than 1,300 manufacturers worldwide have now joined the Bluetooth family. For further discussion on Bluetooth, please refer to Chapter 13.

The following subsections highlight popular uses for Bluetooth.

Conferences

In meetings and conferences, you can transfer selected documents instantly with selected participants and exchange electronic business cards automatically, without any wired connections.

Phone

At home, your phone functions as a portable phone (fixed line charge). When you're on the move, it functions as a mobile phone (cellular charge). And when your phone comes within range of another mobile phone with built-in Bluetooth wireless technology, it functions as a walkie-talkie (no telephony charge).

Internet Access

Use your mobile computer to surf the Internet wherever you are, regardless of whether you are connected cordlessly through a mobile phone (cellular) or through a wire-bound connection (such as PSTN, ISDN, LAN, or xDSL).

Headset

Connect your wireless headset to your mobile phone, mobile computer, or any wired connection to keep your hands free for more important tasks when you're at the office or in your car.

Data Synchronization

Bluetooth can be used for automatic synchronization of your desktop, mobile computer, handheld device such as PDA, and your mobile phone. For instance, as soon as you enter your office, the address list and calendar in your notebook will automatically be updated to agree with the one in your desktop, or vice versa.

Wireless LANs

Wireless LANs (WLAN) combine data connectivity with user mobility. A wireless LAN is generally implemented as an extension or alternative to a wired LAN. Wireless LANs use radio frequency (RF) technology to transmit and receive data over the air. Many vertical markets, such as healthcare, retail, manufacturing, warehousing, and academia, have implemented wireless LAN solutions, as you will see in the later chapters of this book.

If you are a corporate network manager, you can set up or augment wireless networks without installing or moving wires using a variety of technologies. You can use a narrowband radio system to transmit and receive user information on a specific radio frequency. Privacy and noninterference are accomplished by the use of separate radio frequencies. This is similar to having a private telephone line in a home. Most wireless LANs, however, use *spread-spectrum technology*, which uses wideband RF techniques developed by the military to trade off bandwidth efficiency for reliability, integrity, and security. Spread spectrum technologies are either *frequency-hopping spread-spectrum* (FHSS) or *direct-sequence spread-spectrum* (DSSS). FHSS uses a narrowband carrier to change frequency in such a way that a single logical channel is maintained; DSSS generates a redundant bit pattern (chip) for each bit to be transmitted. You may also implement a wireless LAN using infrared technology, although this is rarely used in commercial wireless LANs. There are two types of IR-based WLAN systems: The direct IR WLAN systems have a limited range of about three feet and are therefore only used for personal area networks or fixed sub-networks. The other type of IR WLAN is the diffuse or reflective IR wireless LAN system that can be used for networks limited to individual rooms.

A typical wireless LAN configuration consists of an access point (a transceiver device) that connects to the wired network using cables. Access points, which receive, buffer, and transmit data between the wireless LAN and the wired network, are installed at fixed locations. An access point has a range of less than 100 to several hundred feet and can support a small group of users. At the user end, notebooks or handhelds have a PC card implemented or integrated into them that acts as a wireless-LAN interface between the client *network operating system* (NOS) and the airwaves via an antenna.

NOTE: Having had its roots in the military, complex encryption is typically built into wireless LANs, making it difficult for eavesdroppers to listen in on network traffic.

CAUTION: When implementing a wireless LAN network, security enable all individual nodes before allowing them to participate in the network traffic.

Preferred Wireless System for Mobile Applications

Based on the preceding discussions, one can conclude that some applications are better suited to certain networks than others. Table 5-1 shows which network types work best for each application.

Application	Preferred Bearer
Audio	GPRS, HSCSD (High Speed Circuit Switched Data), 3G
Chat	SMS, GPRS
Collaborative working	GPRS, 3G
Corporate e-mail	SMS, GPRS
Customer service	SMS

Table 5-1. Preferred Wireless Systems for Mobile Applications

Application	Preferred Bearer
Downloadable ring tones	SMS
Dynamic authoring	GPRS, 3G
Dynamic images	3G
Electronic agents	GPRS, 3G
Electronic commerce	SMS
File transfer	3G
Home automation	GPRS, 3G
Instant messaging	SMS, GPRS
Job dispatch	GPRS
Location tracking	SMS
Mobile banking	SMS, GPRS
Over the air	SMS
Person-to-person messaging	SMS
Prepayment	SMS
Qualitative information services	GPRS
Quantitative information services	SMS
Remote LAN access	GPRS, 3G
Remote monitoring	SMS, GPRS
Remote point of sale	Circuit switched data
Software downloads	3G
Static images	GPRS
Unified messaging	SMS, GPRS
Vehicle positioning	SMS
Virtual Home Environment	3G
Voice and fax mail notifications	SMS
Voice over IP (VoIP)	3G
Web browsing	GPRS, 3G
Wireless web mail	SMS, GPRS

Table 5-1. Preferred Wireless Systems for Mobile Applications *(continued)*

Case Studies

The following case studies further discuss real-life wireless technology scenarios.

Charity Institutions   A Canadian-based charity uses a dispatch system running over BC Tel mobility's CDPD network that has improved response time, efficiency, and customer service. With CDPD, maps can be updated with new destinations, rerouting trucks in as little as 15 minutes while the trucks are in motion. The charity receives hundreds of calls daily for furniture and clothing donations. With the CDPD service, they can change planned truck routes in seconds for last-minute pickups or delivery requests. CDPD has also improved response time, efficiency, and customer service, allowing dispatchers to better plan the pick up of donations from the public.

A computer screen at the charity's head office displays detailed maps of the region with a database of street names and numbers. Dispatchers can easily direct drivers to any of the calls they receive on a daily basis for furniture and clothing donations. They can also change planned truck routes in seconds for last-minute pickups or delivery requests. When the charity started its donation drive several years ago, the staff had to track pickup and delivery destinations separately. Each driver would spend the morning planning his route for the day from a map book, which usually took about an hour and limited truck stops to a maximum of 20 per day. The old system could take as much as ten days before a truck was available to pick up donations. With CDPD, maps can be updated with new destinations while the trucks are in motion.

CDPD also allows the charity to better utilize their trucks by coordinating pickup and delivery routes together, thus keeping all vehicles busy. At the end of the day, it means more donations for those who really need it.

Concrete Companies: Vehicle Management   Real-time communications in the concrete industry is vital to the success and existence of a company. Each time a concrete company loads one of its trucks with concrete, the clock starts ticking, and the company has a set amount of time (sometimes as little as 90 minutes) in which to deliver its product. Once the time period has passed, most inspectors will reject the load—and in some cases, it could mean having to remove the concrete from the truck with a jackhammer. The quest for a better way to manage its large fleet of trucks and reduce product loss led a particular concrete company to develop an innovative CDPD network–compliant wireless data solution. The result is a state-of-the-art automated vehicle-location system, utilizing customized hardware and software, that runs over a CDPD network. It allows the concrete company to track its drivers accurately in real time, thus preventing product loss and dramatically increasing driver productivity. The concrete company's CDPD-compliant vehicle-location system helps its drivers navigate new subdivisions and building sites where there are no street signs. Now when drivers lose their way, the dispatcher can locate their vehicles via a tracking mechanism and navigate them to the intended location. Each precious minute can mean the difference between saving the concrete and the customer or losing both.

The new system also allows the concrete company to get more trips out of each truck, because dispatchers receive real-time advanced vehicle tracking information (via a GPS) from each truck. Using a status box located in the truck, drivers indicate the status of their job by pressing buttons such as "leaving plant" or "starting job." This kind of information prevents inefficient return trips to one of the concrete company's many concrete plants for dispatch to the next job. This is particularly useful since a large percentage of the concrete company's customers schedule orders the day of delivery, often just minutes or hours before they are needed.

Previously, this information was sent to the dispatcher over an 800 MHz radio system and could often take 20 minutes to get through. It is now sent via CDPD, which relays the message in less than a second. CDPD allows the concrete company to respond to customer requests more quickly, thus improving customer service and reducing costs.

CHAPTER 6

The Horizontals Part 1: Mobile Security in Commerce Applications

Advertising, trading, and banking, as well as the credit card industry (albeit to a lesser extent), have always used new technologies to reach more people and reduce costs. The mobile world is a simple extension of modern day techniques in the wired world. However, just as we all realized with the commercialization of the Internet, security becomes a standard issue that has to be managed.

Security for these applications covers several basic areas: privacy, integrity, secrecy, and nonrepudiation. *Privacy* for mobile commerce generally centers on the physical movements and activities of individuals. This is far more complex than simply protecting someone's e-mail or postal address because an individual can be tracked by hackers or even by governmental organizations. *Integrity* ensures data has not been modified in transit. *Secrecy* involves ensuring transactions are not seen by malicious parties. Given that wireless applications can be used by everyone, it's a given that anyone can attack a network. Finally, *nonrepudiation* is similar to the wired or physical world in that we must prove with reasonable effort that a particular party has willfully conducted a particular transaction. In the wireless world, though, this gets slightly more complicated because the tested and tried methods of nonrepudiation available to the wired/physical world are not available as easily in the mobile world. Security solutions are restricted in the mobile world mainly due to size and mobility requirements of mobile devices.

MOBILE AND WIRELESS ADVERTISING

A new media such as wireless is destined to attract push and pull advertising—the possibility of which taps into commerce (an example is shown in Figure 6-1). Three distinct mobile advertising models have lately been seen coming into force:

▼ Broadcast advertising to the whole consumer base

■ Targeted advertising to a specific location or consumer demographic

▲ Yellow Pages advertising targeted in response to customer queries

Figure 6-1. Example of a real-time coupon advertisement on a mobile phone

An example of wireless advertising is Spotcast, which has leased its technology to SmartTone and PeoplesTel in Singapore to allow users to get free "call minutes" in exchange for listening to a few seconds of advertising. Most mobile advertising applications work in the following ways:

▼ The consumer signs up and receives points for each promotional message received from a mobile advertising portal provider on his or her cellular phone, PDA, or alphanumeric pager.

■ The consumer gets points and rewards for receiving a set number of promotional messages/coupons per day on any text-capable wireless device of interest.

■ The consumer can earn points per month by creating his or her own "pals network."

■ The consumer can control the number of promotional messages received per day.

▲ The consumer can save discounts on the wireless device for later use.

Mobile advertisements can lead to savings for the consumer in the form of redemption through mobile e-mail, text message, and toll-free number redemption schemes. For example, consumers can select a highlighted link provided in any e-mail advertisement sent to them. The link directs the user to a mini web page where the offer can be redeemed. In the case of text message redemption, the consumer can visit a participating retail location offering the advertisement portal provider's discount. The phone or alphanumeric pager discount can then be used at the point of sale. Finally, pressing "TALK" on a cellular phone will automatically dial a toll-free number embedded in a text message. Consumers can also store text discounts and coupons automatically on their wireless devices and recall them for use when needed.

Such redemption schemes bring up strong privacy issues. Most companies track their campaigns, when using discounts, to determine the most effective types of campaigns and the buying patterns of consumers. For example, some large U.S. grocery store chains print out a competing product's coupon on the back of the store receipt when a particular product is purchased. Similarly, data mining and buyer behavior will become an issue when redemptions are used.

NOTE: Merchants need to determine methods for authenticating digital coupons or time-based discounts.

For the merchant, the authenticity of the redemption must be addressed. One-time passwords of redemption numbers, use of digital signatures, and other mechanisms will need to be implemented for good security management.

WIRELESS AFFILIATE ADVERTISING NETWORK

Wireless server-side applications make use of a wireless affiliate network through which wireless portals, service providers, and operators can drive merchant traffic to their wireless sites on a pay-for-results basis. Content-rich wireless information and entertainment site affiliates can generate a revenue stream through advertisements placed on their sites. The applications are built to have affiliate payment modules that handle all merchant payment processing. The affiliates get a monthly commission check, sometimes subject to a minimum payout cost. A few companies in the wireless advertising space include PlayAdz, Airvertise, SkyGo, Vicinity, and Mobile-Affiliates.

Mobile advertising brings up major issues of privacy. Much of the mobile advertising of today and the future will be based on the physical location of the user. As a result, a user's location might be tracked and cataloged by advertisers. All this brings up ripe data for criminals—especially data on high-profile individuals such as politicians and CEOs. We discussed this concept of location privacy in Chapter 4.

Additional implications include maintaining the integrity of online, mobile coupons. Some attacks may center around the creation of fake coupons and cashing them in. One scheme for protecting against fake redemptions would include the use of unique, random codes created as a hash of the promotional code, date, time, and possibly other unique factors.

MOBILE AND WIRELESS BANKING

Wireless banking services are poised to become a significant market for two inherent reasons: People need to constantly manage their money, especially checking their bank balances and accounts, transferring funds, and making bill payments, and financial data is perfect for wireless display and optimization. In the U.S., however, financial companies have to contend with too many technical standards to deliver information on mobile devices, forcing them to limit which kinds of devices will receive their services. Users of certain devices will receive error messages if their service provider does not offer its services on the same network as the device.

Getting access to bank accounts from a wireless hand-held device requires a wireless data service. Such services are provided by operators such as AT&T, Sprint, Verizon, Cingular, and many other wireless communication service providers. In general, the mobile banking services most major banks aim to offer include account inquiry, funds transfers, PIN changes, online rates, loan rates, financial news, bill payments, and ATM and branch locations.

In most cases, customers can log in to their web banking accounts and register for wireless banking. In many cases, if consumers are using certain specific wireless devices (for example, a Palm hand-held device), banks can have their customers download a customized security-enhanced browser. That way, fund transfers and interactions can take place within an end-to-end secure connection. Most service providers, such as EDS, w-trade technologies, Consolidated Data, Aether Systems, and 724 solutions offer services and solutions at least for the Palm OS–based PDA. One example is EDS's wireless banking products for the Palm platform. This service offers most banking services currently available to users on the wired Web. Other institutions, such as Juniper Financial, offer services through the Blackberry PDA from RIM as well as devices running the Palm or Windows CE operating system.

CAUTION: Security of information on a mobile device varies from device to device, based on physical capability and the network used to service the mobile device. Chapter 7 details some popular mobile devices and possible security issues with them.

Another example is Alltel's wireless banking solution, whose core processing systems are interfaced through Open Financial Exchange (OFX), Interactive Financial Exchange (IFX), and Wireless Access Protocol (WAP) gateways to their customers' wireless devices. Customer profiles are constructed by the customer and stored on the network, not on the device, so the customer experience is the same no matter how they access information. In general, the wired world has not succeeded in achieving similar personal storage profiles. The concept of cookies, where data about a user is stored on the user's machine for access by a web site at a later time, itself has come under attack by data privacy groups. However, with strong privacy statements and regular third-party security audits, this may be an acceptable compromise between data privacy and improved performance.

Most current mobile banking application architecture is template based—that is, it can be implemented across multiple mobile devices. Microsoft provides an example of a template-based architecture, as used in BankInfinity's software applications. Although BankInfinity uses a proprietary, digital Net-based processing system that is compatible with several banks, it also utilizes Microsoft BizTalk Server for integrating manifold business processes within and between organizations. BankInfinity's software applications have been employed by Wells Fargo, Harris Bank, BankBoston, Bank of Montreal, and Wachovia, as well as smaller community banks. Other popular development tools for wireless banking include the IBM WebSphere Transcoding Publisher and the IBM WebSphere Application Server, Enterprise Edition tools on the IBM Netfinity Server platform. IBM WebSphere Transcoding Publisher can dynamically adapt content for a variety of pervasive devices by transcoding HTML code into standard formats for wireless, such as WML, HDML, and i-Mode, which reduces the need to create different versions of a web site for pervasive devices.

A good configuration for mobile banking application development might be a combination of IBM- and Microsoft-based solutions, where web content can be transcoded using WebSphere Transcoding Publisher to run as a servlet within IBM WebSphere Application Server, Enterprise Edition. Transcoding Publisher and WebSphere Application Server can run on a couple of IBM Netfinity 4500R servers in a RAID-5, high-availability configuration, and the WAP-enabled channels can utilize the IBM WAP gateways. The Web-enabled channel for the wired Internet can use WebSphere Application Server and Microsoft IIS Web server. Both the Web- and WAP-enabled channels access an application layer that provides the Internet presentation and runs transactions. This layer of Internet business logic can reside on a Netfinity 7000 server and communicate with the bank's back-end systems to provide the HTML web site content that WebSphere Transcoding Publisher extends to wireless devices. Many banks have also found that device-neutral XML technology is quite good for mobile banking application development.

Security Implications for Mobile Banking

Many of the security implications for mobile banking are similar to those for banking done on fixed lines. The added elements include how to manage breaks in connections and ensuring only the proper user gets reconnected. The security implications for mobile banking can be summarized as follows:

▼ Nonrepudiation

■ Encryption

▲ Transaction states

Nonrepudiation

Normally, nonrepudiation refers to the ability of a party to sign or commit to a transaction and not be able to deny having conducted that transaction later. Generally, this will be for the sender or initiator of the transaction. However, it is possible that the bank may want to create some type of integrity around, for example, mortgage rates. Especially for a new medium such as mobile devices, it may be important to convince customers that rates and information are valid.

Encryption

Naturally, all financial transactions will need to be kept secret, or *encrypted*. For mobile devices, this will occur through the use of WAP and Wireless Transport Layer Security (WTLS). As explained in previous chapters, WTLS, along with other functions, will allow the user to encrypt transactions and provide nonrepudiation through digital signatures.

Transaction States

One of the issues with conducting transactions in a volatile connection medium such as mobile devices is that an open connection may allow a hacker to take over an established, authentication session. In a good system, this will not occur. To protect against such a threat, an mCommerce merchant/bank server would need to conduct transactions in such a manner to ensure that a terminated connection also terminates any authentication associated with that connection. A polling system would be required to determine when a connection has been terminated.

MOBILE AND WIRELESS TRADING

From complex options and commodity trading to simple stock quotes, mobile trading has carved out an eager market for itself. In B2B finance, a proliferation of wireless trading devices has been integrated with existing trading systems, thus interacting directly with each other. An example of an innovation within the mobile trading sector can be seen in the New York Stock Exchange, where the brokers now access information from servers through their hand-held PDAs connected to a wireless network. Now most major financial institutions and brokerage houses offer wireless trading services so that investors can use their wireless devices to do the following:

▼ Create alerts that track the markets for trading opportunities

■ Receive alerts (from an online broker) when customized buy/sell prices are reached

■ Get real-time quotes and financial information

■ Trade securities with trade verifications sent to the customer's wireless device, fax, or e-mail

▲ Manage positions across any number of accounts

NOTE: Although many brokerage firms now offer online and mobile trading, very few provide robust support for the mobile platform. Some, including Schwab, waive all liability for mobile trades.

Many products and technologies in the market address the wireless trading sector; however, many of the key suites and services are hosted Wireless Application Service Provider (WASP)

solutions that offer trading account access (WAP session enquiries and transactions) and wireless event messaging ("sessionless" text messages delivered in real time). Most of these systems comprise key modules or subcomponents, such as the following:

- ▼ Trading Account Access Component
- ■ Event Messaging Component
- ■ Notification Component
- ■ Payment Network and Component
- ▲ User and System Admin Interface Component

A popular platform for the development of such trading components is the Java 2 Enterprise Edition (J2EE), which runs in an application server environment. The Enterprise Java Beans (EJBs) are known to be efficient, task-oriented programming objects designed for scalability and maximum system uptime. The IBM servers and the WebLogic Enterprise Application servers (the two largest market-share holders of this space) are also popular hosting platforms for such trading systems. Because Java applications are portable across multiple hardware platforms, the hosted ASP solutions are generally not platform specific, and some installations have been deployed on the Windows NT platform and even the Sun Solaris platform.

To ensure system security and system performance, a dedicated circuit is generally required between the WASP's financial network control center and the customer premises. This dedicated circuit can be a T1 or fractional T1 private line or a Frame Relay connection, the sizing of which is directly related to the anticipated customer transaction volume. For the notification system, the alerts consist of content that is stored in a template database, along with relevant customer data that can be tailored and even branded to match a financial institution's needs. The systems can communicate to external databases using native JDBC interface calls.

Trading components are also being built using Microsoft technologies, mainly by extending the Microsoft .NET Enterprise Server applications using the Mobile Information Server, a secure mobile proxy server positioned behind a firewall. The architecture is based on Windows 2000 and supports standard WAP/WML v1.1 and Openwave HDML browsers. It also supports common industry standards such as DAV, HTTP/HTML, XML, SSL/HTTPS, WAP/WML/WTLS, and ADSI/LDAP, and uses both SMTP and SMS for trading system notifications. Because the architecture is based on Windows 2000, it supports Windows 2000 Active Directory and clustering services.

In complex mobile architecture systems such as these, security is often left to the underlying middleware software. BEA's WebLogic Server, a popular server for this space, relies on SSL certificates to ensure communication to and from the server is encrypted. Authentication of the connection is not done; rather, integrity and privacy is maintained through SSL encryption.

The Security Behind Popular Mobile Trading Software Platforms

Having discussed the security behind mobile trading application technologies, we now focus on a few popular trading platforms, such as Schwab PocketBroker, MSDW TradeRunner, and Reuter's Internet Finance Platform PDS, to see how these platforms handle security issues.

Schwab PocketBroker

The Schwab PocketBroker service provides access to a Schwab trade account, real-time stock quotes and news, execution of equity trades, stock performance alerts, a list view, and the use of a wireless web portal using a Palm organizer or RIM pager.

Note that although Schwab does provide some username/ password schemes to access data, no liability protection is provided. Schwab's security and privacy policy states that Schwab "cannot guarantee the privacy or security of wireless data transmissions" (see **http://www.schwab.com/SchwabNOW/SNLibrary/SNLib029/ pbcustomer.html**).

Such policies make the PocketBroker a neat toy but not a robust, professional platform. However, for small trades, given Schwab's overall reliability and leadership in the market, this may be a small but acceptable risk. On larger trades, using PocketBroker would not be advisable.

TradeRunner

Using the latest in wireless advances, Morgan Stanley Dean Witter Online and Aether Systems have developed TradeRunner, a new interactive wireless trading system that is connected with the New York Stock Exchange (NYSE), American Stock Exchange (AMEX), National Association of Securities Dealers Automated Quotations Exchange (NASDAQ), and the Options Price Reporting Authority (OPRA) and provides wireless trading capabilities for equities, mutual funds, and options. The information being transferred to MSDW Online is protected by Cellular Digital Packet Data (CDPD) encryption. As a result, the air link portion of the customer's data transmission is supposed to be unintelligible to anyone but the intended recipient. CDPD encodes data into digital transmission bursts (packets) securely and efficiently over the air using a forward error-correction scheme. This strives to ensure that the customer's data will arrive safely at the intended destination. Also, security measures are in place for the individual Palm organizer. Customers are assigned unique wireless PINs that they use the first time they log on to access the TradeRunner service. In addition, each time they access the TradeRunner application, they are asked to provide their MSDW Online account number and password (the same as they would to access an account online). Customers are also prompted to enter their password each time they place a trade.

MSDW Online's TradeRunner takes a different approach to security than Schwab's PocketBroker. MSDW Online's security liability is shifted to the users to ensure they protect their user ID and password. Users are responsible for alerting MSDW Online of potentially fraudulent use of an ID/password. However, MSDW Online does not specifically single out wireless liability and, like Schwab, simply removes itself from any obligation (see **http://www.schwab.com/SchwabNOW/SNLibrary/SNLib029/pbcustomer.html**).

Reuters Internet Finance Platform Personal Delivery System (PDS)

The Reuters Internet Finance Platform is a suite of technologies that enables institutions to extend their financial applications over the Internet. A key component of this suite is the Personalized Delivery

System (PDS), which enables event-driven or scheduled information updates to be delivered to end users via pagers, cellular phones, PDAs, or e-mail. The following list provides the details of this architecture as based on Tibco (for further information on Tibco Finance Electronic Trading products, please refer to **http://www.tibcofinance.com**):

▼ **Personalization agents**   These agents gather appropriate information and deliver it to the distribution manager. An agent consists of three components: a data source adapter, an operational data store, and a business rules processor. The Agent Software Development Kit (SDK), allows for customization through the development of a variety of personalized reports..

■ **Distribution manager**   The distribution manager distributes messages to gateways and tags received messages with the appropriate client profile. This is similar to the concept of user provisioning.

■ **Presentation gateways**   These gateways deliver the final messages. Each delivery mechanism is linked to a presentation gateway that formats and dispatches the messages. The gateway allows for messages to be routed to a specific type of technology (such as wireless). Additional delivery services are created through SDK.

■ **Client profile stores**   These stores contain individual client profiles stored in an ODBC database. Profile information includes the delivery service, and the time of delivery. Profiles are stored in an ODBC-compliant database.

▲ **Data sources**   Data sources provide the information resource from which clients include preferences.

Most of the security protection afforded to the Reuter's solution is provided via software tools through the SFC Java Edition, a set of Java developer's code. The SFC Java Edition provides for per-user permission (to partition transaction on a per-user basis), firewall compatibility, and data entitlements (assigning security rights to sets of data). In general, such solutions to security (that is, software-based solutions) can be adequate for a large number of situations. However, caution must be used. Although the underlying toolkits may contain useful security features, the implementation of the toolkits and/or the application using the toolkits must be done properly. One notable example is an older version of the Netscape browser in which SSL 2.0 was implemented, but not properly to the specifications. As a result, hackers discovered how to take advantage of a poor programming implementation and crack SSL, which was designed to protect data from a client to a server. Code reviews and security professionals should always be used in reviewing/evaluating software-based security solutions that involve custom code.

MOBILE eWALLETS

Most consumers have dozens of passwords, identification numbers, credit card numbers, and other pieces of confidential information that need to be both easily available and secure. Mobile eWallet (meWallet) is a tool that helps consolidate a consumer's financial information into a PDA for portable use. Mobile eWallet is a small, fast, single-file database, with options to secure all or segments of the database. This lets consumers keep all kinds of confidential data (including numerous passwords) under the lock and key of a single meWallet database file, protected by a master password. Most Mobile eWallets offer the ability to categorize information, such as placing all credit cards in one folder and all office-related passwords and codes in another folder. Mobile eWallets have the ability to sync consumer meWallet information with their Windows desktop or notebook PC (or vice versa) and share it with an meWallet on a Pocket PC, Palm device, or hand-held PC.

Figure 6-2 shows an example of an eWallet (note that meWallet is a combination of "mobile" and "eWallet").

One of the main meWallet products available in the market today is Ilium Software's eWallet. This product stores a user's important information in a format that's secure, easy to access, centralized, and portable on all handheld devices based on the Palm OS platform, including all Palm series hand-held devices, the Handspring Visor, the IBM WorkPad, and the Sony CLIÉ. The eWallet can store credit card numbers, calling card numbers, usernames and passwords, pin numbers, lock combinations, bank account information, emergency

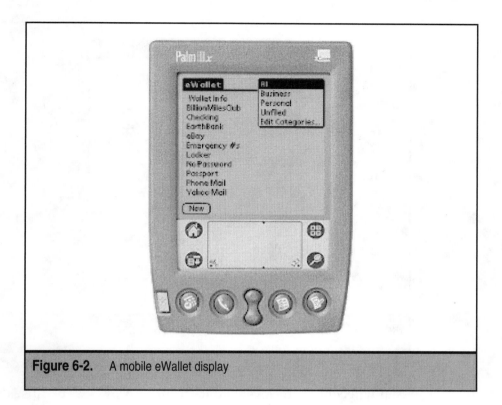

Figure 6-2.   A mobile eWallet display

and medical information, serial and registration numbers, and travel club memberships, among many other types of personal and confidential user information. The eWallet protects user-data in two ways: It requires a password before displaying cards in protected categories, and it encrypts the protected data using an RC4 encryption algorithm with a 128-bit key. Users can set password protection for specific categories so that nonsensitive data can be accessed quickly, without having to enter a password.

meWallet Security

Mobile eWallets use 128-bit key RC4 encryption for security. The easiest way to break into an encrypted file is to simply guess the password. In addition, generally only *cards* (or groups of related information) in password-protected categories are encrypted (see Figure 6-3 for an example of creating a card). Note that the password

Figure 6-3.   The meWallet card-creation screen

used will control the level of data security provided. Because the password is used as input in determining the encrypted data output, a good password is important.

Note, however, that if the password is limited only to numbers, the security of the data will be greatly reduced. The password is simply an input to create a hash that's used to generate the final encrypted data. However, guessing the password (and therefore the ability to duplicate the hash and decrypt data) becomes simpler with fewer choices. For this reason, a good password is required despite the level of encryption performed.

SECURE MOBILE PAYMENT TRANSACTION PROCESSING AND CREDIT CARD AUTHENTICATION

Any mobile payment processing network has various nodes that need to be secured individually before the system itself can be deemed secure. These nodes include the customer devices, authentication service provider systems, and mobile communication links. Despite the release of new standards each year, no single all-encompassing standard exists that renders all of these nodes secure. Having said that, a number of industry groups, such as MeT, Mobey, GMCF, and Radicchio, are addressing the secure mobile payment processing market. For example, phones compatible with the widely praised MeT payment protocol are being developed by companies such as Ericsson.

In any mCommerce payment processing system, three key entities are involved: the customer, the merchant, and the Mobile Payment Processing Agent. The payment service provider and the authentication service provider are peripheral entities. The Mobile Payment Processing Agent connects all these external entities to create a payment transaction network. Figure 6-4 displays how these entities interact with each other. Each of the entities in the mobile payment processing system has its own unique security requirements in addition to relying on the common basic protocols of authentication, authorization, integrity, confidentiality, and nonrepudiation.

Of course, there are other security considerations that are not unique to the Mobile Payment Processing Agent. For example, the agent's operator, the customer, and the merchant will each have their own physical security considerations. The customer's security will rely on his or her handheld being secure. However, seeing as mobile phones are "on" most of the time, server side security implementations have to fill the physical security void. Numerical information, such as credit card numbers, bank account numbers, passwords, PKI key rings, and so on, are only as secure as the customer keeping them. From the agent operator's point of view, the operator should host the agent programs only on servers located within a physically secure network operating center. In addition, consumer handheld devices connecting to the Mobile Payment Processing Agent system should be protected by secret PIN numbers. From the merchant's point of view, the agent operators and other entities, such as the authentication service providers, should place the services they provide behind a firewall with rules programmed in a way that no unnecessary remote access is allowed to the system.

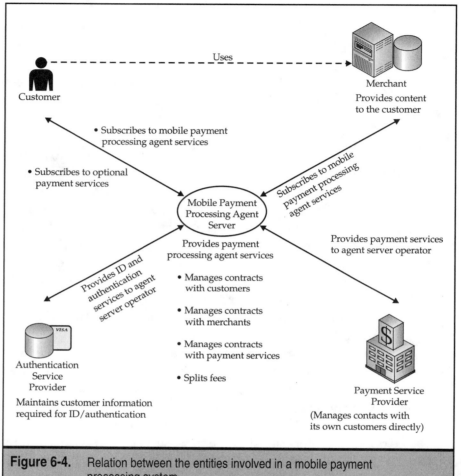

Figure 6-4. Relation between the entities involved in a mobile payment processing system

CAUTION: If there is an error in the dial-in wireless modem pool configuration, the firewall will not be able to secure the mobile payment processing transactions and services.

Now let us look at the security behind each of the key entities in the mobile payment processing system and specifically at how the customers and merchants interact with the agent.

Customer Security in a Mobile Payment Processing System

The Mobile Payment Processing Agent provides the customer with various forms of authentication. For example, WAP gateways can provide the telephone or Mobile Subscriber Integrated Services Digital Network (MSISDN) number. In cases where automatic authentication is neither available nor safe to use, the customer can enter username-password combinations or PIN codes that can be validated against the agent's internal or external registration databases.

TIP: A combination of both automatic and username/password authentication methods can also be used for customer authentication. Sometimes special PIN codes or one-time passwords, commonly known as *transaction authorization numbers*, can be used to improve the authentication sequence.

Mobile payment authorizations can be set up using a combination of services. For example, payments below $1 can be automatically confirmed (provided authorization has already been authenticated in that session). For payments between $1 and $2, the customer may need to enter his or her username and password, and for payment authorizations above $2, an additional PIN number may have to be entered.

Mobile credit card payments can be approved from any WAP-compliant mobile phone through the WAP processing services offered by the Mobile Payment Processing Agent operator. Customers log in using a pre-assigned username and password to process the credit card transactions through a mobile phone. They can even configure the data-entry fields that appear on their WAP phones to be different from those that appear in their operator's desktop mode. The customers' mobile payment transaction history is maintained in their online payment profile for later review. In their payment profile (accessible through a web browser), as shown in Figure 6-5, they can choose to add fields, such as Invoice Number and Store Name, to display on their phone when entering payment details. All information

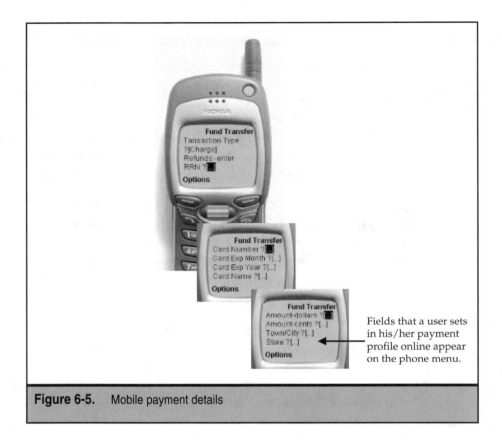

Fields that a user sets in his/her payment profile online appear on the phone menu.

Figure 6-5.   Mobile payment details

entered is stored in their online payment profile on the Mobile Payment Processing Agent operator's server for later use. After the customer has completed all data fields, they can select the specified option to process the payment from the menu using the scroll bar or buttons. The phone will display the transaction status and amount. Each approved transaction receives its own unique identifier (or approval number) that can be noted on invoices and customer records. This number is also generally recorded in the customer's online payment profile, attached to the payment it relates to. After confirmation is received, the phone is now ready for the next transaction.

One form of mobile credit card authentication is to hold the customer's partial credit card number on the Mobile Payment Processing Agent server. In an interactive session, the customer enters the missing credit card numbers to complete and validate the transaction. Using this method, sensitive credit card data can be authenticated without having to store the entire credit card number on the Mobile Payment Processing Agent server. On the merchant's side, practicing a similar authentication technique can enable credit card authentications without having to reveal the card number to the merchant.

Integrity and confidentiality are difficult to achieve in a mobile payment processing system. Because there is no common standard, end-to-end security cannot be standardized for all participating entities.

Unlike the wired Internet, WAP neither requires strong cryptographic authentication nor does it ask for nonrepudiation. Nonrepudiation is only supported by handheld devices that come with SIM cards. In such cases, the merchant has to send the transaction ID over to the Mobile Payment Processing Agent server that stores this ID and then retrieves it later to track and confirm that the merchant did deliver the requested content. Thus, complete transactions can be reconstructed in this way.

Some payment systems are programmed such that they place charges on the mobile phone bill, rather than actually deducting electronic cash. In such cases, the liability is somewhat limited, because the scenario is very similar to a credit card situation.

Merchant Security in a Mobile Payment Processing System

Before a payment transaction goes through to the merchant for acceptance, the Mobile Payment Processing Agent server has to have the customer confirm the payment parameters: the payment method, amount, product being purchased, and identity of the merchant receiving the payment. Once the customer has confirmed all payment parameters, the Mobile Payment Processing Agent server can inform the merchant application about the success or failure of the customer's payment. This way both the customer's payment is authorized and the merchant's content delivery is authorized. So that the customer does not have to validate every single payment parameter within a session based on the dollar value of the transaction amount or the trust relationship associated with a particular merchant, various rules and business logic can also be programmed into the system. Of course this compromises security, but it increases customer convenience. By keeping the security lapses closely linked to the dollar thresholds of the transaction amount, the compromise can be kept to a minimum. A certain level of trust is, however, necessary between the merchant and the Mobile Payment Processing Agent server operator because otherwise the merchant may generate fraudulent charges. The Mobile Payment Processing Agent system can detect these charges, especially when the contested charges are cross-referenced with the logs held on the agent's server.

TIP: To help with risk analysis and combat fraud, always build a business model where detailed transaction logs are maintained and backed up from time to time.

CAUTION: Mobile Payment Processing Agent server operators should not store any complete credit card numbers, passwords in plain text, or any other authentication information on the server, so as to secure themselves from malicious employees. This information can be requested from the customer in real time and the hashed value compared with the hashed values stored in the Mobile Payment Processing Agent server database.

Although currently still a novelty, mobile payment authorization and transaction processing algorithms implemented by the merchants at point-of-sale sites (POS) typically come in the form of mobile e-payment terminals, boasting broad wireless coverage and high-performance multiapplication functionality. Such mobile terminals have a magnetic-stripe reader, primary smartcard reader, and internal PIN pad to support the full spectrum of applications, including credit, debit, and smartcard-based transactions. The smartcard reader is compliant with Europay, MasterCard, and Visa (EMV) standards, which ensures global interoperability between chip-based cards and terminals, both today and in the future. The terminals are loaded with e-payment software programs built on a customized operating environment. The general system for transmission is the nationwide Cingular Interactive Intelligent Wireless Network from Cingular

Interactive (formerly BellSouth Wireless Data), a business unit of Cingular Wireless in the United States. The all-digital core network's Mobitex technology is the de facto international standard for wireless data communications. In addition to its core technology, it offers connections with complementary networks and several host connectivity options. Europe, Asia, and Latin America utilize the GSM wireless network to offer merchant-side mobile payment options. Generally, for such systems the security lies in the use of the smartcards themselves. When smartcards are well designed, it's very difficult, if not impossible, to tamper with the data on these cards. The challenge in this space has always been poor adoption in North America and varying standards across the globe. More recently, Java cards have become popular due to post-issuance capability. Through the use of post-issuance capability, users can store one-time password tokens, static passwords, loyalty programs, and other applications.

TICKETING

Wireless booking and ticketing is still a new area of development and essentially involves communication between standard and previously discussed components of transactional mobile commerce, such as WAP phones, PDAs, content/transaction servers, and credit card–processing algorithms. Flight bookings provide a good example of wireless ticketing, where customers have to first register to activate their wireless service at the airline's web site. Customers with WAP-enabled cell phones can then easily access the mobile site by launching their phone's mini web browser. Once Web access is established, customers can use the keypad to type in the airline's wireless URL. From there, the menu allows travelers to book flights as well as check flight status, flight availability, and mileage account summary. Additionally, customers can register for flight paging, locate an airport code, and contact the airlines. Customers can also view their itineraries, enabling them to check their departure time and seat assignment, select preferred seating, place meal and wheelchair requirements, all while booking a flight through their WAP. What's more, they can make changes to any flights previously booked, just as they would from a wired computer-based web browser.

The technology and system that enable this transaction to take place is similar to what's used in credit card processing, wireless transaction processing, wireless content delivery, and wireless SMS. Most of these topics have been discussed in some detail previously in this chapter. For the sake of flight travel services, most mobile handhelds can be generically divided into four major types of devices: alphanumeric pagers, i-Mode phones, web phones, or wireless PDAs. Each of these devices typically provides access to a variety of flight travel features, as shown in Table 6-1.

Consumers can also download electronic timetables for their PDAs as well as link their awards to their ticket bookings for savings and discounts. Currently, United Airlines offers a comprehensive wireless flight-booking service to its customers. Wireless check-in capabilities for e-ticket holders are offered by many airlines, including Alaska Air, Deutsche Lufthansa, and Swissair, among many others.

Travel Features	Alphanumeric Pagers	i-Mode	Web Phone	Wireless PDA
Flight booking			X	X
Personal itinerary			X	X
Flight availability		X	X	X
Flight status		X	X	X
Flight paging	X	X	X	X
Mileage summary		X	X	X
Mileage upgrade status		X		X
Mileage awards and availability		X		X
Contact airlines		X	X	X

Table 6-1. Common Flight Travel Features Accessible Through Handheld Devices

Wireless ticketing options have also been used by parking enforcement officers for quite some time. For example, using a handheld device and access to a mobile server, parking enforcement officers can have instant access to the state's judiciary mainframe computer and wirelessly transmit tickets over the system in real time. The timely data allows parking enforcement officers to know the status of parking tickets at all times. The system runs on a Mobitex wide area network (WAN).

In general, security for most ticketing applications can be managed through the use of transport layer security. In addition, audit trails can be created through the use of SMS messaging to mobile phones (the main target for such applications).

Currently, some large movie theater chains allow for secure ticket transactions via the Internet and give the user a confirmation code for the transaction. The user then goes to a physical terminal at the venue, enters the code, and inserts the same credit card used in the original transaction (as physical proof of identity). The terminal then prints out a physical ticket. Security in this manner cannot help mobile commerce grow because physical interaction and the use of physical ticketing prevents a scalable approach.

Additional security might rely on a PIN code required to activate the mobile device and possibly another PIN code to access the S/WIM card in a mobile phone, for example, that may contain the relevant ticketing data.

MESSAGE FOR THE IT MANAGER

For most financial-oriented transactions in the mobile arena, mobile phones are still the most poplar device. As a result, the bulk of security lies in the WAP Forum standard for security (that is, WTLS). Additional security mechanisms could include device PIN/passwords and smartcards. Further risk from fraud can be mitigated by tying the transaction together with the actual carrier's bill for the use of the mobile device. In this manner, fraudulent charges can be disputed and reversed.

Many complex payment systems use a variety of middleware software applications. This increasingly compromises security because not only is the mobile device a security risk point but so is the middleware software. To minimize risk, it is important to perform third-party code reviews or at least have internal code-management processes. Even since the days of COBOL (a very old computer language that was used heavily by financial institutions), many banks have had strict audit and code-review processes.

Finally, because most firms use outside assistance for developing such complex architectures, it is important that the consulting agency go through a strong selection process. The following list summarizes the important actions you need to take when working with outside agencies on mobile financial-oriented systems:

▼ Insist on security and background checks

■ Require detailed hour-by-hour work documentation

■ Ensure internal personnel are part of the development/implementation team

■ Consider bringing another, different third party onboard for an independent code/architecture review

▲ Keep regular audits planned

CAUTION: Numerous mobile infrastructure companies and many mobile consulting companies are proving to be financially unstable in the most recent downslide. Ensure the vendor for any platform used is fiscally sound, especially mobile companies.

Case Study: Wireless Bank, Inc.

Company	Wireless Bank, Inc.
Application	Wireless trading and banking
Business benefits	Thirteen-week development cycle for wireless solution; one source of XML code that addresses many wireless formats
Software	IBM WebSphere Transcoding Publisher, IBM WebSphere Application Server (Enterprise Edition), and Microsoft IIS Web server
Servers	IBM Netfinity

The emergence of mobile commerce and the wireless devices built for it has created an intense market for wireless banking and trading. Banks and financial institutions are trying to offer the best services supported by the most stable and scalable technologies in order to retain customers and gain further market share.

In this case study, we discuss the technologies behind implementing a wireless trading and banking solution for an imaginary bank—Wireless Bank, Inc. Through its several member organizations, Wireless Bank offers services for trading, fund and asset management, insurance, credit, leasing, and retail and corporate banking.

Wireless Bank's aim is to offer services through all its Web-based channels—the wired Internet and WebTV as well as the wireless Web. The next step for Wireless Bank is to develop a solution for transcoding HTML that's compliant with a wide range of mobile devices, such as WAP phones, personal digital assistants (PDAs), and other pervasive devices. A technology platform has to be selected and used that's able to dynamically adapt content for a variety of pervasive devices and transcode HTML code into standard wireless formats, such as WML, HDML and i-Mode. As a result of a lack of knowledge of the wireless protocols that will be dominant in the years to come, another need for the bank is to be able to integrate new transcoders into the technology infrastructure using a rapid development methodology.

The technology architecture has to support the bank's customers accessing its servers from a variety of WAP-enabled phones as well as through the wired Internet and WebTV. The goal is to offer customers banking services to obtain account balances, request checks, get exchange rates, research and trade stocks, and sign up for mutual funds.

To implement and support its wireless vision, Wireless Bank has developed a software infrastructure using the IBM WebSphere Transcoding Publisher in around 13 weeks. The bank has experimented with building custom Java technology-based solutions for its WAP-enabled information channel, but that proved costly and slow because it involved totally custom development. Therefore, Wireless Bank is using the WebSphere Transcoding Publisher platform to customize devices and its style sheet association feature to address the slightly different implementations of the WAP protocol that the various phones support.

To transcode the web content, Wireless Bank has installed the WebSphere Transcoding Publisher to run as a servlet within the IBM WebSphere Application Server, Enterprise Edition. Both the Websphere Transcoding Publisher and the Websphere Application Server run on two IBM Netfinity 4500R servers in a RAID-5 high-availability configuration. The bank's WAP-enabled channel utilizes two IBM WAP gateways.

Wireless Bank's Web-enabled channel for the wired Internet uses the WebSphere Application Server as well as the Microsoft IIS web server. Both the web- and WAP-enabled channels access an application layer of Internet business logic that resides on a Netfinity 7000 server and communicates with the bank's back-end systems to provide the HTML web site content that WebSphere Transcoding Publisher extends to wireless devices.

Security Concepts   The majority of this architecture is based on the security afforded by IBM's WebSphere Transcoding Publisher software. IBM has incorporated the Two Party Key Distribution Protocol (2PKDP), which enables bidirectional authentication of the client and server through a challenge/response method. This ensures that the gateway and clients in use are both legitimate, protecting the user and the financial institution providing the service. In addition, the architecture allows for WAP-based security (WTLS) and Point-to-Point (PPP) connection security. PPP is a protocol method for exchanging encryption keys between two parties (as opposed to a PPP connection over dial-up).

Three security options are available with the transcoder system:

▼ Client validation

■ Administrator access

▲ Data traffic control

Client Validation   Client validation determines whether a valid client is connecting to a system and creates an audit trail for transactions/connections. Each client is tracked by a unique username. The audit trail adds to nonrepudiation claims because each device can be tracked through its transaction to an address later disputed. An additional feature that might be useful is a digital signature of the audit trail (which is currently not provided).

Administrator Access   IBM's software allows for the separation of administration domains to enable different administrators to focus on different areas (a fundamentally important security practice). For example, the banking division of the system could be administrated separately from the brokerage division of the same company (as regulated in some countries/areas).

Data Traffic Control   Data traffic control allows for standard packet filtering, as might be provided by most firewalls. This can prevent known malicious clients from accessing the system. In addition, if it's used as an internal system, this ability can restrict the system to only predetermined devices/users, for example.

Data traffic control has the same "gap in WAP" problem as WAP gateways, as described in previous chapters. This problem involves data encrypted with WAP's WTLS being decrypted for a short period of time as it gets reencrypted using SSL.

CHAPTER 7

The Horizontals, Part 2: Mobile Security in Information Applications

It may appear at first glance as if there are no security implications with information-only applications. However, most useful information applications create data to be used for commerce or other financial transactions. Dependence on such data creates the need for the reliability of the data. An example of such a problem can be depicted with a traffic scenario. Imagine one scenario in which you arrive at a traffic intersection knowing all lights are unreliable and therefore all parties stop and err on the side of caution. A second scenario is that all lights are green for all directions of traffic, and no one is aware of the fault. In the second scenario, people make decisions on what they believe is correct information, not knowing there could be any problem. Likewise, in the use of mobile information, it is important that the data be attributed to a reliable source and that the data is acknowledged to maintain its integrity. Although various hardware devices attempt to resolve security through various methods, they typically focus on encryption and nonrepudiation (the ability to link a transaction to a single user).

A famous example of information forgery that caused financial harm was the August 2000 release of a fake press release about Emulex Corp. That release caused the Emulex stock price to drop dramatically. Once the release was established as fake, the stock recovered. However, during the time when the release appeared to be legitimate, over $2.5 billion dollars of market capitalization were lost through traders believing the company was on hard times.

THE BASICS

In general, we can conclude that security, as related to financial information on a mobile space, revolves around the following key areas:

▼ The integrity of the data (ensuring the data is not modified in transit)

■ Authentication/nonrepudiation (conclusively determining the source of the information)

▲ Liability (covering areas that the data provider is unsure can be secured)

Integrity

Data integrity has been addressed in the wired world through Secured Sockets Layer (SSL), a secured method of transmitting data between servers and clients. In the mobile word, Wireless Transport Layer Security (WTLS) and SSL provide data integrity through encryption of data from source to destination. In general, most financial data providers of information such as market data do not use WTLS/SSL. Because today's use of WTLS is riddled with compatibly and usage issues, the use of data provided via WTLS/SSL would be limited. In addition, the use of SSL on the data provider's server creates additional processing burden. This results in a slower throughput and may need to be resolved through additional investment in hardware. Therefore, the increased cost of using WTLS/SSL prevents many data providers from implementing this technology.

Authentication

It is a given that if a data source is not authenticated, even if the data integrity is maintained, the data cannot be trusted. WTLS/SSL do provide a measure of authentication because of the issuer of the digital certificate (the main component used to generate the WTLS/SSL).

Liability

Because we discuss security in terms of the mitigation of risk rather than the elimination of risk, it is important to note some features of liability in mobile information applications. Generally, most financial information and other types of information delivery of high-value content in the mobile space have very poor (for the consumer) liability statements. Charles Schwab nearly removes itself of any liability to customers using wireless trading (and thus related information). Because Service Level Agreements (SLA) and other guarantees cannot be made (from the data provider), the widespread use of professional reliance on mobile devices for high-valued information will be quite low.

CAUTION: If you are using mobile platforms for financial data, carefully read liability statements because they usually differ from the policies for phone and wired access. Most companies will not be liable for more than the commission of the transactions, and they likely won't be responsible for any losses incurred through reliance on incorrect information.

SECURITY OF WIRELESS INFORMATION DELIVERY MODELS

At the crossroads of today's wired Internet and narrowband wireless networks sits a wireless information gateway that facilitates the delivery of information from a source to a wireless network and its users. The gateway also optimizes the information for the devices being used and enhances data packets for faster transmission over the network. Information gateways solve interoperability issues among the various wireless networks. Although made-for-wireless information-delivery models are now being developed, a lot of the information that mCommerce users want to access is either existing enterprise data or data that has already been placed on the Internet or is accessible on a server somewhere. This data can be location specific, in which case the information-delivery architecture involves the use of location-based technologies and servers. The problem is that this information is not optimized for presentation or delivery to the small screens of today's mobile wireless devices. Therefore, the information gateway has to be compliant with common Internet programming standards, such as HTML, XML, J2ME, and Java MID, and common e-mail protocols, such as SMTP, POP3, IMAP4. It also has to be able to interoperate with popular corporate operating systems such as Windows NT/2000, Unix, and Linux. As a result of these various requirements, these systems are vulnerable to security risks due to the various layers of software and hardware that need to be integrated.

Mobile Internet information delivery models generally rely on a version of HTML or on XML. HTML only deals with data presentation and not the substance of the data itself—in other words, it merely arranges text, images, and buttons in a graphic environment. This has given rise to XML, the popular standard that can interpret information beyond the display parameters, allowing information providers to also define the "functional attributes" (that is, the rules for operations on the formatted data). For example, if the information is going to a wireless screen, it is stripped of any graphics and so on.

Newer options may assist in securing the authentication of a source. One example is the XML Key Management Specification (XKMS), a XML-based protocol for public key infrastructure (PKI) functions such as digital signatures. Through the use of XKMS, users can simplify the validation of the signature of web pages, for example, to ensure the integrity of a document has been maintained (to prevent a fiasco such as the Emulex hoax).

NOTE: XKMS is a protocol created by Microsoft, webMethods, and VeriSign with further extension proposals from Entrust and Baltimore.

Types of Models

In today's environment, the delivery of wireless information is based on three primary business models: the service provider, the information source, and the wireless ASP (WASP). Each model presents various security issues based on the various placement of components.

Service Provider

In the service provider model shown in Figure 7-1, the mobile server is hosted by the wireless network operator or service provider. Many current commercial information-delivery models follow this pattern. A mobile server (at the service provider) performs many functions, such as data translation, formatting, compression, and routing. In this model, servers are provided by companies such as Nokia, Ericsson, and other infrastructure companies that also supply browsers for mobile devices. Because the sources of information are many, the information residing on an enterprise server (at the customer's site) can be preformatted for wireless devices and served over the Internet to a service provider's mobile server. The challenge is the ability to get content from the customer's site to the mobile server at the service provider in a secure manner. As you will see in the "Dealing with WASPs" section later in this chapter, secure transmission may not be an option on all mobile servers. As a result, you may have to investigate your WASP and ensure there is some way of transmitting data securely. In addition, it is important to figure out whether changes need to be made on the mobile server and, as a customer, how you can initiate those changes securely. The WASP may provide some username/password–type access, but will it be secure? These are some of the questions that need to be asked of your potential WASP.

Information-Based Model

In the information-based model (both the mobile and information servers are at the customer site) displayed in Figure 7-2, the advantage over the service provider model is that information can be delivered to many wireless networks, not just those that have a mobile server, thus giving the information provider greater control over its product.

This model has the most secure setup because both the information (content) server and the mobile server are at your site. Access control and secure communication methods are up to you. This is recommended if you have in-house staff to run these systems.

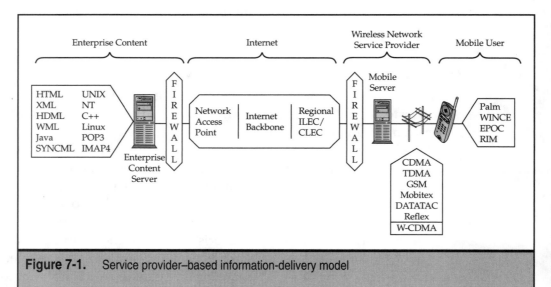

Figure 7-1.   Service provider–based information-delivery model

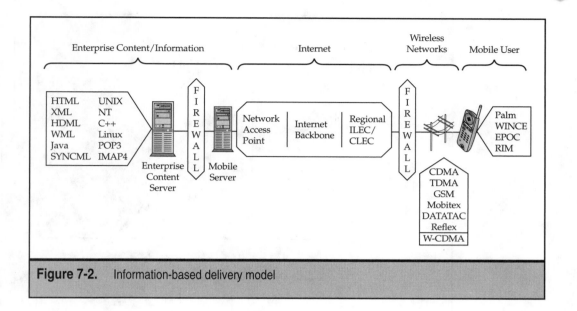

Figure 7-2.   Information-based delivery model

WASP Delivery Model

Lately, the wireless ASP (WASP) model of information delivery has been increasingly popular among many verticals (as shown in Figure 7-3). The WASP either develops applications in-house or sources them out to a third party. These applications are aggregated in a secure data center and packaged as outsourced service solutions for the WASP's customers. These solutions include provisioning, secure links to enterprise information, hosting services, customer service, the provision of wireless bandwidth, wireless network interconnection, co-marketing, and service development.

Dealing with WASPs   To avoid being "stung" by WASPs, you need to note some key areas of security concern, including viruses and administrator access. One challenge with transcoding is that some transcoders interpret code that they view from a source file. For example, JavaScript or some other malicious code could be written in the source file. When the transcoder reaches this code, the code may be executed and infect the WASP server. When this occurs, the WASP then risks infecting all its customers. This implies that the WASP user must be fully aware of various security processes and

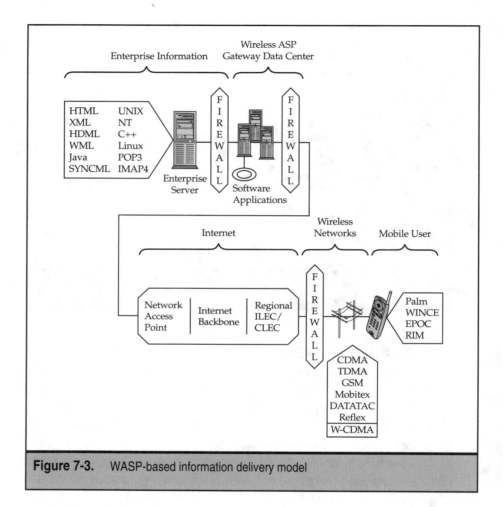

Figure 7-3. WASP-based information delivery model

methods to deal with viruses in these situations. Then comes the issue of how to administrator the service from a remote location. For example, Oracle's 9iAS wireless edition software requires a username/password, but this data is transmitted in the clear from the Oracle software to the WASP (by default). As a result, for complete confidence and security, users must run their own wireless infrastructure.

Given the multitude of information-delivery scenarios, gateway capabilities, and wireless network standards, for any enterprise or company to keep track of all the changes so as to keep up with the evolution is a mammoth and daunting task and also prohibitively expensive. Therefore, for most businesses, the ability to outsource wireless information delivery is a valuable alternative. As a result of this rapidly growing need, a new breed of wireless ASPs have developed that essentially perform application and web hosting (shared, dedicated, and co-location) for wireless devices, similar to what ISPs have done in the wired world. For information from an enterprise (Unix, NT, or IMAP4) to get to a mobile user's device, it needs to be translated to be compliant with wireless network standards (CDMA, TDMA, GSM, and so on) and formatted to the particular operating system of the receiving wireless device (Palm, PocketPC, and so on). Wireless ASPs provide this capability by creating a virtual private network (VPN) with the enterprise and undertaking the daunting tasks of wireless integration.

MOBILE SERVERS SECURITY FLAWS

One aspect of the security of a mobile server is its placement in the network, as you saw previously in the three models. However, some issues are common to all the models, which increases the risk of compromise. We address specific examples with two of the leading transcoding (or mobile) servers—IBM and Oracle. However, some of these weaknesses can be found in other vendor solutions as well.

Administrator Weaknesses

Although weaknesses do vary from vendor product to vendor product, the most common issue is the lack of security in administering a mobile server machine. Several vendors have default port addresses, server names, and even default passwords. In addition, either passwords are stored in plaintext or there are no login privileges, especially for the mobile server.

IBM Transcoding Processor, for example, has no admin-specific login. IBM makes the assumption that whoever has access to the server the transcoding processor is hosted on should also have access to the administrator features of the product. This, of course, is a poor assumption, because many organizations separate application-level administration and server-level administration as a matter of good security practice.

CAUTION: IBM does not perform secured transcoding if the network model is used in its implementation. This means that if data between the user and the web server is to be transcoded, it must be unencrypted!

Another area of weakness is IBM's replay feature. This feature allows the administrator to capture a series of commands/actions and replay them to replicate server configuration on multiple machines. However, passwords and other sensitive information are captured as a result of this process and may be used to compromise the system.

CAUTION: The default port for Oracle's Wireless Edition is 2008, and the default server name is PanamaServer. This should be changed to something different (and more cryptic) immediately.

Database Access

Most of the mobile servers access databases on other servers designated as database servers. Many of the mobile server products have poor security in exchanging authentication information between the mobile server and database server.

IBM's Transcoding Server stores the database access username ID/password in encrypted form. However, it sends this ID/password in *clear text*. At the very least, administrators should ensure this ID/password is a read-only privilege password for the database that is being accessed.

Oracle's Wireless Edition stores its passwords in clear text by default in the System.properties file. To secure (and encrypt) this information, you need to run the command

```
encryptPassword.sh WE_HOME/<server path>/admin
```

and then set the following property in the System.properties file to indicate to the server that the password is now encrypted:

```
passwordEncrypted=true
```

APPLICATIONS

Let's examine some common examples of applications in the information space.

Stock Quotes

Wireless stock quotes are available in delayed format or in real time through most major online brokerage houses. In general, most stock quotes can be viewed on a variety of wireless devices, such as web-enabled cell phones (with wireless web services from providers such as AT&T PocketNet, SprintPCS Wireless, or Verizon Wireless Web Access), RIM two-way pagers (two-way paging service, such as GoWeb from GoAmerica), Palm series PDAs (Palm.Net), and PocketPC devices. In most cases, an online account with the financial broker is required before an existing customer/account holder can sign up to receive wireless stock quotes and alerts. The wireless stock quote service is really an extension of the online financial portfolio of a customer who can opt to extend their reach to their portfolio by setting up features within their online stock account. The services that a customer may access through a wireless device can be broken down into four primary categories:

▼ **Customer-initiated stock quotes**   In this case, the customers can access quotes for securities and indices (delayed or in real time) by typing in a symbol on their wireless devices and initiating a search transaction on the financial provider's server. The server returns the results in the form of formatted quotes that are readable on the search-initiating wireless device.

■ **Alerts**   In this case, the customers can set alerts to notify them when specific securities and market indices rise or fall by a percentage or point limit that the customers set in their online profile or through their wireless devices.

CAUTION: If hackers are able to access a list of alerts and determine a pattern (data aggregation), they could take advantage of an upcoming market situation.

- **Personal stock portfolio** The customers can set up and monitor one or more stock portfolios for equities traded on the NYSE, Nasdaq, or AMEX. The portfolio is created online (wired web site) and then a simple command from a wireless device can access quotes for every stock in the portfolio.

▲ **Market summaries** From their wireless devices, customers can initiate and view information about volume leaders and top percent and dollar gainers and losers for NYSE, Nasdaq, and AMEX stocks.

Wireless stock quotes have to abide by the same restrictions as the wired Internet versions. Although real-time quotes are available for equities and indices, some institutions apply real-time quote bank restrictions by offering a set number of real-time quotes per customer or for each new order placed by the customer that is executed. Alternatively, customers may also buy a set of new real-time quotes, and the purchase amount can be automatically deducted from their account online. These restrictions vary from one financial institution to the other.

NOTE: Wireless communication may cause longer transmission delays of stock quotes than are common on the wired Internet. As a result of intermittent breakups in communication, ensure your provider does not leave a communication session open when your connection breaks up. By default, a broken or dormant connection should be terminated to avoid the possibility of anyone else taking over.

Access to wireless stock quotes is generally offered free of charge by a financial house to a customer who maintains an online trading account with the financial institution. In most cases, however, this does not include any charges imposed by the customer's wireless communication provider. Stock quotes available to most wireless customers by leading financial institutions are generally in the form of indices and equities, each holding certain information. Here's the information held by equities:

▼ Bid Price

■ Ask Price

■ Last

■ Change

■ Volume

■ Bid Size

■ Ask Size

■ High

■ Low

▲ Tick

Here's the information held by indices:

▼ Market Symbol

■ Last Value

■ Change

■ High

■ Low

■ Open

▲ Last Close

Many financial institutions also allow multiple online accounts holding multiple stock portfolios to be consolidated within one unique username and password. These accounts can be physically located on multiple servers or on the same server. The consolidation of information held within multiple accounts is generally accomplished by initiating a compounded search from a server holding one user account to the servers holding all other accounts that are to be part of the multi-account setup. Information from these accounts is consolidated and sent to the search-initiating server, which in turn transmits the information (stock quotes and so on) to the wireless devices after reformatting it by passing it through a mobile server. This model, of course, requires strong data storage protection and good security policies because data from multiple sources is now aggregated, thus increasing the collateral damage of a break-in.

Security Implications

Most information-based services use a common set of mobile devices. We will briefly highlight the most popular devices and discuss some of the basic security issues around those devices.

Web-Enabled Cell Phones

Security between the wireless device and the carrier's server is implemented by over-the-air encryption and authentication. Security between the carrier's server and the web servers is provided by standard Secure Sockets Layer (SSL).

Palm VII (Palm.Net)

Security between the wireless device and the Palm.Net proxy server is implemented by over-the-air encryption and authentication. Security between the Palm.Net proxy and the financial service provider's web servers is provided by standard Secure Sockets Layer (SSL). Further details can be found in the Palm VII white paper from Palm Computing (www.palm.com).

Windows CE Handheld PC and Cell Phone (CDPD/Mobitex)

The customer's data transmission over the Cellular Digital Packet Data (CDPD) network is encrypted and hence indecipherable to anyone but the intended recipient. CDPD encrypts information and account data in digital transmission bursts (packets) securely and efficiently. This ensures that the customer data is not transmitted to anyone but the intended recipient.

An example of a CDPD is the Sierra Wireless Aircard (for the Compaq iPaq), which uses 163-bit Elliptic Curve Cryptography (ECC) encryption and 120-bit DESX (a stronger variant of the Data Encryption Standard—DES) encryption on all packets. The strength of these protocols ensures that breaking any encrypted transmission will be difficult.

Mobitex is another mode for wireless communication that can support strong encryption. In addition, Mobitex allows for network security login/logout capability with feedback on the status (such as logged in or logged out). Error checking of transmissions can also assist in detecting tampering with the data packet flow.

Palm III

With a modem and wireless Internet service such as GoAmerica Go.Web, security between Go.Web and the financial service provider is provided by Security Sockets Layer (SSL). In addition, the CDPD network, which the modem utilizes, is secured with advanced RSA public key encryption technology.

RIM Two-Way Messenger

With a RIM device and wireless Internet service such as GoAmerica Go.Web, security between the Go.Web server and the financial service provider's web servers is provided by Secure Sockets Layer (SSL). Also, every Blackberry has a unique PIN embedded in it that is independent of the software or enterprise server version the user may have. This means the user can send a message directly over the wireless network to the unique personal identification number of another Blackberry user without the message traversing through anyone's corporate infrastructure. In other words, the message goes from the sender's wireless device to the receiver's wireless device through the wireless network without hitting either person's Exchange server or desktop PC.

RIM's Blackberry also provides the optional ability to use Simple Network Management Protocol (SNMP) support to define security policies for devices from a central location. In addition, other security features RIM provides are the "instant-on password" feature and message encryption (using the standard triple DES algorithm) through the provider's network. Blackberry's wireless e-mail solutions and other applications for the Microsoft Exchange and Lotus Domino environments incorporate end-to-end, triple DES (3DES) encryption technology as a key component of its security architecture. In some other solution offerings by RIM, the RASP Data Security for wireless applications and message-handling software has also been integrated with the Blackberry wireless e-mail solution to provide secure "always on, always connected" access to corporate servers.

News Headlines

Most current news sites, such as CNN, Reuters, and BBC, offer a service whereby a user can configure their mobile device to receive news content from the online news provider. In many cases, this architecture is based on a screen-scraping methodology that is a variant of the news provider's existing web site and translates the existing Hypertext Markup Language (HTML) to device markups, such as Wireless Markup Language (WML) or Handheld Device Markup Language (HDML), by passing the news content through a mobile server and making the necessary changes to adapt to the wireless device's smaller real estate. News content can be sent to a wireless device using any of the three models explained in Figures 7-1, 7-2, and 7-3 earlier in this chapter.

News is mainly delivered using two screen-scraping approaches, as displayed in Figure 7-4.

Figure 7-5 displays another, slightly enhanced approach to wireless news delivery in which the news text is edited prior to being transmitted over to the mobile devices. In this example, about 25 percent (two out of eight lines) of the news content displayed on the WAP screen has been cut off, thus saving bandwidth, both in the visual sense as well as in transmission of data bytes.

The model of directly extracting information out of the database instead of scraping it from the HTML or web site is also used by many wireless news content providers, and the architecture is similar to any wireless non-scraping content-delivery architecture.

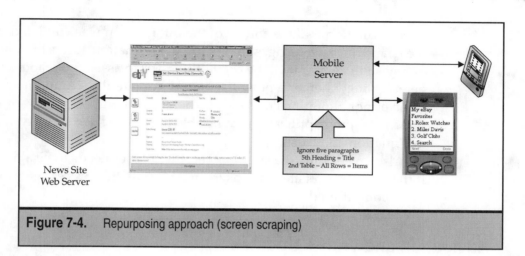

Figure 7-4.   Repurposing approach (screen scraping)

From a security perspective, screen scraping does not usually determine whether the information being gleaned is from a valid source or has not been altered in transit. In addition, most mobile applications with screen scraping do not pass on any authentication

Figure 7-5.   Intelligent scraping of news content

or confirmation that the source of the information was validated. In the near future, web pages that display information such as financial or news information will be digitally signed to assist the reader in determining whether a potential hacker got into the site and made some minor alterations to the site. Therefore, it will be important for screen-scraping applications to be able to convey such security information and trust.

Also, every time the site changes, the scraper needs to be altered. If the scraper is offsite (such as in an ASP site), this process gets even more complicated.

Navigation and Traffic Updates

Mobile devices and services used while driving or walking are known as *wireless motion-based services*. There are two types of mobile traffic services: conventional location-based services and motion-based services. Location-based services focus on a mobile user's static location, whereas motion-based services focus on a mobile user's movement (location, direction, and speed). This is because, in a mobile world, the path of a user determines the information that is most relevant for the user. Many companies currently provide conventional location-based services to customers, and wireless carriers and others are deploying location-determination technologies that will support motion-based services. Location-based mobile traffic services (both conventional location-based as well as motion-based services) can be further broken down into two main categories: navigation and traffic updates. In conventional location-based navigation, if the user deviates from their desired path or direction, the service must be restarted from the new origin. Figure 7-6 displays a case of conventional location-based navigation where automatic rerouting does not take place.

In a motion-based navigation service, a mobile user can receive directions based on their movement in a particular direction. If the user makes a wrong turn or encounters heavy traffic and decides to change direction, the system will reroute the user as needed. A case of automatic rerouting is displayed in Figure 7-7, which shows motion-based navigation.

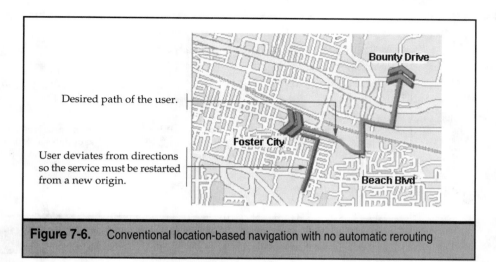

Desired path of the user.

User deviates from directions so the service must be restarted from a new origin.

Figure 7-6. Conventional location-based navigation with no automatic rerouting

Now, in the case of traffic updates, a motion-based traffic information service will send traffic information to the mobile user ahead of the user along the path they are traveling (see Figure 7-8). This is not quite the case with conventional location-based traffic information services, which scan a "zone" around the user's location and send information that may sometimes not be relevant to their path of travel (for example, sending traffic information close to but behind the user).

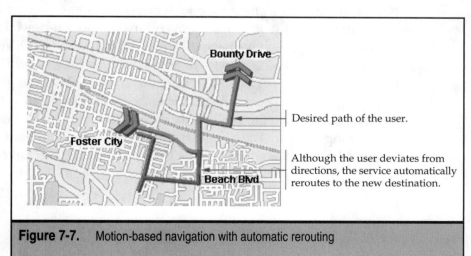

Desired path of the user.

Although the user deviates from directions, the service automatically reroutes to the new destination.

Figure 7-7. Motion-based navigation with automatic rerouting

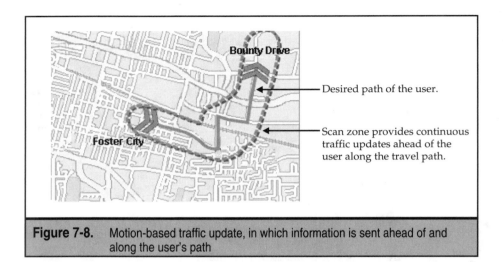

Desired path of the user.

Scan zone provides continuous traffic updates ahead of the user along the travel path.

Figure 7-8. Motion-based traffic update, in which information is sent ahead of and along the user's path

This service and motion-based spatial search technique can also be used to determine a business that is optimally located ahead of the user along the user's path, rather than one that is close but behind the user (it is assumed that the user is driving ahead and wishes to avoid making a U-turn).

Most location-based traffic and navigation applications support both thin- and thick-client mobile devices, and some even have an automatic built-in switch from conventional to motion-based services. Many such services have been developed using standard XML and Java APIs with a voice-, WAP-, or SMS-based user interface. They are linked to online maps as well as national address database providers over secure links. The address database has real-time connectivity with the application for intelligent address geocoding to accommodate a user's input error. The applications also have online mobile location-based access to the area's yellow pages and are linked to other advertising systems that offer local shop discounts and specials. The applications provide extensive search criteria for finding a route or destination, such as minimal radial distance, minimal driving distance or time, minimal number of turns, or within a certain distance. Every user can also have their own "personal profile" online at the application provider's web site, where a user can store their own personal maps with frequently used addresses, locations, businesses, and so on, and then initiate searches on this stored profile from their mobile devices to request information.

Supporting Technology Overview

Location-based navigation, traffic, and business information applications utilize coordinates provided by the location-determination infrastructure to pinpoint a mobile user's trajectory—including location, direction, and speed. The system then allows the user to request and receive information based on the user's movement along the path.

Most current location-based application platforms are generally supported by XML and Java-based architectures designed to handle a large number of users. A typical architecture is generally modular and can consist of many layers. Figure 7-9 displays a sample architecture with four layers: the Common layer, the Engine layer, the API layer, and the Media layer.

Security Implications for Location-Based Technologies

As described in previous chapters, the main security issue with location-based technologies is the lack of privacy and/or fear of being tracked by governmental organizations. For mobile phone

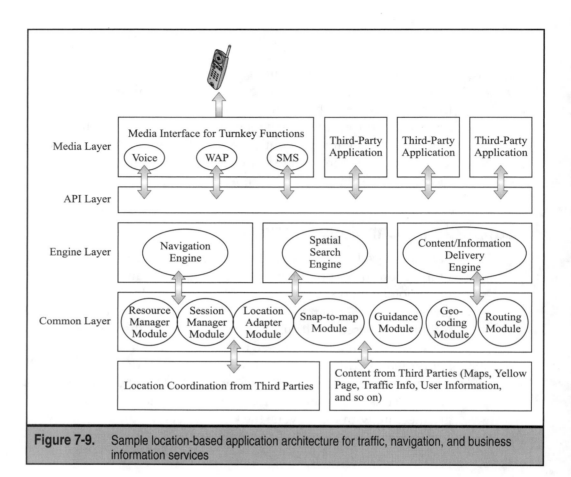

Figure 7-9. Sample location-based application architecture for traffic, navigation, and business information services

(e911) applications, the tracking of the phone can be done to within a few feet of the phone itself, and presumably the owner. For location-based advertising or push information, advertisers may want to tie in geophysical information to determine how best to position sales strategies. For example, if a large number of coffee shop customers go to a bagel shop right afterwards, then perhaps the coffee shop may consider selling bagels. Such data mining, while providing rich information, compromises the privacy and possible security of the users. What's more, hackers, having access to such tracking systems, may be able to physically track certain high-profile individuals.

On the flip side, location-tracking capabilities can provide for improved physical security of assets such as automobiles, because now a stolen vehicle can be tracked by law-enforcement agencies. Various applications such as OnStar have provided for a whole range of new services for consumers. For example, with an OnStar system in the car you can simply press an I or SOS button in your vehicle to connect to a trained advisor who will assist you with directory listings, information, accident assistance, emergency services, roadside assistance, remote door unlock, remote diagnostics, and stolen vehicle tracking in addition to many other functions such as route assistance, maps, and concierge services. The vehicle is fitted with a GPS system that instantly informs the advisor of your physical location. Should the airbags deploy for any reason, the OnStar system will automatically trigger an alert. The advisors will call your car to check on your safety.

The following extended case study describes a wireless information-delivery portal solution based on the WebSphere Everyplace Suite (WES) 1.1 and Tivoli SecureWay Policy Director 3.7. The case study focuses on the architectures and infrastructure requirements and discusses deployment and security details. Refer to Figure 7-10 as you read through the case study.

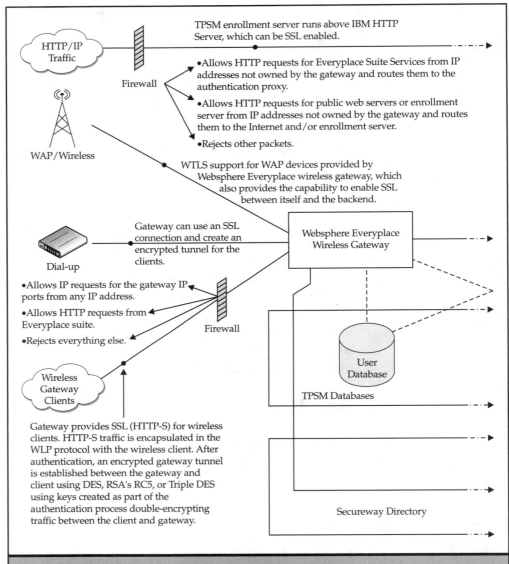

TPSM enrollment server runs above IBM HTTP Server, which can be SSL enabled.

HTTP/IP Traffic

•Allows HTTP requests for Everyplace Suite Services from IP addresses not owned by the gateway and routes them to the authentication proxy.

Firewall

•Allows HTTP requests for public web servers or enrollment server from IP addresses not owned by the gateway and routes them to the Internet and/or enrollment server.

•Rejects other packets.

WAP/Wireless

WTLS support for WAP devices provided by Websphere Everyplace wireless gateway, which also provides the capability to enable SSL between itself and the backend.

Gateway can use an SSL connection and create an encrypted tunnel for the clients.

Websphere Everyplace Wireless Gateway

Dial-up

•Allows IP requests for the gateway IP ports from any IP address.

•Allows HTTP requests from Everyplace suite.

•Rejects everything else.

Firewall

Wireless Gateway Clients

User Database

TPSM Databases

Gateway provides SSL (HTTP-S) for wireless clients. HTTP-S traffic is encapsulated in the WLP protocol with the wireless client. After authentication, an encrypted gateway tunnel is established between the gateway and client using DES, RSA's RC5, or Triple DES using keys created as part of the authentication process double-encrypting traffic between the client and gateway.

Secureway Directory

Figure 7-10. Security overview of WebSphere Everyplace Suite

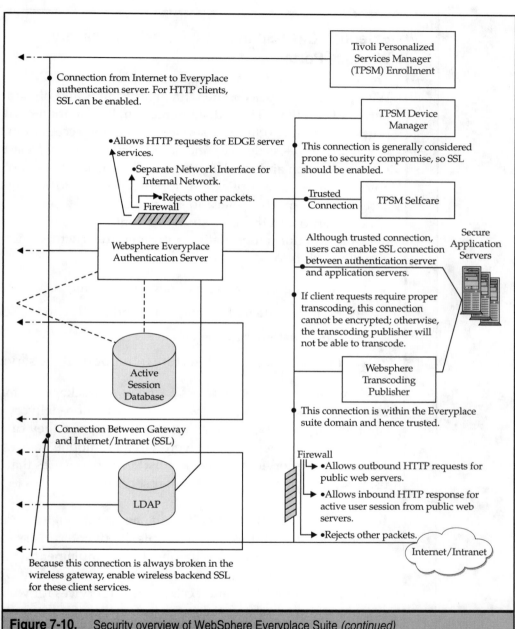

Figure 7-10. Security overview of WebSphere Everyplace Suite *(continued)*

Extended Case Study: An Information-Delivery Wireless Portal

This case study is based on implementations of the IBM Websphere Everyplace Suite with architectures and illustrations derived from IBM/Tivoli documentation. Information-delivery portals must now offer new services to include access from both wired and wireless devices, increased security, and wireless self-registration and service selection. The portals must also be able to deliver new applications rapidly; this includes providing access to third-party applications if necessary.

The purpose of this case study is to outline a solution for building an information-delivery portal infrastructure, the aim of which is to

▼ Facilitate easy creation of new content and services

■ Facilitate efficient maintenance and production of services

■ Offer customer management services

▲ Provide a secure architecture to support all the services

Applications for the wireless portal use a package of standard building blocks. Users of the wireless information-delivery portal can typically register and manage themselves, and they can select the information they want delivered to their mobile devices by paying for the services online. Robust security ensures that only users who have paid for a particular service have access to it.

Tools   Policy Director is a policy-management tool for wireless applications that addresses the complexity of enterprise security solutions and the difficulties involved with implementing security policies across platforms. As shown here, Policy Director provides authentication and access-control services for web resources from a central, single, logical web space.

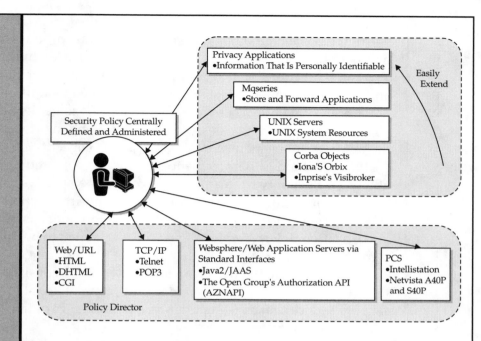

As shown in Figure 7-10, WebSphere Everyplace Suite (WES) is an integrated, secured, end-to-end middleware solution for mobile e-business that provides functions to enable data access and extend e-business applications to wireless devices. In general, IBM and other vendors in this space (such as Bea Systems) have taken care to ensure security is part of the product suite. Overall, IBM has provided security policy management and implementation based on such standards such as Enterprise Java Beans (EJB) security, SSL, DMZ architecture (DMZ or a *demilitarized zone* enables a company to offer a public presence without compromising the security of its internal network), support of Lightweight Directory Access Protocol (LDAP) running over TCP for accessing online directory services standards, and general compatibility with good network security architectures.

In many ways, IBM has chosen to roll into one product suite a number of different core functions with its security architecture. Typically, functions such as user provisioning, entitlements, and user management/delegation are performed by multiple applications tied into a common integration. To some degree, all these functions can be described as attempting to provide the ultimate but ever elusive "single sign-on" concept.

IBM's method is to implement a policy-based solution that allows for flexibility from an IT management perspective, as do most security solutions today. The overall security functions WebSphere provides for include authentication policy/services, authorization policy/services, and what is claimed to be "single sign-on support."

As displayed in the following illustration, WES consists of these major functional areas: connectivity, content adaptation, security services, management services, performance optimization, and common services.

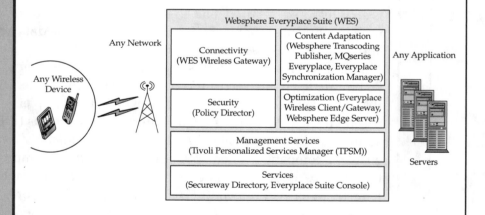

Let's begin with connectivity. The WES Wireless Gateway provides secure connectivity between the IT network and the communications network. It also acts as a WAP gateway by providing protocol translation and as a WAP push proxy gateway by pushing information to the wireless devices. The WES Wireless Gateway also provides support for short messaging (SMS).

The functional area of content adaptation is supported by the following tools:

▼ **WebSphere Transcoding Publisher** Transforms arbitrary content into a form that can be presented on a wireless device.

■ **MQSeries Everyplace** Enables wireless devices to queue messages and ensure their completion only once in both connected and disconnected end-user scenarios. MQE provides for strong security for low-bandwidth applications and for devices low in memory and processing power. One notable feature is the ability to invoke message-level security, which allows application-to-application messages to be encrypted and secured.

▲ **Everyplace Synchronization Manager** Enables wireless devices to synchronize the results of their offline activities with the server database when the device goes online.

Security services for the system are provided by the Policy Director, which facilitates user authentication, provides data protection during transit, and controls access to services. The fundamental basis of this security protection is the use of digital certificates. Certificates are mapped to access permissions so that when a user initiates a session, the certificate is presented not only to authenticate the user but also to determine what that user can do.

The Tivoli Personalized Services Manager is responsible for the functional area of Management Services. It provides content personalization, enrollment, customer care, self-care, interfaces to external billing systems, reporting, software distribution, and customer updates (for example, information on upgrades, software patches, and other personalized data relevant to a particular customer).

The Everyplace Wireless Client/Gateway and the Websphere Edge Server optimize system performance:

▼ **Everyplace Wireless Client/Gateway**   Provides wireless optimizations for standard Internet Protocol (IP) communications as well as Transmission Control Protocol (TCP) optimization.

▲ **WebSphere Edge Server**   Provides caching functions on a server to improve response times when processing web addresses.

Lastly, the SecureWay Directory and the Everyplace Suite Console handle the common functional services within the system as explained here:

▼ **SecureWay Directory**   A central Lightweight Directory Access Protocol (LDAP) repository that contains runtime information about active sessions, users, devices, and networks. Also, the digital certificates used in the authentication can also be stored here, if desired. LDAP does allow for a secure method of communication between the directory and the application.

▲ **Everyplace Suite Console**   Provides a single console for system administrators to perform installation and carry out diagnostics and maintenance as well as routine administrative tasks.

Logical Architecture   The following illustration shows the logical architecture for the wireless information portal infrastructure.

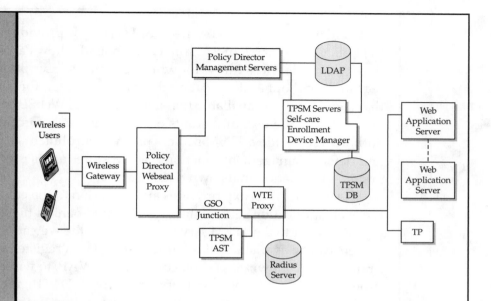

WebSEAL and Web Traffic Express (WTE) are reverse proxy servers. In other words, each appears to the client to be the origin (content) server, whereas in reality the request is sent to another server. The WTE proxy is placed behind the WebSEAL with a Tivoli SecureWay Policy Director Global Sign-On smart junction established between WebSEAL and the WTE proxy. This TCP/IP connection between a WebSEAL server and a connected server allows WebSEAL to protect web resources located on that server as well as protect its own resources.

The Global Sign-On junction provides username and password information to the WTE proxy that authenticates the user to the RADIUS server and creates an entry for the user in the Active Session Table (AST). This table maintains the user state so that information such as device type is forwarded as part of each request to the back-end web application servers (for transcoding purposes, for example).

NOTE: The WTE proxy does not provide authorization functions.

Content authorization on the TPSM servers is provided by the Policy Director WebSEAL proxy. WebSEAL allows access to unregistered services (those for which a formal subscription is not required) without authenticating the user. However, for content that should only be available to registered users, WebSEAL authenticates the user and grants or denies access according to its authorization policy. TPSM servers provide enrollment, self-care, and device-management functions. TPSM stores all its user and system information in its own database.

The WebSEAL proxy provides authorization to the content on the Web application servers that are stationed behind the WTE proxy. Similar to the TPSM servers, content on the web application servers can be available to both unregistered and registered users. Translation from wireless protocols, such as WAP, to wired protocols, such as Hypertext Transfer Protocol (HTTP), is carried out by the wireless gateway, which can also authenticate the user if configured to do so. WebSEAL can be configured to receive an authenticated ID from the wireless gateway so that it does not have to reauthenticate the user.

In the WES environment, TPSM manages the users. When a user is enrolled in TPSM, they are automatically created in Policy Director and the privileges are set up based on the user's subscription options. Policy Director uses the LDAP server to store the user's authentication and privilege information. Although TPSM also uses LDAP to store all information about users, it does not use this information internally. Instead, TPSM publishes this information to the LDAP server for third-party applications to use (by billing systems, for example).

Physical Architecture   All communications from the Internet to the demilitarized zone (DMZ) and from the DMZ to the intranet are protected by secure sessions. Secure Sockets Layer (SSL) is used for data security in the wired situations, and Wireless Transport Layer Security (WTLS) is used in the wireless WAP situations. In non-WAP wireless scenarios, security is provided by the WES wireless clients. The following illustration shows the physical architecture for the wireless information portal infrastructure.

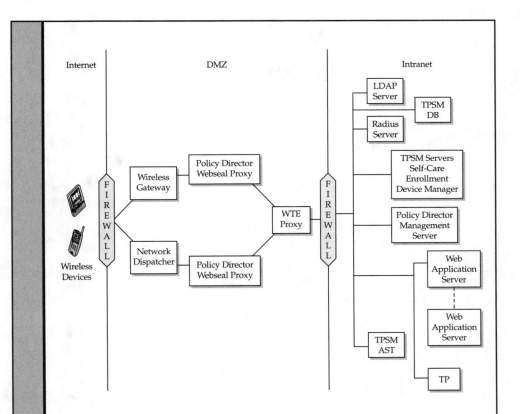

The flow of data from one region to the other is controlled by a firewall that separates adjacent regions. The firewall helps detect intrusions in the DMZ before the data reaches the back-end intranet. Wired users are routed to the Policy Director WebSEAL proxies in the DMZ, which ensure that only authenticated and authorized users get access to protected resources. If the content being accessed is public in nature, the WebSEAL proxies also allow unauthenticated access to that content. This way, all the critical components of the intranet are protected from the Internet by the firewall, WebSEAL, and WTE proxies.

The system also uses the Transcoding Publisher, which is installed as a plug-in on the web application servers. The wireless information-delivery portal was built on the Sun E220R and E420R servers running Solaris 7, with all the latest patches.

CHAPTER 8

The Horizontals, Part 3: Mobile Security in Communications Applications

Customer Relationship Management (CRM) and Sales Force Automation (SFA) are two of the hottest areas in the mCommerce space. Both of these applications allow organizations quicker and easier access to data as the sales and support forces interact with the customers. The challenge is opening up such confidential data to the mobile sales force without compromising security in shuttling this data around the wireless airwaves.

An important aspect of Customer Relationship Management is communication. This chapter, therefore, also discusses the Instant Messaging (IM) and Short Messaging System (SMS) applications, both of which, when used in conjunction with CRM and SFA applications, can greatly enhance the end user's experience. Of course, both IM and SMS have their own security issues, especially since they can circumvent well-designed and guarded firewalls as well as other wired security infrastructure.

MOBILE CUSTOMER RELATIONSHIP MANAGEMENT (MCRM)

CRM has become one of the hottest and fastest growing markets for mobile enterprise applications. Many companies that have realized the business significance of CRM are now seeing a need for wireless extensions to their customer management cycles. The Aberdeen Group states that more than $15 billion of investments have been made in Customer Relationship Management (CRM) applications, infrastructure, and services in 2001 alone—and more than $30 billion in cumulative investments since 1998. Mission-critical CRM applications have been used extensively in the last few years, with companies such as Siebel realizing mammoth growth and success. Modern corporate business models are becoming more and more customer focused as they try to retain their existing consumer base and attract new ones.

Given the business significance of mCRM, it is essential to focus on the security for mCRM applications since much of the mCRM business model centers around the customer accessing sensitive product-, finance-, and company-related corporate data from a PDA over a wireless network. With the ability to be mobile, salespeople can have an increased selling advantage, but this also creates a number of security risks in the process.

mCommerce Security: A Beginner's Guide Blueprints

Table of Contents

Secure mCommerce End-to-End Architecture

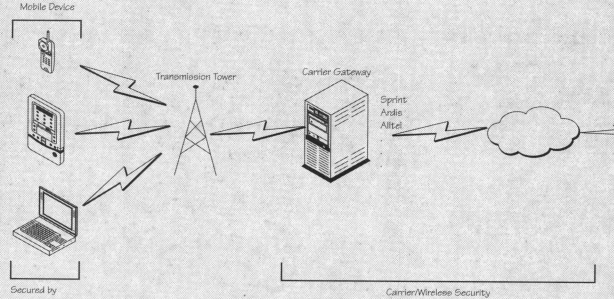

Mobile Device

Transmission Tower

Carrier Gateway

Sprint
Ardis
Alltel

Secured by
- Biometrics
- Username (password)
- Smartcards
- PIN

Carrier/Wireless Security
- GSM Authentication
- Data Encryption

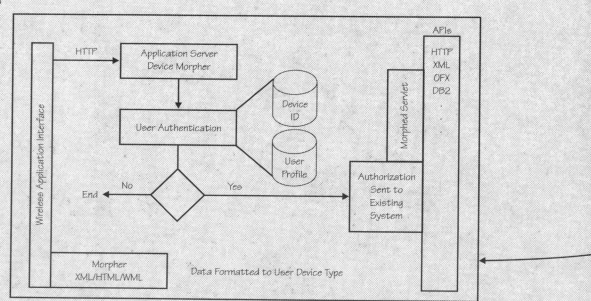

Wireless Application Interface

HTTP

Application Server
Device Morpher

User Authentication

Device ID

User Profile

No → End

Yes

Authorization Sent to Existing System

Morphed Servlet

APIs

HTTP
XML
OFX
DB2

Morpher
XML/HTML/WML

Data Formatted to User Device Type

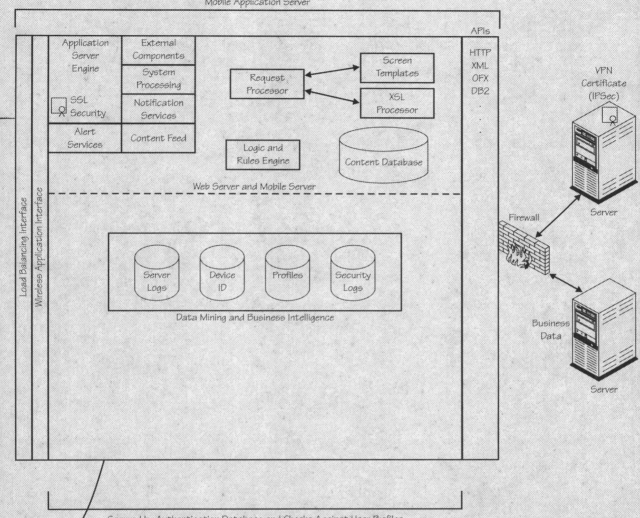

Mobile Application Server

Load Balancing Interface

Wireless Application Interface

Application Server Engine

External Components

System Processing

SSL Security

Notification Services

Alert Services

Content Feed

Request Processor

Screen Templates

XSL Processor

Logic and Rules Engine

Content Database

APIs

HTTP
XML
OFX
DB2
.
.
.

Web Server and Mobile Server

Server Logs

Device ID

Profiles

Security Logs

Data Mining and Business Intelligence

VPN Certificate (IPSec)

Server

Firewall

Business Data

Server

Secured by Authentication Database and Checks Against User Profiles

Process Flow

The mobile device connects via a carrier network to the mobile application server. The application server checks against the user profiles and access control lists. Data is then morphed to the correct format. Using API's, the mobile device is given access to the business data. In addition, a VPN tunnel can be created from the mobile application server to the business server.

3

Vulnerability Points in an mCommerce Network

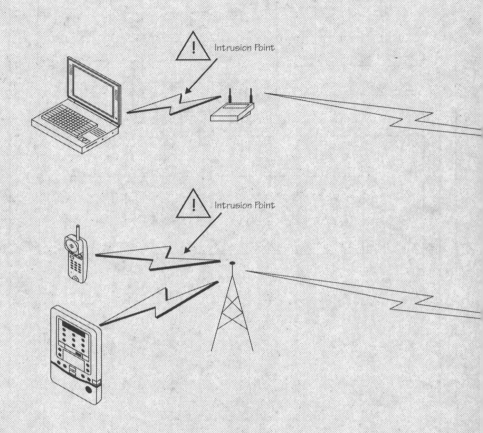

 Indicates points at greatest risk to hacking. These points must be especially secure.

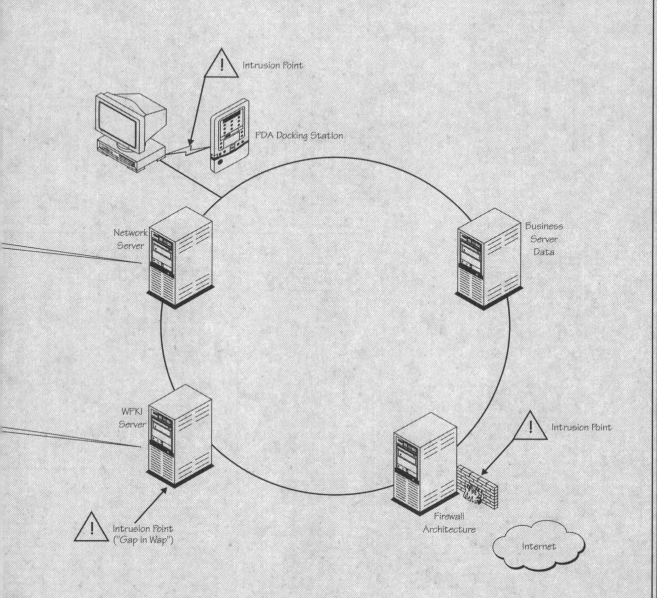

Intrusion Point

PDA Docking Station

Network
Server

Business
Server
Data

WPKI
Server

Firewall
Architecture

Intrusion Point

Internet

Intrusion Point
("Gap in Wap")

5

Secure Wireless Local Area Network

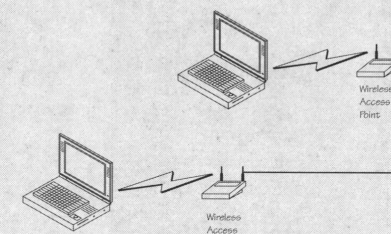

Wireless
Access
Point

Wireless
Access
Point

Internet

Wireless access points should be segmented to ensure
minimal impact in the event of a security breach.
Intrusion detection systems (IDS) should also be in
place to take action should a breach occur.

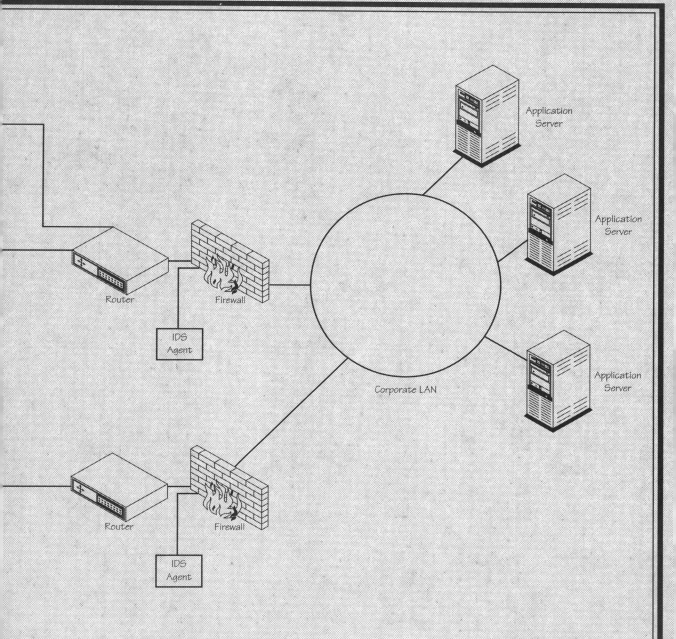

Application
Server

Application
Server

Application
Server

Corporate LAN

Router

Firewall

IDS
Agent

Router

Firewall

IDS
Agent

Steps of a Secured Mobile Payment

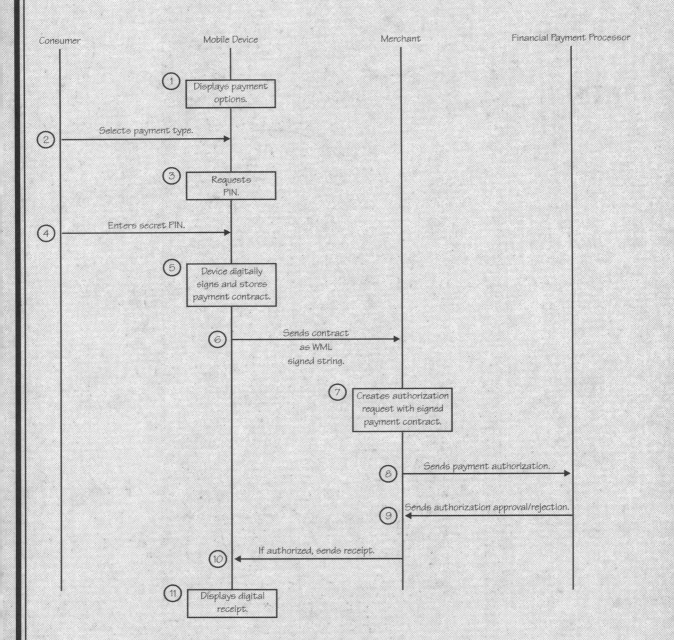

Consumer	Mobile Device	Merchant	Financial Payment Processor

1. Displays payment options.
2. Selects payment type.
3. Requests PIN.
4. Enters secret PIN.
5. Device digitally signs and stores payment contract.
6. Sends contract as WML signed string.
7. Creates authorization request with signed payment contract.
8. Sends payment authorization.
9. Sends authorization approval/rejection.
10. If authorized, sends receipt.
11. Displays digital receipt.

The previous chapters have shown that wireless data is highly successful in many business applications today. Using wireless has significantly improved worker productivity, increased customer satisfaction, and, in many cases, provided a competitive advantage. Most of the success of wireless data to this point has been in the operational side of business. However, wireless data is starting to be more widely adopted by enterprises to provide real-time access to information for field salespeople and mobile business professionals. The most complicated aspect of security is to provide protection against real-time threats. Because CRM relies almost exclusively on the latest, most accurate information, it requires strong data security. In the past couple years, new tools have made fundamental customer relationship management principles achievable, such as knowing who the most valuable customers are and treating each customer as an individual. Web technologies, for example, enable call center staff to access any number of corporate databases from a single browser interface, giving them a complete view of a customer's value to the enterprise. Self-service web sites automatically consult customer profiles before selectively displaying ads or making product recommendations.

TIP: If you need justification for management to get funds to provide increased security, point out that customer profiles and data can be considered assets (intellectual property). Assets have a material value; therefore, real financial loss can be suffered if the data is not protected.

Mobile CRM Security Techniques

As we have discussed throughout this book, security techniques and solutions are based around the type and value of data a system must hold. In the CRM space, customer data and related information needs to be protected. Generally, customer data is considered a strategic and competitive advantage. With the ability to use mobile devices to access CRM data, the security risks extend not only to the access of the data but also to the protection of the data itself.

CRM security protection can be classified into four main areas:

▼ Access to network protection

■ Protection of data

- Thin-client approach
▲ Dial-back

Access to Network Protection

CRM systems are primarily accessed on laptops and increasingly on PDAs. Typical security measures for such systems include VPNs and dual-factor authentication.

Virtual private networks (VPNs), as described in previous chapters, are secured tunnels that allow protected and secret communication from the end-user device to the corporate server. In this manner, the user can be sure the data is not seen by any third party in transit. Most VPN solutions require a VPN client, which is generally a piece of software located on the end-user device. This client software prompts the user for a username/password or requires the presentation of a digital certificate to initiate the VPN connection. Furthermore, VPN client software has the ability to "time out" the connection. This means that after some period of inactivity, the connection can be terminated. Such an instance may happen, for example, when a PDA is suddenly switched off, without being logged off the network. This feature reduces the risk of an attacker hijacking an open connection. Generally, the VPN software is not part of the specific CRM software security. For example, Oracle has its own username/password mechanism for signing in.

The VPN runs underneath applications on the network level so that applications have no idea they are running over a VPN. The whole idea is that you are part of the corporate intranet (behind the firewall), even though you are on the public Internet. The secured connection and strong (and encrypted) authentication makes this possible.

Other methods of protecting access to the network include guarding access to the device itself. As you have seen in previous chapters, biometrics is one method of protecting (physical) access to mobile devices. This topic is covered in detail in Chapter 14.

Protection of Data

Because most CRM systems are based on modern relationship database management systems (RDBMS), such as Oracle, DB2, or Microsoft SQL Server, it is possible to restrict access to each piece of data by authority level. For example, a West Coast sales manager may be restricted to access customer data for West Coast customers only. Furthermore, individual sales territory reps may have access to only their named accounts.

> **CAUTION:**   Never allow all employees unrestricted access to your CRM database. Limit access based on need. Remember that most security threats come from within the organization.

So, the question is, why restrict access in this method? In general, the amount of risk is limited in case a mobile device becomes compromised. In addition, it is widely accepted that the risk of a security compromise is much more likely from an insider, such as an employee, than from an external hacker. In this manner, by restricting access to the CRM data, a disgruntled employee could not copy and eventually steal it. Data can be restricted by role (for example, manager or director) or by context (for example, region or customer name), thus giving an organization flexibility in how to protect its data.

What's more, encryption at the mobile device could be used to further protect the data in the event a mobile device is compromised. Public key infrastructure (PKI), for example, could be employed by using digital certificates to encrypt data as it is stored on the mobile device.

Thin-Client Approach

One method in which CRM data and access can be protected is with the use of thin-client methods of access to the back-end CRM system. A *thin client* is a piece of communications software that sends information to and from the mobile device, but the actual CRM software and commands run on the remote server. The thin client simply transmits the commands and responses to the server. In this manner, data is not actually being stored on the mobile device, except in memory.

> **NOTE:**   Many thin-client solutions can significantly degrade performance of a CRM application. Ensure that your chosen thin-client solution can be usable in a typical sales environment—that is, on the road using a 56 Kbps dialup connection.

One of the more popular thin clients is a product called ICA by Citrix, a company well known for providing thin-client systems. In addition, the thin-client approach generally requires fewer resources on the mobile system, because only small-footprint software needs to be set up.

Dial-Back

For more secure options, organizations can use dial-back techniques. Dial-back systems require users to identify themselves initially. Then, based on known information such as a particular telephone number, a central computer calls back that number and connects to the device. With the popularity of Internet access and more advanced wireless networks, dial-back networks will remain useful for only the most extreme cases of required security. In general, most corporate organizations will not use this solution due to the expense of such a system. Perhaps government and defense contractors that have CRM systems will require a system like this. In addition, the challenge with mobile users is that they might not always be at a fixed location for long. Dial-back systems rely on being able to find that same user at a predetermined phone number.

Best Practices

To help you assess how to go about closing any security loopholes, we will discuss some best practices concerning security policies in this section.

Who Owns the Customer?

Although a salesperson may collect and access data on a customer, that data belongs to the organization. When the salesperson leaves the organization, that CRM data should be destroyed and/or prevented from leaving the organization. Techniques such as thin-client networks, mentioned earlier in this chapter, allow for the control of access to data in this regard. One method of establishing ownership of customer data is through strong corporate user policies.

Your policies should state (at a minimum) the following:

▼ How the data is used

■ Who can access the data and under what conditions

■   What happens to the data when the customer is no longer an active customer

▲   The user's role in protecting and securing the data

NOTE: It is important to include in your privacy policy how customer data is being used. This includes CRM data for sales and marketing purposes. Some governments are now requiring full disclosures around CRM data (for example, the European Union Data Protection Directive).

Syncing Standards

In general, because most mobile sales users will not be concerned about the technical aspects of security, it is important to maintain consistency across the organization in the tools and technologies being used. In this manner, security issues can be resolved quickly and efficiently because all systems will have similar architectures. First off, it is recommended that your organization actually own the mobile devices and allow employees to use the devices, much like desktops or even laptops are dispensed in organizations. Aside from the ability to standardize on a set of technologies, the mobile device could be taken back when an employee leaves the organization.

Syncing policy should indicate the following (as shown in Fig 8-1):

▼   Which systems to sync against.

■   Whether network syncing is allowed (not recommended).

■   How the system being synced to (the host) is backed up.

▲   The host system should have actively running antivirus software to catch any transmitted viruses from the mobile device.

Synchronizing is important because data from the mobile device is transmitted to the host. If viruses or corrupt data are transmitted back to the network, they will possibly be bypassing normal firewall protections.

Standards for Power-On Protection

Most mobile devices have the ability to block access to them at the time of power-on. Written policies as well as the standard

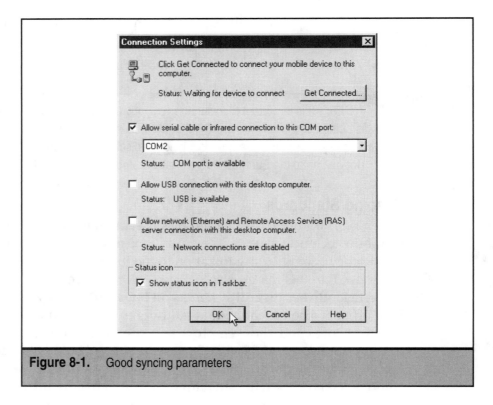

Figure 8-1.   Good syncing parameters

configuration of corporate mobile devices should incorporate the
following key strategies:

▼   Require a nontrivial password or other authentication
mechanism at power-on.

▲   Ensure that startup information does not reveal personal details
about the owner. Startup display data should state that "This is
a private device and unauthorized use will be considered an act
of trespassing. Please return this device to …."

To provide an end-to-end multichannel solution that covers
all aspects of the customer relationship cycle, many organizations
in markets such as insurance, healthcare, and finance are looking to
extend their CRM systems into the field. Mobile CRM products are
being developed that enable sales personnel in the field to carry out
complex tasks straight from their PDAs, for instance, accessing customer
information residing on corporate servers, querying the server database

to check on the availability of a particular product, filling out customer orders or checking the status of an order, generating quotes on the fly by wirelessly querying the servers, as well as accessing product documentation, and even renewing customer contracts while meeting with the customer! Solutions such as these extend customer relationship management data and processes literally into the hands of the frontline staff. With the ability to synchronize hand-held devices with desktop PCs over a wired connection as well as corporate servers over a wireless network, mobile users can interact with CRM and other critical enterprise applications anytime, anywhere. Whether they are in a restaurant having a meeting with a prospect or under a desk diagnosing a faulty hard drive, hand-held users not only have two-way communication with enterprise applications and databases but also have the ability to pull information from web sites. They can access historical customer data, decision-support aids, and company policies in a few simple steps, just as if they were in an office.

As discussed in previous chapters, the mobile phone is one of the wireless touch points for all mCommerce applications, not just in terms of customer care and relationship management but also in information, advertising, transactional, and payment-based applications. In the case of mCRM applications, the mobile device becomes a constantly accessible point of contact between the customer and the company making the device a 24/7 customer care center. Such a mobile access device will not likely be a shared utility and will therefore carry the identity of its user; this will enhance the authenticity of interactions on the mobile network as well as create the ability to build targeted services. Moreover, with the global marketplace building consensus around data encryption based on public keys, the transactional mobile environment will very likely address the five key security requirements (access control, confidentiality, data integrity, authentication, and nonrepudiation) very early in its evolution and therefore will affect directly e-service strategies. One of the areas where mCRM has gained respect is the travel and tourism industry. mCommerce applications can be used to support most aspects of the travel industry value chain; for example, they can help customers define and decide on a tour or trip or experience the trip itself. From a CRM perspective, mCommerce becomes a boon for this industry since it allows travel companies such as Expedia, Travelocity, and many others, to establish and maintain the relationship with the traveler after the travel experience has been completed. The companies that will attract and retain the maximum number of satisfied customers will be those that are able to successfully deliver a real-time customer experience at all points of the journey, as displayed in Figure 8-2.

In conclusion, mCRM provides access to accurate corporate and customer information at any time and from any place, including retail sales floors and especially from environments where laptops are difficult to have or carry. mCRM gives field care and support professionals the ability to immediately answer customer questions as they come up, tailor deals to customer needs, compute totals, capture customer approvals, and confirm orders as well as delivery schedules on the spot (see Figure 8-3).

MOBILE SALES FORCE AUTOMATION (SFA)

With the recent slump in the U.S. and global economic climate, many companies are feeling increased pressure to improve the value and effectiveness of their face-to-face selling. As markets become more competitive and transparent, especially with the rise of the Internet, the sales representative's role has become critical to differentiating quality, adding value, and building customer loyalty for the company. Mobile commerce brings with it a breath of new life into face-to-face selling allowing field representatives equipped with handheld devices, the ability to orchestrate greater responsiveness for customers, expand the pool of resources that can be brought into selling discussions, and broaden the scope of customer relationships.

NOTE: By extending their CRM initiatives to mobile devices and implementing smart mCommerce applications to layer on top of the existing CRM value chain, companies can elevate their sales forces from lone disconnected representatives to always-connected team players with anytime, anywhere access to the sales resource pool.

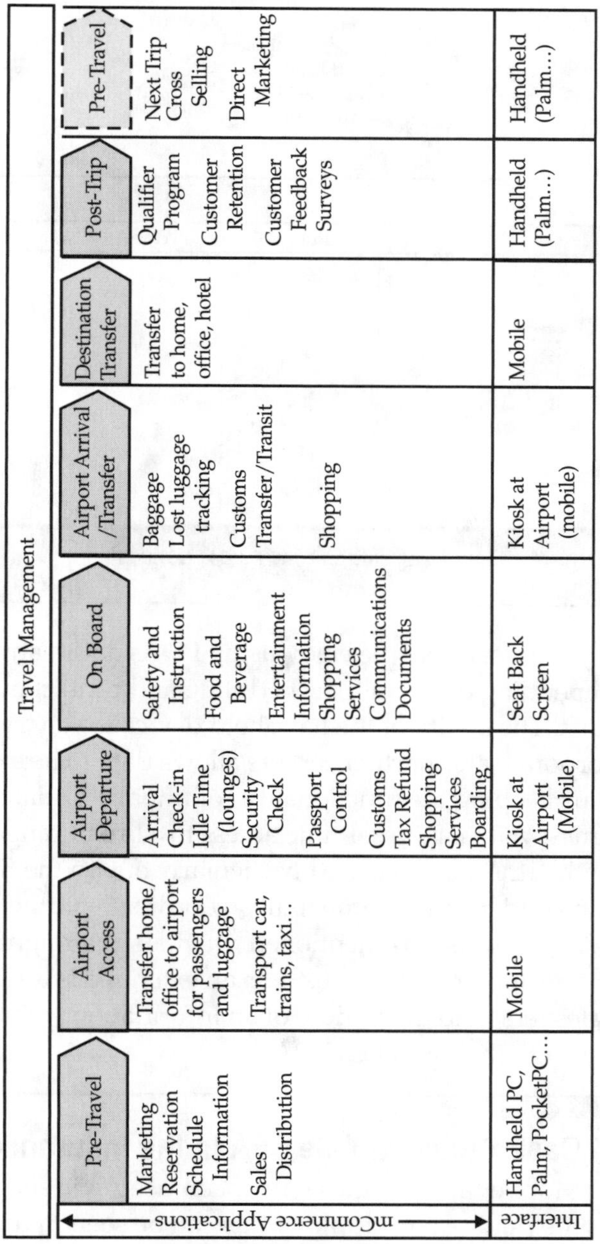

Travel Management							
Pre-Travel	Airport Access	Airport Departure	On Board	Airport Arrival /Transfer	Destination Transfer	Post-Trip	Pre-Travel
Marketing Reservation Schedule Information Sales Distribution	Transfer home/ office to airport for passengers and luggage Transport car, trains, taxi...	Arrival Check-in Idle Time (lounges) Security Check Passport Control Customs Tax Refund Shopping Services Boarding	Safety and Instruction Food and Beverage Entertainment Information Shopping Services Communications Documents	Baggage Lost luggage tracking Customs Transfer/Transit Shopping	Transfer to home, office, hotel	Qualifier Program Customer Retention Customer Feedback Surveys	Next Trip Cross Selling Direct Marketing
Handheld PC, Palm, PocketPC...	Mobile	Kiosk at Airport (Mobile)	Seat Back Screen	Kiosk at Airport (mobile)	Mobile	Handheld (Palm...)	Handheld (Palm...)

mCommerce Applications ←——→ Interface

Figure 8-2.   Mobile CRM value chain in the travel and tourism industry
(Source: Arthur D. Little)

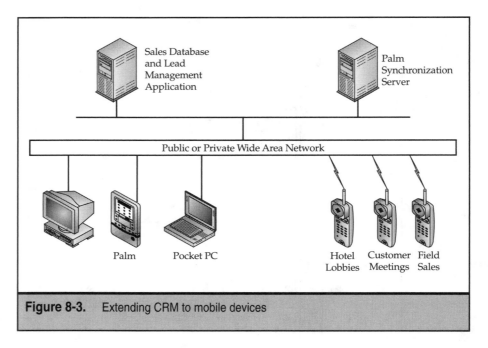

Figure 8-3.   Extending CRM to mobile devices

Most salespeople enjoy using PDAs and many have already started depending on them for scheduling and contact management at the very least. The ability of the handheld device to stay synchronized with the corporate and partner servers allows data to be exchanged in real time, thus keeping the functionality continually updated and improved at all times. With easy, real-time access to a broad range of services, both within the company and particularly out on the field, the salesperson can check product availability, coordinate partners, explore options, and get approvals—as mentioned previously, straight from the PDA, all in the customer's presence. Such an extended business model moves the salesperson to the middle of an information web that they can manage through their wireless PDA.

Case Study: Mobile SFA in the Insurance Industry

Mobile technologies have been used widely by sales forces in the field. An example of this can be seen in the insurance industry, where field agents with wireless Internet capability are being empowered to create new value for their customers, their firms, and themselves. In this case study, we will take an example of a fictional agent, based on a large firm's actual operations. Security issues will be highlighted throughout the process to indicate how critical good security is to mobile SFA and CRM applications.

Amrita, an insurance agent, has just sold a homeowner's policy to Daniel, a busy middle-aged corporate executive who is closing on a new home for his wife and two teenage children. Amrita has stopped by Daniel's office to quickly review his homeowner's insurance application and get his signature on it. At Daniel's office, Amrita offers him a 10 percent discount on his auto insurance if he were to sign up along with his homeowner's policy. She has to show Daniel that he could save money by doing so. Amrita proceeds to enter information on Daniel's car, such as the make, model, and year, into her PDA. Because Daniel's kids are only 12 and 15, she also enters this information into her PDA—*there is a copy of Daniel's life on her PDA now.* This initiates the agency's "teenage driving safety" program that gets triggered when the first child turns 16. Besides building good will with the parents, this also positions the agency as a key contender in insuring the children's cars when they acquire them. Amrita also uses her PDA to get an instant DMV report—*she used a username/password scheme for identification (not very strong)*—on Daniel and his wife's driving records. Based on the consolidation of all this information—*this is how to prove to management to spend money on security; there is a financial impact based on the security of Amrita proving her identity*—Amrita is able to offer discounted rates to Daniel and show him the math on her PDA screen. She is also able to compare those figures to what Daniel is currently paying by selecting his current insurance provider from a pull-down menu and have her agency system automatically price the same policy from the competitor. In addition to this, Amrita bids—*in this case, software agents are used that are remote pieces of code that follow certain business rules (need to ensure there is very good, solid code)*—Daniel's policy to a list of major Internet insurers straight from her PDA and shows him all the corresponding rates on her PDA screen. Because some cheaper options are available, Amrita initiates a feature comparison query between the insurers displayed and her own company's offerings, displaying them side by side on her PDA screen. Once Daniel is convinced, she taps a selection on her PDA and the proposal begins printing on Daniel's fax machine—*even printing can pose a security risk because the document may be read in transit by a hacker.* Amrita goes one step ahead and has Daniel sign directly onto her PDA screen—*this is a literal signature on the PDA; however, this is dangerous because the signature could then be copied and reused.* This sends out a message to her insurance company's servers to automatically cancel Daniel's old policy and put the new one into place—*a database query and action is initiated here, so security is critical.*

Mobile SFA Application Service Providers (ASP)

Companies that are successfully implementing mobile SFA solutions may find themselves in a hot business zone; with a bit of planning and change in their business model, they can convert their corporate mobile SFA application server into a shared application server thus opening up a new line of business—that of being the primary Wireless Application Service Provider (WASP) to independent, mobile salespeople in their industry. For example, independent insurance agents could pay a monthly subscription fee to have an account and profile on the SFA WASP's application server so that when they are meeting with their customers, they have the ability to shop multiple underwriters, configure products, work with experts, and orchestrate instant services directly from their handheld devices. Besides allowing the WASP to build relationships with the independent sales agents, this business model also opens new doors for the WASPs in areas such as business intelligence (BI). For example, the WASP already capturing detailed data on its subscribers' usage and access patterns across the industry can charge for specific information mined from this data, such as information that encourages desired purchase behaviors.

Besides the insurance industry, several industries are apt for mobile SFA WASPs to target. The product sales industry comprises field sales agents spread across the country trying to sell, for example, industrial equipment and office products to a broad range of customers. Such field agents could use a handheld device to do a variety of tasks, such as get anytime, anywhere access to updated pricing and product information, orchestrate special services, view inventory, and confirm orders. Another industry that could be targeted by mobile SFA ASPs is the realty sector. Real estate brokers are constantly on the move and require instant access to changing information to help orchestrate deals with their clients onsite.

One of the key differentiators of these WASPs is the way they deal with security. One of the challenges facing most organizations involves dealing with outsourced agencies and sensitive business applications. In general, with mission-critical applications such as SFA or CRM, it is important to check them out thoroughly on the ASP. The following are the key questions you need to ask before selecting an ASP:

▼ **Security policies** How do they guarantee the safety of your data? Are there insurance policies to mitigate the financial loss in the event of a disaster?

■ **Backup/restore policies** How quickly can data be restored from backup? Does the ASP have a backup site for a hot or warm standby switch over? Three to six months worth of backups is minimum; one year worth of backups is ideal.

■ **Physical security** How does the ASP hire and screen its staff? How are the physical servers protected?

■ **Data migration** What are the policies of the ASP for switching to another ASP in case of poor service or changing business conditions? Ensure the data still belongs to you.

CAUTION: With the bankruptcy of data host providers such as Exodus Communications (ranked number 1 by IDC with annual revenues in excess of $1 billion) in the *new* new economy, it is critical to ensure that you are able to migrate your data in the case of disaster, whether physical or financial! Such clauses should be in any service contract.

■ **Audits** How often does the ASP perform audits to ensure security systems are functioning as expected?

▲ **Data provider** Ensure that your contract ASP is in fact the data provider hosting the physical servers. Many times, ASPs will subcontract the actual data server storage operation to another vendor. In that case, both the ASP and the data host provider must be checked out.

MESSAGING

To support mobile CRM (mCRM) and mobile SFA (mSFA) applications, two key messaging tools are needed: instant messaging (IM) and Short Message Service (SMS). Although both are being used to support mCRM and mSFA applications, they do have some major security implications.

Instant Messaging (IM) Security

Any network dependent communication mechanism is faced with Internet routing bottlenecks that cause delays in exchanging information. Such bottlenecks are generally avoided by instant messaging (IM) algorithms that attempt to take the more attractive aspects of e-mail as a communications tool. Since IM is based fundamentally on a closed system, where a user can only send an instant message to another user on the same network, it can prove useful for CRM applications, where instant communication with a customer can be established. IM has become extremely popular over the wired Internet as is evident from services such as AOL, MSN Messenger, and Yahoo! Messenger. It is expected that this phenomenon will repeat itself in the case of the wireless Internet. The International Data Corporation (IDC) has estimated that by 2004 there will be 43 million wireless IM users.

NOTE: Modern technology makes entering text on a handset easier by recognizing that the device at the other end is wireless. Although IM subscription services were being provided by the carriers and network operators up until now, this trend is gradually changing towards mCommerce portals that are being set up as special wireless web pages that wireless Internet users can access from a handheld device such as a Wireless Application Protocol (WAP) or HTML phone. By accessing the portal's special wireless web page for instant messaging, a user can IM the portal's other messaging subscribers. In this case, the end users' presence will likely be determined when they log in to the wireless web page and not only when their handsets are turned on.

The popularity of IM systems, especially in the mass market, gives rise to security flaws within IM. Some of the key IM flaws include the following:

▼ Clear text messages (no privacy or data integrity).

■ Encryption that is provided uses proprietary methods (which in general are insecure relative to known standards such as the Triple Data Encryption Standard (3DES) and Advanced Encryption Standard (AES).

■ IM uses nonstandard ports, which forces an organization to open up ports on the Internet firewall for IM communication.

▲ IM attachments can introduce infected documents that do not pass through the corporate firewalls that check and disarm viruses.

How can you disable or prevent IM and its security flaws? Realistically, the safest policy is to prevent IM use in the organization. To prevent IM through the firewall, ensure you do the following:

1. Turn off any high ports that are used by IM clients.

2. For IM clients that use port 80 (the HTTP port), disable access by IP address to the host for the IM server.

If you cannot turn off the firewall access completely, then ensure that the IM clients are configured securely, as follows:

1. Ensure that file-transfer options are set to request user approval (for example, in the Yahoo! Messenger, set the option Ask Me for Permission to Get Files instead of the weakest option, which is Allow Users in my Friend List to Always Get My Files). See Figure 8-4 for an example.

CAUTION: Always set your IM ID and password to something other than your e-mail ID. In this manner, if the IM account is compromised, it will not compromise other web-based accounts. In addition, ensure the ID does not indicate personal information (such as your name, sex, age, or organization affiliation).

2. Ensure virus checking (after attachments are download) is enabled (assuming a virus checker client is enabled for the device). Also ensure the antivirus program is always on. Norton's AntiVirus program, for example, has a feature that blocks write operations to the registry (many attacks embed or modify the registry).

3. Create a separate directory for downloaded files. This makes it easier for the virus scanner to always scan that directory and makes it easier to quarantine suspect files.

4. Avoid extensive "buddy" or "friend" lists because many worms use these lists to propagate by sending themselves as attachments to these trusted clients (on mobile devices, for the sake of screen real estate, it is probably not feasible to have too many concurrent discussions in any case).

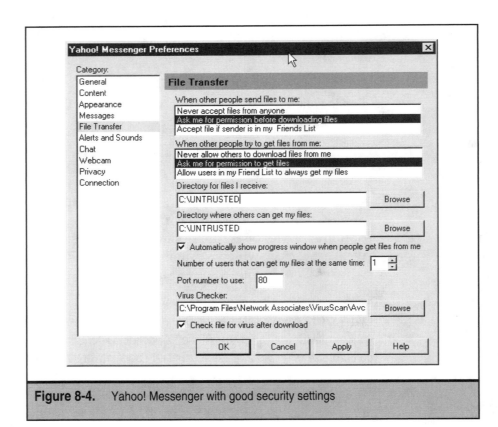

Figure 8-4. Yahoo! Messenger with good security settings

Wireless Short Messaging Service (SMS)

As described in the previous section, IM can greatly enhance end-user functionality in CRM and SFA applications. In this section, we will see that SMS is also a player in this space, alongside the CRM and SFA applications, enhancing the functionality of these systems. The lowest common denominator of wireless messaging data is *simplex-mode* (one-way) numeric paging that evolved into one-way alphanumeric or *text messaging*. SMS capabilities are now enabled in many digital wireless phones and devices, with most digital cellular operators also offering, at the very least, SMS as a one-way communication service, generally limited to around 150 characters. Because most other mobile forms of messaging for laptops and PDAs use standard e-mail packages such as Microsoft Outlook and Exchange 2000, they do not need messaging in the form of SMS. However, one thing all platforms share is their vulnerability to security risks.

Wireless Short Messaging Services appeared on the wireless scene in 1991 becoming a part of the European standard for digital wireless (now known as the Global System for Mobile Communications (GSM)) right from the beginning. In North America, SMS was made available initially on GSM, Code Division Multiple Access (CDMA), and Time Division Multiple Access (TDMA) digital wireless networks built by early pioneers such as BellSouth Mobility, PrimeCo, and Nextel, among others. The SMS service makes use of an Short Messaging Service Center (SMSC), which acts as a store-and-forward system for short messages being sent to and from wireless devices. The mechanisms required to find the destination station(s) and transport short messages between the SMSCs and wireless stations are provided by the wireless network. The mechanisms and service elements involved in SMS transmissions guarantee the delivery of text messages to their destinations, as opposed to other existing text-message transmission services, such as alphanumeric paging.

SMS Security Issues

Alongside the use of SMS are the security risks involved. SMS has some key characteristics that make its misuse result in significant impact:

▼   Many providers charge for SMS messages on a
    per-message basis.

- SMS messages have a relatively short length.

- A user cannot block an incoming SMS message.

▲ SMS messages take up memory in a mobile phone.

These characteristics make the abuse of SMS messages financially severe. SMS messages can be compromised in the following ways:

▼ By viruses

▲ Via message bombs

As has been discussed, the nature of SMS initially allowed it to support only limited-size messages, mainly notifications and alphanumeric pages. However, SMS is evolving with the times to exploit more recent niches, in addition to supporting its traditional notification and paging roots. A variety of SMS-based services have been introduced, including wireless e-mail, fax, and paging integration, interactive banking, information services such as stock quotes, and integration with Internet-based applications.

At the heart of most applications that are built for wired networks with fixed terminals attached to a local area network (LAN) or wide area network (WAN) is the messaging concept of having short bursts of data flow. The real value of such applications, however, can only be seen when this data flow or communication is extended to the wireless network, that is the data communication capabilities can be added to the mobility of the station. SMS is an efficient means for transmitting short bursts of data since the two main SMS characteristics that support such bursts are out-of-band packet delivery and low-bandwidth.

Such data communication has minimal security implications since the data is only useful for such a short period of time. Ideally, the shorter the usefulness of the data, the easier it is to protect and/ or go without security controls. Therefore, a waiter who can charge a customer's credit card right at the table, instead of going to a fixed POS terminal located by the register, will be able to help customers in a faster, more convenient manner. This way, after the transaction has been completed, the data is no longer needed and can be erased.

The ability to track the location of a moving asset, such as a truck or its load, is also valuable for the service providers and clients from a security point of view because the amount of information being interchanged in such applications is quite small. The type of information that may be passed could be the longitude and latitude at a current time of day and perhaps other parameters, such as temperature and humidity. Such an approach would be, perhaps, less intrusive then using the location-tracking mechanisms of mobile phones and PDAs. In this manner, the user can choose to share location information rather than be tracked using the currently technology designed to track mobile phones.

SMS-based industry applications now include the downloading of subscriber identity module (SIM) cards for activation, debit, profile-editing purposes, wireless points of sale (POS), and other field service applications, such as automatic meter reading, remote sensing, and location-based services. An example of an industry whose applications can use SMS as a data-transport mechanism is banking. We all know that using a bank's automated teller machine (ATM) or conducting a transaction over the wired Internet is less costly than over-the-counter transactions completed at a branch. In fact, Internet transactions are often cheaper than ATM transactions. Therefore, enabling wireless subscribers to check their balances, transfer funds between accounts, and pay their bills and credit cards using their handheld devices is valuable, not only for the subscriber but also for financial institutions. These types of applications have given rise to a series of data aggregators. These data aggregators display different account information on a single interface (such as a mobile phone or PDA). The user then avoids having to log in to various systems (which can be very slow on a mobile phone). The problem with these systems is that the aggregator requires the user to give it all the usernames and passwords so it can log on, on behalf of the user. These systems are, therefore, not generally recommended from a security point of view.

CAUTION: Think about the consequences to your confidential data if an aggregator goes out of business or is bought by another company. You should ensure that the aggregator employees have gone through rigorous security background checks. This includes acquired or merged company personnel.

However, if you need to implement aggregation services with SMS or other methods, the following guidelines should help minimize security concerns:

▼ Create an obscure and unique password (relative to all the other passwords you use in other systems) for all accounts the aggregator may access.

■ Disable all account functions that allow for funds transfer or withdrawal (if possible).

■ Disassociate all username and passwords with any personal information (that is, avoid using names and places).

▲ Check directly with the aggregated site on a regular basis (through direct login) and ensure nothing has changed without your knowledge.

Another good driver of SMS usage is entertainment for purposes of *texting* (exchanges between two parties) and *chat* (exchanges between multiple parties). The proposition that would appear attractive to an mCommerce user, however, would be the ability to have SMS alerts customized to fit a person's individual lifestyle.

SMS Viruses   Like viruses for wired e-mail systems, SMS viruses can be transmitted and cause data and service loss.

TIP: The best protection from such viruses is choosing a carrier that scans for this type of activity.

At the operator level are solutions such as SMSafe, a product and trademark of WhiteCell. SMSafe allows its scanning module to scan all SMS traffic against established security policies. These policies force updates and settings for network- and device-based agents that enforce the polices. Type, length, and frequency, for example, can be used to determine unusual activity.

Message Bombs   The other area in which SMS is vulnerable is message bombs. Message bombs attack a system by sending so many messages to a particular destination in a short amount of time that the receiving device fails to receive any more. In corporate mail systems, message bombs can stop all e-mail from going out or into the organization. Because many operators charge on a per-message basis, an SMS mail bomb could cost the user a great deal of money. Another interesting use of SMS bombs is being used by the Dutch police. To help combat mobile phone theft, the Dutch police send out an SMS message to the stolen phone that it was stolen and how the purchase of the phone is illegal. The number of arrests has gone up partly because of this SMS technique.

Local proxy or scanning agents, yet to be developed, could help in determining abnormal SMS messages, which could indicate SMS bombs. However, SMS mail bombs are best protected at the operator level, because the offender can be more easily tracked and stopped by the operator.

Information Services

SMS applications have been successfully developed to provide a variety of information services such as weather reports, traffic information, entertainment information, financial information, and directory assistance. In Chapter 6, we discussed the differences between push- and pull-based advertising approaches. Since much of wireless advertising occurs using SMS, we can safely infer that the same push and pull approaches are supported by SMS-based information services to allow not only delivery under specific conditions but also delivery-on-demand as a response to a request. However, delivery-on-demand services, as opposed to push services, can decrease the impact of message bombs.

WAP Notifications and Transport Mechanism

SMS can not only deliver WAP message notifications to wireless subscribers but also be used as the transport mechanism for those WAP messages. These messages can contain information from diverse sources such as databases, the World Wide Web, e-mail servers, and so on.

CAUTION: SMS cannot provide a high degree of confidence of the sender and therefore should not be used for mission-critical applications.

Although applications can be written to transport, for example, database queries via SMS/WAP integration, this is *not* recommended because the security around this is weak.

Mobile Data Services

There are many types of interactive mCommerce services where SMS is actively used, such as fleet dispatch, inventory management, itinerary confirmation, sales order processing, asset tracking, automatic vehicle location, customer contact management, interactive gaming, instant messaging, mobile chat, query services, and mobile banking services. This is accomplished using the SMSC that provides the short wireless data in the aforementioned examples of interactive services especially where voice calls are involved. The SMSC is used in the event that you wish to run an ASP script and push out the results via SMS. The SMSC does the actual translation of the ASP to SMS. Again, security of both ASP and SMS are not considered sufficient for mission-critical applications, and such applications should be avoided. If SMSC must be used, you should make sure secure methods are used in ensuring data integrity. See Figure 8-5 for an example of a secure architecture.

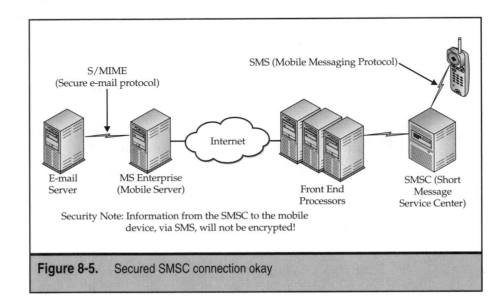

Figure 8-5. Secured SMSC connection okay

Customer Care and Management

One method that carriers and network operators use to administer and manage their customers is to have a mechanism by which they can program the mobile devices. Such mobile device programming allows customer profiles and subscription characteristics to be downloaded to the mobile device (customers can be activated/deactivated based on the data downloaded), and customers to be advised of charge, which enables the SMS to be used to report charges incurred for the phone call (for example, calls made when roaming). The mechanism to program the mobile devices is supported by the SMSC that is used to transfer binary data that can be interpreted by the mobile device without presentation to the customer. Although it may seem obvious, this method is nearly a given for viruses or Trojan Horse attacks. After all, how many of us can read the 1s and 0s of machine language and immediately know that we have downloaded a virus? We recommend that you accept updates from the operator of the mobile network on an occasional basis and confirm they are in fact pushing out an update by contacting them out of band.

Notification Services

Notification services are currently the most widely deployed SMS services. However, because message bombs and viruses are a danger for SMS, it is not recommended that you enable these features. Examples of such notification services using SMS include the following:

▼ Voice/fax/e-mail message notification, which indicates that voice, fax or e-mail messages are present in a user's mailbox

▲ Reminder/calendar services, which enable alert reminders for meetings and scheduled appointments

Paging Interworking

Paging services integrated with SMS allow digital wireless subscribers to be accessible via existing paging interfaces as well as escalation of messages. These services are also suspect to message bombs. With escalation features, a message bomb can increase the reach of its effect because it may trigger a message on one system that may be escalated to many, thus causing all systems to overload on SMS messages.

Other Messaging Issues

A number of other issues arise when it comes to dealing with customers or IM use. The main difference in privacy issues between standard wired messaging and mobile messaging is that the third dimension of a user's location in mobile messaging adds not only more rich content, it also creates, privacy issues.

Presence Detection

Knowledge is power. A major issue in wireless messaging for carriers, advertisers, and even other wireless users is the ability to know that someone's handset is turned on or is available to receive messages. In the wired world, users create address and buddy lists linked to their online profiles, so when someone from their buddy list logs in, they receive a pop-up message on their computer screen. It is expected that the same mechanism will be used for the wireless Internet as well in that a user shall receive an SMS alert based on an entry in his/her buddy list.

Network operators and carriers, however, cannot build buddy lists. They use more scientific methods to detect a cell phone's presence and status; the carriers do this by accessing the home location register (HLR) to determine when a handset on their network is switched on. The HLR database is used for completing calls and creating call detail records that are used in billing. When a handset is turned on, it must communicate with the HLR. If the handset is roaming, it has to access the visitor location register (VLR) in order to place and receive calls. The HLR can be queried to develop address and buddy lists, and it can also be used for presence detection. There are two types of presence detection: *automatic* and *manual*. Automatic detection allows a handset to be automatically registered on a network the moment it is switched on and detected by the network.

NOTE: The use of the HLR poses a strong security risk because the user can be located (physically) and call patterns established.

Whenever users roam, their profiles are sent to authenticate their connections/accounts. 3G networks improve the security and handling of such data.

To decrease the risk of identity theft or other similar attacks on mobile systems, disposable, prepaid phones are becoming very popular. The idea here is that the user can prepay for a certain number of minutes and then dispose of the phone once the minutes expire. This avoids having to associate an identity to a user. This concept is still relatively new and not available in all mobile markets.

Manual detection fosters more privacy because it requires users to do something more than simply switch on their phones to register their presence. To be detected as available, users may, for example, have to enter a sequence of digits on their keypads. Manual detection does not work well within a system where carriers want to have their customers available for messaging most of the time. However, since privacy becomes an issue in an automatic registration system, carriers will probably offer a combination of the two, a system in which handsets are detectable unless the user enters a sequence of digits to remove presence detection. Portals and carriers will treat presence detection in different ways. A carrier such as AT&T Wireless will likely offer detection of other AT&T wireless subscribers whose phones are turned on in the AT&T network, while a wireless messaging portal may offer presence detection only of those phone users who have subscribed to the portal's messaging service and are accessing the portal's messaging service currently through a wireless device. In other words, a messaging portal's wireless users will only appear as being available if they use their handsets to access the Internet wirelessly. The winner in the end will offer presence detection of not only the subscribers on its own network but also users on other networks in addition to offering some sort of privacy solution to presence detection.

Interoperability

Even in terms of offering interoperability among carriers, one of the issues that will arise will be in presence detection among carriers, because each carrier has access to its own HLR to determine users' availability but cannot determine the presence of other carriers' subscribers. Other interoperability issues will include getting presence information from and enabling communication among the major online portals that offer messaging. Reasons exist for both sides of the coin when it comes to deciding whether to work out interoperability issues among carriers. Carriers will want to offer universal messaging because it will increase the viability of their wireless messaging offerings. Carriers will likely not charge for messaging but will make money from companies that want access to their customers' presence information. Therefore, carriers must ensure that the vast majority of their customers are open to giving out their presence information. Various opt-in clauses will need to be set up so that users can decide how their information is shared among operators.

Enhanced Wireless Messaging Services (EMS)

Since wireless messaging has already been around for a while with a large cross section of applications built for mobile users, the demand is now emerging for enhanced messaging services offering additional value such as the following:

▼ Unified Wireless Messaging. One mailbox for all wireless communications—voice, fax, and text messages, as well as other information

■ Wireless access from any mobile device. Auto device configuration that involves configuring a device on the fly (analogous to plug-and-play)

■ Integration of the user's mailbox with the wireless Internet

▲ A single and unique mobile number for every subscriber, no matter where they are

WhiteCell, a company mentioned earlier, also has a solution for EMS as well as SMS to allow the mobile operator to filter out and block spam. It is strongly recommended that carriers use similar protection against SMS/EMS bombs and other types of spam (and that users choose these carriers).

MESSAGE FOR THE IT MANAGER

CRM and SFA applications are seen as the key to increasing customer satisfaction and therefore increasing sales. It is important to understand that wireless extensions to these systems can allow security risks to appear and bypass well-established, secure network perimeter defenses. The security risks around these and supporting systems demand that organizations follow specific guidelines to minimize exposure to security compromises. The best practices we can identify are as follows:

▼ Use thin-client systems whenever possible to minimize the amount of data stored at the mobile device.

■ Define strong corporate policies on the ownership for the CRM data and the mobile devices that store the data.

■ Avoid using instant messaging (IM), because it bypasses the corporate firewall and can introduce viruses and other issues directly into the network.

▲ Use mobile operators that can take steps to minimize the possibility of SMS message bombs through scanning tools.

CHAPTER 9

The Verticals, Part I: mCommerce Security in the Service Sector

As a service industry, the financial sector has always been on the cutting edge of technology. Given the magnitude of mistakes in IT architecture in this area, the financial industry has also had some of the most stringent backup and security requirements. The mobile sector of the financial industry has led to an additional set of security issues. In general, most mobile financial systems are systems designed with multiple, complex components. These components range from Wireless Public-Key Infrastructure (WPKI) servers to Enterprise Application Integration (EAI) systems. Because data flows through all these systems, in addition to the possible software or functionality at the mobile device itself, there are numerous areas in which a security risk may be established. In addition, because so many vendors and product types are used in developing these complex systems, security becomes a challenge because product variations and revisions change constantly from one financial institution to another.

The other vertical service industries covered in this chapter have similar issues in the way that information needs to be captured and mined to adequately target the customer or recipient. As a result, privacy and data-aggregation attacks are potential issues for these areas. Furthermore, the wide range of standards and methods make these industries ripe for complex mobile architectures and therefore ripe for security compromises.

We can address security issues in these various industries at three basic levels:

▼ **Middleware security** These are web server applications or EAI applications that perform the business rules. Data gets moved from lower-level (data) storage to higher-level applications and eventually to the data-delivery layer.

■ **Data delivery security** This is the actual transmission of the data from the source to the destination through a set of various protocols and physical media. With complex architectures in the mobile space, the transmission covers not only wireless transmissions but also queries or transmissions to legacy systems to obtain additional data. Many retail and travel systems still rely heavily on legacy systems or legacy integrations.

▲ **Data storage security**   This refers to the storage of data, whether temporary or permanent. All the industries in this chapter require large databases to track massive amounts of information.

RETAIL

When people think of wireless commerce, many, if not most, think of shopping. Online shopping has already gained tremendous popularity on the wired Internet. Although there have been security issues and concerns from wireless end users regarding the use of mobile media to conduct commerce, most believe that retail eCommerce over the wireless Web will eventually become as popular as wired eCommerce, if not more. The IDC forecasts the U.S.-based wireless retail market to grow (in millions of dollars) as displayed in Table 9-1.

Wireless retail shopping on the Web is, however, not going to be the same as shopping on the wired Web. User shopping habits on wireless media may slightly differ from that on a wired connection. It is doubtful that consumers will browse the wireless Internet to buy something the way they do on the wired Web. However, if they know what they want to buy and if they also know that the item can be easily bought from their wireless device, then it is likely that they will purchase the item over their wireless device, especially in a situation where access to a wired connection is not as easily available. Another important aspect of retail mobile commerce is time-sensitive threshold purchase. For example, if an airline ticket hits a certain price, an alert-notification is sent to the consumer's mobile phone or handheld device. If the user likes the price and has a way to purchase

2000	2001	2002	2003	2004	2005	2000–2005 CAGR (%)
$6.4 million	$24.9 million	$52.6 million	$104.7 million	$201.9 million	$491.7 million	138.1

Table 9-1.   Growth of U.S.-Based Wireless Retail Market (Source: IDC)

the ticket from his/her handheld device, it's likely that the transaction will take place. Retail stores can also send electronic discount coupons to users' handsets as the users approach the vicinity of these stores. A user can receive an SMS displaying a $10 coupon off a pair of jeans and then proceed to the store to purchase the jeans using a mobile phone or by paying through the vendor's wireless point-of-sale terminal (POS).

This concept of *just-in-time* (JIT) inventory has been popular in the manufacturing sector. Less inventory on-hand means less costs and therefore greater profits. In the consumer market, given the range of products, people, and geographical regions, it is much more difficult to maintain a JIT system. Some time ago, grocery stores started a popular clipless coupons concept. In this scheme, a consumer presents a card attributed to that consumer's identity in lieu of a coupon. As a result, stores can change discounts within an hour without the overhead of printing coupons. However, in the mobile space, the additional component of having to prove that a particular wireless offer is legitimate is a further complication. It is possible for users to receive digitally signed messages from a sender and present them in the physical store. Other methods allow the user, once the message is received, to call right from the mobile device (such as on a phone) and present some type of authentication code. However, as we have seen with all such authentication mechanisms, checksums and such predictable, generated codes can be broken. For example, the Internet contains many credit card number generators. Knowing the checksum routines the card makers use, they simply generate random numbers in the known ranges of credit cards. Those numbers, along with the expiration dates, appear legitimate.

When department stores receive merchandise from their vendors, they have to check the packaging and tagging of the merchandise in order to pass them on for sale to the sales floor. For example, a vendor may have agreed to ship its merchandise with hangers because it is to be displayed on hangers at the department store. However, if the merchandise arrives without the hangers or is in violation of some other requirement, the department store has to deploy staff to make the corrections, thus ending in wasted time, not to mention financial loss associated with the error for the department store. This could result in a delay in merchandise presentation on the sales floor, thus leading to business loss. Many stores use handwritten review procedures, resulting in manual data entry into the corporate mainframe computers. This also results in data backlogs. Therefore, implementing a wireless solution to reduce the time lag between the identification of the problem and transmission to the vendor becomes very important. A possible solution is to use hand-held devices with built-in barcode scanners. The hand-held devices could be running any of the leading wireless operating systems. When incoming merchandise does not meet the store standards, the store workers can use their hand-held devices to scan the shipping label and product code (UPC) of the items. The hand-held devices can also display a drop-down list from which problem descriptions can be selected and additional information entered. When all scanning for the day has been completed, all that needs to be done is to synchronize the hand-held devices with the desktop PCs and upload the data to the corporate mainframes, where the managers can analyze it.

Price verification for retailers is another sector where mobile technologies can offer tremendous value. Correct pricing is critical to the success of any retail store. Many stores are nationwide retail chains, with hundreds of stores spread across the country. Such stores have traditionally spent many wasted hours every week changing and verifying prices using laborious, paper-based processes. This has resulted in errors, such as tagged prices that didn't match the advertised specials or match the register at checkout. In most instances, because the lower price is generally honored, the store has lost revenue. A good solution for such a retail chain is to implement and use a wireless price verification application that enables store personnel to determine current prices by simply scanning the merchandise with a hand-held device. The device can connect via radio frequency (RF) to a wireless LAN station in the store. The challenge with wireless is that security has many points of compromise. In the case where a mobile device syncs up with a base station, that is usually the weakest point in the link. Most sync systems either use RF or infrared for syncing. Some consumer mobile devices use serial or fixed cables. Most will probably use Bluetooth in the future, but we will not see that in the majority of devices for at least another two to three years (due to cost). Bluetooth will offer slightly better security for the syncing process. Infrared (IR) can be picked up from several feet away, although IR does require a line-of-sight connection for information transfer. In some cases, this is an asset because the information does not radiate freely, as can occur in RF. On the other hand, the line-of-sight requirement limits the uses and environments in which IR transfer can be used (for example, in poor weather).

CAUTION: Many laptops now offer IR capability, usually enabled by default. IR ports should be disabled and/or physically covered to avoid a hacker from penetrating a laptop in a public area such as an airport. Some consultants advise putting electric tape over the IR port to ensure it has been disabled.

This allows for an IR sniffer to pick up data and, either in real time or at a later time, mine the data captured. In the simple case of a grocery list, peoples' personal habits, financial information, and even addresses may be picked up by hackers. For the retailer, if a competitor picks up information regarding inventory levels or promotions, that could lead to a loss of competitive advantage.

The information is then transmitted over Ethernet to a router with a Frame Relay connection to the retail chain's corporate headquarters, where pricing is maintained in a centralized database. Generally, most companies looking for increased security and guaranteed service level agreements (SLAs) will use private leased lines. Other technologies, such as public key infrastructure (PKI), make the use of leased lines (at least for security) an unnecessary option. The database sends back the correct pricing for the product, which displays on the hand-held browser within seconds. The central database also transmits to the store hand-held device the color of the sticker that the price should be printed on (for security). In some stores where this type of solution has been implemented, the store clerks carry a small RF printer on their belts for automatic sticker output.

Wireless technologies are also ideal (and have proven so in many cases) in the online food and grocery delivery business. Many online grocers have the big problem of successfully fulfilling customer orders in the least amount of time and with minimal paperwork. When a customer places an order at an online grocer's web site, the system generates a corresponding "pick" sheet for the placed order. This is used by the online grocers to select and fill the order. When the order is filled and completed, the order information is manually entered into a computer located at the distribution center. This data is then fed into the corporate back-end database. With the increasing volume of online orders, many grocers have felt overwhelmed by the sheer amount of paperwork, requiring hours of data entry thus opening them up to errors. Errors in which the grocer mispicks orders turn out extremely costly for the grocer. In such cases, the grocer generally has to redeliver the missing item, thus having to make an extra delivery trip to the customer's home or office. Therefore, an accurate way to pick and track grocery orders is to use wireless technologies. Hand-held devices can be used at the grocer's distribution centers onto which customer grocery orders can be downloaded from a database at the corporate office. This is normally done using a syncing process. Many hand-held devices come with integrated barcode readers. This way, each item can be scanned as it is picked from the shelf, making sure that the grocery item matches that on the customer order. All order information can be uploaded to the corporate back-end systems at the end of the day, again using syncing technology. A setup such as this can greatly reduce the cost and turnaround time for order fulfillment, thus leading to a dramatic increase in customer satisfaction.

Gathering accurate, detailed sales and inventory data on sold merchandise for any retail chain is a major task. Many retail chains can track gross sales, but not specific colors, sizes, and styles of items sold, or lost or missing inventory. Many point-of-sale (POS) and back-end processes are paper based, leading to great difficulty in tracking the amount of merchandise given to each stand, accurately forecasting and replenishing the right merchandise, and accurately reconciling the inventory and accounting systems. Therefore, a mobile inventory-management system can be very useful in such a scenario. Palm Computing has been very popular in this sector of mobile technologies. Symbol hand-held devices equipped with barcode scanners are being used by many retailers to collect POS information. As each item is scanned, data is collected and stored in a database, such as Oracle8i Lite running on the Palm OS. The data is then uploaded to an enterprise database, such as Oracle8i, using a syncing technology such as Palm's HotSync. Symbol hand-held devices are also used at the loading dock. Once merchandise data is synchronized with the purchase order, the purchase order can be closed on the spot by the receiving manager, who can sign for the order directly on the hand-held device. Scanner technologies are also being implemented by agencies such as the U.K.'s Royal Mail, which uses Compaq Aero 1550 Pocket PCs with plug-in compact flash barcode scanners from Socket Communications (called the *Socket In-hand scan card*, based on Symbol IS5000). The Royal Mail uses the Pocket PCs as scanning devices as well as to record notes on them, which are then fed back to the database. The Pocket PCs run Microsoft Windows SQL Server for CE, which can record all the input information just as the regular SQL Server can. Engineers can sync up the information they gather on the Pocket PC SQL Server via a docking cradle using Microsoft ActiveSync technology. The information is synced to a TBS TaskMaster host system, which in turn feeds into a Windows NT 4.0 Server and Microsoft SQL Server 7.0 database. Such solutions have also been seen to connect to incorporate Enterprise Resource Planning (ERP) systems, such as SAP R/3.

Players and Examples

In this section, we will highlight some of the key players with mobile infrastructures and various architectures they chose to ensure smooth customer experiences and secure delivery of information.

Amazon.com

In September 1999, Sprint PCS launched its Wireless Web, and a couple of months later, it introduced *wireless duplex* (two-way) transactional Internet shopping in conjunction with Amazon.com. The idea was for customers who are registered with Amazon.com to be able to purchase items directly from their Sprint PCS Internet-ready handsets. Customers could also set up new Amazon.com accounts from their handsets. This mCommerce service provides Amazon.com's customers wireless access to some of its features, including the Gift-Click feature, Personal Recommendations, and Best Seller lists. Hand-held users can also search for specific products, compare prices, and check on order status. The wireless application development for display on the wireless devices was a joint effort between Amazon.com and Openwave. When a Sprint PCS customer purchases a product on Amazon.com over the Sprint handset, Sprint receives an affiliate fee from Amazon.com. Besides Sprint PCS, among the other Amazon.com partners are Bell Mobility, Motorola, Nextel, Nokia, and Palm VII. For example, using the Palm VII connected organizer, users can process purchase requests wirelessly from anywhere in the United States if they have set up their 1-Click Settings associated with their Amazon.com online accounts.

BANKING AND FINANCE

Wireless banking and finance is revolutionizing the financial industry. Customer expectations have risen dramatically in the past couple of years in societies around the globe. Consumers are beginning to demand access to their money and financial information anytime, anywhere. The IDC forecasts the U.S.-based wireless banking and finance market to grow (in millions of dollars) as displayed in Table 9-2.

In Europe, the situation is expected to be even more dramatic, attracting one-third of the European population into the wireless user base. With the speed of growth of the user base, it will surely get difficult for financial institutions to keep pace with the changes demanded. Connectivity issues, new protocols, and even newer devices coming into the market will pose a challenge for enterprise

2000	2001	2002	2003	2004	2005	2000–2005 CAGR (%)
$8.9 million	$49.8 million	$141.8 million	$428.3 million	$812.8 million	$1311.1 million	171.7

Table 9-2.   IDC Forcasts for Growth of Wireless Banking and Finance Market (Source: IDC)

IT managers to be able to deliver across every platform, protocol, browser, and service provider.

Unlike in Europe and Asia, U.S. financial companies have to deal with multiple technical standards to deliver information on PDAs, thus limiting the customers they can serve. There is a conflict among the basic technical standards and networks for transmitting data on PDAs—Code Division Multiple Access (CDMA), Time Division Multiple Access (TDMA), and Global System for Mobile Communications (GSM). However, WAP is now gradually taking over as a higher and more consistent standard, so as not to inhibit growth in the financial wireless sector. The WAP standard adopted by Nokia, Ericsson, Motorola, and most other major players is supported by all three networks. Many interfacing technologies are rapidly coming up, especially in the financial and banking sector, that enable account access from any wireless device.

Many banks and financial institutions are inclined to use the Open Financial Exchange (OFX) as a standard interface for wireless financial transaction processing. For example, The Bank of Montreal, Harris Bank, and First Tech Credit Union all use the Open Financial Exchange protocol as their enabling technology. The OFX server was initially set up to support personal financial management software such as Quicken and Money; however, the idea behind it was to offer a standard platform for use across multiple channels, thus setting the stage for wireless. The key advantage to using standards such as OFX is having a uniform entry point to legacy transaction systems. By using standard interfaces such as OFX, banks and financial houses are able to add and reconfigure wireless interfaces without having to go back and modify or rewrite their core systems.

OFX has been built to incorporate security issues using standards such as X.509 v3, which is the general standard most digital certificate certifying authorities (CAs) use. CAs issue special OFX server certificates for this purpose. OFX provides for two types of security protection: channel level and application level. Channel-level protection is basically protection of communication from end to end, providing a secure tunnel. The application-level protection centers on protecting the password from the client application through to the server application performing the authentication. A summary diagram of these concepts is show in Figure 9-1.

CAUTION: By not using a standard interface such as OFX, you have to "screen scrape," or write software code to link up with a proprietary interfaces, which can be very expensive given that there are so many different proprietary interfaces in the financial industry.

In general, screen-scraping applications do not provide any security. Screen scraping delivers raw content without integrity or encryption. In sensitive financial applications, transmissions of data such as account numbers and balances can prove to be a severe security compromise. Some institutions have stopped the ability of screen scrapers with the use of biometrics or digital certificates. In addition, some companies, such as data and account aggregators, rely on screen scrapers to consolidate information. Although several lawsuits brought against data aggregators using screen-scraping techniques have failed, the risk for the ability of these companies to create a single, golden pot of sensitive data makes hacking attacks very scary. Yodlee, an example of a data aggregator, has worked with Citigroup to create a data/account aggregation site that relies on screen scraping.

If consumers are worried about their data being screen-scraped, it is important to use financial institutions that require strong security, such as digital certificates or biometrics. As described previously, XML can provide similar capability, but with more security. Some

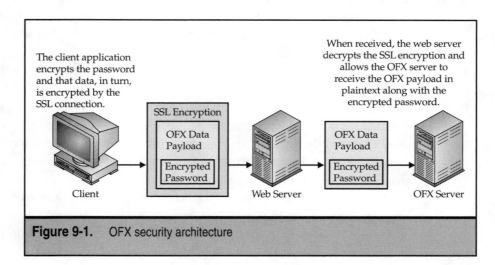

Figure 9-1. OFX security architecture

tools, such as FileFrameVX by Ascend Software, is a legacy system sync software that is specifically designed to combat screen scraping. This software does not send clear username/passwords.

Although financial institutions have control over standards used in the data-transport layer between the wireless application provider and host system, the wireless carriers themselves use conflicting standards, especially in the U.S., where there is limited control. As mentioned earlier, the U.S. has four major competing wireless standards: Global System for Mobile Communications (GSM), Code Division Multiple Access (CDMA), Personal Communications Services (PCS), and Time Division Multiple Access (TDMA). There are many application service providers and *data intermediaries* (also known *as traffic cops*) that interface with all the carriers, thus shielding the financial houses from these competing standards. (The traffic cops take care of all interstandard discrepancies.) Initially, many financial institutions were using alphanumeric pagers with streaming stock quotes for wireless access, but the pagers didn't deliver enough information or any interactive capability. Then came the next generation of access devices in the form of the PDAs, such as the Palm. For example, Deutsche Bank uses Palm hand-held devices with Reuters software and a Minstrel Wireless IP modem. This interactive wireless financial system delivers Reuters real-time U.S. equities data on the Palm. Among the many services, customers can call up detailed information such as quotes, headlines, market alerts, 15-minute intraday and 20-day historical charts, and summaries. In addition to these, two-way data exchange lets them input the specific stock quotes or portfolio values they need.

Interestingly, although the technology shifted from one-way devices such as pagers to two-way devices, many of these firms were faced with developing new policies. In general, many companies now have policies that cover security and liability issues on how employees may use mobile devices for business. However, most companies have very weak (for the consumer) policies and liability protection for nonemployees, including for customers.

Wireless payment processing is also a key component of financial systems within the banking and finance industry. Wireless payment is the ability to initiate and/or confirm a payment transaction from a wireless hand-held device. This not only involves bill payments but also the ability to purchase merchandise using one's mobile phone or hand-held device. The example frequently cited is the ability to purchase drinks from vending machines using a mobile phone. Pilot schemes for parking payments are also running in some Nordic countries. Here are the key components of a wireless payment transaction:

▼ *Consumer/buyer initiates a transaction.* The consumer enables their hand-held device to transact a wireless payment by entering into an agreement with a financial authority. The consumer can also load a trusted token to sign the promise to pay for goods. This is analogous to using a credit card—in this case, a virtual credit card.

■ *Consumer/buyer exchanges a transaction.* The consumer exchanges value or a promise to pay for goods or services. This can be done using a prepay or postpay method.

▲ *Seller realizes the transaction value.* If the transaction is prepaid, this happens directly. If it is postpaid, the payment is realized after an elapsed amount time, via some intermediate billing or payment-processing authority.

The preceding financial exchange and processing can take place within open or closed communities. As the name implies, in a closed community, the consumer, seller, and payment-processing authority form a binding agreement to exchange value for goods or services only within their community. Open-community schemes become convenient for the consumer because their payment methods are generally accepted at a large number of places. This is analogous to using credit cards that involve a "risk sharing" agreement between the banks and merchants. In mobile commerce, such agreements also need to be in place, especially in terms of verifying the consumer and authenticating the electronic payment device. This implies that the consumer, seller, and payment-processing authority must have a trust relationship with each other. This may be accomplished by using digital certificates as a secure way of engendering trust. These digital certificates must be accessed by every potential point-of-sale and payment device, requiring a secure network of trusted authorities and protocols—in other words, some type of global wireless PKI.

It is also worth noting that the medium of transmission and transaction processing can be different, involving varying communications media. This depends on the capability of the initiating device and receiving machine, and anything from a wireless LAN, Bluetooth, or infrared can be used as a local (or peer-to-peer) transmission mechanism. The devices may also use a cellular network to communicate the payment transaction via the carrier's system. The type of network and carrier being used will determine the security characteristics of the transmission media. Although network service providers have the technology to support a payment system and the business purpose to fuel such an initiative, they do not have regulatory approval to process payments the way a bank does. Many also do not have a trusted brand name similar to a bank and therefore face customer trust problems. Network providers also do not have the expertise and experience in financial risk management; this expertise resides more with banks and financial houses. Therefore, traditional banks and financial institutions are better suited for offering mobile finance and banking services. These include card issuers such as Visa and MasterCard. Credit Companies such as GE Capital and HFC also manage a number of store cards on behalf of retailers and are therefore also part of this segment.

Wireless payment processing is also valuable to retailers because it makes the customer transaction quick and location independent, thus leading to impulse payments. It is perhaps also more secure than credit/debit card payments because the use of a PIN to open the device, authenticate the payment mechanism, and to enable the transaction leads to stronger cardholder verification. This results in increased security, reducing the risk to the merchant of processing a fraudulent transaction.

In recent times, the payment-processing sector has begun to upgrade its systems to EMV (Europay MasterCard Visa) standards, which have been built with security capability. Most mobile phones in use today are not EMV compliant for card authentication. If in-phone credit card processing via Bluetooth or IR is to be adopted widely to communicate with a POS device, then either the mobile device has to be upgraded or the standards have to be modified. Other devices, such as SIM cards and dual slots in mobile phones, allow for other types of payments based on smartcards, which are becoming much more prevalent.

NOTE: EMV standards, popular in Europe, compete with other standards such as American Express's Blue card. In addition, standards vary from smartcard to smartcard, including Java Open Platform and Multos.

Several types of mobile wireless payments are available, including debit and credit solutions. Debit micropayments are popular because anonymity can be maintained and the low values placed in such applications limit the liability of the loss of the cards. Generally, payments on mobile devices tend to use smartcard or similar media in which account information or encrypted schemes are used to store micropayment information, using standard schemes such as EMV.

The implementation of a wireless financial or banking system is complex. To ensure the longevity, scalability, security, and robustness of a wireless implementation, justifying the long-term viability of the investment, open mobile systems need to be constructed that use standard protocols, independent of the network operator or type of wireless device. Figure 9-2 displays the various components that make up a wireless financial system, including the wireless hand-held devices, financial gateways, middleware financial web application engine, formatting engine, API connections, and back-end financial systems. From the consumer side, the wireless device accesses a local cell tower that delivers local geographical coverage in the defined hexagonal region of the financial service provider. Consumer data from the cell tower is sent over to the base station, where the data is transferred to the mobile switching center. This center connects all base stations together. When a user makes a request from a PDA or other device, its identity (electronic serial number and mobile identity number) is sent to the financial gateway for user authentication. The data is then formatted by the financial application server to be sent back to the user's unit to be displayed. Most financial wireless networks are compliant with common protocols such as GSM (huge

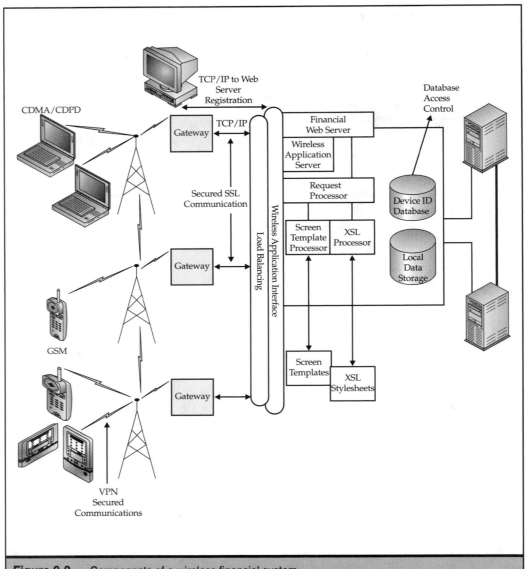

Figure 9-2. Components of a wireless financial system

in Europe but not big in the U.S. yet), Cellular Digital Packet Data (CDPD), CDMA, and Ardis.

The hub of the wireless system is the financial web application server, where all rules are set, financial dataflow is controlled, and configuration files are executed. Most financial web application servers use XML APIs to communicate with the back-end systems. XML extracts and delivers the data, and Document Type Definitions (DTDs) are used to make sure that the XML conforms to the specifications of the tags, attributes, and relationships set forth in the DTDs. The transformations are performed by the Extensible Stylesheet Language (XSL).

XML issues can focus on two key areas: the security of XML instances and the security of applications using XML. In summary, we can address XML issues as follows:

▼ Because XML runs on the same ports as HTTP, it will be difficult for firewalls to stop malicious XML traffic. Because many firewalls do not stop XML traffic, viruses and other types of code can be embedded in the XML tagged area of a web document.

▲ The manipulation of XML traffic eliminates integrity and nonrepudiation. Realistically, the only way we can mitigate this is to only accept XML code from trusted sources and/or use only encrypted/signed code packages. In 2001, the XML Key Management Specification (XKMS) standard picked up momentum, as it addressed specific security requirements by defining XML for PKI. With key industry players such as Microsoft and VeriSign backing the standard, most applications are likely to go this route. It is yet to be determined how this will translate to the smaller mobile devices, such as mobile phones.

The database resides in the financial application server layer and stores information such as user IDs and device IDs. The database is accessed by the application server when a login request is received. The middleware database prepares and formats the data for the device requesting the login.

Many security breaches actually occur not in transit but at the merchant's database. There are many cases in which crackers have broken into merchant databases and stolen huge amounts of financial data of consumers and businesses. Many commercial databases are used for multiple functions in a typical commerce architecture: for e-commerce via the Internet, mCommerce transactions, and so on. As a result, a compromise of the database means a compromise of an entire merchant's site. Most of the popular databases, such as Oracle and Microsoft, have gone through some level of National Security Agency (NSA) certification, at least for older versions, and have achieved a slightly better than minimal level of security (which for commercial purposes is good enough).

However, to ensure databases are secured, let's discuss some basic areas in which databases in mCommerce transactions may be compromised:

▼ Ironically, the most insecure chain of a company's defenses tend to be their backup systems. A skilled hacker can use backups to re-create the original data. Use only reputable backup companies that have sufficient security and auditing capability for you to track where your data is at any moment.

NOTE: As we have seen with recent disasters, business continuity planning (BCP) is a must. Just as important is choosing a reputable backup provider/storage facility. Consider encrypting all your backup material.

■ Most databases have some type of default admin login. Change the default login ID and passwords.

■ Keep database table names and their locations on a need-to-know basis. If someone doesn't know what each table's name and purpose is, especially in a large database, it makes their attack all the more difficult because they can't target their attack on a single area.

■ Enable auditing. Ensure you can audit your users and your DBAs. Never trust anyone is the basic rule of thumb.

■ Separate staging or test servers from production servers. All servers hosting databases should be *hardened* (in other words, configured to reduce the amount of security risk) to remove unnecessary software and commands.

▲ Encrypt all communication between servers and the database by using integrated capabilities that ship with the database. (for example, encrypted named pipes with SQL Server 7.0 and 2000).

NOTE: The financial application server also compares the registered device ID to the user ID for additional security verification.

The financial application server and the gateway server for the request-initiating device communicate with one another, during which the information is pushed to the hand-held device by the financial gateway. Figure 9-3 shows a typical communication process

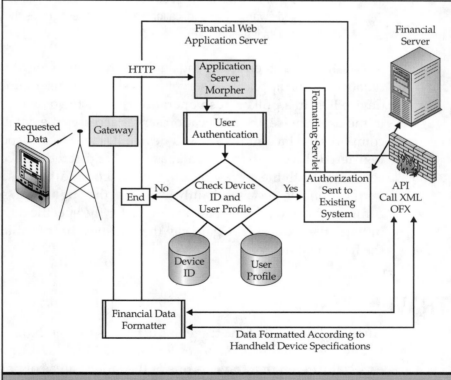

Figure 9-3. Communication process between financial web application server and the outside world

between the various components of a financial application server layer and the outside world.

In financial systems, control of the communication link determines whether push or pull technology is being deployed. When a data request is initiated by the wireless hand-held device through its financial gateway, pull technology is deployed. In this case, data is pulled from the financial application server layer down to the hand-held device. In situations where the financial application server makes basic content decisions and pushes data to the hand-held device without waiting for the client's request, push technology is deployed. In this case, the financial application server is in control.

NOTE: In either method, device authentication must take place first. The gateway transfers the hand-held device's request to the financial application server (middleware). The application server then recognizes the device type according to its identifier.

The server authenticates the device in the following way: The database at the application server level stores the username and device IDs. In a pull or push operation, before the data is sent across to the user device, the application server accesses the database and compares the incoming user and device IDs to the corresponding registered IDs stored in the database. The registered device ID is also compared with the corresponding user ID for additional security verification. On successful authentication, the application server communicates with the gateway server for the specific device that initiates the request. The gateway then pushes the information to the handheld device.

TRAVEL

Analysts believe that the travel industry has tremendous opportunity to develop content and services for hand-held wireless devices, especially given that travel is one of the largest areas of online consumer spending.

One of the largest travel-processing systems in the U.S., Sabre Holdings, offers wireless services in which customers can create, access, and change flights as well as car and hotel reservations using WAP-enabled hand-held devices. The company also makes its consumer web site, **www.travelocity.com**, viewable on mobile devices. Many other companies offer wired versions of their travel sites to be viewable from a PDA. The Air Travel Center is one such company that offers wireless access to their online travel content and services by making as much of the online information and services compliant to WAP standards for delivery to wireless hand-held devices. Expedia.com also gives its customers WAP access to personal travel information such as itineraries, alternate flight schedules, hotel availability, driving directions, flight status, frequent flyer account numbers, and maps. Some sites offer wireless synchronizing of their customers' online web travel profiles to their wireless devices using syncing tools. Many airlines offer wireless services with alert-based travel updates, arrival and departure information, safety warnings, airport alerts, and special deals on travel. Users are also able to update their itineraries from their WAP phones or PDAs. In most cases, leading airline sites and online travel providers such as Expedia, Travelocity, Worldspan, and Getthere.com offer the following wireless services:

▼ Flight arrival and departure information

■ Reservation changes

■ Ticket purchases

▲ Cancellation information

Expedia.com, for example, offers a service along with its interactive service partner AvantGo, called Expedia To Go. Users of PocketPC, Palm, and Windows CE devices can download personalized travel information onto their wireless or desktop-connected PocketPC, Palm device (version 3.0 or higher) with HotSync Manager (version 2.0 or higher), or Windows CE device—with or without modem. Figure 9-4 displays some of the Expedia wireless services.

For web phone users, Expedia.com partners with Cingular and all AT&T PocketNet web phones. With AT&T PocketNet web phones,

Figure 9-4.   Expedia.com To Go wireless services

users can access Expedia To Go from the AT&T PocketNet Travel menu. With Sprint, Verizon, and Nextel web phones, users can access Expedia To Go through MSN Mobile. On Cingular, a user can reach Expedia To Go by entering **expedia.com/daily/html/default.asp** on their phone's web browser. Some web phones use Wireless Markup Language (WML) for which access to Expedia To Go can be obtained by entering **expedia.com/daily/wml/default.asp?tpid=1** on the phone's web browser.

The technology supporting these services is very similar to that explained in previous chapters (covering a variety of applications), where content is accessed directly from the database to be displayed on a hand-held device.

MANUFACTURING

Mobile commerce technologies have also been leveraged in the manufacturing industry to optimize and streamline business processes and improve production efficiency. In the past, import/export records for car manufacturers used to be written on clipboards for a large number of different items. An external vendor would do the database entry, and information would be given to this vendor in the form of hand-separated forms. Weeks would pass before the data was compiled. The challenge would be exacerbated when inspection forms would have to go through frequent updates in order to meet current inspection criteria. Therefore, a need grew for the automated collection and compilation of data. Mobile technology is ideal for such an automation project, where inspectors can record information on handheld devices using pick lists and check boxes. At the end of the day, syncing technology can be used to transfer the data to a central location for consolidation and analysis. Inspection results are therefore also immediately available. Using hand-held devices coupled with the right software can also help managers modify inspection points for a particular automobile model or make, at any time from anywhere.

In general, much of the competitive intelligence in the automotive world centers around the sale price of the vehicle as well as its design and production quantities. From this information, a competitor can derive costs and possibly material types used. As a result, using RF scanners, wireless laptops, and other mobile devices can allow for valuable information to leak to a competitor.

NOTE: Many wireless systems in the manufacturing sector now either use encrypted VPNs or limit the range of exposure by using line-of-sight synchronizing methods (such as IR).

Mobile technology can also be beneficial in the tire inspection and manufacturing business. The success of a tire manufacturer depends on their ability to demonstrate superior cost and safety performance of their tires to their customers. Therefore, tire manufacturers continuously inspect tires mounted especially on their customers' commercial carriers, such as trucks making multiple calls per day, and inspect tires on multiple vehicles per site. Tire inspection data keeps the customers apprised of tire performance and maintenance needs. Until recently, many tire manufacturers were using manual paper-based processes for consolidating such data. Inspection data such as mileage, make, model, wheel/tire position, and tire wear was captured using separate paper forms for each truck. The forms were mailed to the tire manufacturer's corporate office and the data manually entered into a database. Reports were then generated by a desktop-based application residing on the corporate office servers. This process caused disconnection between the field-based data collection system and the data consolidation, analysis, and reporting tools, thus leading to critical loss of data. Some tire manufacturers now use forms-based applications running on hand-held devices for carrying out tire performance analysis. These applications use custom onscreen menus with graphic displays of the trucks and wheels to automate the collection of data and to update fleet tire maintenance records. The data is uploaded into the sales force automation systems using a syncing technology, thus allowing file sharing for fleets with multiple locations. The fleet inspection data collected on the field is also synced onto data warehouse application servers, where it is used to enhance the development of the manufactured tire. In addition, some manufactures uses mobile devices for digital authorization or signatures for "in-the-field" decisions to ensure quick decisions can be made at the factory floor level.

A different version of this example is also being used in auto racing. When a car makes a stop during a race, design team members measure the temperatures and pressures of the tires and combine that information with data about lap times, track temperature, and weather. This allows designers to analyze how well the tires are holding up, and the data provides valuable information to the manufacturer to improve its next generation of tires. Until now, the data-collection process was manual or laptop computer based, but these solutions were ruled out as being too expensive, too large, and too fragile for the racing circuit. Therefore, mobile technology is now used, whereby team members record temperature and pressure gauge readings on hand-held devices and, using syncing technology, transfer all the data to a database on the company's global network. Many racing circuits now use applications such as Versid Temperature Acquisition Module from Tangent Systems, for which temperature and pressure settings are automatically read from test probes attached directly to the hand-held devices.

Another small example of how even in car racing security is an issue is the reoccurring Solar Car Race. In this competition, universities and automobile companies from around the world compete to design the fastest car run only on solar energy. For one American university, the University of Michigan (Ann Arbor, Michigan), the Solar Car Team designed two sets of wireless telemetry systems. One system, using encrypted traffic, relayed vital statistics to strategists in a chase car. The other one, sent in the clear, generated false telemetry so that when competing teams tried to get information, it would be inaccurate.

Generally, manufacturing has very few applications for an end consumer. As a result, the security issues can be more easily controlled. In such business applications, the wireless components can use secret or proprietary wireless frequencies in addition to encrypted traffic. Furthermore, most devices in this area do not have to be as small as consumer devices do, thus allowing for more options (such as using SSL instead of WTLS for security).

DISTRIBUTION

Mobile commerce technologies can be effectively utilized in the distribution industry. Here are some of the areas where mobile computing can be used:

▼ Activity monitoring

■ Inventory control

■ Route optimization and mobile delivery functions, including vehicle tracking

▲ Load and checking functions

The distribution industry has become a complex one, with transaction quantities increasing, order turnaround times undergoing pressure to decrease, and customer service constantly becoming a high priority. Mobile technologies have been, and are, playing a key role in streamlining the processes and functions governing distribution. The task of automating part or all of a company's route sales process, making key information available anytime, anywhere throughout the sales flow—from the initial order through the load creation, to delivery and adjustments at the customer site—has become a driving force behind mobile technology use. Various methods are available for communicating all this information to and from the hand-held devices in the field, such as batch upload/ download, cellular communication, wireless packet data, and satellite. Although most distribution data from the delivery standpoint should be handled with an end-of-day upload/download at the distribution center, there are some types of data for which wireless transmission directly from the field may be necessary. This data might include the following:

▼ Same-day or next-day priority orders

■ Messaging to or from drivers for routing information or pickup requests

▲ Problems at customer sites with deliveries

The common standards that support wireless transmission within the distribution industry are the same as those that support many other verticals. These standards are cellular, CDPD, PCS, RAM, Ardis, radio, and satellite. An overview of mobile technologies in the distribution sector is also given in Chapter 2.

Other areas of distribution control include the power industry. Due to the costs associated with calibrating and reporting meter reading, some power companies have resorted to using wireless systems to relay information back to a central station, to better plan for the distribution of power. Such real-time information not only saves money in billing but also provides for real-time allocation changes of power consumption. Companies such as Energy Tracking, Inc., create wireless solutions for reading a whole host variable, resource consumption.

CAUTION: Not all wireless data acquisition services use encrypted wireless traffic. Some only provide basic username/password access into a merchant profile to see the data.

MESSAGE FOR THE IT MANAGER

In general, many security issues in the financial vertical can be mitigated through strong auditing and control processes. Some of the more important ones can be summarized as follows:

▼   Separating the production, test, and development environments with appropriate access control

■   Employing strong security policies

■   Using technologies such as OFX

▲   Being aware of the dangers of XML, including the ability for XML to carry malicious code

The travel industry utilizes security technologies similar to many other industries and therefore does not have specific, unique issues. One area that may be of concern is that the travel industry does deal with a large amount of legacy data; therefore, connections to the legacy data may be insecure. The auditing and use of good security practices can minimize such compromise.

In the other verticals mentioned in this chapter, manufacturing and distribution, security is the greatest issue at the time data is synched. Therefore good security policies for syncing and methods of syncing are important. In these verticals, data has a strong competitive value, so the syncing of the data must be done using a secure method.

Case Study: Wireless Extension to Online Book Store

This case study is based on an online wireless implementation of a large national bookseller. Although the bookseller's web site is colorful, comprehensive, and easy to navigate, little of this site, beyond its data, has been used to create their wireless shopping extension. The web site's data resides on a Microsoft SQL Server database running on Microsoft NT servers, which can access the book title database through data feeds. This data and infrastructure is leveraged by the wireless shopping service.

Initially, the bookseller's wireless division decided to move ahead with implementations for Palm VII hand-held computers and WAP phones. The team's two main initial problems to be solved were data access and data presentation. One option was "screen scraping," which takes data straight off the web site. However, the team decided that it would make them overly dependent on the web site pages, and any changes to the web site would also necessitate changes to the application in order for the data to be presented.

The technology decision was made to access the SQL data directly, rather than through the web site, but eager to get to market and establish a wireless presence, the integrators took a shortcut with their initial Palm VII implementation, using the web site as the interface to the data. They stripped away all the nonessential information, leaving only those elements deemed necessary for selecting and purchasing book and music products, either by searching or browsing top-10 lists.

As you have seen from our earlier discussions, due to the lack of security of screen scraping (as well as the lack of reliability if web pages change), using direct SQL queries is the best route, as the bookseller has chosen. Their next set of security issues centered around the database itself.

The initial version of the Palm VII implementation was implemented over Palm.Net. It was also available for the Palm V, using the OmniSky service. Initially, the Palm VII book software had to be downloaded onto a PC and then synchronized with the Palm device to install the software on the Palm hand-held device.

Users of the Palm V could add a wireless modem to gain access to the service. Such a service and modem for the Palm V is marketed by OmniSky, through which users can access the bookseller's wireless site.

In the meanwhile, the need to access the back-end database for wireless applications was felt. For the purpose of this data access, XML was used, initially formatting only for web-capable mobile phones. An application program interface (API) and XML front end was created to transact data between the wireless environment and the Internet, working as a conduit. Note that that there is no communication between the actual web site and the wireless environment. The development was carried out in such a way so as to minimize the number of steps required to place an order over a web phone or Palm device. For example, the standard delivery shipping option was already hard-coded into the program, not allowing the wireless users to select any other shipping options. It was also more complex to develop the web phone application than the Pam hand-held device because of the small real estate of the phone screen and keypad-input limitations. This led to clever programming features that enable users to use their phone buttons for various product selections or drill down under keywords using their phone cursors.

The system also offers "cool" features such as a wireless e-card, which enables users to send greetings from an embedded drop-down list from their wireless devices. Another feature offered is a wireless listening wall, where users can click on top-10 music titles and hear clips. A store locator can help the user find and contact a local bookseller (brick-and-mortar store) with one click to check real-time inventory for the desired product. Users also have the option of opening a new account right from their hand-held devices.

The order-placement process works in the usual way. The data stream from the hand-held devices is transmitted to the appropriate wireless tower, on to the WAP gateway or wireless server, and on again to the Internet via landlines. Once the signal reaches the Internet, it is immediately routed through the application program interface through the XML layer for interaction with the database, where the transaction is effected. Confirmation simply reverses the process.

After this, it was time to take the wireless application implementation to the next level—that is, to use a standard wireless server-based technology to offer enhanced services to the customers, provide for easy back-end administration, and also offer the services across the board to all major available wireless hand-held devices. The company selected a set of tools and platforms that would avoid screen scraping and integrate with the database directly from the hand-held devices as well as send data to a variety of devices, such as those compliant with HDML, WML, Palm's PQA, and other proprietary languages.

XML was used in an innovative way, and custom development was avoided to quite an extent. The team used existing infrastructure as much as possible. For example, an account on mobile device is the same as on the Web. The catalogs are also the same as on the Web. Solutions to the business problems had already been inserted into the initial wireless effort. These rules were all leveraged for the new wireless development as well. It is also worth noting that the wireless transaction server also has to interact not only with the RDBMS database feeds but also directly with other data sources, such as live feeds, HTTP-based HTML servers, flat files, transaction engines, and even e-mail systems, to securely transfer content from the source. The wireless transaction server automatically detects the protocol and device making a content request and then generates content into standards-based markup language appropriate for incoming wireless requests. All markup is generated to the specification relevant to each device—PQA for Palm VII, WML/HDML for WAP-compatible devices, compact HTML for WinCE devices, and Short Messaging Service for SMS-compatible phones, pagers, and so on. The following illustrations display the implementation architecture for the bookseller's wireless site:

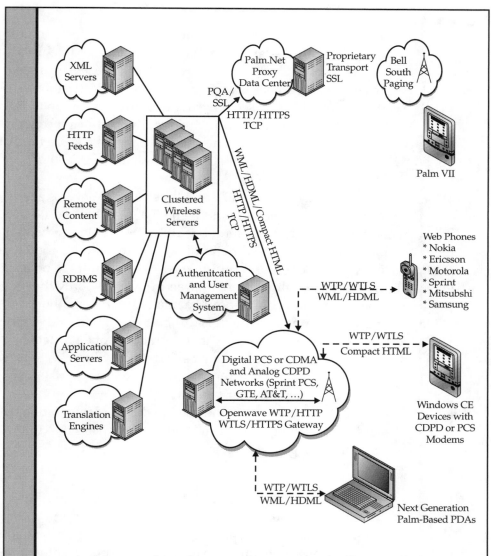

Architectural implementations such as buffer management, dynamic loading of shared objects, and content caching were also used, contributing to a high-performance solution and reduced data-transmission time delays.

Because the bookseller's data resides on different platforms, including Windows NT, Sun Solaris, and Red Hat Linux, the transaction server had to use replicated configurations in order to map the multiple data sources onto the handheld devices.

The preceding implemented system has three levels of security: front-end security, back-end security, and application-level security. Note that this security architecture is common to most implementations—wired and wireless. The mobile piece varies from the wired components because there will be some type of wireless gateway or similar security mechanisms.

Front-end Security   Three different types of web servers are involved in this implementation—IIS 5.0, Apache, and iPlanet. Therefore, security considerations from the wireless server's point of view had to be different for each. In general, good security practice requires multiple types of vendors to be used in the same implementation. In practice, though, only the most competent organizations should actually use this method across the network infrastructure. It is difficult enough to understand the flaws and good implementation practices of a particular vendor, let alone replicating that effort across many systems. Using many different vendors avoids being open to risks caused by using just one particular vendor.

Of the three types of servers used in this implementation, we'll discuss IIS first, then Apache and iPlanet. Here are the different aspects of security involved in IIS (as taken from the IIS Help pages):

▼ **Digest authentication**   Allows for secure and robust authentication of users across proxy servers and firewalls. In addition to this, anonymous, HTTP-basic, and integrated Windows authentication (challenge/response authentication and NT LAN Manager or NTLM authentication) are also used. In general, digest authentication ensures integrity of transmitted messages. The basic operation is that the sender generates a hash code based on a selected algorithm (such as MD5). The receiving party performs the same algorithm and verifies whether the result it received matches the sender's hash.

- **Secure communications**   SSL 3.0 and TLS provide a secure way to exchange information between clients and servers. They also provide a way to verify the client, before the user logs on to the server. In IIS 5.0, client certificates are exposed to both Internet Server API Specification (ISAPI) and Active Server Pages (ASP) to track users through the sites.

- **Server-gated cryptography (SGC)**   An extension of SSL that allows systems with export versions of IIS to use strong 128-bit encryption. Although SGC capabilities are built in to IIS 5.0, the implementation described in this section used a special SGC certificate. In general, this is not much of an issue today, because export encryption laws have been significantly relaxed. Events such as the World Trade Center bombing have caused a resurgence in the government restricting encryption export or otherwise making encryption easier to break (for law-enforcement officers and therefore criminals).

- **Kerberos v5 authentication protocol compliance**   IIS is integrated with the Kerberos v5 authentication protocol implemented in Windows 2000, allowing authentication credentials to be passed among connected computers running Windows. Kerberos is basically a ticketing protocol that allows for one, easily used credential (a *ticket*) that can be presented to all systems on the Windows NT network. This protocol is only used for back-end systems and would not be applied to mobile devices.

- **Certificate storage**   This is integrated with the Windows CryptoAPI storage. The Windows Certificate Manager provides a single point of entry that allows for the storage, backup, and configuration of server certificates. In the later versions of Microsoft's OS, certificates can be stored in their Active Directory and be accessible by all applications. Some vendors do provide their own certificate provider (rather than using Microsoft) because they may provide additional checks, such as password length, used to protect the activation of a certificate. Because a certificate relies on the existence of a private key known only to the owner of the certificate, loss of the private key means loss of the certificate and all the information it may access. Encrypted data could be forever lost without the associated private key. Key-management systems may be required to avoid such scenarios.

▲ **Fortezza**   This is a U.S. government security standard supported in IIS 5.0. This has been implemented in the bookseller's system, both in the server and browser software as well as the PCMCIA card hardware.

Due to that fact that Apache is a free web server (open source), it has become one of the most popular web servers in use today. The base version of Apache does not include SSL support. You have to get Apache-SSL (or similar free variants) to get SSL support. Further information about Apache-SSL can be obtained at **www.apache-ssl.org** web site.

The Apache-SSL implemented in this scenario is a secure web server based on Apache and SSLeay/OpenSSL. Its main features are as follows:

▼ 128-bit encryption worldwide

■ Client authentication

■ Full source code availability

▲ Modular extension API

iPlanet, the evolution of the Sun/AOL/Netscape alliance, contains equivalent security functionality as other web servers on the market. Information about it can be obtained at **http://docs. iplanet.com/docs/manuals/enterprise/41/ag/esecurty.htm#1068714**.

Back-end Security   At the back end, for negotiating SSL over HTTP/HTTPS, the wireless transaction server in the sample implementation utilizes an open-source toolkit library from

OpenSSL (which implements complete SSL 3.0 and is backward compatible with SSL 2.0).

Server and Application Level Security   Once the data is encrypted in the application server, any payload on the disk that the request may contain is not logged. The web server and application server also run on separate machines; therefore, that communication is secured via SSL. It is important to note that due to the large transactions these servers receive, disk caching of memory is inevitable. As a result, any unencrypted data in memory may be stored, albeit temporarily, on the servers. If routine cleanup routines get rid of these temporary files, such as credit card processing data, a hacker could access the data through this backdoor. In addition, most operating systems do not actually delete data; rather, they simply mark the data so that future data may overwrite it. Skilled hackers can get at this data even though the OS has cleaned up temporary files. The only way out for this higher-end solution is to use programs that write garbage data on top of files to be deleted. This prevents any remnants of useful data from being left on the disk.

Sometimes the protocols and markups provide ways to minimize security risks. In WML, for example, you can look up the HTTP Referer Header to make sure that the request has originated from a friendly domain (the server must send sendreferer="true" for this to work).

Comments on the Security Used   From the wireless transaction server's perspective, any implementation of SSL can be used—SSL PLUS, RSA-BSAFE, OpenSSL, or any other implementation. Although there are differences among the cipher suites supported by these products, this support is needed only for the back-end interfaces of the wireless transaction server, where the data source interfaces are very standards based. On the front end, most wireless gateways and user agents are SSL (TLS) compliant. Additional client authentication (where the users prove their identity to the merchant) could have been used with WTLS.

CHAPTER 10

The Verticals, Part 2: mCommerce Security in Healthcare, Public Services, and Hospitality

There are few areas of computer security regulations that are required by the government for the non-government sectors. One key area of regulation has been created through the adoption of the Health Insurance Portability and Accountability Act (HIPAA) regulations. HIPAA basically mandates the integrity, availability, and confidentiality of medical records and information to protect people's rights and privacy. As a result of HIPAA, an entire industry has been created in helping companies become compliant. The impact on the mobile sector has also been significant, especially in the area of biometrics. Biometric devices are devices that can identify people with relative ease because these devices use the physical characteristics of a person in the identification process. Many new devices using radio frequency (RF), infrared (IR), or other means have resulted in the ability to help healthcare companies comply with HIPAA regulations for privacy and security.

The public sector uses mobile technology for defensive means to protect public officers by providing them with sufficient information in real time at the point of a conflict. In many ways, the mobile technology used is similar, although not as sophisticated, as what is used by the military.

Other areas we cover in this chapter also have strong needs for privacy and security, but they go one step further and attempt to use mobile technologies to generate additional revenue. The hospitality sector looks to mCommerce—whether it is generating revenue from wireless services for guests or the casino industry's use of information to help make gambling easier (we reserve judgment as to whether this is a good thing). mCommerce is significant in these areas, because these industries can increase revenue without the usual methods of building or heavy capital improvements.

HEALTHCARE

The healthcare industry has a lot to benefit from the use of mobile solutions. Healthcare providers are increasingly using mobile devices to deliver on-the-spot care to patients, by having anytime/anywhere and instant access to the critical data they require in order to dispense medical care. Mobile technology is, therefore, gradually becoming a part of the healthcare system, allowing, among many other functions, medical professionals secure wireless access to patient records and test results, the ability to enter diagnosis information on handheld devices during patient visits, the ability to consult drug formularies by initiating wireless queries from their PDAs, and also the ability to handle charges and capture medical insurance payment data when needed. The International Data Corporation (IDC) forecasts the U.S.-based mobile healthcare market to grow (in millions of dollars) as displayed in Table 10-1.

HIPAA

HIPAA is the major factor driving the healthcare industry to use computer security. The Health Insurance Portability and Accountability Act of 1996 is the U.S. government's set of regulations that dictate how patients and hospitals treat data related to medical scenarios. HIPAA has established strict privacy and security guidelines. In addition, the European Union (EU) has even more strict regulations on how patient privacy and data is safeguarded. As a result, many companies and solutions are focused on achieving HIPAA and EU compliance with healthcare privacy and security.

We can examine HIPAA as requiring the following main categories as related to security:

▼ *The need for administrative procedures to guard data integrity, confidentiality, and availability.* This guideline is the basis for creating a set of information security policies. Such policies would dictate the requirements for the other guidelines listed and indicate penalties and remedies for failure to comply. Audits and similar checking mechanisms would be defined to ensure that the policies are enforced.

■ *Physical safeguards to guard data integrity, confidentiality, and availability.* This guideline refers to the physical access to computer systems and facilities that host computer data of a confidential nature. This includes protection from physical access to servers as well as protection against (or at least recovery from) natural hazards such as fire.

■ *Technical security services to guard data integrity, confidentiality, and availability.* This guideline helps protect access and control of information, such as patient records.

▲ *Technical security mechanisms to protected unauthorized access to data transmitted over any communications network.* The intent of this guideline is to protect access to systems when data is in transit. In addition, this guideline covers external access points, such as dial-up or Internet connectivity.

Based on these four main categories, we can talk about various technologies that solve these issues. For administrative procedures, procedures for the certification of systems need to be in place to ensure that they are HIPAA compliant. Some companies have developed custom test suites for this purpose. Next, for physical safeguards to be maintained, classic security countermeasures, such as locks, cameras, and security badges, need to be in place for access control. The third category is the technical security, which is where computer security has an important role. Devices such as biometrics, digital certificates, and other mechanisms to tie access levels to individuals are used. Finally, the last category of the technical security mechanisms refers to protecting data in transit as well as protecting remote access entry into protected systems. Firewalls, encryption, and related technologies are all used to protect unauthorized access.

So how does this all relate to mCommerce security? As it turns out, due to the key factors of the healthcare industry, such as mobile personnel and the need for high security and simple technology, it is

2000	2001	2002	2003	2004	2005	2000–2005 CAGR (%)
$41.9 million	$199.2 million	$394.2 million	$680.7 million	$1211.3 million	$1966.6 million	116.0

Table 10-1.   Growth of U.S.-Based Mobile Healthcare Market (Source: IDC)

necessary to implement strong mobile security solutions. Devices such as PDAs, RF emitters, IR transmitters, and even Bluetooth all do or will play a major role in healthcare. In addition, the HIPAA standards make U.S.-based companies more in line with the traditionally higher European standards of individual privacy. Considering the higher adoption of mobile devices and technologies such as smartcards, HIPAA will lead to a boon in healthcare-related technologies in the mobile space all over the world.

Biometrics

Biometrics can be defined as the ability to authenticate an individual's identity based on something physically unique about the person. Fingerprint scanners, hand geometry, retina scanners, and other types of technologies all authenticate users with, presumably, something that cannot be easily changed. This, in combination with something you have (for example, an access badge) and something you know (for example, a password), can make security extremely strong.

Biometrics is popular in healthcare applications because it allows for quick and reliable authentication. Many biometric devices designed to authenticate medical personnel can be used to help healthcare facilities meet HIPAA regulations. Devices are usually combined with an access/photo badge and are small enough to clip on or hang around the neck of medical personnel. Some devices have fingerprint readers on the badge that, when authenticated, transmit RF signals to allow a user to use a PC terminal, for example.

NOTE: There are companies that provide biometrics solutions based on an individual's fingerprint, hand geometry, retina/iris, face, signature, and voice. The particular solution to be used will depend on the consumer and the requirements for accuracy and speed of authentication. In addition, mobile devices have fewer choices due to their small form factor.

The real challenge with most medical institutions is that they are not quick to adopt new technology. Hospitals, for example, still do quite a bit of manual data entry and process paper forms. HIPAA will create even more hurdles in achieving technology adoption, but because it's the law, medical facilities will have to do what it takes to overcome these hurdles.

Other biometric solutions focus not just on the desktop PC but also on the mobile device itself. For example, Applied Biometrics has produced a fingerprint-recognition system for PDAs that uses Palm and WinCE devices. Its a stand-alone solution, and it has its own battery, making it portable. The hardware may use a wired or wireless connectivity solution. However, because the device must accompany the PDA, the practical use of this is most likely restricted to high-end applications, such as those in the healthcare sector. See Figure 10-1 for an example of the flow of the fingerprint-matching process.

Another biometric example for protecting access to the mobile device is the solution from Communication Intelligence, which provides for signature matching in order to access the PDA. This product is more portable than the Applied Biometrics solution because it does not require external hardware. However, fingerprint matching is more convenient and more accurate than signature matching capability.

Although we present biometrics as the solution for increasing security for the healthcare market, the biometrics field does have markets in other verticals as well. Healthcare happens to be synergistic vertical between the needs of the users and the devices' capabilities. The area of caution for biometrics is that, depending on the architecture, the database that stores the matching information (such as a thumbprint in a database) must be very well secured. If security is breached in the database, an even greater problem arises, because identity theft could become a disastrous consequence. In the healthcare market, many of the solutions are distributed so that if a particular device is stolen, the exposure is limited to the individual's information on that device (versus centralized systems that may yield a compromise of many individuals' information).

Because of the rising costs of specialized and emergency healthcare, many hospitals and medical centers are turning to smarter ways of dispensing medical care, mainly through the use of technology.

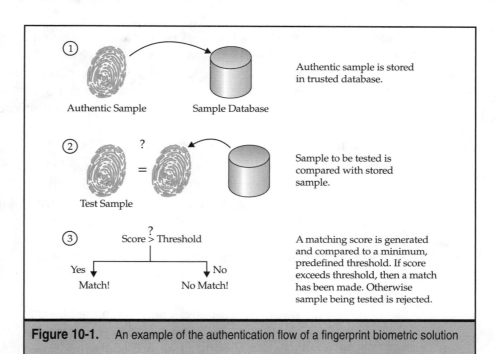

Figure 10-1.   An example of the authentication flow of a fingerprint biometric solution

Mobile commerce has become one of the key contributors in this area, proving beneficial to the healthcare industry as discussed in the following sections.

Point-of-Care Service Delivery

Mobile technologies are being used to deliver medical care at the point of care (POC) itself. In many cases, doctors and caregivers use handheld devices to record patient information and history, remotely monitor vital signs, as well as deliver remote care to an ambulance from the hospital premises itself:

▼   *Recording patient information at the point of care.* This includes the use of wireless devices such as a Palm Pilot. Many hospitals using these systems do not have adequate security to protect such data in transit. The use of Wireless Transport Layer Security (WTLS) or a related technology would provide a basic level of protection.

■ *Gathering patient history.* This is the concept of being able to transmit an entire history to anywhere in a medical facility. For example, a doctor could get notes when with a patient, or a lab technician could get a history while doing a blood sample. In this case, the data is usually tagged with a code or patient number. In this manner, security compromise is limited because no names are used.

■ *Remotely monitoring vital signs.* Due to managed care cost cutting, there are fewer support staff members to monitor patients. As a result, a single person can now monitor more people because the employee can move around with wireless monitoring devices. Security is also improved in this manner because there are fewer access points to equipment (which provides for privacy and physical security).

▲ *Remotely administering ambulance care.* This involves sending electronic updates of a patient's status to the hospital while in transit so that the doctors can remotely monitor the patient's health and have the right staff and equipment ready for the patient's admission when they arrive at the emergency room (ER). The location and estimated time of arrival of the ambulance is generally detected using the Global Positioning System (GPS). Again, the use of tagged or coded data with a patient number allows for the privacy of the patient.

Physician's Orders and Test Result Handling

Mobile technologies are also being used for optimizing prescription- and test result–handling procedures. Using handhelds, doctors can write prescriptions that are automatically sent to a central drug-dispensing server. The server can monitor drug doses and send alerts to practitioners based on set thresholds. Such technology can also be used for tracking lab specimens and reviewing patient's test results as well as interacting with the medical insurance carrier's servers to inform them of the patient's condition. Using mCommerce, caregivers can work with the insurance carrier to get preapproval for procedures and the hospital's billing office can work out payments for care. A hospital's staff is mobile; mCommerce helps them do their job no matter where they are within the hospital. A few of these remote care procedures are highlighted next along with their security implications:

▼ *Writing prescriptions.* Some of these applications are being ported over to PDAs. With the use of digital signature technologies, doctors can authorize medications in real time. This allows for lower billing and administrative costs as well as quicker medication delivery times.

■ *Collecting laboratory specimens.* Specimen data can be transmitted to the laboratory for analysis. The data can be encrypted but is usually tagged with a patient number instead of a name to maintain privacy.

■ *Tracking samples from bedside to lab.* A history of all tests conducted on the patient is stored on a central server in the hospital. A wireless device at the patient's bedside keeps a tab on every test result and displays the ones requested by visiting doctors. Doctors can also use the devices to request additional tests on a patient that are automatically allotted a test number by the patient's profile administrator residing on the hospital's mobile server.

■ *Reviewing test results.* Doctors and care givers can initiate wireless queries to the central mobile server and receive and review results stored within the patient's central profile. Security is built in to the system such that only authorized personnel can view the appropriate results and patient information. Usually these devices need to be physically secured, because most PDAs and similar devices used in hospitals have very minimal encryption or logical security. As a result, a device could be stolen, and later brute-force hacking methods could be used to obtain the data.

▲ *Capturing payments.* These are basically point-of-sale (POS) terminals generally found in hospital reception areas that can handshake with the patient's insurance provider's servers and receive/capture payments from the insurance company for services rendered to the patient. Usually, this can be done through a payment gateway that uses its own encryption schemes to protect data in transit. Unfortunately, most of these systems do not store the data in encrypted format at their origin or destination.

Medication Monitoring and Diagnostic Devices

Mobile technologies can also be used in dispensing medicines, monitoring patient statistics, such as blood glucose and temperature, sending out alerts based on preset thresholds, and diagnosing primary and secondary illnesses. A few of these uses are discussed next, with the discussion highlighting their security implications:

▼ *Diagnosing illnesses.* Mobile devices can be used to help diagnose illnesses—for example, the doctors can enter the approximate symptom data onto their handheld devices and initiate queries to the central medical server. The system basically assists doctors in honing-in on the actual illness diagnosis. Given that doctors rely on this system for critical decisions, the accuracy of the data is essential. As a result, some high-end applications include the ability to verify that data has not been altered after it was created (through digital signatures).

■ *Monitoring blood glucose.* Data from glucose monitors can be transmitted to central servers that conduct analysis and return results. This can help reduce risk because a doctor can be alerted if there may be any secondary illnesses that should be tested for based on what is revealed from the historical data match. Due to legal and financial requirements, test results must be stored for a period of time. As a result, databases of this information are usually created and secured by some type of access control, such as a username/password scheme.

▲ *Dispensing medication.* Special devices can be used to dispense medications based on a certain threshold being reached. Security here is generally physical security and error checking to ensure that devices function correctly and are not modified in some way so as to produce dangerous levels of a medication.

Sales Force Automation

In general, the sales cycles in the healthcare sector are very long. The pharmaceutical industry spends quite a bit of money on advertising and influencing spending to convince medical professionals to recommend their products. However, due to legal requirements, much of this activity must be carefully controlled and monitored. In addition, medical equipment can be difficult to sell because hospitals may be regulated by a managed care provider. As a result, salespeople need to have as much knowledge as possible to reduce sales cycles and delivery times.

The mobile space has become ideal as a way of providing solutions for these areas:

▼   Pharmaceutical sales

▲   Medical equipment sales

In the next section, you'll see how mobile equipment is laid out in a hospital running mobile servers and other devices to assist in secure, on-the-spot delivery of medical services. The security holes in these layouts are then discussed.

Equipment and Personnel Tracking

Mobile solutions can and are being implemented in various ways for tracking equipment and personnel.

Using an Ethernet-Based Controller

Using this location-positioning solution using radio frequency (RF) technology, a hospital can continuously track equipment and personnel on the premises. An Ethernet-based controller is used for this purpose. Figure 10-2 displays how this location determination takes place using a series of components. Note that this solution uses radio frequency tags (RF tags) that are affixed to objects for tracking and identification purposes. The tags receive RF signals from the RF reader and return back to the reader the identification information of the object to which they are affixed. The positioning antenna in the diagram simply acts as a tower that collects and transmits terrestrial radio waves for location triangulation determination of the hospital assets and personnel. These solutions are more popular outside of the U.S. because privacy and other issues have hampered widespread adoption of such technologies in the States.

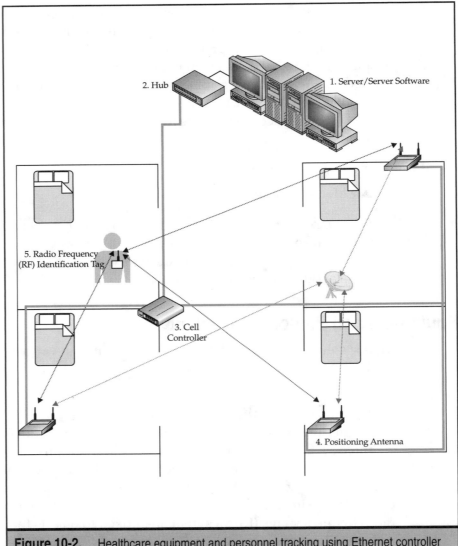

Figure 10-2. Healthcare equipment and personnel tracking using Ethernet controller

Using Infrared Technology (IR)

In this solution, which allows a hospital to track equipment and personnel on the premises, infrared (IR) sensors are wired to a collector to detect signals from the IR badges that are forwarded to the concentrator for processing. The concentrator processes the information and transmits it to the mobile server and host computer for viewing. Versus Technology, Inc., manufactures a widely used IR/RF badge in hospitals. The IR/RF badge emits both infrared (IR) and radio frequency (RF) signals and is used for locating applications that require direct, instant two-way communication between two individuals, such as a patient and a caregiver. The system can be configured to initiate a discreet page directly to a specific individual when the call button is activated. This opens a direct, discreet communication channel with the other individual.

Using IR as a method to protect access to data is important because IR is a line-of-sight technology. Authorization through this mechanism implies the user is physically close to the device (such as a computer) being accessed. Once the user leaves the presence of the secured area, the connection terminates. This is very important in most hospitals and clinics because systems are usually shared among various levels of personnel, including doctors, nurses, and administrators.

NOTE: IR systems do not work as reliably outdoors because they may be affected by weather and interference.

The line-of-sight requirement of IR reinforces access rights and privacy that is restricted by role (doctor, nurse, and so). In addition, attacks on IR-based systems are limited because the attacker must be in line of sight of the system and within very close proximity to the emitter.

Using Radio Frequency (RF)

In this solution, hospital equipment and personnel tracking is done using a series of RF readers that wire the tracking area to a controller. Radio frequency ID (RFID) tags are placed on the medical personnel or hospital equipment, and the RF readers detect signals from these tags, passing the data on to the mobile server. The server contains special software that can display the location of the assets. Figure 10-3 displays how the data flows from one device to the other, reaching the mobile server for location display.

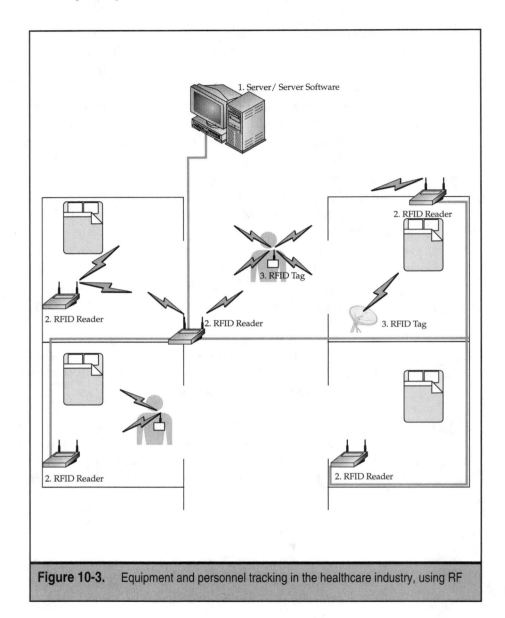

Figure 10-3.   Equipment and personnel tracking in the healthcare industry, using RF

Patient Data Access and Maintenance

Mobile solutions can and are being implemented in various ways for
maintaining patients' records and personal information.

Patient Data Access and Maintenance over an RF LAN

In this solution, client software is embedded in the handheld device that is used by the healthcare professional to enter data regarding a patient. The handheld device then synchronizes with the central hospital server database over the internal radio frequency LAN. Figure 10-4 shows the device layout and flow of data.

NOTE: Many RF and wireless-based applications in the healthcare space lack strict security. RF and wireless communications can extend beyond the perimeter of the healthcare facility, which increases the risk of eavesdropping.

Patient Data Access and Maintenance Using Diffused Infrared (IR)

The function of this solution is the same as the preceding solution; the only difference being that the handheld device updates the central server database over the internal diffused infrared LAN instead of an RF LAN. Figure 10-5 displays how this works. As you can see, the solution uses an infrared hub that acts as a multiport connection point for local devices that communicate using IR. The IR interface adapter acts as the bridge between the handheld device and the local access point and also with the second IR interface adapter at the top-left corner of the hospital.

NOTE: IR communications are slightly more secure than the more common RF communications. IR requires line-of-sight for communications and, therefore, does not propagate beyond the perimeter of the healthcare facility.

Alerts and Notification

Mobile healthcare solutions can and are being implemented in various ways for alerting and notifying healthcare professionals about vital patient statistics and signs.

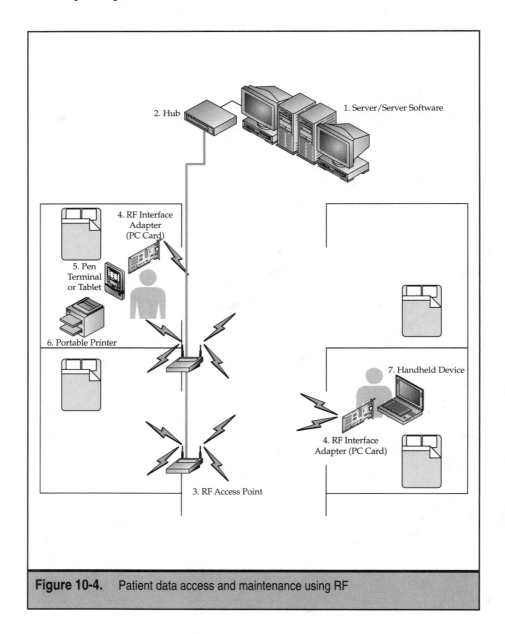

Figure 10-4.   Patient data access and maintenance using RF

Alerts and Notification for Indoor Use

In this solution, healthcare professionals can set up special medical thresholds (such as body temperature, heart rate, and so on) that,

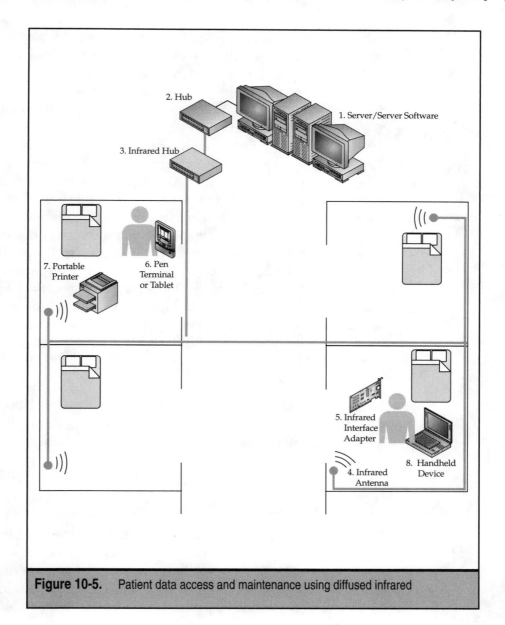

Figure 10-5.   Patient data access and maintenance using diffused infrared

when reached, will have the messaging server software transmit alert notifications to the doctor's handheld device. The alerts or messages may contain important information about the patient, including vital signs, so that the healthcare professionals can respond accordingly. Because these alerts have to be in real time, the services and devices have to be sensitive to the critical nature of each alert. The solution uses the existing infrastructure to send messages to the handheld devices. Figure 10-6 displays how this solution works. Note that the RF interface adapter (ISA/PCI) sits in a PC's ISA/PCI slot and interacts with another interface adapter (or in the case of this figure, with the RF access point in the middle of the hospital ward). These interactions take place over an RF LAN. You also see the doctor carrying a pager that receives the alerts. The way this works is as follows: When a threshold is reached, the messaging server transmits an alert notification to a ground station with a transceiver or satellite. The alert then gets sent to the base station that governs the paging network in which the doctor's pager belongs. Because the alert includes the identification number of the doctor's pager, the pager activates when there is an ID number match, and the doctor receives the alert. The doctor can then respond to the message using a handheld device and/or pager in different ways, as described in the preceding scenarios.

Alerts and Notification for Both Indoor and Outdoor Use

The aim of this healthcare solution is exactly the same as the preceding one, with the only added feature that the alerts and notifications can be sent to devices out in the field.

Wireless Voice Access to the Phone Network

Mobile healthcare solutions can and are being implemented in various ways that provide healthcare personnel with wireless access to the phone network. This network can be in the form of a Wireless Private Branch Exchange (WPBX) or a nontrunked radio network. In the WPBX solution, healthcare professionals can use both wired and wireless handsets for voice access inside the hospital environment. Figure 10-7 displays the architecture and information flow. In this figure, you will notice a wireless private branch exchange that serves to basically connect all the hospital extensions with each other and to the public telephone network. Because the solution has both a local

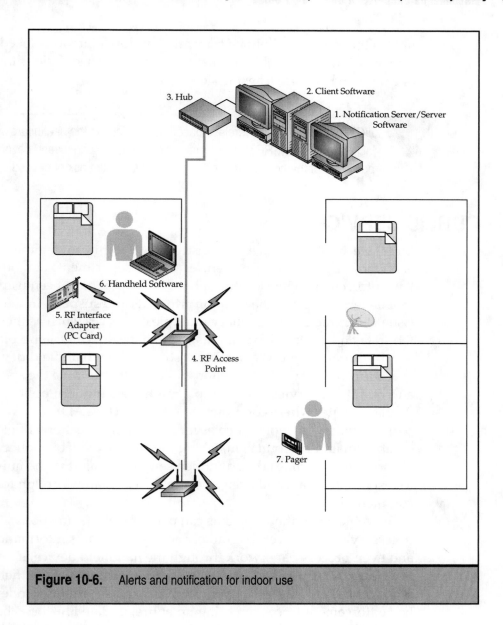

Figure 10-6.   Alerts and notification for indoor use

area network and wide area network, it requires a Channel Control Unit/Data Service Unit (CSU/DSU) to allow for data transmission between these two networks. The voice muliplexer that sits between the WPBX and CSU/DSU is simply a splitter/consolidator that either breaks the high-speed phone transmission down into low-speed transmissions or consolidates many low-speed transmissions into one high-speed voice transmission.

NOTE: Many RF and wireless-based applications in the healthcare space lack strict security. RF and wireless communications can extend beyond the perimeter of the healthcare facility. This increases the risk of eavesdropping.

PUBLIC SERVICES

Mobile technologies have been instrumental in improving the efficiency of public service agencies. Police departments and other law enforcement agencies throughout the nation have been using mobile technology to check up on criminals and suspects in the field, issue electronic citations, query multiple databases (such as those of the state and federal departments), automatically run license plate checks through the DMV databases straight from handheld devices, and perform many other functions that greatly improve the speed and quality of service. An example might be a modern police dispatch center where computer-aided dispatch (CAD) systems perform many functions, such as monitoring the location of field equipment and personnel, matching the closest available police squad unit to a crime scene and then sending an alert to the unit to respond to a call, and even tracking the call status through to completion.

In-vehicle handheld systems can perform all the functions necessary for an officer to remotely access a civilian's information and even process paperwork through the handheld device, if necessary. The other side of this access to information in the field is the concern for the security and privacy of individuals. Modern law enforcement forces can bring up entire, updated histories based on vehicle or individual identification to assess the potential for a threat. One example of how law enforcement uses secured mobile technology is Datamaxx's product called Cyberforce. This product allows officers to access person, vehicle, firearm, and other databases in a secured fashion, using ECC encryption technology. The form

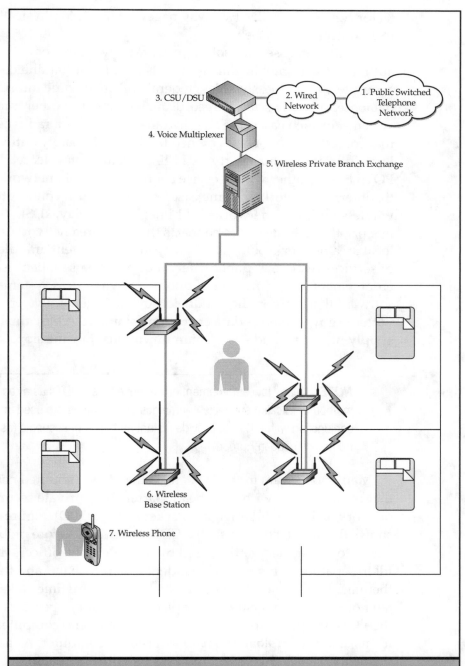

Figure 10-7.   Wireless voice access via a Wireless Private Branch Exchange (WPBX)

factor consists of a RIM two-way pager designed to physically attach to an officer's utility belt.

Mobile public service solutions have allowed law enforcement authorities with mobile data terminals (MDTs) or handheld computers to wirelessly access federal and state crime information databases as well as access records management or other internal systems. In such cases, the data is transmitted over a radio network that consists of frequencies owned by the public safety entity or leased through a third party. A T1 line, Frame Relay, leased line, POTS line, or other wired service connects the radio network to the internal network. In some cases, the MDTs also connect to the wireless wide area network. A T1 line, Frame Relay, xDSL, or ISDN line or other wired service connects the wide area network to the local area network. Some third party–related content, middleware, or services relative to public safety may also be used. Because law enforcement is a prime user of public safety wireless systems, the software that runs on the handheld devices is generally compliant with the government's data encryption standard (DES), thus supplying secure and silent communications transmission.

NOTE: Many law enforcement officers use these MDTs as a regular method of tracking suspects. Biometrics and cameras are used in conjunction with MDTs to provide instant matching of suspects (as is frequently used in Europe).

Many police cars in the U.S. and Canada use mounted consoles that communicate with their headquarters on a private secure network, using Cellular Digital Packet Data (CDPD). Figure 10-8 shows the architecture of such a CDPD network. Before mobile technologies started getting used by the police, the officers had to fill in separate forms for each incident report by hand and then turn them in at the end of their shift, which could sometimes take up to ten hours after the incident took place. Data-entry operators would then take the paper incident forms, type them onto computer-based forms, and then upload them all to a central computer. As a result of the delays caused by this manual system, officers would not get the right material at the right time for investigation purposes. Sometimes the police department would be lagging behind in data entry by up to a week. In this manual system, if an officer needed information about a suspect or case, they would need to call in by radio, and if the information was available in the central computer, it would be relayed back to the officer according to their number in the backlogged request queue. Therefore, a new mobile system was implemented whereby officers could initiate request queries directly from their handheld devices that would seek information from the local and national computer systems. Officers could also upload incident reports, witness statements, narratives, and other types of data from their handheld devices without having to go through the pain of manually writing them.

Many law enforcement bureaus can also connect via interserver messaging over the Internet to other agencies. Interserver messaging enables two or more message switches to send and receive messages between the servers. Public safety departments can be linked via a wide area connection (such as the Internet) to other agencies. One such example of interserver messaging is the Valley Emergency Communication Center (VECC), a large multijurisdictional, integrated public safety telecommunications network. Many states currently have Integrated Justice Information processes planned or underway. The U.S. Department of Justice, the National Association of State Information Resource Executives, the International Association of Chiefs of Police (IACP), the Association of Public-Safety Communications Officials (APCO), and the National Association of Counties are a few of the organizations leading the development of a comprehensive national plan.

Here are some of the other areas where mobile systems have been useful:

▼ **Parking enforcement** Mobile units are being used to facilitate the dispensing of parking tickets based on threshold alerts. The parking meters can emit, via IR, a signal to a passing ticket-collecting agent and alert them to an expired meter. This speeds up the checking process, and as you can imagine, increases fine revenues.

- **Vehicle checks** Generally, most traffic stops are preceded with some type of real-time database check on the vehicle/person being detained. RF-transmitted information can give officers a quick background of the situation they are about to enter.

- **Fingerprint matching** A suspect's fingerprints scanned into a handheld device can be sent to the crime database server, which cross-references the incoming data with the fingerprint records on file and returns a result back to the handheld device. Increasing cooperation between agencies can allow, for example, federal agents to search against INS or other governmental records quickly.

- **Vehicle tracking, antitheft** The most famous product in this market is the Lo-jack tracking system. Lo-jack can alert officers that a car has been stolen. Using GPS, it can give officers a second-by-second update on the vehicle's location. Other products, such as OnStar, that also use wireless communications can also act as vehicle locators and even remote activators of vehicle functions (such as locking/unlocking the vehicle).

CAUTION: These systems are only deterrents. Many high-valued cars are stolen by simply towing them away and disabling the transmitter in transit.

- ▲ **Facial recognition** The U.S. Army's military police have conducted field trials with a wearable computer that uses mobile communications to relay people's faces and get back information on those persons. This application is being considered by some other law enforcement agencies. Officers wear a head-mounted display to see the status and other information about the individual being scanned. The wearable computer is currently manufactured by ViA, Inc., a Minnesota-based provider of body-worn mobile computers. With a copy of Visionics' FaceItsoftware embedded in it, the ViA wearable computer automatically captures an image of a person's face and immediately conducts a one-to-many match with the

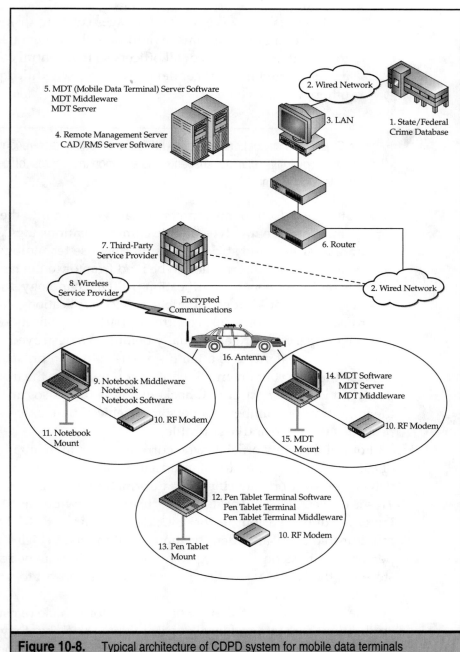

Figure 10-8.   Typical architecture of CDPD system for mobile data terminals

central database server of facial images running Visionics face-recognition programs. In addition, the system uses GPS to indicate the location of all officers so that central command can be alerted if an officer deviates from a scheduled patrol or otherwise faces danger.

NOTE: The city of London in the U.K. uses advanced face-recognition technology to flag criminal suspects and summon the nearest officer by wireless communication.

Another new form of mCommerce that is coming into the public service marketplace involves mobile communications tags. These tags are paper thin and sticker like, and they use technology that allows user-defined information to be read from or to the tags. Using wireless radio frequency identification (RFID) technology, these tags can be used for a variety of public service applications, such as electronic toll collection, access control, or parking applications. These tags are tamper resistant and usually default to a destroyed or non-usable state if physical attempts are used to manipulate them. Because the tags contain only identification numbers, the information they emit is not very useful to hackers unless they also can associate the identification number to a person or vehicle (that is, access the receiver's database and user profile).

For public-safety officials who currently have to manually key in or call in and request motorist information, they can now, via RFID vehicle registration, have the same information within a few seconds. This is especially useful as airport security worldwide has been increased due to various terrorist incidents. In airports, RFID can monitor frequency and identification of authorized vehicles and/or personnel. Emission or safety program information can be read and stored in the tag for later wireless retrieval—in contrast to labor-intensive manual monitoring.

The technology also offers an alternative for vehicle registration applications for state and local governments. The technology is based on a 902–928 MHz wireless communications reader that generates an RF signal that is specially coded to communicate to a sticker tag. The tag reflects the RF signal to convey information back to the reader.

The reader passes the tag information to a local host computer for processing.

Public service technologies and software packages are being developed that enable data collection, reporting, and analysis related to contacts between police and citizens. Such applications run in the form of software programs embedded in the handheld devices on which police officers input citizen contact data throughout their shift. The collected data is then exported to the agency's central database server via mobile syncing programs for analysis by law enforcement administrators who proactively manage how their departments engage with the public. Technologies are also being researched for providing secure messaging and alarm capabilities for connected mobile users, as well as data collection and reporting functionality to address concerns relating to racial profiling. Secure, real-time data access and covert mobile communication tools are being developed to arm out-of-vehicle personnel, such as detectives and officers on foot as well as bike and mounted patrols, with handheld devices so that they can access the National Crime Information Center, National Law Enforcement Telecommunications System, and the Department of Motor Vehicles databases over a secure wireless network to check the status of vehicles, persons, articles, and guns. System-wide alarms can be sent to all users, including both handheld and laptop units, as well as dispatch personnel, in case there is a need. This is being accomplished using digital text messaging support to provide secure broadcast of messages and user-to-user communications.

Tools are also being developed to provide police officers in the field with direct access to motor vehicle and warrant information. Officers can tap into a wireless computer network from laptop computers in their cruisers to get complete motor vehicle and warrant information. Such technologies are being developed to work on most public or private wireless networks.

Another area of wireless research is mobile field reporting, which offers the capability of conducting field interviews, preparing reports, carrying out mobile reviews and approvals, and remotely managing incident and accident reports. Technical research is being carried out to develop products that provide wireless access to records-management systems (RMS), computer-aided dispatch

(CAD) systems, and other information networks. The resulting technology will enable in-field officers and supervisors to create, review, approve, and store reports directly from their handheld devices.

Research is also being carried out in mobile technologies for the fire brigade personnel that would extend fire records-management systems (RMS) and other in-house data sources to a mobile environment—in other words, to develop a wireless computer-aided dispatch solution that delivers critical information to mobile devices fixed onto fire engines, ladder trucks, and supervisory vehicles. Such mobile technology will enable on-the-scene reporting and free resources for fire prevention and other community-based programs.

HOSPITALITY

It is a known fact that in the hospitality industry, service and margins are the name of the game. Business survival depends on serving customers lavishly around the clock while keeping operations lean and efficient. Therefore, point-of-activity services and the technologies supporting anytime, anywhere customer access become vital. Mobile technology is a relatively new entrant to the hospitality industry. Many useful nonwireless hospitality applications are being developed for Palm, iPAQ, and Symbol hardware. Wireless applications are also being developed and implemented that make near-real-time communication possible. Communication is generally accomplished either by putting a nonwireless unit in a cradle connected to an on-property server and syncing the handheld's data with the server, or by wirelessly transmitting data by radio. Small, cabled send/receive units or cradles placed around the hotel are used for syncing the data. Many hotel chains are implementing cradle-based handheld technology to organize and track housekeeping inspections and quality checklists. Wireless check-in/check-out modules are also in the pipeline that incorporate key cutting and credit card processing straight from a handheld unit. A few hotels have implemented handheld housekeeping applications that use standard wireless platforms such as Palm to automate housekeeping inspections, manage property-created inventories, and provide curbside check-in and wireless guest services.

Already, many hotels today offer connectivity services, where guests can plug in to a hotel network to check e-mail or surf the Internet. Not only does this offer guests added convenience over using conventional dial-up lines, but it also acts as a revenue generator for the hotel because connection time is billed to the guest. Now hotels are looking at mobile technologies to improve flexibility and raise margins on the network connection offerings. For example, InnTechnology provides wireless printing solutions for hotel guests in their rooms. With such short-range applications, security is almost a nonissue because a potential threat would need to essentially be in the room to steal transmitted data. Billing and other information associated with the system is hardwired to the hotel's central computer database so that information cannot be attacked through wireless means.

NOTE: Many major hotel chains are now offering temporary offices on the hotel property for traveling business people. Use of wireless technologies lowers the cost of setting up these offices.

For most hotels that have gone mobile, they have had to first "wire themselves" by installing receiving stations to pick up the handheld devices' signals. These access point receivers have been placed throughout the property and wired back to the server with CAT-5 cables. Besides implementing their own wireless handheld information-management systems, providing instant access to vital guest and corporate information, many hotels have also commenced building a wireless LAN architecture. Such solutions are aimed to free telephones from walls and wires, all the way from the curbside to the top of the tower. Hotel chains are experimenting with new mobile software programs for various handheld devices. Hotel personnel carrying these handheld devices can perform a variety of services, such as checking in guests at the curbside the moment they arrive and taking food and drink orders at the poolside by recording the order details on the handheld and sending it up to the kitchen for fulfillment. The staff can also check inventory levels, for example, tracking the number of mini-bar items used and replenishing them, reordering hotel supplies, and making purchases. Housekeeping can maintain housekeeping ledgers for purposes of recording the number of sheets used, supplies replenished, and rooms cleaned.

Mobile technology is also becoming an integral part of casino operations. Pagers, radios, cell phones, and other niche devices have used their own individual networks to communicate across and among casino properties to enhance security and service. New standard mobile architectures are being developed, offering casinos the ability to move slot carousels at any time, without cabling, check in guests from anywhere on the property, and allow floor hosts to provide "on the spot" services. Guests can pay for gaming using their handheld terminals, which are temporarily linked to their credit card or bank accounts or a line of credit provided by the casino itself. The handheld devices can also be used as mobile financial transaction devices, downloading all wins and losses from the gambling host's handhelds based on the results of a particular game or gambling deal. Therefore, a guest's financial gains and losses can simply be stored in the form of numerical data on their personal handheld device for the entire duration of stay at the gambling resort. The guest can pay for services, gamble, order drinks or food, rent cars, and register gambling gains and losses straight from the handheld device. During checkout, a simple click of a button can settle the bill both ways (that is, a debit or credit of funds).

Currently, the gaming industry uses smartcards or loyalty cards. These smartcards contain the guests' personal information, preferences, and sometimes loyalty program points. Many large, chain casinos can access a common database anywhere in the world. As a result, when guests use their smartcards, a particular casino machine will know exactly the type of player and the value of that player to the casino. Smartcards can have fairly strong security through the use of digital certificates and encryption. Wireless solutions in the gaming sector will not easily be able to take advantage of smartcards because, in North America, use of mobile smartcard applications is very low. In Europe, some phones do have dual slots for smartcards or use S/WIM cards, but they are not heavily being used for gaming or loyalty applications.

The casino industry is now going for a total wireless cross-property solution. Spectrum24 from Symbol Technologies has been a technology echoing in the casino and hotel industries. Some casinos and hotel chains have implemented Spectrum24 wireless LANs, extending the reach of their existing wired LANs by using frequency-hopping spread-spectrum cellular technology operation within the 2.4–2.5 GHz unlicensed frequency range reserved worldwide for data communication.

Hotels are also implementing Voice-over-IP technologies to support data transmission of both voice and data messages over their wireless LAN or internal TCP/IP network—or even over the Internet. In general, security is provided for through standard VPNs or other related encrypting technologies. In addition, spread spectrum can also add an additional layer of security, provided that the hopping sequence is not predictable (otherwise, an attacker could guess the next frequency the channel may hop to). The particular implementation of these WLANs will determine the level of security of these systems. Many casino regulars carry frequent visitor or player cards generally unique to a particular casino. These cards generally maintain a profile of the cardholder's playing habits, gambling history, and other information. Although such information is not stored physically on the card, as soon as the card is entered into a special reader, it contains data that can be wirelessly sent to a central mobile server that maintains extensive information on the cardholder's playing habits. Swiping the card through the handheld reader can also establish a temporary credit line for the cardholder, depending on their creditworthiness and relationship with the casino. Technologies are being implemented that provide the player with credit, right at the casino door, for immediate play. Maintaining statistics on a player's habits and history with the casino can also help alert the casino management to greet good customers as soon as they swipe their card anywhere in the casino or play at a slot machine using their loyalty card as a credit card. Because all data is centrally stored on a mobile content server, it can be accessed by floor hosts using handheld devices to answer questions and provide guest services on the spot. On the wireless LAN side, because there are no cables or wires to worry about, casinos can move their tables and slot machines around whenever they want.

Mobile technologies are also beginning to be used at conventions, meetings, and tradeshows. Convention organizers are starting to provide services such as the following:

▼ **Internet access**   Exhibitors, customers, and the media can access the Internet via the wireless network, thus avoiding having to set up wired Internet access sites within their booths at tradeshows. Due to the direct connection to the Internet, the exhibitors must rely on the host facility to provide firewall and virus-scanning protection. Additional security can be provided through locking down terminals and software firewalls on each terminal. In addition, many setups like this today do not address cached information from one user to the next (because these terminals may see hundreds of different people accessing them per day during large conventions).

■ **Lead retrieval systems**   Generally at tradeshows and conventions, there ends up being a sizable exchange of business cards between corporate professionals and executives. In most cases, the data on the business cards has to be manually entered into a contact-management program such as Outlook or even onto the PDA. This generally ends up becoming a cumbersome task, especially if you have collected 500 cards! However, now with the use of wireless technology, convention exhibitors are been given handheld devices to gather lead information and business cards in real time and then transmit them to a common database. The general security compromise of private information in this case is minimal because the actually syncing occurs with a certain physical proximity to a trusted host computer (either through short-range IR or through some type of cable/cradle setup).

■ **Electronic newspapers**   We are all aware of the sheer number of brochures, pamphlets, and advertisement printouts at tradeshows, not to mention the convention directory and the cumbersome maps that we end up accumulating while attending them. A new and easier solution to this problem has been implemented in the form of a light mobile device that can be given out at the front door to convention and tradeshow attendees so that they can view exhibitor locations and other helpful information on the handheld screens instead of carrying half a pound of papers. Because the entire convention is on a wireless network, the attendees can see the schedules and timetables of potential business prospects, send mobile meeting requests to these prospects, and manage their meeting schedule for the day.

▲ **Instant payment**   Some exhibition organizers are also developing handheld software that can allow attendees with handheld devices to purchase a product after they have seen a demo at a booth or panel discussion. Companies can allow organizers to connect handheld devices to a bank account for one-way payment processing of all on-the-floor product purchases. Payment processing in such an environment can be handled as it is anywhere in the wireless mCommerce world through WAP, WTLS, and related technologies.

Mobile technology has also penetrated the food-delivery marketplace. Customers are ordering meals to be delivered to their homes and offices within a short amount of time and are also demanding that the food not show up cold! For a delivery company (there are many online delivery companies that collect orders from different restaurants in a region and provide home or office deliveries for a set fee), this is not an easy task, especially during the lunch hour, when the demand is heavy. Therefore, many such companies are now equipping their drivers with portable smart phones or handheld devices that work over a wireless IP (CDPD) network. The handheld devices are integrated with the delivery company's existing customized dispatching software and GPS-based vehicle-location system. When an order comes into the company's dispatching center from their web site, the computer system locates a driver in the area of the delivery address, notifies the driver of when and where to pick up the order, and then faxes the customer's order to the restaurant (some startup companies are now developing business-to-business wireless networks where local restaurants can communicate with one another and with the delivery center). Drivers use their handheld devices to signal their arrival at the restaurant and notify the dispatcher once the food has been delivered.

A new generation of wireless handheld POS (point of sale) ordering systems have also been developed that transmit the customers' orders instantly to the kitchen, bar, or register. This allows the wait staff to instantly move to the next table and take the next order while the last order is being cooked. Wolfgang Puck Restaurants, Hudson News' Euro Cafes, Carnival Cruise Lines, and Princess Cruises are among the restaurants and companies implementing such front- and back-office mCommerce systems, particularly using mobile solutions provided by Symbol Technologies. In such order-management systems, security is not generally found to be a major issue, because most of these systems do not process credit payment from the terminals. In addition, very little information could be gained by intercepting the wireless communication, because someone would have to aggregate information over a long period to gain any trade secrets based on sales patterns and order types.

Back-office automation has also been at the forefront of wireless restaurant management industry. Many restaurant chains and companies have wired back-office systems that perform bid analysis, e-procurement, receiving, inventory management, menu engineering, labor management, food production planning, and enterprise reporting. Integrating these functions with mobile handheld technology can allow many new functions to open up, such as mobile inventory management, purchasing, receiving, inventory adjustments, internal requisitions, and web-based reporting using a mobile device. Some restaurant corporate headquarters are using mobile inventory managers that integrate with major POS systems, handheld computers, and accounting systems. The mobile central purchasing module can request product and pricing information and, upon receipt or proposals from multiple vendors, select the best vendor based upon preestablished relationships, product quantity, availability, and price. Some system can also include bar-coding capabilities. Some restaurants are now using mobile commerce technologies to manage their distribution processes. Many of these back-end systems use traditional security and payment processing systems. These back-end systems simply sync up with the mobile devices and process orders as other wired network systems might. Therefore, from a mobile perspective, the security is minimal, provided that auditing is in place to ensure even internal staff do not compromise the back-end systems.

Healthcare Security Case Study

A Rochester, New York–area health insurance company that provides insurance for hundreds of thousands of members in six New York counties has implemented a mobile solution to provide its authorized physicians with detailed medical information and HMO guidelines. The HMO physicians can now carry a Palm handheld device to access medical reference applications, search specialist and pharmacy listings, and search a database of commonly prescribed drugs and clinical guidelines. The handheld PDAs have power-on passwords that are assigned to the doctors by the IT department. Furthermore, asset tracking allows a particular PDA to be tied to a specific doctor, ensuring each doctor is responsible for the security of the data given on the PDA.

Using the mobile system, physicians can print discharge instructions for patients simply by pointing their handhelds at infrared (IR) devices located at the nursing stations. The devices used are infrared so as to minimize anyone nearby from trying to also capture the transmitted data. Because IR is limited in range, the doctor has to physically be near the nursing station, where the employees would be able to verify the credentials that doctors carry visibly. Every 90 days, the Palm handheld devices are synchronized with the health insurer's web site to obtain the most current content. The doctors simply place the handheld in a HotSync cradle next to their office PC, log on to the secure site, and download the updated information. Physical syncing, again, limits access to the wired data because the stations are near where only trusted employees (identified by their security access badges) have access.

The health insurance company is also exploring a biometric-based access badge. In this solution, the doctors would put their fingers on the badge, which in turn would transmit an IR signal to communicate with a local PC at a nursing station. In this manner, data can be accessed from a fixed workstation for applications that cannot be done easily through PDAs. Such access control can be used to limit access to the healthcare data of patients, which would help the hospitals/doctors come into HIPAA compliance, thus keeping insurance costs down.

MESSAGE FOR THE IT MANAGER

Mobile communications is a valuable tool in the healthcare industry, public sector, and hospitality businesses. Concerns about security are especially acute in the healthcare industry due to HIPAA governmental regulations. However, concerns over consumer privacy and identity theft also occur in the public sector and hospitality businesses. The main mobile technologies to resolve these issues have been around for quite some time, although their application is relatively new.

We can summarize the key areas of concern in the mobile space by dividing the applications by verticals.

Healthcare

Concern   Conforming to HIPAA regulations.

Solution   The use of various Internet security technologies, including biometric devices, enabled for wireless applications. Additional requirements for using wireless LANs and other transmissions include VPNs and digital certificate technologies. We recommend using an experienced consulting company to assist in determining what needs to be done to be HIPAA compliant because the costs of compliance can be high.

Public Sector

Concern   Providing real-time information to field officers.

Solution   Using network protocols such as CDPD and other protected RF transmissions that allow for real-time data to be sent to mobile terminals in field agents' cards. RFID tokens and GPS devices can assist in asset tracking to provide physical security and/or recovery of stolen assets.

Hospitality Industry

Concern   Increasing offerings to guests while maintaining security.

Solution   Generally, most applications can implemented with Bluetooth or IR solutions, which will minimize the risk components. Wireless printers or Internet connections can provide for additional revenue sources. The security risks are minimal because most of these applications are close-proximity wireless solutions, making it difficult for hackers to get any information from them.

CHAPTER 11

The Verticals, Part 3: mCommerce Security in Entertainment and the Military

Given that there are many more vertical industries in the mCommerce space, we have elected to focus on some key ones in this book. This chapter discusses the remaining two verticals we will address as examples of security techniques for mCommerce verticals. The two verticals we will address are, in fact, opposite ends of the need for mission-critical reliability in mCommerce applications: entertainment and the military. Entertainment relies on consistent delivery, especially in scenarios of gambling, for example. Incremental revenue from gaming applications make this is a very lucrative market. Due to their low financial cost per transaction, entertainment applications have more leeway for reliability than our next topic, military applications.

The military sector relies on mobile applications as a matter of life and death, thus making reliability essential. In this chapter, we have concentrated our efforts more toward discussing the mCommerce side of military applications than highlighting their pure wireless usage. Applications such as messaging and planning logistics are some of the mCommerce applications discussed in this chapter. Many of these applications are used with commercially available products to help keep military costs down. Case studies are provided at the end of this chapter to show how mCommerce applications are being developed and implemented in a variety of military situations, such as in the creation of a global distributed database application to support the U.S. Army's war reserve equipment prepositioning strategy.

ENTERTAINMENT

The growth of the mobile Internet has created a plethora of business opportunities for players in the entertainment arena. The development of high-speed network systems, such as GPRS, EDGE, and 3G, coupled with cutting edge gaming application environments, such as WAP, CHTML, and recent advances in new devices and wireless operating systems, have led analysts to believe that mCommerce hosts a bright future for the mobile gaming industry. Datamonitor recently estimated that four out of five mobile phone users will be playing mobile games by 2005. The advantage of mobile gaming is the market reach of mobile technology. Analysts estimate it took Nintendo ten years to sell 100 million Game Boys, whereas four times as many mobiles phones are estimated to sell each year, forming a potential worldwide market of 950 million mobile subscribers. The mobile gaming experience is therefore expected to be worth $5 billion, with over 100 million players by 2006, according to a study released by the consulting firm Strategic Analytics. The entire mobile entertainment industry is based on a fundamentally secure infrastructure, because many of the revenue opportunities are based on reoccurring revenue from gaming.

Privacy Rights

Given that gaming appeals to a younger audience, a whole host of privacy and legal issues are brought up due to various laws about content that can be shared with children. In the U.S., the Children's Online Privacy Protection Act of 1998 (COPPA) mandates specific rules on how interaction and data collection with children can be conducted. Basically, U.S. law mandates that online services seek parental approval to collect information about children under 13 years of age. It is important to understand COPPA, and its derivatives in various forms around the world, before you can use or implement a gaming site.

In order for a mobile gaming site to function within accepted privacy guidelines, you must do the following:

▼ You must have a privacy notice on the site, stating how information is used and how the site deals with information on children.

■ You must obtain verifiable parental consent—some type of proof that a parent has consented to allow their child to continue with the electronic interactions.

▲ You must provide a parental notification and an opt-out method when signing up children to mailing lists or protected areas of a site.

The idea of determining age for gambling is another issue. Because gambling is not legal without regulatory clearance in the U.S., many Internet gaming sites are based offshore, which effectively makes them legal. How can you ensure a gaming site has the correct age audience? One easy option is to use age-verification services, where developers can tap into data providers such as Aristotle that provides 18/21 age verification for adult or gaming sites.

The U.S. $20 billion adult entertainment industry is also poised to benefit from the growth of mobile technology. There are portals that serve as an mCommerce portal delivering information on venues, products, games, and adult services (that is, provide adult entertainment via download or real-time wireless delivery). Because such adult portals gather certain types of information about their users pertaining to their choices and preferences, the issue of security and privacy surrounding the capture and use of that information comes into play. Most adult mobile portals collect anonymous information (via IP addresses and opt-in e-mail addresses) that enables the portals to analyze the user experience. A user's IP address is used to gather broad demographic information from log files. Log files are used to track and monitor traffic patterns throughout the mobile site. These logs pose a risk of being used to track or monitor personal identification information. Most mobile portals use cookies to save the user's password (so the user does not have to reenter it each time they visit the site). During the installation process and subsequent synchronizations, many mobile adult entertainment portals note the kind of PDA operating system a user has and the amount of free memory available on the system.

Additionally, the portals use a temporary session cookie that is active during the registration process to monitor the download process during installation. Although this temporary session cookie is not stored on the user's computer and/or PDA once the user leaves the portal's web site, there is a risk of the cookie information being captured by intruders or the portal company itself and then used for malicious purposes. Many terrorist organizations have been known to communicate via coded information encrypted within adult entertainment sites. Such sites can also collect information about the user's PDA device, the other applications used, or the data on the user's device outside the portal's host of services. Because adult mobile portals maintain profiling records on each visited user, as well as the user's IP address and sites visited, much of this information gets backed up automatically on a periodic basis to the backup servers. For privacy reasons, many users like to have their personal identification information removed from such backup databases; however, this is a tedious task, and despite reasonable efforts to comply with user requests, the provider might not erase all the backed up information on the user.

CAUTION: Some user profile information is automatically stored in backup copies of the adult mobile entertainment site databases that the portals keep for access only in case of emergency. In many cases, such backups cannot be edited, so there may be residual information that will remain within the portal's databases, access logs, and other records, which may or may not contain such personal information.

Convergent Gaming

One of the new and upcoming areas of wireless gaming is *mobile convergent gaming,* which is based on the idea of a player being able to play anytime, anywhere, against anyone. The game is resident on the server, and all the devices are merely portals into the game. Each device has a unique client, and the server simply tailors its output to match each client. Security becomes more difficult to manage here because the masses of gamers could elect to use the system in so many ways, including maliciously. To protect convergent gaming systems, it is necessary to address the following issues:

▼ **Strong web server security** Most of the systems require a web presence for the portal; therefore, that will be the first line of defense.

■ **The ability to validate a gamer's identity** This will occur either through smartcards (where the identification/authorization data is stored on the card) or by making queries against the owner's credit card (an authorization to a third party) to determine whether the card is valid. Possession of these cards assumes the card's information represents the owner's identity (although this is far from accurate).

▲ **All the privacy issues raised earlier in the chapter** These issues may become even more complicated because there could be a mix of individuals, ages, and countries involved in a particular game. This would require the game operator to run a rules engine to determine what to ask and what can be displayed about a gamer based on the laws of the gamer's country.

Embedded Gaming

There are different types of games, each with its own sets of rules, implementation strategies, and security protocols. For example, the game ExEn, developed by In-fusio, offers a video interface for real-time animated graphics. Many game categories, such as arcade games and multiplayer adventure games, use it. ExEn games, embedded in the mobile, downloaded (via ExEn) or played on a remote server, and connected via ExEn, SMS, GSM data, or GPRS data channels, are downloaded from a GameZilla platform and are executed on ExEn enabled handsets. The most interesting application for ExEn is in the lottery or gambling area. Oberthur Gaming Systems has developed, along with Oberthur Card Systems, the ability to secure lottery transactions using smartcard technology. The smartcard, as it is traditionally used for other applications, acts as the authenticator for payment. The user, being uniquely identified via the smartcard, can claim the lottery winnings with the smartcard as evidence. In this scenario, the only way to "steal" a lottery would be either breaking into the gaming provider's back-end systems or cracking the smartcard technology in use. Either method would be very difficult and not practical for the average hacker.

The idea of using a smartcard as a way of authenticating a user is akin to the games in the 80s that required PCs to have hardware dongles as proof of possession of a license to play the game. With a wider audience, including gamblers, using smartcards will most likely be the only solution that can provide some level of anonymity (versus using biometrics) and yet provide proof of transactions.

Code Breaker

Many games are built on the Java platform. The emergence of wireless technology gave rise to J2ME (Java2, Micro Edition). The first Java-enabled handsets were released at the beginning of 2001 in Japan and later in 2001 in Europe. Only high-end terminals can support the memory requirements of the Java Virtual Machine (JVM) and the processing power required to properly run games.

Mobile platforms are not exempt from the basic security issues that arise from code writing. In fact, the disadvantage of Java is that whatever mistakes a programmer built into the code (or worse, a virus) can now be spread to any device, because Java is meant to be platform independent. Add to this the idea of 2.5G or 3G networks that allow mobile devices to stay on all the time, and we have a situation that's ripe for a "virus wildfire." Due to the relative tight limitations (to desktop systems), mobile devices are especially susceptible to insecure code due to memory and processing tricks used to conserve space or processing power. The same security features found in Java are lacking in J2ME. This is critical when dealing with gaming because performance is an issue, and tight code is necessary. J2ME has been popular because it provides for a protected execution environment. This occurs through a "sandbox" concept, in which programs cannot execute outside a given range of memory. This prevents a poorly written program (or a virus) from accessing other data or programs outside of its intended purpose.

Good Coding Tips

We can identify three key areas in which mobile code using Java can be hacked:

▼ **Memory leaks**   This is the generation or storage of memory variables by a program that does not end cleanly. As a result, the used memory keeps growing until no more memory is available. Viruses may force memory leaks to use up available resources.

■ **Tampering**   This is the manipulation of stored information (usually in memory). This could allow a program to insert itself in a routine. A Trojan horse, for example, could add a few lines to a running program in memory to execute the Trojan horse and then return control back to the program.

▲ **Resource stealing**   This is the use of unauthorized resources, such as memory or CPU (as would be done by a virus).

Some interesting applications with J2ME for security include the creation of a lightweight Secure Sockets Layer (SSL) client. Sun Microsystems Laboratory has built an SSL client-side implementation called kilo SSL (or kSSL). A diagram of SSL based on J2ME is shown in Figure 11-1. The advantage to using kSSL is that the mobile device can have true end-to-end encryption, thus avoiding the gap of

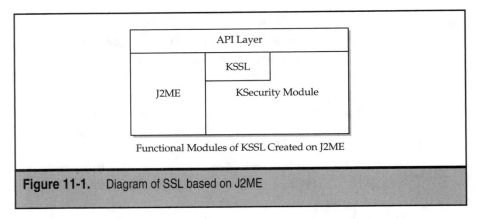

Functional Modules of KSSL Created on J2ME

Figure 11-1.   Diagram of SSL based on J2ME

security at the WAP gateway. The drawback, due to the limited processing power of the mobile device, is that not all standard cipher suites are supported and there's a lack of client-side authentication (that is, the device cannot present a certificate to the server).

Here are some tips for how to write good Java code for a secure, mobile platform:

▼ Ensure your Java classes are private by limiting access to them.

■ Initialize all variables. This will ensure that seed values are not tainted by viruses or rogue routines.

▲ Ensure your classes are not clonable. An attacker could otherwise clone your class and then modify it and replace the original in memory. In this manner, they could create the desired result, perhaps without the user ever knowing.

Code obfuscation can ensure some level of difficulty in reverse-engineering your code. However, keep in mind that obfuscation cannot be considered a serious form of security. This means any cryptographic keys or passwords in your code can be recovered.

Case Study: Implementing Secure Mobile Games

In this case study, we describe some tips to implement secure mobile games using the tools and framework of Nokia's Mobile entertainment Service (MES), which provides a popular tool for building interactive games and content for Internet-connected mobile phones. This service utilizes the Nokia Mobile

Entertainment Platform, which can help you develop gaming applications on the WAP protocol. For players, the platform offers, among other things, the ability to invite other players, enter player and chat rooms, where messages may be exchanged and invitations to other players posted, and read news and messaging. For the game provider and operators, the system provides the ability to deploy entertainment services as a managed facility (for example, manage user groups, user accounts, monitor system and audit information, install game cartridges, and collect data for billing, accounting, and analysis purposes). Developers can take advantage of the system's support for multiplayer gaming, registration, authentication, session management, and management of player communities.

Keep in mind that only a sample of the issues are covered here. This is not a comprehensive introduction to the MES. A fully detailed code and architecture review should be done before releasing any application to production.

The most important aspect of this system is what it offers game developers to implement and deploy wireless games. The system has built-in functionality, such as multiplayer game support, registration, authentication, session management, usage data reports, game features that support player communities, and other software tools for application development and content creation.

You should ensure that all sessions are terminated as users leave a game or terminate the game by turning off their devices. This is important because open sessions may lead to the possibility of a hacker taking over the session In addition, a Denial of Service (DoS) attacked could be launched by generating a huge number of dummy sessions, which would slow down or crash the game server host.

The Architecture   At the heart of your game development architecture lie two functional parts: the wireless application server (WAS) and the portal. The WAS provides the underlying infrastructure and development environment for distributed mobile game development.

The portal, on the other hand, makes game services available to the outside world by providing runtime information and services to your games and by handling the registration and logic of the users (in other words, the users gain access to the game services through the portal).

Keep in mind, however, that the portal also allows for communication with various Internet-bound communications, including e-mail. Although highly unlikely, this could lead to viruses or mail bomb activity.

The game services are integrated with the portal through a registration process. A high-level architecture defining the relationship between the WAS and portal is shown here:

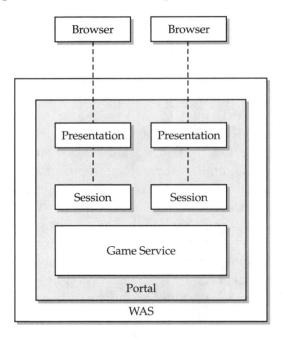

Development Tips   Here are some other key security points to note while developing under this framework:

▼   Keep in mind that MEP Lite is meant for development. This version does not have any authentication mechanism, such as password control. Therefore, putting MEP Lite in a live site opens it up for hackers. In addition, no log files or audit files are generated.

■ The MEP software requires access to an Oracle database instance that requires Admin privileges. Access to the database needs to be secured through some type of access control, such as a username/password.

▲ The MEP software must communicate to the Oracle database via port 1521, which means any firewall in between must have this port open.

The Final Product   As a developer, you will also need to supply some runtime configuration parameters to the portal for it to function correctly. The core of your development will take place when you develop the logic for your game. Any sequence of dialogs within the game home page could be considered a game. You can use either the basic game services framework or the boardgame framework, depending on the type of game you are developing.

Your final product (the game) can be deployed in the form of a game cartridge that contains a set of mandatory and optional files. In order to create your cartridge, you first need to compile all your Java sources, assemble resources in the class directory tree, perform a proxy compilation, and then finally build your cartridge using the WAS Packager tool. Because the Java class files are released as a JAR file, it is wise to assemble them under a different directory tree to the Java source so as to ease the creation of the JAR file. In Java, unsigned JAR files are given the least security access. Therefore, unless there are specific reasons to sign a JAR file, leave them unsigned to reduce their capability and potential security threat.

DEFENSE AND MILITARY

Mobile and wireless technologies have been an integral part of defense and military systems ever since these technologies were invented. In light of the terrorist attacks on New York City in September 2001 and the growing concern with cyber-terrorism, security has undoubtedly become the single most important issue of discussion among national defense officials. The National Security Council, the Department of Defense, the CIA, and the FBI all believe that terrorists may look at online technologies as a means for causing future economic destruction. Because much of defense technology is mobile based, this raises some serious questions regarding the nature of mobile technologies being used in our military and government security agencies. The use of information technology and secure networks in the military and government is intense, to say the least. In this chapter, we discuss the security behind the use of mobile technologies for information analysis and/or cost savings with mCommerce technologies and products used by the U.S. defense and military agencies.

NOTE: Most military technologies use special mCommerce hardware servers with specialized security keys to process their transactions. These custom servers ensure that although the data travels over highly encrypted wireless networks, it is useless to an intruding or eavesdropping party who does not have the custom hardware and software required to process the data.

Mobile Hawks

The General Accounting Office (**www.gao.gov**), which is the investigative arm of U.S. Congress, says that the U.S. Department of Defense has a sprawling computer infrastructure that's spread across some 2.5 million unclassified computer systems, 10,000 local area networks, and hundreds of long-distance networks. The GAO further revealed that there have been nearly 1,400 combined attacks against the computer systems of the U.S. Army, Navy, and Air Force in 1999 and 2000 alone. A large part of these forces use mobile technologies for their day-to-day activities as well as for combat mission planning and execution, not to mention keeping the nation's security intact. Such planning and execution requires the active use of mobile handheld devices initiating transaction requests that travel across a wireless network to an mCommerce server hosting a database. The database and mobile server process the initiated request and return the result to the requesting hand-held device, resulting in a processed transaction.

Security and Terrorism in the Post-September 11th Era

Defense policy analysts such as Martin Libicki of the Rand Corporation believe that mobile devices can be configured by terrorists and hackers to pose threats in three general areas: remote access to networks, electronic eavesdropping, and data removal. In a November 13, 2000, article in *Computerworld*, Dan Verton writes that "Pro-Palestinian hacker groups, some of which have links to international terrorist Osama bin Laden and anti-U.S. terrorist organizations, have vowed to launch a new round of cyber-attacks as part of an ongoing wave of violence that began this fall between Israelis and Palestinians." As we have seen after the terrorist attacks in the U.S. in September 2001, cyber-terrorism again continues at a global scale against powerful democracies such as the U.S. and India. Hacking is no longer just a tool for "script-kiddies" (a reference to amateur hackers that use canned scripts for their attacks), but is now a tool for political and military objectives.

Some specific groups Mr. Verton mentions in his article include:

▼ al-Muhajiroun

■ Arab Hax0rs

■ Dodi

■ Hezbollah

■ PROJECTGAMMA

■ ReALiST

■ Ummah.net

■ UNITY

▲ Xegypt

For example, with the right skills, a terrorist can configure a personal digital assistant (PDA) to download information from the Pentagon and remove it from the building. Defense agencies such as the Air Force Research Laboratory (AFRL), which develops some of the service's most advanced technologies, have also crafted

> policies to deal with mCommerce security risks. For example,
> information stored on PDAs must have a low level of data
> security classification to ensure loss of the device does not
> compromise national security.

Yes, They Are Listening

Many U.S. and other international government intelligence services
use mobile technologies and wireless networks for messaging and
commerce. Advanced security technologies are being developed that
will allow intelligence services to track down mobile network crackers,
computer vandals, and possibly even international terrorists like those
who attacked the United States.

NOTE: *War dialers* used to be a term for computer programs that would
methodically call all phone numbers in a given range searching for a computer.
They would record the computers found for later use to attempt hacks. Today's
systems for hacking wireless networks are called *road dialers* (because hackers
drive around searching for wireless access points) or *snoop dialers*.

The technologies are based on so-called *snoop dialers* that rapidly
dial a series of phone numbers and detect when a computer answers
the phone. Such technologies can be used to launch covert attacks on
computer networks. Other security technologies sniff, capture, and copy
data packets that move across mobile networks; then, using indexing
programs, they sort out the different traffic streams. The system
monitors evidence of network abuse by keeping old records and
matching them with data packet patterns. Figure 11-2 shows how
real-time mobile traffic modeling can help detect an intrusion. The
security technology sniffs, captures, and copies data packets that
move across mobile networks, and then using indexing programs,
sorts out the different traffic streams. The system monitors evidence
of network abuse by keeping old records and matching them with
data packet patterns. A mismatch between predicted and actual
traffic timing or pattern can imply an intrusion.

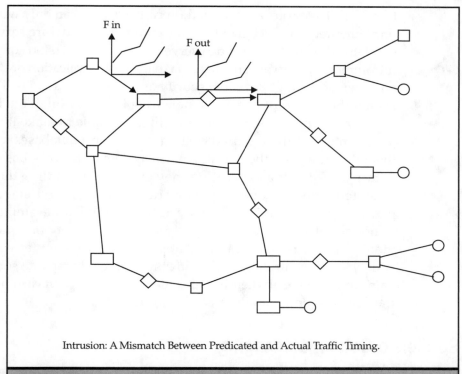

Intrusion: A Mismatch Between Predicated and Actual Traffic Timing.

Figure 11-2.   A mismatch between predicated and actual traffic timing can imply an intrusion.

If there were any mobile transactions (wireless communications that occur between New York or Boston and Saudi Arabia, for example), security sniffers would be able to isolate them for analysis. If the sniffing was carried out on one particular user, the system would be able to detect all downloaded files from a remote server or even call up the web sites that the person has visited. The problem with such systems is that they cannot be legally used yet by the FBI because the law forbids the capture of all mobile packets. (However, the terrorist events of September 2001 have resulted in a legal expansion of this capability and have started the reduction of privacy through the monitoring of citizens in the U.S.) The FBI uses a carnivore snooping system, DCS1000, that only detects data packets on a particular person or type of information. Obviously, such security technologies could be very dangerous if they end up in the hands of criminals or terrorists. Therefore, as an added precaution, they can only work when implemented on specialized mobile commerce hardware servers with specialized security keys. Such servers are custom versions of popular mCommerce hardware suites that take the base application or database and then add a high level of security and custom code to it. That way, even if the technology reaches the wrong hands through the Internet or a wireless network, the thieves will not be able to make it work if they don't have the required custom servers and databases to process the data. However, the nature of such systems—to work based on a data-packet fishing expedition they carry out each time they are executed—raises a question: How do we handle the issue of user privacy infringement? Intelligence agencies could, for example, install a snooper black box device into a wireless ISP's network and then monitor traffic remotely. If this happens, the day is not far when an admin who is controlling such sniffer systems could tap into someone's name and receive all their mobile data, including credit card numbers, transactions, and e-mails!

Soldier-to-Soldier Messaging

Person-to-person (P2P) mobile messaging, a good example of mCommerce usage, is also being implemented within the defense sector. The U.S. military is currently researching the use of P2P wireless networking, similar to what the music-swapping service Napster used. P2P is used in real-life military combat situations, particularly to develop training technology that simulates a real-life mission. The aim is to have soldiers equipped with head-mounted displays that broadcast details of a virtual environment and transfer data between each other's mobile headsets. This would allow information to be shared directly among battlefield participants without having to go through a central command center.

NOTE: These soldier headsets can be thought of as mini-mCommerce servers hosting programs and databases that capture, process, transcode, relay, and receive wireless data.

The idea of the mobile program is to simulate an attack scenario. In other words, before a battalion goes and attacks a hill, they could run a simulation of the hill zone with scenarios that may occur—while awaiting orders. This concept of real-time planning and data-packet exchange among soldiers while at war appears to be the Holy Grail of wireless technology for the military. The soldier's headset, acting as mini-mCommerce server hardware, records relevant data that is beamed to it from the soldier's handheld, which is capturing field data at the war scene. This headset then processes the data and relays it to another soldier's headset, informing them of the state of affairs in the transmitting headset's zone. Such P2P mobile transactions are critical to the success of a war mission. However, there is the risk here of enemy soldiers tapping into this data stream or altering the transmitted data in such a way that the data being captured by the receiving soldier's headset is not the data that was relayed from the transmitting headset.

Soldiers could also capture vital data and beam it up to a server that could be synced with the defense computers at headquarters. Officials could analyze the data sent from different battalions and act accordingly, based on their consolidated analysis of data from the entire war zone, not just one field. The advancements in 3G/4G networks and 802.11 Wi-Fi technologies could make this an achievable goal.

CAUTION: In a military context, having a centralized receiving and syncing mobile server may be considered a critical point-of-failure node, because if that server gets taken out, you've got a lot of blind people with a lot of useless electronics.

Secure Group Computing

Another research area where mCommerce security is being explored in the military is secure group mobile networking. An example of this is displayed in Figure 11-3. Secure group communication management is an area of defense security research where the focus is to create a hierarchical group key distribution service that adapts to changes in network topology due to mobile users and nodes; in other words, as a military truck or tank (user) crosses (that is, joins/leaves) administrative domains, thereby causing system re-keying, the secure mobile multicast protocol minimizes the transmission outage due to this event taking place. This way, ad-hoc coalitions can securely share sensitive data.

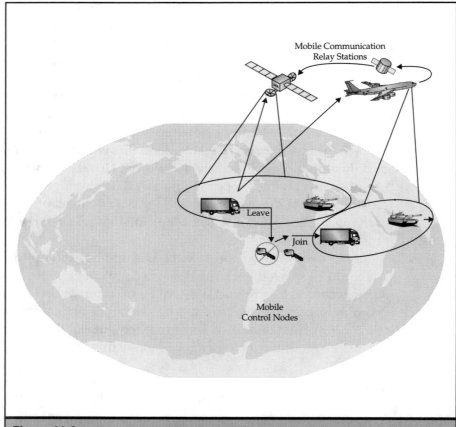

Figure 11-3.   Secure group mobile military communications management

The technology also aims to implement a secure multicast routing infrastructure that protects routing information (such as control messages) from attacks.

As the mobile Internet becomes a popular medium for conducting business among defense and military personnel, the use of encryption keys to carry out secure group discussions and/or operations also becomes increasingly important. In a commercial network, when a connection is initiated, terminal authentication is carried out by the base stations for billing purposes. In the Department of Defense's networks, mobile unit authentication by base stations ensures the legitimacy of the transmitted data. At the same time, the mobile units also authenticate the base stations to ensure the trustworthiness of the receivers. Because symmetric key authentication protocols almost always require a trusted authority, this is often a source of vulnerability.

TIP: An authentication protocol should use both the public key and symmetric key cryptographic protocols.

In addition, because encryption and authentication both depend on symmetric key cryptography, the problem of key management becomes an important issue.

CAUTION: Trusted authorities should not be blindly relied on for the distribution of group and individual keys.

The key distribution protocol should also include mechanisms for revoking compromised keys. Key update algorithms should take information such as unit identity, original group keys, and new data through the broadcast channel as parameters in the computational equation.

TIP: It is best to have a distribution protocol that distributes the initial conference keys through a trusted authority's secure channel and then periodically updates subsequent keys through broadcast channels. Alternatively, an off-the-shelf solution such as public key infrastructure (PKI) can be used as the basis for such a system.

The use of mobile communications in military and defense ranges from tactical radio communications and data management, to integrated airborne, spaceborne, and ground-based communications. Mobile image mapping and dissemination technologies are also used by many members of the intelligence community, national policy makers, military services, and other defense agencies. Most mobile devices, hardware, products, and mCommerce networks involved in defense use top military-grade encryption, key management, and host-interfacing capabilities. The U.S. government's Commercial Communications Security (COMSEC) Endorsement Program (CCEP) is the seal of the demanding military mobile security marketplace.

Solutions such as the Citadel engine, the Fidelis chip, and the Sierra reprogrammable module are examples of National Security Agency–approved, military-grade algorithms. Besides providing top encryption for wired Internet devices, the Citadel cryptographic engine also provides military-grade protection for mCommerce transactional applications with the option to use the standard Citadel high-grade algorithm or have a custom algorithm configured. All Citadel cryptographic algorithms are based on a mixed-mode, arithmetic block cipher and support both mobile communication security and transmission security functions. The solution provides half-duplex encryption and decryption. Besides Citadel, another military-grade programmable encryption option is Sierra, a solution with the capability to program Type 1, Type 2, and Type 4 algorithms and the capability to switch between them. Sierra can also run various *vocoding* algorithms, which compress voice data in digital communication.

The preceding cryptographic solutions are produced by the Harris Corporation. The company also builds an embedded military-grade security module endorsed by the National Security Agency (NSA). This Presidio key generator, embeddable module encrypts and decrypts voice and data communications, providing embeddable Type 1 COMSEC for mobile networks (the solution also works for wired networks). Another NSA-endorsed Type 1 cryptographic key generator module that can be embedded into communications equipment for COMSEC applications and encrypts and decrypts communications over mobile networks is Fidelis. The security module can also be embedded into military telephones, radios, modems, computer systems, and other defense telecommunication products, for both wired and wireless networks. For further details on these cryptographic solutions, refer to **www.harris.com**.

Scotty, Beam Me My Orders!

mCommerce technologies are rapidly being introduced in mission-critical defense operations. The following case study highlights a few such scenarios and their security implications. However, mobile devices are not being used just in the trenches. The armed forces are also gradually realizing the convenience and speed of using mobile technologies, an example of which is the U.S. Navy. Even in the most routine training missions, U.S. Navy pilots and their crews have to complete many forms and checklists before, during, and after every flight. However, some naval bases, such as the Naval Air Station in North Island (NASNI), California, are beginning to use hand-held computers in their day-to-day operations. The pilots and aircraft support personnel at NASNI use SHARP (Sierra Hotel Aviation Readiness Program), a Palm-based daily flight-tracking program to enter information such as flight times, maintenance records, and crewmen names into the system. The information the pilots enter into the hand-held computers is transferred into SHARP using Palm's HotSync feature. SHARP, which produces reports for the base and Command Naval Air Pacific, was built using Microsoft's Visual Basic platform to track operations of NASNI's air fleet, which includes advanced strike fighter aircrafts as well as unmanned vehicles.

Another system similar to this has also been deployed by the U.S. Navy guided-missile destroyer USS McFaul that uses Palm V hand-held computers across all departments of the ship. The vessel has installed infrared ports from Clarinet Systems all over the ship and deployed Aether's ScoutWare, including ScoutSync software, to link the devices into the ship's intranet, back-end business systems, and various databases. In a way, the mobile system is a client/server and mainframe solution for the ship's mobile workforce. Using the system, officers and crewmen get access to information such as the day's plan, onboard e-mail, training applications, consolidated checklists, and even HTML-based documents, thus making it a full-fledged mCommerce information access, maintenance, and processing system.

NOTE: For security reasons, infrared (IR) data transfers are restricted in certain compartments aboard the ship. The advantage of IR transfers in a military setting is that they require a line of sight between the two syncing devices, which makes it harder for spies to pick up data.

Military leaders in the U.S. Army have also been seen using an integrated mobile product called Platoon Personnel for handling their daily administrative tasks. If you are a small unit military leader and want to use this product, you can do so by installing it on both your desktop computer as well as your hand-held device, which can be from Palm, Handspring, Symbol Technologies, Sony, or any other leading provider.

NOTE: Platoon Personnel is not currently available for Pocket PC devices (as of the date of publication of this book, as mentioned by the product manufacturer).

You can use Platoon Personnel on a PC as a stand-alone, integrated data-management tool through which you can view, update, add, delete, and print information without the need for a hand-held device. However, if you have a handheld PDA, you can do the same remotely in the palm of your hand and then electronically synchronize the data to your PC. The syncing is bidirectional, meaning you can also have your data residing on your PC beamed to your PDA! Military personnel will have access to cool little features on this product. They can maintain and capture information about their soldiers and search through the records stored on the PDA. They can also generate many reports about their soldiers, such as a listing of their GT scores, promotion status, injuries, and other items. As an extra add-on to the hand-held, they can get a complimentary platoon leaders' guide, which contains current doctrines on fighting as well as checklists and memory aids for routine operations in the field and in training. For further details or to buy the product, go to **www.warriorsolutions.com**.

Case Study: U.S. Army War Reserve Logistics Management

This case study highlights the security features behind an mCommerce implementation for two U.S. Army War Reserve Mobilization Logistics Management applications.

Challenge   The challenge was to create a globally distributed database mobile application to support the U.S. Army's war reserve equipment prepositioning strategy. The use and management of data in a cost-efficient manner created a need for a commercial-ready solution. This became an mCommerce project because it required up-to-date information for tracking and delivery, and it needed to able to execute orders, which resulted in financial decisions of moving/buying/tracking inventory.

Solution   The solution was based on Sybase SQL Anywhere Studio, SQL Anywhere Studio running on 24 Windows NT–based central servers, SQL Anywhere Studio running on 2,500 Windows-based PCs, applications written in Delphi.

Results   In the past, the U.S. Army's War Reserve Support Command relied on six-month-old paper inventory reports to manage its equipment inventory logistics. Two mCommerce applications running on replicated and distributed database technologies now provide the Army with equipment inventory and readiness information that is updated every few hours to a central server in Virginia. The War Reserve Support Command can now save on logistical costs during combat mobilizations.

Discussion   The U.S. Army has intense inventory-management and maintenance requirements for all its equipment and needs to ensure their quick availability and readiness in the event of a war or for combat or humanitarian operations. This makes them a mission-critical requirement. The Army wanted a mobile application solution that would enable it to quickly dispatch brigade-size forces of 10,000 to 12,000 troops with all the equipment and spare parts they need to sustain themselves. In response to this need, two mobile applications were implemented: The U.S. Army War Reserve Deployment (AWRDS) and Automated Battlebooks Systems (ABS). Built on the Sybase SQL Anywhere Studio Database platform, these applications maintain inventory information on military equipment prepositioned in over a dozen sites in the United States, Europe, Asia, and the Middle East, as well as aboard many ships at sea. The Automated Battlebooks Systems distributed Sybase Adaptive Server application allows U.S. military personnel on land and sea, globally, to get the status on current military equipment availability and readiness. The Adaptive Server Anywhere (ASA) databases run on Windows PCs. Communication between the servers is carried out over FTP. During the inventory- management routine, the military personnel around the world enter updated information into their local ASA databases from their hand-held devices. This updated information is replicated from their local machines to the central Army War Reserve Deployment server in Virginia every few hours, using SQL Anywhere Studio's SQL Remote capability. SQL Anywhere has built-in local data encryption and server- side encryption for data syncing to mobile clients. This is a key element in any secure application.

Using the logistics-planning PDA tool, soldiers around the world can query their local or location-specific War Reserve databases to determine whether a specific piece of equipment is available and in working order. Because the War Reserve network has no direct WAN links and some of the sites are poorly connected at best, it becomes critical that the mobile application's replication solution be able to work in a batch mode without requiring the overhead of a direct database connection.

One interesting note is that a distributed database system has one key advantage that's also a disadvantage: It is dispersed among many systems. Given that this is a mobile system, a distributed system minimizes the amount of data each individual has access to in the event of compromise. On the other hand, local cached data is stored on the mobile system. This may allow the capturer of a solider carrying a mobile device access to a limited amount of data. As we saw in 2001, when Chinese planes shot down a U.S. military surveillance plane, the first action of the personnel was to destroy all data, including encryption equipment. Similarly, soldiers would need to be trained to destroy their mobile devices and the devices' contents in the event of capture. Remember, breaking encryption is difficult—not impossible.

MESSAGE FOR THE IT MANAGER

Let's examine some important points from the relevant discussions of mCommerce security in entertainment and the military, as discussed in this chapter.

Entertaining Lessons

Mobile security in the entertainment space is perhaps the most difficult of any application in the mobile world. Protecting applications and infrastructure in the mass-consumer market is always difficult because nearly every possible attack has to be considered. The best defense is to ensure good processes for code development and to ensure privacy policies are well thought out and easily accessible.

To address mobile security for the entertainment space, it is always recommended that hiring an outside, trusted firm to perform code review and/or testing should be part of any general availability of a product and/or service. In addition, regular ongoing testing should be established as a method of catching problems after release. Another useful technique is creating a developer community. Such communities not only can help a vendor spread the word about a product or platform, but can also provide ongoing feedback about various security issues.

Finally, it is important to determine the payment strategy for the game being developed. If you're developing casino-type gambling games, strong payment options must be used. This could include micropayments, smartcards, debit cards, or even credit cards. For the casual gamer (nongambling gamer), a simple addition to the service bill by the operator could be arranged for a subscription-based method of revenue.

Corporal Corporate

What can the corporate world take away from our discussion on the military space? The main lesson is that mission-critical applications can be supported through off-the-shelf mCommerce solutions, without significant compromises of security.

Specifically, a distributed database model can allow field agents (sales, marketing, consultants, and so on) to be equipped with the latest information, yet protect data in the event of compromise. Furthermore, it should be noted that security is no longer just a hacker's game—it has become a political and social vehicle for change. Corporations need to accept that fact and prepare for cyber-war and cyber-terrorism consequences. Government-sponsored hacking and intellectual property theft is a given in today's environment. Are you taking the steps to ensure your mCommerce implementation is protected in this new war?

CHAPTER 12

Security
Considerations in
Other mCommerce
Applications

The latest fad in the mobile world is the 802.11b wireless technology. This new set of standards allows for the creation of a wireless LAN. (We sometimes in jest refer to our ideal working scenario as being outdoors on the LAWN—local area wireless network.) Advantages of 802.11b wireless technology include quick setup of networks and greater mobility. We will address, at a high level, how these networks work and some key issues surrounding them.

Other applications we discuss are perhaps the least sexy apps in the mobile world, but very important for business. These applications, such as environmental and energy management, can allow for lower costs and improved efficiencies. Other traditional technologies, such as vending machines, can use new wireless capability to conduct mCommerce transactions and/or maintain inventory and distribution. This creates lower costs from the same set of merchandise. You will see that some of these applications have more security uses than others. The fundamental principal in security is that damage to an application due to a security breach is proportional to the value of the data/platform being attacked. In pure information-only systems, fewer incidents of hacking occur because the value is minimal.

802.11B WIRELESS APPLICATIONS AND SECURITY

802.11b is a wireless LAN technology that is also known as Wi-Fi in the mobile industry. Wi-Fi provides for wireless Ethernet transmission, primarily between laptops and local access nodes that attach to a standard corporate LAN. Initially, speed posed a problem; however, today's 802.11b products, which transmit in the unlicensed spectrum at 2.5 GHz, are capable of speeds of up to 11 Mbps (although, practically speaking, many networks will not achieve that speed). As technology has evolved, corporate laptop users have found it convenient to be able to move around the office (or campus) without the need for a physical LAN connection (for example, Dell laptops ship with Wi-Fi embedded). Facilities' personnel have begun to realize the benefit of not needing wires and cables when provisioning new offices or even adding new users. Universities are also becoming huge consumers of the Wi-Fi technology. With thousands of students now getting on the Internet, it poses a challenge for any university to be able to retrofit tens of thousands of

Internet connections throughout the campus, which in many cases are required in very old buildings. Some of the largest active Wi-Fi networks are now installed at American university campuses such as Stanford, the Massachusetts Institute of Technology, and Carnegie-Mellon University, allowing students to access the Internet from almost any place on campus, including the common spaces outside the buildings.

Like other technologies, Wi-Fi is working its way from the office into the home. Although home networks are still in their infancy, the benefits of a wireless architecture in the home may be even higher than at the office. It is often impossible to rewire a whole house. Another less obvious advantage is that of the aesthetic gain by installing a Wi-Fi home network rather than stringing wires halfway across the various rooms.

Having entered our homes, Wi-Fi networks are now slowly creeping into public places. In Chapter 10, we saw how mobile technologies have entered the public services and hospitality industries. Well, many airports, hotels, and restaurants are installing Wi-Fi access throughout their facilities as the underlying infrastructure upon which to build their mobile applications. Coffee houses have become places for students and researchers to meet and exchange ideas, as well as for professionals to discuss business plans. What if they could bring along their laptops and simply continue working at their café table, the way they were at home or at the office? Installing a Wi-Fi network to access the Web would be of great value in this case. Well, Starbucks aims to offer Wi-Fi access to its customers in each of its coffeehouses, thereby making its stores into Wi-Fi Cyber-Cafés!

Companies such as Newbury Networks are addressing some of these concerns in an interesting way. Newbury offers technology that breaks up security by space (through location awareness), by services (that the mobile application is capable of), and by user role (administrator, user, guest, and so on). In this manner, a solution can be created to distinguish, in a granular manner, the presence of a device and/or user and understand what access privilege that entity has.

Wi-Fi Architecture Overview

An 80211.b wireless LAN consists of two main components, as shown in Figure 12-1: a Wi-Fi access point and a Wi-Fi wireless LAN card (a PC card for notebooks or a PC card and a PCI adaptor or USB device for desktops).

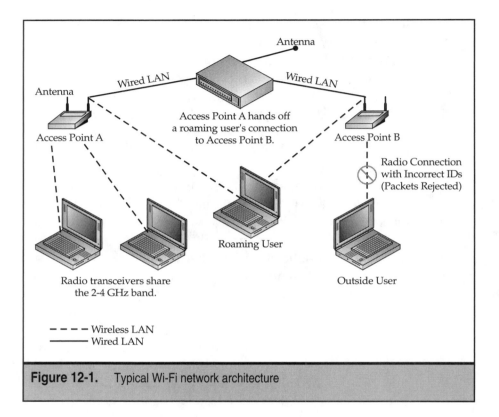

Figure 12-1.   Typical Wi-Fi network architecture

The Wi-Fi access point is a box that plugs in to the LAN on one end and communicates with the Wi-Fi LAN card–equipped notebook and/or desktop on the other. This enables the user to walk around the office campus and access whatever is on the LAN (such as e-mail, Internet, and files) as long as the user is within proximity of the access point. In the case of a desktop PC, a Wi-Fi wireless LAN enables the user to get network access into conference rooms or hard-to-wire areas. Setting up file and print share information within an office is as easy as it is for a wired LAN. An alternative to the traditional access point for a small network is the PCI card. If a desktop PC and adequate software is already available, a PCI card can be plugged in to it, and essentially the PC can be used as an access point.

Many access-point applications available will forward the data communication from one wireless computer to another. The wireless network can be extended by adding more of these access points. The access points include built-in modems that allow for the sharing of an Internet connection among multiple computers. The system also allows for the ability to connect a workgroup to the Internet. Some access points come with dual PC card slots, enabling users to double their network capacity; two PC cards can be used on different frequency channels, enabling more users to utilize a single access point. Access points also have Ethernet controllers that run at speeds of approximately 10 Mbps, half duplex, and allow for shared Internet access among many users.

Some laptops and desktops now also come preinstalled with Wi-Fi WLAN cards that can enable them to communicate wirelessly without having to utilize an access point. This way, small wireless workgroups can be set up for file and print sharing needs. As long as the stations are within range of one another, this is by far the easiest and least expensive way to set up a Wi-Fi wireless network.

NOTE: In terms of market size, Frost & Sullivan forecasts that Wi-Fi manufacturers' revenue will reach $884 million by 2002, and Cahners In-Stat Group forecasts that more than 10 million Wi-Fi products will be installed by the end of 2001.

Wi-Fi Issues

The main issue with Wi-Fi technology is that the proliferation of Wi-Fi in the corporate world has led corporations to totally bypass the security and network design practices that have been built over the last several years. Here are some other important issues the Wi-Fi technology faces:

▼ Signal interference issues

▲ Various security issues (discussed later in this chapter)

Signal Interference Issues

Weather issues can affect Wi-Fi signal strength. In addition, wet walls, tinted windows, and other similar obstacles can reduce signal strength and/or decrease network throughput. To compensate, an increased number of access points are needed with overlapping coverage.

Multipath loss, caused by obstacles in the path between a Wi-Fi client and the access point, results in lower bandwidth due to the out-of-order signals to the access point caused by timing delays when obstacles are encountered. In this case, the access point has to perform additional computations to reassemble the signals. In addition, the speed of the mobile devices also affects the throughput. This might occur, for example, in a warehouse where personnel are traveling from place to place on a forklift.

Security Challenges

Many "ethical" hacks have been done to highlight the problem of poor security in the wireless world. A number of these wireless hacks found nearly 50 percent of all Wi-Fi networks do not have any encryption enabled—not even the Wireless Encryption Protocol (WEP) standard that has been provided for the Wi-Fi networks (see Figure 12-2). As a result, some of the biggest problems with Wi-Fi applications involve the weak security inherent in the Wi-Fi protocol and the poor security practices used in setting up Wi-Fi networks.

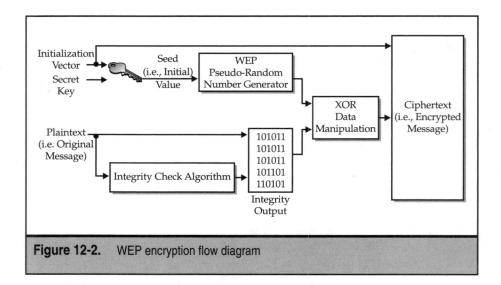

Figure 12-2. WEP encryption flow diagram

Vulnerability of Your Wi-Fi Network

How can you determine how vulnerable your network is? Try using public domain hacking software! Recent tools such as AirSnort have made it easy for hackers to sniff the wireless airways and pick up data traffic. With certain tools, real-time decryption of WEP is also possible. Other hacking tools, such as WEPCrack, can also assist in cracking Wi-Fi networks.

To set up AirSnort, you need the following items:

▼   The AirSnort kernel code (Linux based)

■   A wireless card with the Prism2 chipset

■   The PCMCIA CS software package

■   The wlan-ng software package

▲   The wlan-monitor-airsnort patch

Set up your device, compile the code, and you're off! For more details, see **http://airsnort.sourceforge.net/**.

CAUTION: Although the next version of the Wireless Encryption Protocol, WEP2 (due out sometime in 2002), may address a number of these issues, in the interim, wireless networks are not going to be very secure.

As is the nature of many security professionals, we are paid to be skeptics and discover possible issues. These professional skeptics point to many challenges, including the following:

▼   Limited authentication options

■   Default ESSID setup

■   MAC attack

■   Schlepping WEP

■   The bunny hop attack

▲   Checksum attack

Limited Authentication Options   The current standards for 802.11b provide limited authentication options. Client-based authentication can be done using a shared-key mechanism. Remote Authentication Dial-in Server (RADIUS), for example, provides for user-based authentication and is typically used today for remote access authentication and therefore can be used in conjunction with traditional VPN authentication in addition to wireless authentication.

Default ESSID Setup   One of the most basic security mechanisms in the 802.11b standards is the use of the Extended Service Set ID (ESSID). The ESSID is an alphanumeric code that is used in the access points and wireless clients in the same network. This is somewhat akin to computers being part of the same network in an NT domain. Each Wi-Fi vendor has a default name.

NOTE: The default EESIDs used are "tsunami" for Cisco equipment and "101" for 3Com equipment. Remember to change the default right away.

The first step to protect against a wireless attack is to change this ESSID to something cryptic and difficult to guess.

MAC Attack   Wireless networks have something akin to an access control list (ACL). This list is basically a list of Media Access Control (MAC) addresses of trusted and allowed systems (MAC addresses uniquely identify the nodes of a network). However, attackers could sniff out valid MAC addresses and configure their own systems to spoof those addresses.

Schlepping WEP   The Wireless Encryption Protocol (WEP) is a shared secret encryption algorithm designed to protect wireless communications. WEP can provide 40-bit (by default) or 128-bit encryption. Although you would think WEP should be run all the time, the maximum throughput on a wireless network decreases dramatically with 128-bit WEP enabled versus not using WEP at all. In addition, WEP itself has a number of flaws that make the protocol suspect to begin with.

In August 2001, the *EE Times* reported that the RC4 algorithm had been broken and, worse yet, could be cracked in less than half an hour. WEP is based on this RC4 cipher. Other ciphers are being considered for a new WEP version, but until then, WEP provides some, albeit not too much, comfort to users that their wireless networks are not being monitored by potential attackers.

The Bunny Hop Attack 802.11b uses frequency hopping to, in theory, help increase security by leaving a would-be attacker to guess at the frequency being used to transmit the data. The problem with this is that a sophisticated attacker could, in theory, record transmissions on all known frequencies for the 802.11b specification and decode these transmissions at a later time. To make this even easier, the protocol actually transmits the hopping sequence and timing of hops repeatedly. In fact, the hop frequency is relatively slow, making it even easier for attackers to predict the sequence and steal data.

CAUTION: Using frequency hopping alone is not a viable security method. It can, however, help improve signal quality and prevent degradation, as might be found with using only a signal channel.

Checksum Attack One of the most common flaws in any protocol is the ability for an attacker to change the data in the payload of a data packet and change the checksum corresponding to that data packet. By changing the data and checksum, the receiver device is lead to a false sense of confidence that the data being sent has maintained integrity. However, 802.11b does not check to see whether the data and checksum have been changed. Future versions will have some type of integrity check for the data as well as the checksum.

Wi-Fi and Wired Networks

Like hard-wired networks, Wi-Fi networks are as secure as network administrators make them. This is because of an inherent security feature of the 80211.b networks—spread spectrum modulation. For many years used only by the military for top-secret communication, this method of putting information onto the airwaves has only recently become available for civilian use and is now used wherever secure transmissions are required, including Bluetooth, wireless LAN, and wireless WAN radio transmissions. It makes the signal difficult to recover without knowing the spreading sequence code.

NOTE: At this lower layer, hard-wired networks are inherently insecure. All it takes is the phone number of a server or the location of a LAN connector to start communicating.

Compared to hard-wired networks, 802.11b networks provide additional lower-layer security features. Because of its flexible security architecture, Wi-Fi offers different security options at the link layer for a wide range of applications. These include public-oriented usage modes, such as exchanging business cards, and very secure usage modes for applications such as financial transactions and data exchange between two devices programmed to communicate only with one another.

802.11b WANs provide security at this level by utilizing carrier-provided authorization via a unique electronic serial number (ESN) and IP address assigned to each PC card. A typical 802.11b wireless LAN PC card can provide MAC address–based access control at the link layer. This allows the user to restrict access to the access point—the wireless hub based on the unique hardware ID of the wireless network interface card (NIC). If the ID of a particular NIC is not listed in the access point's address list, that NIC cannot become associated with the access point. This prevents unauthorized attempts to access a network by visitors with their own wireless devices. If a laptop is stolen or misplaced, the unit's MAC address can be quickly deleted.

802.11b networks provide data encryption immediately before the signal is transmitted over the air. Once wireless LAN access has been granted, the data is protected via 40-bit WEP encryption. Some companies are doing research to provide 128-bit encryption. Wi-Fi WLANs and WWANs can use the same upper-layer security options as their hard-wired counterparts. Protocols such as Internet Protocol Security (IPSec), Secure Sockets Layer (SSL), and application-layer logins may be employed for complete end-to-end encryption and access control. Enterprise security solutions can also be used.

The point of susceptibility for a Wi-Fi WWAN occurs when it connects to a hard-wired network, between the cellular base station and the enterprise LAN. Most IT managers don't want to open up the firewall to enable access out of the LAN. The solution is to use a virtual private network (VPN) to provide an encrypted tunnel through the corporate firewall.

The Wireless Ethernet Compatibility Alliance (WECA) is the standard governing the wireless fidelity compliance of the applications. In general, most Wi-Fi certified solutions can interoperate with one another.

ENVIRONMENTAL MONITORING AND ENERGY MANAGEMENT

Wireless technologies have played a key role in many areas of environmental monitoring and energy management. Measurement and radio transmission systems have been providing results in the logging of underground and surface water levels, current speeds, water pressure in pipeline systems, air and water quality recording, and general environment monitoring. Wireless applications carry out data logging, data transfer, and data visualization. Different sensors constantly monitor relevant environmental parameters that are transmitted to a central visualization point where the data is then analyzed. Important data, monitored by various sensors, is transmitted via remote terminal units (RTUs) to a telemetry gateway that is connected directly to a PC. The RTUs work as relay stations. Therefore, large-scale wireless measurement networks, such as one displayed in Figure 12-3, can be set up. If a relevant parameter hits a preset threshold, it triggers an alert, and the data is sent to the PC. Most environmental monitoring systems are connected to third-party systems such as weather forecasting systems, GIS mapping systems, water supply control systems, and various others.

A description of how mobile technologies are being used in various sectors of the environment and energy industries follows.

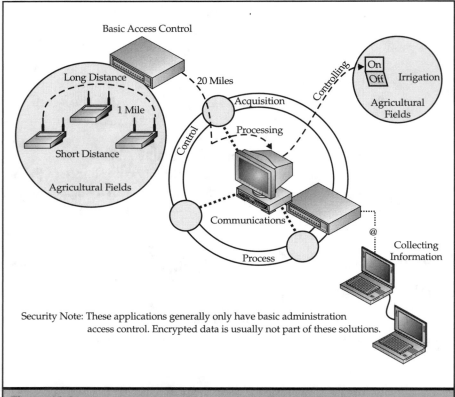

Figure 12-3. Environmental monitoring measurement network

Agriculture

Wireless technologies are used in agriculture to monitor microclimatic parameters in order to provide early pest and disease forecasting as well as detailed treatment recommendations, irrigation management, and industrial meter reading. For example, falling producer prices and rising costs of production are increasingly forcing agricultural businesses to optimize their costs. Therefore, precision farming—the selective use of inputs such as water, fertilizers, and chemicals—is now becoming a part of the agricultural process. The growing environmental awareness of consumers further accelerates this process. Wireless solutions in this sector comprise agro-meteorological measurement networks (weather stations with different sensors) with radio data transmission, combined with software-supported consulting systems that help farmers solve their day-to-day problems. The solutions help in many ways. Here are two examples:

▼ **Fighting plant disease and pest infestation**   Chemical usage can be reduced by up to 40 percent in certain cases.

▲ **Irrigation management**   By optimizing irrigation measures, water usage can be reduced by up to 30 percent while producing the same harvest.

The RTUs and sensors constantly monitor and transmit important information, such as temperature, precipitation, wind speed and direction, leaf wetness, solar radiation, soil moisture, soil temperature, and barometric pressure.

In the case of pest/disease forecasting, wireless technologies and software can calculate the infection pressure and notify the user at an early stage about the potential risk of disease outbreak. Chemical treatments can be made at the right spot and at the right time, thereby significantly reducing the amount of chemicals. The control of chemicals is done through secured auditing systems to ensure compliance with federal safety standards. In the case of irrigation management, two approaches are generally used that, when used either separately or in combination, help farmers in determining when and how much to irrigate:

▼ **Direct soil moisture monitoring with different sensors**   Soil moisture sensors and probes can be connected to RTUs. When the refill levels are reached, the user receives a wireless alert.

▲ **Calculating daily water consumption via evaporation** Water consumption probes and sensors record the rate of water consumption and evaporation, and transmit this data via remote terminal units (RTUs) to a telemetry gateway that is connected directly to a PC. The data can then be analyzed on the PC and appropriate action taken based on the results.

In addition, irrigation efficiency can be wirelessly monitored by integrating additional sensors, such as level sensors for monitoring ground or flow water and sensors for flow speed, water pressure, and conductivity. All collected data can be transmitted via radio, thus offering the possibility to choose different monitoring points. Signals can also be sent out informing the user of the opening or closing of irrigation valves.

Geographic Information System (GIS) mapping is also a powerful tool for the visualization of complex databases. A GIS is a computer system capable of assembling, storing, manipulating, and displaying geographically referenced information. In agriculture and in many other environmental and energy applications, GIS systems can provide the user with an instant and condensed overview when standard ways of data visualization might not meet the user's need. Raw data collected in the field is wirelessly exported to various GIS mapping packages. Many environmental administrating networks, such as the hundreds of weather stations, use standard GIS packages. In addition, laws in countries such as the U.S. have become more liberal over the past decade, allowing for accurate GPS uses. By waiving these security restrictions, farmers can also tap into GPS to help guide the maintenance of crops.

In general, we find that data used by farmers, especially for corporate farming, does not have a high risk for security. Because most farmers are subsidized by the government, there isn't much competitive intelligence to be gathered by viewing a particular farmer's data about his land.

Energy Meter Reading

Getting regular and online information about water and power consumption is crucial for efficient power plant and supply management. Today, important information on industrial consumers is still collected manually in large intervals—an expensive and inefficient way of operation. This has led to research in the development of sophisticated wireless systems for automatic meter reading (AMR) in cooperation with leading manufacturers of industrial meters. The

Agricultural Security Solutions

An example of a solution in this space is the IP2 Port solution, which is basically a multifunctional box. This solution provides a web server, router, and wireless access point all in one device. It has been built with applications such agricultural monitoring and systems control in mind. Users can either hardwire the box to the Internet or use its Global System for Mobile Communications (GSM) option to place the box anywhere necessary. The purpose of the box is meant to be as a bridge between the actual sensors or measuring devices and a TCP/IP-enabled network. In this manner, using standard interfaces such as web browsers, the information the sensors provide can be accessed.

The IP2 Port solution has some basic, rudimentary security protection. It uses the Password Authentication Protocol (PAP), firewall filtering for network access control, and three levels of password-protected network security.

industrial meters' pulse outputs can be connected to wireless data acquisition units, initiating a continuous flow of information, such as water or power consumption, into the data-processing center's computers.

Wireless meter reading has led to huge cost savings and more accurate billing. Part of this savings has come from allowing consumers to log on via the Internet and view/pay their bills. This provides more control for a consumer over automatic payment services (APS), in which the amount owed is deducted directly from the consumer's bank account. However, as we have seen with a number of emerging technologies, there have been glitches. In 2000, PowerGen, a large United Kingdom utility, inadvertently made available thousands of its customers' personal financial details via its site. Although precautions have been taken to avoid such problems, lack of security in this case was perceived as a lack of trust of the system.

Energy Management in the Hotel Industry

The wireless energy-management industry is offering hoteliers a wide array of alternatives and control. Stand-alone infrared energy-management sensors, digital wireless thermostats, and many other systems help save large amounts of energy within the hotel premises. Such systems can effectively control virtually every electronic or electrical appliance found in a hotel room, including lights, HVAC (heating, ventilation, and air conditioning), radio, television, telephone, and others. Occupancy-based wireless thermostats can automatically relax the HVAC when a guest leaves and then return to a comfortable temperature in a fixed amount of time upon guest arrival. Being wireless allows these smart units to be easily installed above the foot of the bed for a bird's-eye view of the room, continuing to sense and monitor even when guests are sleeping and mostly covered up and still. Such systems offer variable temperature setback in which microprocessors gauge how hard the HVAC system is working, prohibiting the setback temperature to drift above or below a point in which recovery would take more than a few minutes—unless the hotel operator wants to allow this.

Generally, security issues here are limited to a possible hacker being able to manipulate the functionality of a hotel for criminal purposes. There are plenty of cases in which hackers have been able to control airport towers, power grids, and other systems that can affect a large group of people. Most of these control systems generally have poor security, usually limited to a password-protection scheme. Sniffing or capturing the data in the system does not provide much valuable information; therefore, security is only necessary for preventing control to an unauthorized agent. Suggestions for better control include the following:

▼ The biometric lockdown of terminals to ensure that only authorized operators may access the system. This helps mitigate insider attacks or at least creates an audit trail should an inside attack occur.

■ Ongoing audits of the system and its performance to ensure unusual behavior is noted.

▲ Independent networks so that systems that control
environments in hotels are not linked to other data networks
or even the Internet. If reporting or other features are needed,
they can be manually transported from the control systems
network to other data networks. Otherwise, there is very little
reason to mix networks. In the security field, we refer to this
as "air gap protection," with the idea being that a physically
separate network has very little chance of being broken into
from the Internet.

VENDING

Wireless technologies have penetrated the vending and bottling
solutions industry, offering a range of services. In fact, over two
million bottles were tracked last year for inventory purposes using
mobile technologies in the U.S. alone. One such service utilizes
hardware, software, the Internet, and wireless networking services
to monitor and control remote vending machines. Such wireless
Internet-enabled vending information services allow its users to be
able to track and retrieve information remotely in real time about the
status of a vending machine. This capability allows vending machine
owners and product suppliers to efficiently schedule delivery routes
and detect problems such as equipment malfunctions and products
being out-of-stock before they affect end users.

Using a Wireless Data Protocol, the wireless vending system
works using Motorola's ReFLEX protocol, implemented by two-way
transceivers to seamlessly move data through a ReFLEX two-way
wireless network and onto the wireless solution provider's network
operations center.

NOTE: The ReFLEX protocol provides security via simple scrambling or
through the use of symmetric key (that is, shared key) algorithms.

The vending operators can securely interface with the network
operations center through leased lines or via the Internet to administer
the vending machines or incorporate their vending machine data

directly into their existing enterprise systems. This allows vending operators to retrieve real-time information, including sales history, inventory, maintenance indicators and alarms, and general status for any of their vending machines. Among the companies that utilize wireless vending management and information retrieval technologies is the Coca-Cola bottling company. The company uses the aforementioned wireless technology to monitor its vending machines for out-of-stock conditions, increasing replenishment rates, and out-of-service equipment.

Long a reality in some Scandinavian countries, the U.S. is now getting to the stage of installing e-commerce devices that can be attached to point-of-sale terminals such as vending machines and gas pumps. The technology enables unattended e-commerce transactions when the consumer swipes a credit card and supports micro-credit transactions for as low as $1.

This obviously leads to the idea of controlling a soda machine with a smart phone. There are device-networking software architectures being researched and implemented that integrate with standard wireless portal and application platforms to allow for the control of a soda machine with a digital smart phone—with, of course, the implication that virtually any device with a built-in processor can be controlled from afar. The WAP-enabled browser on the cell phone acts as a user interface to allow commands. The technology underlines IP-based access to any intelligent device from any mobile phone. Such mobile commerce technologies allow an 8-, 16-, or 32-bit-based electronic device to be controlled remotely over the Internet without requiring a real-time operating system or even a memory- or process-intensive TCP/IP stack in the device. There are two main components to the process: a networking software component that acts as a tiny device object server that resides on the 8-bit microcontroller in the vending machine and uses 1KB to 4KB of memory, and another component that is essentially a gateway that provides Internet connectivity to existing closed-loop and proprietary networks (in other words, it bridges large networks such as the Internet to lightweight device networks). The technology also supports alerts for outages, coin and column jams, and door openings.

Payments for Vending Machines

When mCommerce and vending machines are being discussed, the ability of being able to pay for a drink using the mobile phone springs to mind. After all, a payment mechanism must be integrated with the aforementioned architecture to be able to complete the mCommerce transaction. In general, such a transaction takes place through a clearinghouse, such as Sonera, that collects the money from the users and credits it to the service providers on a periodic basis. This system relies almost exclusively on the phone system security and billing processes. Very similar to a person denying ever making a phone call, someone could repudiate a vending machine purchase when simply using a phone number billing method. Other methods include some type of SIM or smart card (stored value) card for micropayment solutions.

To purchase a beverage through such a system, a customer simply uses their mobile phone to dial a phone number indicated on the vending machine. The drink pops out automatically and the purchase is confirmed through a short message to the customer's mobile phone. The cost of the drink is charged to the customer's mobile phone bill. This is one way of purchasing the beverage. Another way to order a product is by dialing a premium rate number, with the price set for each individual product. The caller dials a prefix given by their own operator plus a premium rate number to indicate that they want the product to be charged on a separate bill from ordinary phone calls (for example, if an employer pays for the caller's business calls but not for their leisure activities). The prefix service can be ordered from the appropriate operator. As an alternative, the caller can make an agreement that they want to pay with a credit card or direct debiting. In case of higher amounts, a PIN may be requested. Payment mechanisms and related security for mobile purchases are discussed in the banking and finance vertical section in Chapter 11.

Some vending solutions use wireless technologies to provide more than just the packet-level data security afforded by systems such ReFLEX. One vendor, United Wireless, provides application-level security (encryption) for wireless vending systems. This can allow the customer to create encrypted tunnels to track inventory supplies.

Remote Device Control Architecture

Figure 12-4 shows an infrastructure diagram for how any client can be configured to control any device (such as a vending machine) that has a microcontroller embedded in it. Generally, the microcontroller will need input from a security component to make a determination on whether to relay the signals. This security component will vary from application to application (based on the vendor).

Figure 12-4 shows five key components of a device networking infrastructure:

▼   The client application and interface

■   The Internet or a corporate WAN/LAN

■   The variety of gateway implementations

■   The device subnet, made up of protocols and physical media

▲   The network-enabled devices

Clients

As shown in Figure 12-4, there are several types of client applications. For example, designers may use web browsers, database applications, PDAs, cell phones, telephony servers, and custom applications to communicate with, monitor, and control embedded devices.

Internet or WAN/LAN

The Internet or a corporate WAN/LAN is the primary conduit between the gateway and the client applications. TCP/IP is used to communicate with the gateway.

Gateway Platforms

The gateway is the heart of the device network. It is the software bridge that connects a lightweight device networking protocol to the Internet or WAN/LAN. Microcontroller-based devices such as vending machines are controlled within such a device network. This is where, if the vendor provides the facility, security can be monitored and audited.

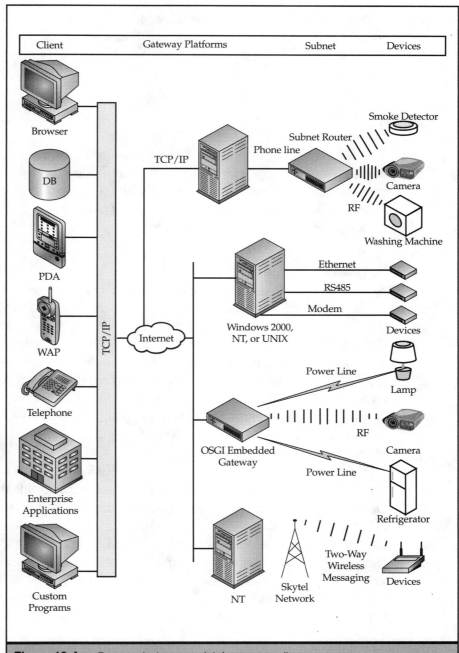

Figure 12-4. Remote device control, infrastructure diagram

Some different kinds of gateway platforms are shown in the middle of Figure 12-4. For example, AT&T runs enterprise-class gateway software on its Global Network. When using this gateway, a device connects through a modem, and users license the gateway services from AT&T.

Subnets

A subnet is the communication link between the gateway and the devices or from device to device. Most embedded devices don't communicate large chunks of data, so they usually don't need a high-bandwidth communication channel. In fact, several devices can even share communication through a subnet router.

Network-Enabled Devices

Network-enabled embedded devices differ from traditional non-networked devices in that they expose information and functionality that can be used in new ways. Examples of typical network-enabled embedded devices include household appliances, vending machines, environmental controllers, energy-management devices, and medical instruments, to name a few. These devices are typically controlled by an 8-, 16-, or 32-bit microcontroller unit. They can be slaves to an external or designated master, or they can communicate with each other in a peer-to-peer environment, depending on the capabilities of the protocol or physical media.

Generally, when referring to network-enabled devices (especially for the business sector), some type of electronic firewall is necessary. Depending on the application, a traditional firewall may be possible at the gateway; otherwise, an authentication mechanism needs to be used in each device being controlled (usually via an identification sequence). Security generally for these and similar devices is relatively low—except for vending machines, there isn't significant cash to steal.

The standards governing the device networking and wireless vending systems are emNet, SCP, UPnP, Jini, CEBus, Echonet, and EIB.

Case Study: Vending

The use of wireless technology in transferring data to and from vending machines and accepting mobile phone noncash-payment mechanisms for dispensed goods has been a popular application in countries such as Finland. The technology has caught global interest, and now companies all over the world are implementing such solutions. A major online vending services firm offers such wireless vending applications and operating systems to its customers. The system offers noncash mobile payment options, including secure credit card, debit card, PIN card, radio frequency identification (RFID) tags, and the ability to offer customers both cash and noncash payment options on one machine. The benefits of noncash mobile phone transactions include the ability to offer customers the option of selling more expensive, nontraditional items and the safety of the accruing revenue from potential theft.

The wireless vending operating system includes transaction-management software that does cash and route accounting, reconciling the vending machines to the actual sales system data, instantly transmitting the data, storing it in a database, and then exporting it directly to the customer's current system in a variety of formats. Additionally, the system offers the ability to remotely monitor in real time, the return on investment (ROI) for each individual vending asset whenever an item gets sold at the vending machine.

In general, using an electronic payment mechanism allows for greater security and better audit trails, because with physical cash, there's a large reliance on paper audits and trusted vendor maintenance personnel. Generally, billing appears as a line item on the mobile phone user's bill, for example. North American users, more than the other region of the world, have more concerns over privacy. Because cash payments do not tie a person's buying behavior to individual purchases, the use of noncash methods of payment can lead to the loss of privacy.

The system wirelessly tunes the space-to-sales for each asset to the product mix best suited to the customers buying at each location. This allows the vending machines to be adequately stocked with the best-selling product mixes, thus minimizing sold-out and overstocked conditions. Because the system wirelessly monitors the supply-and-demand shifts at the machine's point of sale, if habits change or demand surges, the operating system can adjust the mix automatically or send a wireless alert to the operator, giving the option to tune the results to their needs. For example, the system can send information to the seller regarding their machine's days of remaining inventory based on predictive sell through. Because data is transmitted with each sale, the sellers can learn about the nature of their highest-selling machines and products and wirelessly change product prices by pushing them straight from their PCs to the vending machines, to be updated instantly or with the next fill.

Security is a concern for merchants, because manipulation of information can lead to improper dispensation of goods or inaccurate relay of information to the supplier. Generally, authentication on such wireless networks is fairly poor because hacking would possibly require knowledge of the specific network carrier, the format and technology being used, and some account information. In addition, the value of the transactions is fairly low, so the actual theft would not result in much material loss. Companies such as AES Corporation have generic wireless transmission products for which vending machine inventory can be used.

The wireless nature of the transactions also helps lengthen the service cycle and reduce downtime by automatically flagging service conditions for applicable assets based on the seller's preferences. The seller has real-time wireless access to vending machine service problems and therefore can tackle the situation should one arise. The wireless vending operating system can generate inventory control and service alerts to inform the seller when and exactly how a machine needs to be serviced. Such wireless inventory control and alert services are being deployed in several programs, including the Eastman Kodak Vending Program, to realize greater efficiencies. The network infrastructure supporting such a wireless vending program is based on the networks of Motient, Weblink Wireless, and Aeris.net.

Also, as mentioned earlier, the technology of mobile phone–enabled cash-free payments for goods is becoming very popular among many corporations researching in the wireless sector. For example, NTT DoCoMo, Coca-Cola (Japan) Co. Ltd., and Itochu Corp intend to launch trials of a new system that allows users to pay for goods with their cell phone handsets, using a small number of equipped vending machines. Similar trials with mobile telephone companies in other parts of the world have been launched by Coca-Cola. An example is a service recently on the market, in collaboration with Singapore Telecommunications Ltd., that enables users to buy drinks by making telephone calls to vending machines. The price of the drinks purchased is simply added to the telephone bill. The new I-vending service in Japan is expected to be different and more sophisticated, allowing i-Mode users to load credit into electronic wallets in their telephones using the vending machines. Users can then buy drinks using this credit. The users will also be able to collect loyalty points in exchange for free drinks or promotional merchandise.

Another example involves the use of wireless technologies for the transfer of data to and from remote vending machines and power meters. By accessing wireless application services provided by a third party, companies who use vending machines to sell products will be able to access vital data about their products, such as the amount of funds collected and cans sold by a machine as well as current inventory. The companies would not even need to send a person to the machine's location. These services, known as *Remote Asset Management,* are to be offered through a joint venture between Motorola and Tecnocom. Called *T.M. Data,*

> these services are based on the ReFLEX technology, a high-speed paging protocol created by Motorola to handle wireless communications. Because the value of the data can be substantial in asset management, they will take advantage of the shared-key encryption provided by ReFLEX.

MESSAGE FOR THE IT MANAGER

This chapter has summarized a varied group of applications in mCommerce. The most important is the application of 802.11b (or Wi-Fi). The usefulness of being able to set up wireless LANs has been shown through the speed of deployment and the lowered cost of deployment. However, we have noted that there are some severe security issues with the current implementation of 802.11b. Among the security concerns are the following:

▼ A breakable WEP protocol standard, which encrypts information over the wireless network.

■ The ability to capture MAC addresses to pose as a legitimate node on the wireless network.

■ The default Extended Service Set ID (ESSID), which is preset by the wireless equipment vendor. This information can allow an easy way for a hacker to know which network name to use when joining a wireless LAN.

■ The bunny hop attack, which basically describes how predictable and slow the frequency-hopping mechanism is, thus making it effectively useless as a method of data security.

▲ Checksum integrity issues, where the data and the newly calculated checksum can be manipulated so that it isn't possible to detect a change in the integrity of the checksum.

Our recommendation is to wait for forthcoming improvements to the 802.11b standards before basing an entire corporate network on 802.11b. However, if business needs require the immediate use of such networks, PKI-related technologies should be used to provide additional security, above and beyond the minimal level provided by the 802.11b components. In addition, despite the weakness of WEP, it should nonetheless be used. Although this weak protocol will not stop a determined hacker, it will prevent the casual passerby or hacker from accessing your data.

The other applications discussed—environmental monitoring and energy management—use traditional wireless technologies and provide no significant security threats beyond what we know of wireless networks (as discussed in the previous chapters). Vending machine applications, on the other hand, have a slightly greater security threat because they serve the consumer market, and there is inherent value in the inventory. ReFLEX is a common network that can provide some basic security protections for such applications, although nothing on the order of what might be used in a PKI infrastructure.

CHAPTER 13

Bluetooth

One of the challenges in the mobile field is the need to perform specialized functions, yet with strict form factor and power consumption requirements. As a result, most individuals have many specialized mobile devices. A corporate professional, for example, may have a PDA, a mobile phone, and a laptop. When traveling, carrying all three devices is quite burdensome, and the challenge of keeping all three devices in sync is even more difficult. Solutions such as infrared ports and web synchronizing can be employed to attempt to keep the devices all connected.

The problems inherent in the use of multiple devices and the desire for a wireless solution led to the creation of Bluetooth—an architecture that allows devices to communicate within a specified physical range of each other through radio frequency (RF) signals. Bluetooth can allow for a mobile phone to look up a number from a PDA stored in a person's jacket pocket, for example. It also allows for useful applications such as cordless headsets and cordless PC accessories.

NOTE: Bluetooth was named for the 10th-century Danish King Harald Blatand (a.k.a. Blue Tooth), who united the modern day countries of Denmark and Norway. This unification is a symbolic representation of what is proposed for specialized mobile devices—a way to unify all devices through a common mode of communication. The original concept was started by Ericsson as a way using a hands-free and cord-free headset with a mobile phone up to 10 meters away.

One of the reasons Bluetooth may have success in wide adoption (although not necessarily *quick* adoption) is that it draws from existing sets of standards, and it mixes and matches these as needed. Standards such as TCP/IP, WAP, and PPP are integrated with the Bluetooth specification. Bluetooth provides the basic underlying architecture; then, developers can pick the set of protocols to design their applications, as shown in Table 13-1. The Bluetooth Special Interest Group (SIG) has identified a number of usage profiles that specify the protocols and structure required for particular applications.

Application	Description	Protocols Required
File transfer	Transfer files from one device to another	OBEX, RFCOMM, SDP, and L2CAP
Intern bridge (remote modem)	Use a mobile device, such as a phone, to connect to the Internet.	AT commands, PPP, SDP, RFCOMM, and L2CAP
LAN access	Access a LAN	IP, PPP, SDP, RFCOMM, and L2CAP
Synchronization	Sync data between a mobile phone and a PDA	IrMC, OBEX, SDP, RFCOMM, and L2CAP
Smart connecting phone	Use the same phone as a mobile, residential phone, and office phone, making the calls from the appropriate base to maximize bill savings potential	TCS-BIN, SDP, audio stack, and L2CAP
Mobile headset	Wireless headset for mobile phone	AT commands, RFCOMM, SDP, audio stack, and L2CAP

Table 13-1.   A Survey of Applications and Protocols Required (Based on "Bluetooth Protocol Architecture," Version 1.0, August 1999)

This chapter will cover the highlights of the Bluetooth architecture and focus on the security elements. Although there are many details to the Bluetooth architecture, this chapter will keep a high-level view of the main components. The intent of this chapter is to make you aware of the basic components and possible opportunities and weaknesses of the architecture. In this manner, you can decide what applications Bluetooth may be suited for within your particular organization. One other note to keep in mind for any emerging technology: standards and market potential change quickly. Therefore, establishing details of such an emerging technology in a published book is always risky. You are encouraged to supplement and update your knowledge of the Bluetooth architecture and its security elements from various sources, including the Bluetooth SIG.

ARCHITECTURE OVERVIEW

Bluetooth uses a concept known as a *piconet*, which could be described as a personal area network (PAN). This PAN has a range limited to 10 meters from the Bluetooth device. The 2.4 GHz range allows multiple Bluetooth devices to be in the same PAN because they hop different frequencies in different sequences. These piconets can merge into what's called a *scatternet*, which can consist of up to ten piconets and act as a electronic bridge between networks.

Bluetooth Core Components

The Bluetooth technology is broken down into the following key components:

▼ Radio unit

■ Baseband unit

■ Link Management Protocol (LMP)

■ Logical Link Control and Adaptation (L2CAP)

▲ Service Discovery Protocol (SDP)

These pieces are shown in Figure 13-1.

Radio Unit

Bluetooth devices operate on a multihopping frequency mode over the 79 defined frequencies in the industrial, scientific, and medical 2.4 GHz band range. A time-duplex division (TDD) method is used for transmission that provides a full-duplex speed of up to 1 Mbps. This hopping is spread-spectrum technology that transmits data over multiple frequencies at one time, switching frequencies up to 1,600 times per second. The frequency hopping is regulated by an internal software switch based on the particular country's regulations, although

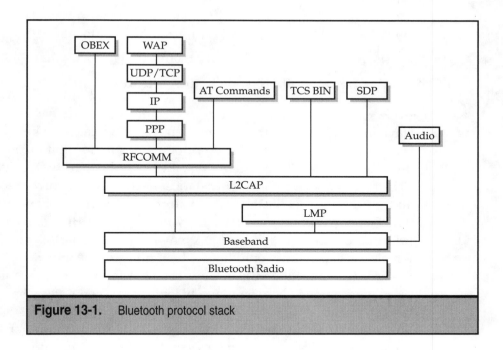

Figure 13-1. Bluetooth protocol stack

the vast majority of countries allow for the 79 hops. Currently, the range between devices extends up to 10 meters. However, it is possible, by using the baseband unit and/or increasing power consumption, to link Bluetooth networks to extend this range much farther.

Baseband Unit

The link controller (LC), as defined in the Bluetooth specification, is the hardware that performs the actual RF transmissions and performs the Link Manager (LM) routines. The LM provides the method for setting up and tearing down links between Bluetooth devices.

When two or more devices are present, one Bluetooth device acts as the master, and the other devices act as slaves. The master device dictates the frequency-hopping characteristic. The link processor part of a Bluetooth device conducts the following tasks:

▼ Does the voice-to-data conversion

■ Performs packet segmentation

- Enables master/slave communication protocols
- Allows devices to identify themselves to each other
▲ Controls authorization to these devices

One area of weakness occurs when a master device becomes a slave in a piconet. For the information from the master to be transferred to the slave, all encryption must stop for that piconet in order for this transfer to occur. Say, for example, that two devices (a PDA and a mobile phone, for instance) need to be synchronized at all times. A user walks through an airport and wants to have both his PDA and mobile phone in sync with, say, the airline departure information. In this case, the PDA may be the master of its piconet, which consists of only one slave—the mobile phone. However, as the user walks through the airport, the PDA (and, thus, the mobile phone) becomes a slave on many piconets and then reverts back to being a master once its out of range of these other piconets (such as the airline departure information network). During the master-to-slave switching, any syncing between the PDA and the mobile phone will not be encrypted, so other people in the airport piconet could potentially pick up information, such as phone numbers, from the mobile phone.

Bluetooth devices can switch to several different power states to conserve power. As a result, a set of protocols has been developed to manage multiple devices in a piconet with differing states of power conservation. The two main states are *standby* and *connect*. Other substates exist for intermediate functions. The two substates we will address are the *page scan* and *inquiry scan*. A page scan checks for the Device Access Code (DAC) and sets up a link between devices. An inquiry scan checks for the Inquiry Access Code (IAC), which helps determine what devices are in range and the devices' addresses.

An inquiry scan will check for one of four states: *active, hold, sniff,* and *park*. Active implies the device is active and transmitting. In this state, the master synchronizes with the slaves. Through the use of a Active Member Address (AM_ADDR), the master can handle up to seven other (active) slaves. Additional slaves will not be given an AM_ADDR and therefore are not considered active and cannot participate in the piconet. Hold indicates the device is in a lower power state usage but can still retain its AM_ADDR and flip to an active state. This mode is also used to perform page and inquiry scans. A sniff state keeps the AM_ADDR and simply reduces the cycle time it uses to check for the slave's listening activity. Finally, the park state gives up the AM_ADDR and is assigned a Parked Member Address (PM_ADDR). The park state allows for sharing of a piconet with a greater number of devices. A park state device can still synchronize to the frequency channel and listen to broadcast messages.

Link Management Protocol (LMP)

LMP's responsibility is to set up connections and implement security tasks such key exchanges and encryption. In addition, LMP controls the power modes and connection states of devices in a piconet.

Logical Link Control and Adaptation (L2CAP)

The Logical Link Control and Adaptation (L2CAP) layer manages the upper-layer protocols over the baseband component. This layer manages services to the higher layers with various types of data manipulation, including segmentation and reassembly. Specific tasks that L2CAP manages include the following:

▼ **Multiplexing**   Allows multiple software applications to use a single link between two devices.

■ **Packet segmentation and reassembly**   Due to the differing requirements of packet sizes among the layers, L2CAP creates the appropriate-sized packets.

▲ **Quality of service (QoS)**   L2CAP makes QoS checks to ensure requested services can be performed over the established link.

L2CAP's possible actions can be broken into five categories:

▼ Requests and confirmations from lower layers

■ Higher-layer requests and responses

■ Data from peers (other L2CAPs)

- Requests and responses from peers (other L2CAPs)

▲ Timer-related events (for example, deciding when to stop trying to contact a device)

Service Discovery Protocol (SDP)

The Service Discovery Protocol (SDP) queries for the type of Bluetooth device and the characteristics it may offer. After SDP finishes its job, communication can be established between devices. Only a master device needs SDP because master devices seek out joining slave devices. Slave/client-only devices do not need SDP, and there is only one SDP server per Bluetooth device. An SDP server may perform services on behalf of multiple applications on the same device that may require SDP services.

SDP creates a service record to track what service attributes are associated with what service. Some service attributes may include the following:

▼ **ServiceID** Identifies a particular instance of a service

- **IconURL** Refers to the URL associated with an icon to represent a service offering

▲ **ServiceName** The human-friendly name for the service offering

As you can see, the number and types of services can be extended to include many different things. As a result, the SDP architecture allows for a group of services. This grouping is called a *browse hierarchy*, as shown in Figure 13-2. In a browse hierarchy, the top root of the tree, called the *public browse root*, has subtrees of information.

Network Topology

When multiple Bluetooth devices are in range of each other, one becomes the master and the others are slaves. As mentioned previously, this miniature wireless network is called a *piconet*. A piconet can be defined as at least one Bluetooth master with one or more slaves all sharing the same hopping frequency (that is, they are

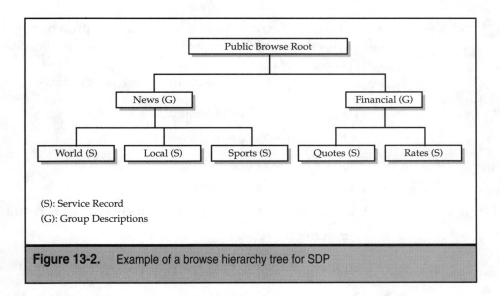

Figure 13-2.   Example of a browse hierarchy tree for SDP

all synchronized to the same channel). Several connected or overlapping piconets are called a *scatternet*. Each piconet maintains its own unique frequency-hopping sequence through its respective master. This overlap can actually allow a device in one piconet to be the master and allow the same device to be a slave in another piconet. A scatternet of up to ten piconets with the maximum number of slaves can provide up to 6 Mbps of bandwidth.

SECURITY OVERVIEW

As with any mobile devices, Bluetooth devices must have strong security to be adequately and safely used. A breach of security could happen in a public place such as an airport, for example. A hacker may come within 10 meters (obviously, very easy in an airport) and access a Bluetooth device without the victim even realizing it. Bluetooth was designed to contain certain key elements around its security architecture. We will focus on the Security Manager and Link Manager components of the security architecture.

Bluetooth addresses security at the link level, offering authentication and encryption. The basis of this link security is the use of a secret link key shared between two communicating devices. A procedure is defined to generate this shared key the first time the devices communicate in the initialization phase of communication.

The general flow of an initialization phase is as follows:

1. The initialization key is generated.
2. Authentication occurs if necessary.
3. The link key is generated.
4. The link key is exchanged.
5. Encryption key generation occurs if encryption is required.
6. Communication begins.

To be precise, at the lower link layer, four key elements are used:

▼ **The device address (BD_ADDR)**   A 48-bit address that identifies each Bluetooth device uniquely

■ **Private link key**   A 128-bit random number used for initial authentication

■ **Private encryption key**   An 8- to 128-bit number used as the basis for encryption

▲ **RAND**   A 128-bit random number

Link Keys

Four types of link keys may be used to cover the various applications: *combination, unit, temporary,* and *initialization.* The combination key is used to devise a link key from two devices, and a new one is generated each time a new pairing of devices is created. The unit key is created when the device key is installed and stored in nonvolatile memory. In the event of a broadcast, a master key is used. The master key is used to establish a common link key among multiple devices in an encrypted broadcast. The initialization key is used when two devices discover each other for the first time. This key is derived from various inputs, such as the device address (BD_ADDR), a random number, and a PIN code. In essence, PIN codes are used to generate the link key, which is used for authentication. Then, the encryption is generated from the link key. Link keys are 128-bit randomly generated numbers and can be temporary or semi-permanent. An overview of this architecture is provided in Figure 13-3.

Security Modes

Security can be broken down into security for devices and security of services. As defined in the generic access profile, a Bluetooth device may use three security modes: security modes 1, 2, and 3.

Security Mode 1

This mode is the least secure of the three and forgoes any security procedures. This is considered a discovery or promiscuous mode, because it allows other devices to initiate connections with it. This mode is, obviously, not recommended for use at all times. Such a mode may be useful during testing phases, but not in most production scenarios.

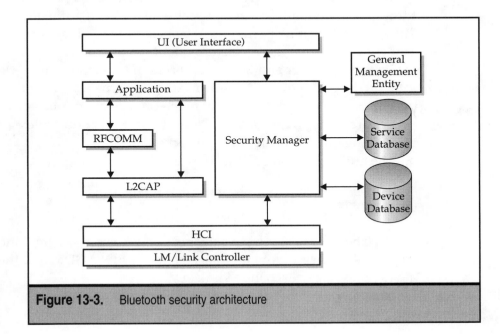

Figure 13-3. Bluetooth security architecture

Security Mode 2

In this mode, security is enforced after the link has been established between the Bluetooth devices at the L2CAP level. Security can be handled through flexible security policies using application-level controls in parallel with the lower Bluetooth protocols. This mode is also referred to as *service-level administrated security*. Basically, this mode establishes security after the channel has been established.

In this mode, two trust modes can be established: *trusted* and *untrusted*. Trusted devices are paired devices that allow for unrestricted access to services. Untrusted services, by contrast, may allow for temporary relationships but not permanent ones. In addition, the untrusted mode restricts access to services.

A trusted mode status is achieved during the initial registration communication of the devices. One of three attributes can be flagged to determine the level of trust: *authentication, authorization,* or *encryption.*

Authentication   Authentication determines the identity of the device making the request. Remote devices must be authenticated before a connection can be established. Authentication can be performed through a stored link key or by specifying a PIN. If authentication fails, a preset waiting period must be passed to reinitiate the authentication process. Each subsequent waiting period is increased exponentially. After another fixed period of time, the waiting time interval drops down until it returns to the original fixed waiting period. Such a method can allow for error-correction time and/or prevent repeated malicious attempts of authentication (for example, by slowing down a brute-force attack).

The authentication scheme goes as follows:

1. A random number is generated by the verifier.

2. A random number is sent to the remote device.

3. The remote device and the host device run the same function using the random number, the host's BD_ADDR, and the previously exchanged link key.

4. The host device determines whether the response sent back by the remote device matches the number it received when it ran its function.

5. If the response from the remote device matches what the host device arrived at, the devices are authenticated.

Authorization   Authorization is the concept of deciding whether a remote device can have access to particular services. Access is automatically granted to trusted devices and can be granted to untrusted devices after an authentication procedure. Authorization always requires authentication.

Encryption   The link must be encrypted before communication can continue. Data in a piconet is sent via data packets. The basic structure of a packet (for connection-oriented applications) consists of an access code, header, and payload. The payload is encrypted to protect user information. However, the access code and header are not encrypted. Encryption takes place with a stream cipher that is resynchronized on every new payload. Although not recognized for highly secure applications, this stream cipher can be used for most basic applications.

An interesting note is that the encryption size is negotiated between the two devices. This, of course, leaves security risks open if the Bluetooth architecture is poorly implemented, because a lower encryption key length may be accepted. Because the key length may be as low as 8 bits, it becomes trivial to crack the encryption for such small keys. However, to prevent a fraudulent device from initiating a weak session, the encryption key length can be rejected by the host device, if the length is determined to be too small. In addition, by separating the key used for authentication from the key for encryption, one can achieve a smaller encryption key without compromising the strength of the initial authentication procedure.

If no registration has taken place, then by default authorization and authentication are required for incoming communications; for outgoing communications, authentication is required by default.

Encryption can take place in one of two modes, with a slave in possession of a semi-permanent key, such as a unit or combination key:

▼ **Mode 1**   No encryption.

▲ **Mode 2**   No encryption for broadcast traffic but encryption for device-to-device communication.

Encryption can take place in one of three modes, with a slave in possession of a master key (a type of key that can replace the current link key during an initiated session):

▼ **Mode 1**   No encryption.

■ **Mode 2**   Point-to-point encryption (in other words, device to device).

▲ **Mode 3**   All traffic, including broadcast traffic, is encrypted.

Security Mode 3

In this mode, the security controls are set up at the baseband level, before any connections are set up. The Security Manager component imposes these policies on the LMP. This can also be described as *link-level security*. In this mode, security is determined before a link can be established (versus establishing security after the link has been established, as in mode 2).

Three types of actions may be taken for services:

▼ Authorization and authentication are required. In this case, trusted devices get automatic access, whereas other devices need a manual authorization.

■ Authentication only is required.

▲ Neither authentication nor authorization is required.

Security policies can be defined to allow trusted devices access to certain services rather than all services. This allows for a very granular approach to security, which is important for good, flexible systems.

Security Manager

The component in the Bluetooth architecture that handles the implementation of the security features described previously is the Security Manager. In simple terms, the Security Manager decides what security policies are to be implemented based on a connection request from a device. The security service type, the device type, and the level of trust of the device helps the Security Manager decide whether to enforce authentication, encryption, both, or none.

The Security Manager is responsible for several tasks:

▼ Storing security-related information for devices and services

■ Responding to access requests by other applications

■ Enforcing authentication, authorization, and/or encryption

▲ Initiating pairing and PIN input (either by the user or another application)

To manage decisions, the Security Manager accesses databases, as shown in Figure 13-4, to determine policy decisions. The two key databases that the Security Manager accesses are the device database and the service database. The device database stores the device type, trust level, and link key. The service database stores the authentication, encryption, and authorization criteria for each service. Note that access granted to a particular service on a device does not grant express permission on the same device to other services. For this reason, the service database is important in keeping track of what can be accessed and by whom. The service database and device database attributes are shown in Table 13-2 and Table 13-3, respectively.

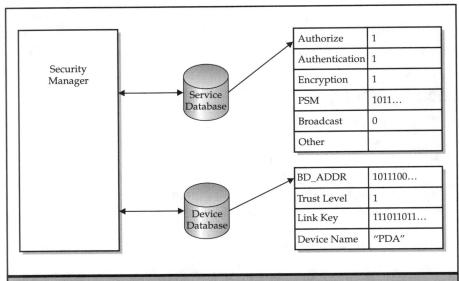

Authorize	1
Authentication	1
Encryption	1
PSM	1011…
Broadcast	0
Other	

BD_ADDR	1011100…
Trust Level	1
Link Key	111011011…
Device Name	"PDA"

Figure 13-4. Security Manager interacts with databases to make policy decisions

Attribute	Requirement	Description
Authorization Required	Mandatory	Indicates whether authorization is a requirement
Authentication Required	Mandatory	Indicates whether authentication is a requirement
Encryption Required	Mandatory	Indicates whether this link must be encrypted
PSM	Mandatory	The identification of the channel

Table 13-2. Service Database Used by Security Manager

Attribute	Requirement	Description
Broadcasting Allowed	Optional	Indicates whether sending messages to all devices in the piconet is allowed
Other routing information	Conditional	Not used yet

Table 13-2. Service Database Used by Security Manager *(continued)*

According to Thomas Muller's "Bluetooth Security Architecture" (Version 1.0., July 15, 1999), here are the general steps the Security Manager follows when a device requests a connection with another device:

1. The device requests a connection.
2. The request is sent to L2CAP.

Attribute	Requirement	Description
BD_ADDR	Mandatory	The unique ID number of the Bluetooth device
Trust Level	Mandatory	Indicates whether the device is trusted or untrusted
Link Key	Mandatory	The bit-level description of the link key
Device Name	Optional	A string (text) description of the device

Table 13-3. Device Database Used by Security Manager

3. L2CAP requests access from the Security Manager.

4. The Security Manager checks the information request against the device and service databases.

5. The device may be asked for further authorization and/or authentication, depending on the contents of the service and device database entries.

6. An untrusted device may have its connection terminated or require authorization. Application-level security may be invoked for schemes such as username/password. Other authentication schemes can be built in through the Security Manager.

7. If the service requires link encryption, keys will be exchanged, as defined at the L2CAP level.

An exception to the preceding flow occurs if the device is in security mode 3. In this case, the Security Manager instructs the LMP to directly require authorization and optionally encryption before the connection to the desired service can be established.

WAP IN BLUETOOTH

Bluetooth has several applications available, such as a wireless headset; however, we will focus on how WAP relates to Bluetooth because WAP is an important part of mCommerce.

Considering the original concept behind Bluetooth was to enable mobile phone–related features, it is important to take some time to understand how WAP will work with Bluetooth. Because WAP was designed for Internet access over a cellular network, given a small form factor, it has specific requirements. Some features of using Bluetooth with WAP include the ability to connect to a local Internet gateway versus a cellular connection. Imagine an airport scenario where Bluetooth kiosks may be set up. Given that piconets may relay each other's communications, it is possible that an area of an airport (for example, a boarding/waiting area) could provide a piconet for Internet access because the piconet would connect to a WAP or similar gateway. This would allow the user to have a good connection without interference (as is the case with cellular in tunnels, airports, and other communication-impaired/limited areas) as well potentially save money by not having to roam or otherwise pay cellular charges. Another feature is the ability to seamlessly traverse piconets and cellular networks. With a mobile phone, a user may be on a piconet one minute, then on a cellular network the next, and then back in another piconet, without ever losing her Internet connection.

In a typical WAP protocol stack, as shown in Figure 13-5, Bluetooth will be positioned as a WAP bearer (as noted at the bottom of the diagram). In order to handle the ability for a WAP client to move into and out of a piconet seamlessly (that is, transitioning from a piconet to a cellular network, or vice versa), management of IP addresses must be done carefully.

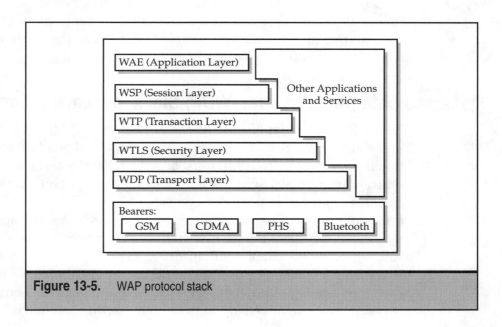

Figure 13-5.   WAP protocol stack

Discovery of Services

The following items need to be discovered by the Service Discovery Protocol (SDP) about the WAP server/gateway:

▼ **Server name**   The name readable by the user.

■ **Server home page document name**   The URL of the start page.

▲ **Server/proxy ability**   To determine whether the WAP server is a content server or proxy. If it is a proxy, URLs not local to the server must be resolved.

Connection Methods

For a PDA/mobile phone to travel from within a piconet range to outside that range and maintain a connection through a cellular network, an IP address must be passed to the device before it exits the piconet. Alternatively, the Bluetooth server may constantly poll the piconet to determine whether a WAP-capable device is in range. If the device is in range, the server may initiate a connection. The server, in this case, would then be able to determine the client name and client capabilities through SDP.

Wireless Datagram Protocol (WDP) Stack Implementation

The WDP Management Entity (WDPME) is a protocol (layer) in the WAP stack structure that handles service requests. For a Bluetooth implementation, the WDPME must be able to handle asynchronous notifications for new client/server node detections, client/server signal loss, and server push detections.

In order to find a particular piece of content (say, a web page) using WAP, the client device first identifies the proxy or gateway available. Next, the client would use SDP to present the user with the servers available. The user then selects a server, and WAP pulls down the web page from that server. Subsequent page navigations are based on the relative path of the initial, starting web page.

This feature also enables the ability to provide location-based advertising or information, without the trivial knowledge of the exact location of a device (and therefore the person), because the granularity can be confined to a distance of a scatternet.

SECURITY WEAKNESSES

Despite attempts to account for security threats, every protocol or standard will have its share of weaknesses. Bluetooth has been widely recognized as incorporating some basic security features in its architecture. The ability to add applications should supplement those features to provide a more reasonable security capability.

PIN Weakness

Because authentication is based on an initial key exchange, the PIN length, as an input into the key-generation process, determines the level of trust that can be achieved. If this initial exchange is done using a PIN, the security is limited in two ways: First, the PIN is usually four digits long, leaving a relatively small space in which to guess the PIN. Second, if the PIN is human generated, trivial PIN codes such as "1234" are possible. This could lead to unintended authorization of a hacker device.

Impersonation

On mobile phones that employ Bluetooth, it is possible for hackers to "datajack" a mobile phone connection and make calls through someone else's phone. A hacker can scan the air for the electronic serial number (ESN) and the mobile identification number (MSN). Then the hacker simply needs to modify the Bluetooth packet frames that refer to the member address (to identify the device in a piconet), the ack (acknowledgement bit), and the error check bit (to make it appear the transmission was not altered). This would lead to a piconet believing that a hacker mobile phone was the intended target and allow the hacker to use the phone.

Replay Attacks

Although not highly likely, it is possible to record a communication between two Bluetooth devices. Given that up to 79 possible frequencies are in use (and in a few countries, fewer than that), all frequencies would have to be recorded. Later, the hopping sequence of those frequencies would then need to be figured out. If all this could be done, the attacker could repeat a particular transaction. For example, an authorization to transfer funds from one account to another could be repeated in its entirety.

Man in the Middle

Because keys are exchanged in the open air, it may be possible, especially in initial key exchanges, that an attacker can intercept sending and receiving communication. As a result, an attacker could intercept the communication potentially without either the sender or recipient knowing about it. There is no concept of certificates at the Bluetooth core architecture level. Therefore, a key exchange is solely dependent on a proper initial authentication and secret communication of the initial exchange between the two devices.

Hopping

In theory, if an attacker could predict the hopping sequence established between master and slave devices, the attacker could then easily intercept communication. Although the Bluetooth specification does have the ability to introduce the concept of a nonpredictable frequency-hopping selection scheme, it is possible to break, as noted by Markus, et al in a paper titled "Security Weaknesses in Bluetooth" (February 19, 2001).

Location Attack

It is possible to determine the geophysical location of a Bluetooth device. Because devices must have (globally) unique identification numbers, it is possible to track a particular device, such as a PDA or mobile phone, and the individual associated with that device. Such an attack would require the placement of many node devices that query a piconet for a device's identification number. This might be practical for an airport location or government organization in governmental espionage.

Denial of Service

The infamous attack method of the '90s that took down marquee web sites will most likely remain the favorite method of attack in the future. Because a piconet relies on communication and control of power states to manage many Bluetooth devices, it is important that the piconet maintain proper control. A denial of service (DoS) attack may occur if transmission frequencies are jammed. It is possible to jam all the known 1,600 possible frequencies that devices use (the ISM frequency ranges are unlicensed currently). In addition, given that the header and access codes are not encrypted, there is a very small opportunity for the hacker to manipulate and impersonate a device.

Another angle of the DoS attack can occur during the authentication process between two devices. In this process, a device must prove its identity to the master. If authentication fails, the waiting period is increased exponentially. However, it is left up to the implementer whether the design includes a list of all the devices that have attempted authentication or are in the process of authentication. Such a list would avoid having to field repeated requests from a group of devices that would be attempting to launch a DoS attack. If we are to take this scenario one step further, even with a list of devices attempting to authenticate, the list is limited to memory capacity. If Bluetooth devices happen to drop significantly in price, it may be possible to set up a large array of devices to force such a list to take up maximum available memory and/or force the computational ability to slow to the point of being unusable. In addition, based on the piconet/scatternet concept, a Bluetooth distributed DoS (BDDoS) attack may also be constructed in which multiple DoS attacks from various piconets are centered on device(s) in a common scatternet.

BLUETOOTH COMPATIBILITY

One of the dangers of emerging technologies such as Bluetooth is that various vendors will create their own set of standards. Such an approach may lead to interoperable devices, devices that are not secure, and market confusion. Bluetooth has incorporated a solution to this problem by introducing the Bluetooth Qualification Program (BQP). The BQP has been designed to test products against a common set of criteria. Typically, vendors will need to be part of the Bluetooth community and will present their products to the Bluetooth Qualification Review Board. Once the product has been qualified, it is listed on the official Bluetooth Qualified Product list.

BLUETOOTH VS. WI-FI

As mentioned in Chapter 12, the IEEE 802.11b (also known as Wi-Fi) standard for wireless LANs provides transmission rates up to 11 Mbps (with fallback to 5.5, 2, or 1 Mbps) at radiated power levels up to 100 megawatt (mW) using Direct Sequence Spread Spectrum (DSSS) modulation. The Bluetooth standard for wireless networks allows transmission rates up to 1 Mbps at power levels up to 1 mW using Frequency Hopping Spread Spectrum (FHSS) modulation. Both operate in the unlicensed 2.45 GHz industrial, scientific, medical (ISM) band, which is available around the world. The similarities end there—both technologies share the same band, but at different power levels and using different forms of spread spectrum modulation. (Both types of spread spectrum modulation serve to minimize interference from other users in the same band.) One of the main problems is that ISM is an unregulated frequency. An 802.11b LAN consists of a fixed access point (wireless hub), which is usually connected to a wired backbone and up to 63 associated wireless stations (STAs) in the form of PC cards or NICs installed in workstations. The combination of the access point and its associated STAs is referred to as a *basic service set* (BSS). The range is up to 90 meters in a typical office setting, depending on the environment and obstacles, such as concrete walls and metal structures. Throughput varies with the distance to the access point (AP) and the number of users. A Bluetooth piconet consists of a least two Bluetooth devices that are capable of establishing at least a point-to-point link. These could be desktop PCs, handheld devices, laptops, cell phones, printers, and so on.

NOTE: Both 802.11b and Bluetooth have extensive error checking and the ability to retransmit packets if an error occurs. Therefore, even if there is interference, the only consequence may be decreased throughput and not necessarily loss of data.

ALTERNATIVES TO BLUETOOTH

Because Bluetooth has been designed as a wireless protocol that can allow devices within a physical proximity to communicate, it faces competition with other methods (as show in Table 13-4). The economic impact Bluetooth will have on other methods of wireless communication has and will continue to be debated.

802.11b is a wireless protocol that can allow PCs to communicate over a wireless network with bandwidth that is nearly ten times faster than Bluetooth. IrDA is designed for communications between devices using infrared spectrum light. IrDA does require a line of

Network Type	Max. Data Bandwidth	Range	Relative Cost	Availability
IrDA	16 Mbps	< 2m	Cheap	PCs, PDAs, and mobile phones
802.11	2 Mbps	50m	Moderate	Various network cards
HomeRF	1.6 Mbps	< 10m	Moderate	Select availability
Bluetooth	1 Mbps	< 10m	Moderate	Various and emerging devices

Table 13-4.   Relative Comparison of Bluetooth and Alternatives

sight in order to communicate, but it can be faster than the Bluetooth bandwidth. Finally, HomeRF allows for multiple communication devices, such as multiple cordless phones, within a residence.

All these alternatives may become more widely adopted due to the higher bandwidth they provide. However, Bluetooth was designed for lightweight, small devices with minimal power consumption. Once the cost of Bluetooth devices falls, Bluetooth will have a clear advantage for short, mobile communications.

3G VS. BLUETOOTH

With the promise of 3G around the corner (perhaps around the perpetual corner), is it possible that 3G services may preclude the need for Bluetooth services? The purpose of 3G is to enable high bandwidth, "always-on" access for mobile devices. However, if we examine this issue a bit closer, we find that there actually may be room for both emerging areas.

Because Bluetooth is limited to a 10-meter range, it implies that the user of the mobile device is within physical proximity of a particular location. In the applications of location-based advertising, this makes Bluetooth cheap and useful. In order to use location-based services, a number of infrastructure-level components must be in place. Another advantage of Bluetooth over 3G is that it will more than likely be cheaper. Although the Bluetooth devices may initially be expensive, the network communications will be free. By contrast, 3G networks will most likely charge a premium when they are fully rolled out (to recover build-out costs).

3G will, however, still take center stage for high-end applications requiring bandwidth because 3G networks provide roughly twice as much bandwidth. This type of bandwidth will allow for basic video and multimedia capabilities. In addition, advertising that provides more details will need to use 3G networks. Machine-to-machine and similar telemetry applications will still belong to 3G due to speed and bandwidth capabilities, in addition to being available over a wider distance.

In conclusion, Bluetooth will still most likely be pervasive in the consumer sector, whereas 3G will most likely dominate in the business sectors.

THE TOOTH FAIRY

As is the case with many emerging technologies, the lack of mass adoption keeps the cost prohibitive. Bluetooth is currently still quite expensive for the devices it is being targeted for. A wireless headset for a mobile phone may run on the order of $200, which may exceed the sale price of the phone itself. However, steps to reduce the expenses involved with Bluetooth production, including a single chip with all Bluetooth functionality, are underway. In addition, the fact that Bluetooth may be used not just in mobile devices but also in fixed devices, such as desktop PC peripherals, makes its appeal much wider.

To some degree, commercial adoption may also take some time (see Table 13-5 for some examples). Due to the rules and regulations of various frequencies, there are differing requirements among countries as to how the Bluetooth frequency range can be used (although Spain remains the only country to this date not embracing the full standard, whereas Japan and France allowed the full spectrum back in January of 2001). For example, in certain countries, the frequency-hopping capacity has a smaller ceiling than the Bluetooth standard allows. In addition, Bluetooth must ensure it does not follow the way of Unix— that is to say, a basic standard that evolved into many variations. The Bluetooth SIG has started the process of a qualification program that can determine what devices are Bluetooth compliant. Finally, adoption may be limited to the main device that Bluetooth is used for. For example, the expense of having multiple-mode wireless mobile phones to cover the American, European, and Japanese standards means many different phone models. Hence, the availability of Bluetooth may be limited to those phones with mass appeal rather than as a standard add-on to all mobile phones.

Company	Application	Description
Nokia/Fuji	Film development	Using a Nokia phone to upload pictures from a digital camera for development
BlueLinx	Q-Zone	Initiates a quiet zone for a certain area to switch mobile phone ringers off or set them to a vibrate-only mode
Johnson Controls	TravelNote	Allows messages to be recorded on a device for playback in a car
Motorola	TimePort phone	Allows for a Bluetooth connectivity kit that can be used with a wireless headset (sold separately)

Table 13-5.   Sample Commercial Products for Bluetooth

How important will Bluetooth be to the future of wireless? The Gartner Group, a technology research firm, bets Bluetooth will play a key role in uniting 70 percent of new cell phones and 40 percent of new PDAs accessing the Web by 2004. Dataquest predicts 200 million PCs will use Bluetooth technology by 2002. Bluetooth is expected to create about $2 billion in 2001, rising to $333 billion by 2006, according to a Frost and Sullivan study (July 2001). In addition, the same Frost and Sullivan study also predicts that 4.2 million products will be using the Bluetooth technology by 2006.

So does this mean that once Bluetooth has reached mass adoption we will see people discarding some of the other wireless solutions? Most likely not. Because Bluetooth has a low-bandwidth transfer rate, the replacement of 802.11b and other high-capacity wireless solutions is not likely. Bluetooth will most likely remain for its original purpose: to provide connectivity to small, mobile devices.

MESSAGE FOR THE IT MANAGER

Bluetooth can allow for efficient use of mobile devices by keeping them always in sync. The fact that Bluetooth has not yet achieved wide adoption indicates that any significant investment in this area is not prudent.

As for security benefits, it is widely accepted that Bluetooth has the necessary basic security protections. The ability to add applications to enhance the security makes Bluetooth an adequate security architecture for basic use. However, caution must be used because applications will play a vital role in strongly securing Bluetooth devices. Application implementation will then become more important; therefore, the vetting of Bluetooth device applications must be conducted carefully before widespread use.

Bluetooth will have minimal impact initially in the corporate sector because the use of mobile devices is still not a general corporate policy. As a result, the actual IT support of a Bluetooth device will take some years to be established. Companies will most likely support initiatives such as 802.11b before Bluetooth, because 802.11b can replace the need for expensive cabling and data connection points.

In summary, it is recommended that IT management wait for a while to adopt Bluetooth. The current costs, lack of extensive deployment, and available wireless alternatives make it prudent to see how Bluetooth emerges before widespread adoption in the corporate environment.

CHAPTER 14

Tomorrow and Beyond

mCommerce technologies progress so quickly that it is difficult to keep up with the security implications around new applications and functions. This chapter addresses some of the key trends in mCommerce technologies and possible security implications. By keeping aware of future technologies, you can be better suited to address security implications as they arise.

3G/4G NETWORKS

Today's mobile networks have limitations in what they can deliver as content and what transactions they can perform due to data bandwidth issues. See Table 14-1 for a list of networks with their current and expected mobile data rates. It can be seen from this table that the panacea of 3G networks may provide increased data bandwidth that will greatly enhance the value of mobile content and mCommerce, in particular. However, the opportunities brought with 3G, as well as so-called *4G networks* even further in the future, also lead to security issues.

NOTE: The Phillips Group forecasts that subscribers to 3G wireless will grow from 1.7 million in 2002 to 38 million in 2007. Wireless operator revenue opportunity will grow from $4.3 billion in 2002 to $63 billion in 2007. Business subscribers will generate most of this growth, and two thirds of the revenue will come from non-voice services. Infrastructure opportunities will grow from $4 billion to $34 billion in the same period of time. More than 60 percent of this growth will be associated with the new capabilities of 3G.

Always on Means Always Paranoid

The real benefit of 3G networks, from an mCommerce perspective, is the ability to have always-on networks without reduced bandwidth. By allowing for constant Internet communication, new services such as streaming media, video conferences, video phone calls, real-time data alerts, and electronic ticketing are all possible. In addition, targeted location advertisement and other context-based advertisement will create new sources of revenue for the advertising

Generation	Technology	Technical Data Rates	Likely Data Rates
2G	GSM	9.6	
	TDMA (IS136)	9.6 Kbps	
	CDMA	9.6/14.4 Kbps	
2.5G	HSCSD	56 Kbps	20–56 Kbps
	GPRS	115 Kbps	
	EDGE	384 Kbps	
	IS-95B	64 Kbps	
	CDMA2000-1XRTT	144 Kbps	
3G	W-CDMA/UMTS	2 Mbps	384 Kbps for outdoor use and 144 Kbps for driving use
	CDMA2000-3XRTT	2 Mbps	
	TDCDMA	2 Mbps	

Table 14-1. Expected Mobile Data Rates (Source: Morgan Stanley)

industry. As noted in Figure 14-1, the potential growth for wireless advertising is so large, significant investment will take place in this area. With 3G and faster networks, we will see the need for protecting against attacks on mobile devices. Therefore, "always on" means "always paranoid."

Due to concerns over speed and constant connections (and therefore exposure), personal firewalls will need to be utilized for mobile devices such as PDAs and mobile phones. In addition, virus scanners will be needed. The challenge with this new technology is that the speed of data transfer will be much faster than even many office networks. As a result, software-based virus scanners and firewalls will need to be designed to operate much faster. We will explore some of these issues in more details in the following subsections.

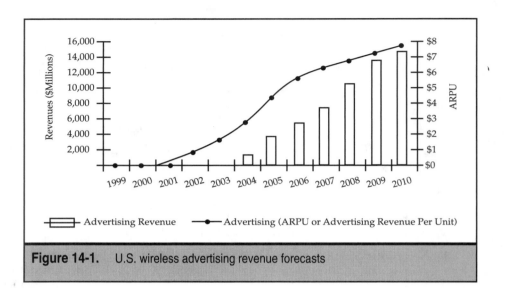

Figure 14-1. U.S. wireless advertising revenue forecasts

Firewall Administration

One of the challenges of any corporate rollout of IT infrastructure is the administration of firewalls and firewall policies. With wired networks, administrators can easily force policies and control a desktop's content. Mobile networks will need to be configured to allow for similar policy deployment and administration. The challenge is this: Because these devices will always be on, and presumably connected to a network, how will administrators force policy changes? Today, policies get updated when a user logs on to a network. However, with 3G+ networks, devices will always be on and presumably always logged in to a network. Therefore, new features of mobile software will need to allow timely and possibly forced updates as per a central corporate security policy.

Content Filtering Based on Context

Given that these devices will always be connected to a network, we can also assume we will get a constant flow of advertisement media or even improper content (for example, pornography). Again, most likely personal firewalls will need to be integrated with these mobile devices to ensure filtering of content. Also, context and geographical information will need to be provided as input to filter out data accordingly. For example, when a salesperson is meeting a customer to make a sale, he may wish to see data and updates related to that customer only. This can be determined by the fact that the salesperson is physically at the customer's site. Customer Relationship Management (CRM) and other applications can be tied to content-filtering software to provide more accurate and relevant data.

Viruses/Worms

Viruses are malicious programs that can destroy files or otherwise damage a computer. *Worms* go one step further than viruses by replicating themselves in addition to damaging computer files. Currently, one of the only reasons that worms do not spread faster than they do is that users log out periodically and disconnect from the Internet.

CAUTION: With always-on devices, worms and viruses will spread with breathtaking speeds.

In addition, we will begin to see the emergence of terrorist or criminal worms/mobile agents. These worms/agents will roam the Internet and either access or destroy critical data based on their particular agenda (versus randomly, as today's malicious software does). Always-on devices allow for a greater timeframe in which to penetrate a system.

Personal Proxies

The future will require every mobile device to have a proxy. This will allow incoming calls or communications to be routed efficiently because it will not be possible to always respond to phone calls, video calls, or incoming live text messages. Therefore, intelligent proxies will need to filter which communications are priorities and deal with them based on existing sets of rules. In addition, proxies can be used to keep user identities (for example, their device MAC or other device numbers) private, behind the proxies. An example of a mobile proxy architecture is shown in Figure 14-2. An advanced example of this concept, known as the *Mobile People Architecture* (MPA), is being developed at Stanford's computer science department. The idea behind MPA is to allow communication to follow users while hiding their personal details (such as e-mail addresses or even names) behind a small proxy-type software.

Roaming

Because many 1G/2G mobile networks and other mobile device networks use various databases to keep track of roaming data, security for 3G networks will have to be carefully protected. Given that users are, in theory, roaming constantly (because they are always connected), operators of wireless networks will need to devise an efficient solution to track roaming and the data of the roaming device, without compromising security.

Digital Rights Management (DRM)

Other challenges in always-on, rich-content networks center around intellectual property protection. An industry called *Digital Rights Management* (DRM) has spawned from the prevalence of stolen

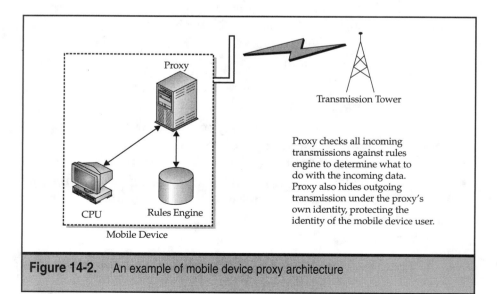

Figure 14-2. An example of mobile device proxy architecture

images and other media on the Internet. DRM's products and services are designed to protect from theft of intellectual property. Currently, most of these DRM services rely on desktop software being modified in some way to read a policy server to access the rights a particular piece of data contains. One challenge with many DRM solutions is that there must be constant communication with a policy server—either a locally cached version or a real-time connection to a central location. 3G networks, being always on, will allow for possible DRM solutions.

Privacy Issues

The other challenge of networks being always on is the decrease of privacy. Recent laws in the U.S. require the ability to track the location of an emergency mobile phone caller. In addition, recent advances in technologies allow for the location tracking of mobile devices even when they are switched off. Some of this technology was used to locate victims in the World Trade Center in the days following the September 11, 2001, terrorist attacks. The search and rescue teams used cutting-edge radio frequency sniffers from Lucent Technologies and other leading wireless companies, such as Verizon, AT&T, Sprint, Nextel, and Skytel, to facilitate tracking down the devices of victims trapped in the rubble.

Current U.S. law requires carriers to have the ability to track the location of an emergency mobile phone caller. However, laws passed in October 2001 now allow law-enforcement agents more access to monitoring and enforcement—sometimes without warrants. These laws were proposed in response to the growing threat of terrorism in the U.S.

4G Networks

Considering that 3G networks are still not in full production, perhaps then it is premature to dream of 4G networks, which promise mind-boggling speeds of 20 Mbps. 4G networks will be based on a technology called *orthogonal frequency division multiplexing* (OFDM). The challenge will be to build mobile devices that can be small enough and last long enough for the additional power requirements of 4G network devices. Although most experts agree that 4G networks are nearly ten years away from being deployed, planning and design for 4G applications has already started. These 4G networks have the same impact that cable modems do today, relative to the standard 56K dial-up modem.

NOTE: The types of security risks will be compounded with 4G networks because the applications will be more complex and more data driven.

Here are some sample applications:

▼ **Virtual navigation** This application allows for a 3D graphical representation for navigational purposes. This requires a central database that will transmit street or internal building layouts to the mobile device. Given that emergency service personnel will be relying on such technology, the integrity of this data will have to be verified at all times. This will require not only encryption to protect the data in transit but also a method of determining when the data was last created to ensure it has not been altered. Such a method will rely on digital signatures for 3D images on a continual basis (that is, a digital signature for each frame of the navigation data being sent). Because the images could be real-time feeds, perhaps from a video feed, it would not be possible to digitally sign a single file.

■ **Tele-medicine** This application allows for a visual description of a medical situation to be transmitted to medical staff physically at another location. A doctor, for example, could guide a paramedic at the scene of an accident concerning how to take immediate emergency action to save a victim's life. This could also be used for doctors and medical personnel to go into the field and retrieve a patient's records. Again, for this application, the privacy of the records and integrity must be maintained and somehow proved to the user. Access to patient and other personal data will also need to be locked down using, for example, biometrics.

▲ **Tele-geoprocessing**   This application describes the ability to vary content based on the geophysical location of a user. A query for the nearest hotel, for example, would be based on the current location of the user. Such systems do bring up concerns of privacy because the location of the user and the queries of the user can be potentially observed by a third party. For example, a medical insurance company may derive certain traits about a consumer's habits based on the restaurants, activities, and other queries made and then judge whether the consumer should be covered under certain medical plans.

WEARABLE COMPUTING

Given the increasing power and shrinking size of computers, it is becoming practical to provide wearable computers. Wearable computers are miniature computer systems designed to fit physically on a person, embedded in clothes or as clip-on/carry-on devices. As mobile networks become faster and standardize on fewer platforms, the idea of having portable computing capability is much more feasible. This concept of a personal area network (PAN) relies on the ability for one PAN to communicate with another and/or a central computer.

From a corporate security and risk-management perspective, wearable computing will become quite a complex issue to manage. Consider that each individual will have a PAN that interacts with many other PANs that, in turn, interact with the wired world. Although practical impacts will not be seen until at least 2005, corporations and individuals will need to start thinking now about the idea of highly dynamic and portable data. Planning around levels of security—to limit types of dataflow and provide automated methods of enforcing data use—will be necessary. If DRM is considered somewhat important today, it will be critical if businesses are to function with wearable systems, given the ease and proliferation of data. In this scenario, a mobile, distributed Napster could be created.

Privacy and security proponents suggest PANs that communicate with each other in a sort of "mobile internet" are preferred over communication with a central station. In this manner, risk is not accumulated by storing people's personal habits or preferences in one location. Risk would be mitigated over smaller communications between PANs.

Other areas of security will arise from applications in augmented reality. This is a newly developing area in which users of wearable computers see the real world with an overlay of information augmented to what is being seen. For example, while taking a museum tour, tourists can wear see-through monitor glasses that allow them to see a painting and a superimposed set of data (such as the painting's history) on top of it. The advantage of these applications is that all sorts of enhancements, including graphics, text, sound, and real-time information, can be applied.

The security implications arise in deciding what information to display, because now the information may have a physical context. Therefore, in our museum example, who is viewing the painting in the museum can affect the data shown. For example, the museum's curator would see items related to donors or maintenance costs, whereas the tourists might see a painter's background and personal history.

WIRELESS LOCAL AREA NETWORKS (WLANS)

The beauty of standards is that there are so many to choose from. Such is the problem with many wireless networks. Currently, it is generally accepted that 802.11b, the main wireless LAN standard used today, is weak. However, new updates to the standards are only beginning to emerge. In addition, newer standards are not compatible with current standards.

It's a given that the major security breaches will be corrected—for example, the wireless encryption protocol (WEP) can be used to provide for encryption over the wireless network connections. Once that occurs, most companies will prefer WLANs over fixed-lined networks. WLANs can easily be reconfigured and are very mobile.

NOTE: In security terms, we judge the level of protection required for data partly based on the exposure time data has to attack.

Because WLANs allow for potentially nonstop exposure, the level of encryption and/or authentication will have to be higher than for the wired Internet. This is also true because WLANs allow access by many more systems than a traditional, wired network would provide.

Generally, WLANs center around the use of laptop computers as the mobile devices because a wireless LAN card is required. As a result, we will see many more laptops with Bluetooth capability to synchronize with devices not using the WLAN network. High-speed transmission capacity is one of the trademarks of WLAN systems, which currently boast transmission rates of up to 155 Mbps (megabits per second). For comparison, dial-up modems transmit at 56 Kbps (kilobits per second; a kilobit is one-thousandth of a megabit), a digital ISDN line transmits at 128 Kbps, and cable modem and DSL connections can transmit up to several Mbps. Given that WLAN can ramp to speeds much faster than other wireless technologies, we will see many more applications from handheld devices that rely on WLAN via the Bluetooth protocol. Figure 14-3 displays an example of the interaction between wired WLANs and Bluetooth networks. Other trends include the creation of public networks, such as in airports. This will allow users, with proper authentication, to work nearly anywhere.

One major challenge with the emergence of these various networks is that there will be a mix of wireless and wired networks. As a result, the network security and related policies must match to accommodate a more complex and possibly more diverse set of security issues. Network architecture will need to separate the wireless subnet from the wired subnet. Internal firewalls will also need to be used in the event the wireless network is somehow compromised (as is very likely today with weak encryption protocols).

NOTE: One key area that will change is how organizations treat and classify data for mobile devices.

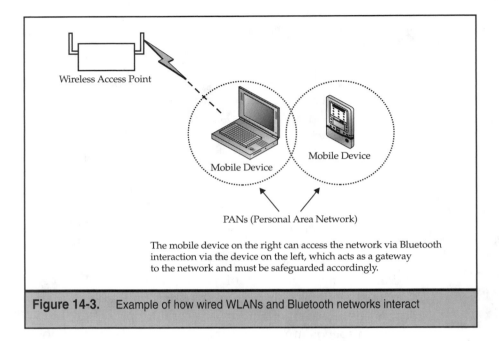

Wireless Access Point

Mobile Device

Mobile Device

PANs (Personal Area Network)

The mobile device on the right can access the network via Bluetooth
interaction via the device on the left, which acts as a gateway
to the network and must be safeguarded accordingly.

Figure 14-3. Example of how wired WLANs and Bluetooth networks interact

For wired systems, such as desktop PCs in offices, backing up and
auditing data is completed within a confined and protected network.
With wireless devices, added complexity arises when a mobile device
is physically lost or stolen. Data in this case is lost, potentially
compromised, and possibly not even backed up. Backing up data
then requires access by a central administrator machine, which in
turn could be a point of compromise. The solution? As mobile devices
become faster, cheaper, and smaller, encrypting all data on a device
will become the easiest and most secure option. In this manner, data
could be uploaded via a syncing mechanism over a wireless network
and stored offsite. Even the data administrators cannot access the
content of the backed up data if it is encrypted.

New standards are in the offing, such as 802.11a, that solve many
of the problems posed by the weaker 802.11b. 802.11a is favored as
the next step in Wi-Fi evolution because it can theoretically reach
speeds of 54 Mbps. This allows for layered security with stronger
encryption. Generally, the more security components we add, the

lower the bandwidth; therefore, many layered approaches to security, such as using public key infrastructure (PKI) and virtual private networks (VPNs), can only be used effectively in higher-bandwidth scenarios. Table 14-2 describes some of the current and future standards for WLANs that will affect how the commercial market for wireless shapes up.

WLAN Standard	Comments
802.11a	Passed standard. Can support up to 54 Mbps.
802.11b	Passed standard. The most common standard used in commercial applications today.
802.11d	Extensions added to 802.11a and 802.11b to compensate for equipment domains outside the U.S.
802.11e	Enhancements to add quality of service (QoS) rules for streaming and other high-quality applications. Not yet ratified.
802.11f	Established extensions to 802.11a and 802.11b to allow users to roam between cell sites.
802.11g	Extension to 802.11b to allow for greater throughput (up to 20 Mbps). Not yet ratified.
802.11i	Provides additional security enhancements to 802.11a and 802.11b but has not yet been ratified.

Table 14-2.   Survey of Existing and Future WLAN Standards

However, as is the issue with all emerging technologies, the battle of standards will rage on. Will 802.11a win out over 802.11g? Will yet another standard appear? We believe that given the delay in 3G rollouts (thus far, limited implementations have only occurred in Korea as of September 2001, with Japan's NTT DoCoMo having delayed its 3G rollout), 802.1x-based wireless standards will dominate. Therefore, corporations will need to address this and take advantage of the benefits of wireless LANs, but also heed the security risks.

WASPS

As we have seen with many IT functions, outsourcing has become popular among CIOs. Wireless Application Service Providers (WASPs) are beginning to gain ground as the outsourced solution to many of the wireless needs of corporations. Analysts believe that wireless ASPs will fall into three main categories: personal, collaborative, and enterprise. The IDC forecasts that all three categories of the wireless ASP space will grow quickly in 2002, totaling $732 million in revenue by 2004. IDC also anticipates that enterprise applications will grow the fastest, achieving a five-year Compound Annual Growth Rate (CAGR) of 125 percent, and that a majority of the revenue will come from companies in the enterprise wireless ASP space. The personal and collaborative wireless ASPs will total $132 million and $211 million, respectively, by 2004. Table 14-3 highlights this further.

WASP Categories	2001 ($M)	2002 ($M)	2003 ($M)	2004 ($M)	CAGR (%)
Personal	14.65	32.46	68.33	131.88	113.7
Collaborative	27.89	63.55	115.47	210.96	119.9
Enterprise	104.35	181.67	281.85	389.31	125.3
Total	146.89	277.68	465.65	732.15	121.4

Table 14-3.   U.S. Wireless ASP Revenue Sources (Source: IDC)

In general, WASPs can be considered quick, thin-client deployments. Applications hosted and served by WASPs include the following:

▼ Commercial applications specifically designed for wireless networks

■ Wireless portal sites

▲ Bridge solutions that provide seamless wireless access to traditional enterprise applications

In general, security for WASPs is very similar to traditional ASPs, consisting of the following measures:

▼ Strong physical security is provided to protect physical access to databases and computer systems. Biometric access is provided to some facilities.

■ Transactions are protected using SSL 3.0 and/or ECC algorithms to ensure privacy and integrity of wireless transactions.

■ Strong Internet protection is provided using IDS, firewalls, strong router policies, and external security monitoring and logging.

▲ Regular audits are provided to ensure that WASPs are security compliant through an SAS70 audit (which provides for best practices in security infrastructure and administrative procedures).

BIOMETRICS

The username/password scheme to protect data is perhaps the oldest known security gate for modern computer systems. Surprisingly, it is still the only security for many companies and applications. Technologies such as PKI help create additional barriers for hackers; however, they are all technologies that are susceptible to attack at the device level. Because mobile devices are more likely to be lost or stolen due to the their small form factor, one must assume that an attack could include theft of the device.

To protect against such attacks, it is necessary to add another layer of security (as shown in Figure 14-4). Well-designed, secure systems must rely on the following:

▼ Something you know (such as a password)

■ Something you have (such as a physical card or certificate)

▲ Something you are (some aspect of your physical body)

Biometrics addresses the last point—something you are. We are beginning to see an increasing number of cases where this technology is being used for security applications, such as tracking criminals. According to the International Biometric Group (IBG), a consultancy in New York, the biometrics space is projected to grow to $594 million by 2003, up from $58.4 million in 1999. Some analysts are even more optimistic. Figures published in the Biometric Industry Report reveal that in 2000, the biometric industry managed to generate a revenue of $196 million, but by 2003, the one-billion dollar mark will be smashed.

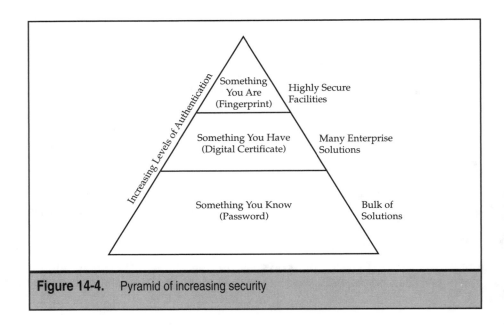

Figure 14-4.   Pyramid of increasing security

Visionics, a company that creates face-matching software, has had its software used to track and match known faces of criminals against real-time camera surveillance in such public places as casinos and sporting events. In cities such as London, every car and person is captured on video at some point in the city limits and matched against a known database of stolen items and criminals.

NOTE: Because changing what you are (for example, your face or fingerprints) is extremely difficult, security based around what you are is considered fairly strong.

So how does this type of technology benefit mobile devices? Mobile devices are becoming increasingly more powerful in terms of processing power. This gives them the ability to perform biometric checks. For example, imagine a mobile phone that activates only after the owner's hand touches the device. Other devices, such as fingerprint-activated badges that emit RF frequencies, can be used in high-traffic areas to create a quick but efficient means of security.

The future of biometrics and mobile devices will converge. Biometrics will become an increasingly useful way of protecting access to devices and thus access to the data the devices contain. In addition, biometrics can provide for protection to mobile devices that are gateways to the networks the devices are part of. One key factor that will increase the adoption of biometrics is the overall cost of these devices. Currently, the price for an average biometric device that reads fingerprints (see Figure 14-5 for an example of a matching dataflow) is about $75–$100 per device.

Considering that high-end PDAs are $500, the cost is still too high for regular use of these devices. As alternatives to fingerprint readers, handwriting-analysis software, for example, is much cheaper since it does not have any hardware components. The downside to this type of software is that it is neither as accurate nor as convenient. One area that biometric devices will be popular in first is as a feature on laptop computers. Identix recently teamed up with Toshiba to deliver a biometric solution as part of Toshiba's laptop offering. When the device debuted, it was around $199. Although high for an add-on, the price is still not too high relative to the $1,000+ price of laptops.

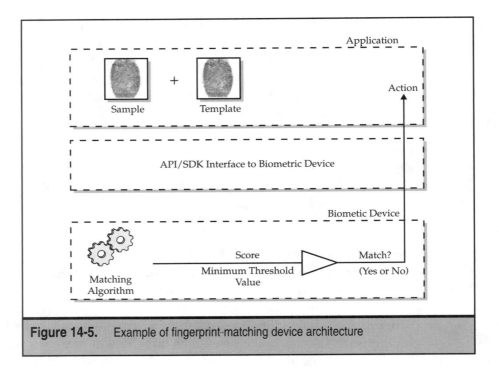

Figure 14-5.   Example of fingerprint-matching device architecture

Just as biometrics is becoming increasingly used, so are attacks against biometric devices. For example, sophisticated criminals can create skin molds to mock certain fingerprints that would pass on the lower-end devices. Lower-end handwriting systems can be defeated through practice. Because many of these attacks will occur on lower-end systems (because the protection will be weaker), biometric attacks are highly likely. The difference with mobile devices is that they will be gateways into corporate or private networks.

NOTE: Attacks on a mobile device in a network can be considered an attack on the network itself.

Other trends in this space include the emergence of biometric aggregators. The concept is that the mobile device manufacturer has to simply work with one company for biometric device use. That one company, in turn, does the work of figuring out how to work with the various devices on the market: fingerprint, iris, retina, hand geometry, and so on. This allows for simpler integration and deployment. Unfortunately, cost and equipment overhead currently make this option too expensive and not practical for mobile devices.

Finally, we will see an increasing trend toward multiple-application integrations. What does this mean for the end consumer? Many headaches! Considering that many devices today are criticized because they do not run all applications smoothly, mobile devices in the future that are considered "secure" will have more of these problems. One example involves signature access to a PDA biometric device. This product works by accepting sample signatures on the PDA. If the sample signature matches a stored, accepted signature, then access is granted. For this solution, Cloakware Corporation, Communication Intelligence Corporation, Neomar, and Certicom all came together to provide a secure way of accessing a PDA to conduct a secured transaction. Changes to one aspect of the solution force all other vendors to possibly adjust their solutions as well, thus creating a chance for a total system failure.

In addition, new trends in wearable computing will also affect the biometric space. As computers become smaller, certain functions can be molded into clothes, wallets, or other common items. Imagine an expensive leather jacket that won't allow any of its pockets to open without the proper person's hand on the zipper! All of this leads to easier access to mobile devices to conduct mCommerce applications.

The use of more advanced and accurate biometrics, such as iris scanning on mobile devices, is still a ways off for everyday devices. Perhaps after the rollout of 3G and more advanced networks we will have devices that have built-in cameras, which may allow for iris scanning. In addition, these devices will have the processing capacity to perform the matching required for such scanners.

Newer technologies such as microelectromechnical systems (MEMS) are micron-sized devices that can measure a user's physical response and act on that response. Because these devices are so small and use less power, there can be significant advances in mobile device features, such as built-in biometrics. According to the Cahners In-Stat Group, MEMS will make up a $1.5 billion market in 2005, showing the potential of their use in all mobile devices.

Companies such as Keyware Technologies and Precise Biometrics are bringing biometric identification to smartcards. In this manner, a card can hold vital information about a device or individual and can then be inserted into a fixed or mobile device after validation of, say, a fingerprint to activate the card. Precise Biometrics' BioCORE is a solution for protecting access to a mobile phone using fingerprint matching.

PUBLIC KEY INFRASTRUCTURE (PKI)

PKI has been described as one of the few solutions that can provide true end-to-end security. Most security discussions thus far have been concerned with protecting data in transit (which PKI does offer as well). However, PKI enables "meCommerce" (mobile/electronic commerce) with the ability to provide nonrepudiation. Nonrepudiation is essential to conducting electronic business because it allows for the legal binding of a person to a transaction.

In the mobile world, as you have seen in this book thus far, the PKI implementation does have some possible security risks. Going forward, many of these risks will be addressed to improve the use of PKI in the mobile world.

One of the first things that must happen for mCommerce to truly thrive will be a narrowing of vendors. Today, there are many combinations and restrictions concerning which mobile devices, browsers, and wireless PKI gateways work together. A consolidation of products and a convergence of standards will allow for quicker adoption. Many vendors currently have to dedicate entire interoperability labs just to determine combinations of the various products. Today, a solution is restricted based on the physical device being used due to compatibility problems.

The other area that will be very important for the development of PKI on mobile platforms is the ability to perform real-time certificate validation. Typically, most mobile PKI implementations deal with the issuance and use of certificates. However, we must also have the ability to check to see whether a certificate is still valid (that is, it has not been revoked). Because certificates are usually valid for up to a year, by default, any event (such as nonpayment of a bill, for example) that might change the status of the certificate needs to be communicated to the relying party. Currently, it is difficult for devices such as mobile phones to download a full revocation list (a.k.a. CRLs). As you have seen in previous chapters, one method to solve this problem is to use short-lived certificates. These short-lived certificates are valid for, say, one day and are associated with a master certificate that would be valid for, say, one year. Although this does work, there is still an exposure period in which the short-lived certificate would be valid versus when the status of the certificate actually changed.

NOTE: The trend in the future will be more powerful mobile devices that can download CRLs very often and/or provide real-time validation of a certificate's validity.

Another topic that needs to be addressed is in the area of key recovery. Mobile devices are small and therefore susceptible to being lost or stolen. This creates a problem when data has been encrypted using a digital certificate, but the private key associated with that certificate has been lost (presumably with the device itself). Therefore, more advanced key-recovery methods are needed. With mobile phones, for the most part, certificates are not being used for the storage of encrypted data but rather to allow for privacy and digital signatures. As mobile devices grow in storage capacity (as is the case with PDAs), the need for encryption and the recovery of an encryption key will be important. Encryption of stored data will also serve (in combination with biometrics) as a method for minimizing damage when a mobile device is stolen.

The last area of the certificate lifecycle that will change in the future is the increased use of code-signing certificates. Code-signing certificates are used in the wired world to indicate the authenticity and integrity of code downloaded or shipped with a computer. As the reliance on dynamic applications and the Internet becomes stronger, it will be necessary for mobile code to be signed and validated. Currently, on most desktop systems, the operating system code and drivers are signed via a code-signing certificate. Today, one of the few mobile platforms that does allow for digital signatures is Qualcomm's BREW developer platform for mobile applications. BREW allows mobile application developers to sign their applications written in this platform via VeriSign Authentic Document Digital ID certificates. These certificates allow the end user to verify the authenticity and integrity of the mobile code. Perhaps over the next several years we will see a trend where devices, including mobile devices, will have the ability to have certificate-signed drivers updated dynamically. The signature of the drivers by the manufacturer will ensure the integrity of the code.

Another area where we will see increased activity is the XML Key Management Specifications (XKMS) initiatives. XKMS appears to have already become a major force in driving easier and quicker certificate enrollment and validation through XML. This will allow for easier portability and use on mobile devices.

Microsoft's initiative, Passport, and competing initiates lead by Sun Microsystems (called the Liberty Alliance) have created virtual identity wallets that can identify a user and his personal details from Internet site to Internet site. This relieves the user from having to log in or enter the same information multiple times. This is perhaps most needed on the mobile space because the form factor does not allow for easy data entry.

It is possible that smartcards could be used in conjunction with the Passport concept. In this scenario, a smartcard would hold personal information that would be forwarded to a merchant using a Passport-enabled site. This would allow the user to take the personal information from device to device.

Finally, the last trend that will affect decision makers is the consolidation and stability of the PKI industry, especially in the mobile market. With the economic and political turmoil of 2001, some financially weak companies are even more suspect for instability.

TIP: Vendor qualification should always include financial analysis and stability.

Table 14-4 shows a breakdown of some key players in the mobile PKI market and how they might fair in continuing their current business.

Company	Financial Stability	Product Offering/Breadth	Customer Base	Comments
Baltimore	Poor	Very good	Popular in Europe and Asia (strong branding)	Near bankruptcy. Has strong branding outside U.S.
Entrust	Average	Good	Good	Products require large upfront investments.
VeriSign	Excellent	Average	Excellent	Leveraging customers base to catch up in mobile space.
Certicom	Poor	Very Good	Very Good	Produces ECC, which is widely used for mobile devices.

Table 14-4. A Survey of Mobile PKI Players and a Snapshot of Their Stability

The trend that must happen to increase mobile security involves mobile devices using Transport Layer Security (TLS) versus Wireless Transport Layer Security (WTLS), which provides authentication, privacy, and integrity for the Wireless Application Protocol based on the widely used TLS v1.0. The "gap in WAP" problem in the WTLS architecture occurs due to the fact that traffic must be translated to/from TLS/WTLS. The "gap" is basically a small fraction of time in which the data is exposed during the conversions. I-Mode, for example, can use TLS, thus not only simplifying the roll out of mobile phone services but also allowing them to be safer.

MOBILE TRANSACTIONS

In the world of mCommerce, money indeed makes the world go 'round. As the prevalence of mobile device increases, so will the use of these devices for micro payments. Visions of paying for vending machine products or petrol purchases make mCommerce ideal because through various options, such as debit cards, smartcards, and even some form of credit card payments, payment processing costs can be brought down substantially. The IDC predicts that by 2004, mCommerce transactions will reach approximately $20 billion in the U.S., with each user spending an average of $75 per month on mCommerce transactions (see Table 14-5).

Payment Strategies

The concept of using mobile devices, such as mobile phones, to pay for goods has appeared in a number of European markets. In the rest of the world, the concept of paying for a vending machine item with a mobile phone is still very remote. However, given the low transaction fees for such methods of micropayment, this will grow in the future as a replacement for payments that are normally done using small amounts of currency.

TIP: Any mobile payment strategy should start in Europe or Asia, because there is a higher adoption rate for such technologies. North America is still highly dependent on hard currency and credit card transactions.

mCommerce Transaction Value per Subscriber	2001 ($)	2002 ($)	2003 ($)	2004 ($)	CAGR (%)
Average value ($)	25.00	40.00	60.00	75.00	58.1
Growth (%)	108.3	60.0	50.0	25.0	

Table 14-5.   U.S. Average Monthly Value of mCommerce Transactions Per Subscirber (Source: IDC)

An interesting twist on payments is provided by a service called CoCyph, based on the work by V-Sync, currently designed for the Japan market. This system works on a device that is clipped onto a mobile phone. When a consumer enters a retail store, he proceeds to checkout at the cash register as usual. The store register transmits the purchase data via IrDA to the add-on device (called Puritama). The Puritama device then sends the payment information, via the mobile phone, for clearing. Once the back-end network confirms proper credit, the response comes back via the Puritama device to the register to print the receipt. Security protection will eventually use RF-ID (the product is still in an evolutionary state), and certification will use so-called *packet keys*. This physical device can also be used for authentication for ticketed events and other functions requiring authentication of an individual.

Another example of future trends includes the Wincor Nixdorf payment-authorization solution. In this solution, the cashier in a retail store scans a computer-generated barcode on the user's mobile phone. Through the PaymentWorks system from Brokat Technologies, the information is sent and reconciled with various payment processors. The assumption in this system is that access to the mobile phone (to generate the barcode, which is scanned at the point of sale) is under the control and access of the phone's owner. Using a PIN or similar scheme, the phone remains locked until the user is ready to conduct a transaction.

Smartcard Roles in the Future

Although the majority of mobile phones use a S/WIM card (Subscriber Wireless Identity Module), there is a trend toward equipping mobile phones and even PDAs with slots for credit card–sized smartcards. In this manner, smartcards can be used for wired and wireless transactions.

Barcode Transactions

An April 2001 IDC study noted that barcodes embedded in mobile phones will be a key trend in the future. The idea of using an embedded barcode scanner in a mobile device provides the ability to scan a product for purchase, research, or related activities. If combined with digital signature technologies (via WTLS), proof of purchase could be strengthened as the combination of the physical scan with a digital certificate signature, and potentially a device certificate that ties the phone to the user, can more easily bind a user to a transaction.

Another unique application is the NTT DoCoMo service of mobile phone vending, released in trial mode back in September 2001. The vending machine authenticates the user by scanning information that appears on the screen of the mobile phone. However, to add personalization to the purchase, the vending machine displays the user's name. Privacy advocates have pointed out that this is a major flaw because vending machines are always in public places. This brings up the concern, in general, that formerly cash transactions, now performed by mobile devices, cause consumers to lose their anonymity.

Mini-servers

One very interesting application of using smartcards and mobile phones is the development of a mini–web server designed by Microsoft. This server, called the WebCamSIM, is designed to run on a Global System for Mobile Communications (GSM) SIM card. This mini-server can serve text to computers over the Internet. Such a server could be used as a platform for dynamic payment applications via the SMS messaging platform used to send messages from device to device. The security of this relies on the GSM security, because a standard GSM mobile phone is used. However, GSM SIM cards generate a 40-bit key that was shown to be crackable as far back as 1999. If these mini-servers do gain in popularity, we may also see mini-server certificates to allow for an encrypted tunnel between the client and the mini-server, as is done with regular Secure Sockets Layer (SSL) certificates and web servers today.

IDS

An intrusion detection system (IDS) is used to detect hacking attempts in real time and to take some action based on the information a system has. Very good systems can tell the difference between a bad query and an actual hacking attempt. Actions can range from prevention and banning of further communication from the malicious source, redirection to another resources, and even real-time paging of key personnel.

In most corporate security infrastructures, intrusion detection systems are placed behind a sensitive network-defense location, such as a firewall.

TIP: A good intrusion detection system employs real-time attack-detection capability. However, you must have a good response team and strategy on hand to fully leverage the capabilities of real-time notification.

However, in mobile systems, many access points bypass the traditional wired security defenses or create problems because the sheer number of perimeter defenses must increase. In these cases, more intrusion detection systems need to be placed around the network.

The trend for perimeter defense will most likely need to evolve to allow for some type of centralized IDS with monitoring agents behind key mobile access points. Perhaps even end-user mobile devices may have agents that can relay back hacking attempts to simply drop that device from the network to avoid an actual compromise. With more prevalent and smaller devices such as mobile phones and wearable computing, this becomes an issue because these devices are entry points into a network, but they are more easily penetrated than wired access points. Therefore, these mobile points are going to be where future attacks will originate. Mobile intrusion detection systems will evolve to address these issues. Figure 14-6 highlights an example of what these new systems might look like.

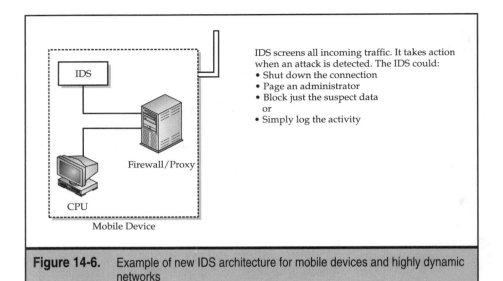

IDS screens all incoming traffic. It takes action when an attack is detected. The IDS could:
- Shut down the connection
- Page an administrator
- Block just the suspect data
  or
- Simply log the activity

Figure 14-6. Example of new IDS architecture for mobile devices and highly dynamic networks

Intrusion detection systems will also have to address distributed denial of service (DDoS) attacks, which will become more prevalent as mobile access to networks becomes increasingly popular. A denial of service (DoS) attack occurs when a particular service is not available to legitimate users of a resource due to maligned or abnormally large numbers of requests from an attacker. A DDoS attack follows the same idea, as shown in Figure 14-7, but it is an attack from many different machines, all targeting the same resource.

In this manner, even if one attacker system could be traced and eliminated, there would be many more performing the same attack. Because mobile devices are expected to exceed the number of fixed wired devices in the future, we can be certain DDoS attacks will take the limelight over the next few years. In addition, DDoS attacks now have many options with wireless/mobile space. The typical TCP/IP attacks are still available, but now RF and frequency jamming, victim calling charges, and so on are new ways DDoS attacks could be launched.

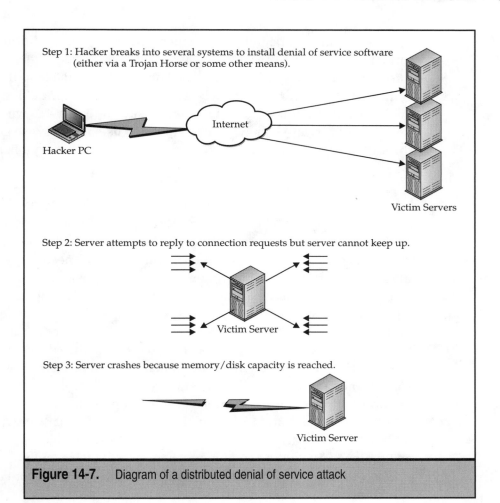

Step 1: Hacker breaks into several systems to install denial of service software
        (either via a Trojan Horse or some other means).

Internet

Hacker PC

Victim Servers

Step 2: Server attempts to reply to connection requests but server cannot keep up.

Victim Server

Step 3: Server crashes because memory/disk capacity is reached.

Victim Server

Figure 14-7.   Diagram of a distributed denial of service attack

RENTING SOFTWARE

The trend increasingly in the wired world has been to rent software
rather than actually sell it for a fixed price and unlimited use. The
concept of "checking out software," much as one would check out a
movie from a video store, is based around the idea that on a per-use

basis, software will be initially cheaper for the user. In addition, each time the user checks out the software, it will be the latest version. The major obstacle here has been the bandwidth available to the computers to allow for such large applications to be updated rapidly. With the advent of fast mobile networks, such as 3G or 4G, we could see mobile software being "checked out" for use or otherwise go through forced updates and accounting via the software publisher.

CAUTION: We have seen with Microsoft that in some cases, new licensing schemes around "renting" software may actually cost more in the long run.

In this model, entirely new security mechanisms need to be in place. The software must maintain integrity in transit, the user must be properly identified to ensure proper accounting/billing, and quality of service (QoS) models must be in place so that if the update of the software is interrupted, the software or data is not left in a vulnerable state. The challenge will be to increase the speed at which this security can be offered, although many of the pieces to this solution already exist for the wired world. For example, a common method of protecting transactions in transit on the Internet is via SSL. SSL, however, adds additional CPU load and usually requires additional hardware and/or numerous servers to be able to adequately serve online customers properly. Likewise, mobile operators may face similar issues with authentication and concurrent sessions.

MESSAGE FOR THE IT MANAGER

This chapter has addressed the security impact of various mCommerce trends. As corporations plan for future IT expenditures, they must recognize that mobile devices will play a significant role in the future of corporate IT. The future of mobile devices will require a new way of thinking to address security concerns. The main areas addressed in this chapter are detailed next.

3G/4G Networks

So how does the IT Manager prepare for 3G/4G network issues? Here are some key areas to focus on:

▼ There's a need for firewalls, content filtering, antivirus software, and personal proxies at the mobile device level.

■ There's a need for secure roaming functions and secure exchange of data while roaming.

■ DRM is necessary because content won't be limited to a small number of fixed workstations but rather billions of mobile devices in a few years.

▲ Privacy will decrease as functions such as location targeting are merged with mobile devices.

Biometrics

Increasingly, biometrics will be needed to secure mobile devices, because these devices will become more powerful gateways into always-on networks. Faster mobile devices will allow for a varied number of biometric options. It is highly recommended that any security infrastructure lock down, at the very least, the most important assets with biometric devices.

Types of biometrics that are feasible include the following:

▼ **Iris scanning**   There's no contact with the eye, so this solution is easy and safe.

■ **Hand geometry**   This solution is not as quick as iris scanning, but it's cheaper.

▲ **Fingerprint**   This is the cheapest and simplest option.

WLANs

The promise of quick and dynamic deployment of wireless LANs is here today. However, the numerous security risks due to a lack of strong encryption implementations has prevented robust, secure systems from being deployed. In general, unless organizations see an absolute need for WLANs, these should be avoided until newer standards address the security risks, or the weak out-of-box security should be supplemented with additional encryption/authentication.

Wearable Computers

As mobile devices become even more portable and, potentially, part of daily items such as our clothes, the risk of security being compromised increases. Again, personal firewalls, proxies, and content filters will be required for these devices, especially because they may participate in dynamic personal area networks (PANs), exchanging data with other PANs many times during the course of a single day.

WASPs

Increasingly, outsourcing wireless functions will become the most feasible option for companies that do not view wireless technology as their core competency. As a result, security is a major issue because many companies are making their core data functions, such as CRM or Sales Force Automation data, available via wireless devices. We expect more consolidation in this space, so if you are considering using a WASP, we suggest you examine the following key points:

▼ The type of architecture (most have their own propriety designs)

■ Security mechanisms (both physical and logical)

▲ Financial stability

PKI

Although PKI may not be the answer to everything, it is a critical component of a secure infrastructure. As weaknesses occur in emerging technologies, PKI becomes even more critical for providing authentication, privacy, integrity, and nonrepudiation. PKI should be part of any IT infrastructure.

GLOSSARY

Meta-Glossary
of Terms

American Society for Information Science and Technology   This site contains a comprehensive glossary of well-defined wireless terms for the communications industry.

http://www.asis.org/Bulletin/Jun-01/wireless_terms.html

BlackHat   The ultimate hacker forum. This site contains information on their conferences and training and is well worth exploring for hackers looking to enhance their knowledge. Keep in mind, however, that FBI agents do attend meetings to keep an eye on the hacker/cracker community.

http://www.blackhat.com/

Cellular Networking Perspectives   This site contains definitions of over 1,500 wireless telecom and networking terms, including many data networking and security terms.

http://www.cnp-wireless.com/glossary.html

Computerworld   The following link takes you to a list of links to security sites, including a number that focus on mobile/wireless security.

http://www.computerworld.com/cwi/research_links/alpha/
0,1897,NAV63-129-1375-1385,00.html

Gartner's 2000 Glossary of Mobile and Wireless Terms   Created by the Gartner Group, this site includes a comprehensive list of most wireless and mCommerce terms in PDF format. The terms are very well explained.

http://www.ecu.edu/si/new_design/pdf/gartner_glossary.pdf

ISC2   Created by the well-recognized security certification organization, this site has information on how to get certified as well as how to train and prepare for the CISSP exam. This site is a good resource for security job posters and seekers.

http://www.isc2.org/

mCommerce Times   This online mobile commerce magazine displays definitions of the latest mobile and wireless terms.

http://www.mcommercetimes.com/glossary

Microsoft Corporation   This web site contains a list of commonly used terms, acronyms, and definitions relating to the emerging mobile and wireless technology industries.

http://www.microsoft.com/business/mobility/moglossary.asp

Mobile Bugs   This mailing list focuses on mobile phone vulnerabilities.

http://developers.of.pl/mobileBugs/

Personal Communications Industry Association   This web site contains a large list of common wireless terms.

http://www.pcia.com/wirelesscenter/resources_glossary_a2m.htm

PKI Forum   Business-oriented site for PKI-related activities. This site organizes material by region and related security issues for that region. The site also lists some of the companies involved in the security space by area of focus.

http://www.pkiforum.org/

Red-Tower   A jargon free source of information on mobile technologies, this site site contains a downloadable glossary of commonly used mCommerce terms.

http://www.red-tower.com/toolbox/glossary.asp

SANS Institute   This site is a good place to learn about various security topics, and the institute also hosts some conferences and tutorials on computer and network security.

http://www.sans.org/newlook/home.htm

Search Security   Security portal with news, links, and technical updates.

http://searchsecurity.techtarget.com/home/0,,sid14,00.html

Security Focus   A good, general security portal that includes a nice set of links based on area of interest. Although weak in the mobile space, this site is a good place to learn about general computer security issues.

http://www.securityfocus.com/

The Wireless Advisor   An online consumer service site for wireless professionals with brief definitions of terms commonly used in the wireless communications industry.

http://wirelessadvisor.com/Glossary.cfm

Webopedia   This site is a comprehensive encyclopedia of mobile and wireless technology terms. In most cases, you should be able to find the definition here. This site contains an easy-to-use text-based search engine to find the term you want simply by entering it into the search window.

http://www.webopedia.com/

Index

NOTE: Page numbers in *italics* refer to illustrations or tables.

 A

▼ D

R

X

INTERNATIONAL CONTACT INFORMATION

AUSTRALIA
McGraw-Hill Book Company Australia Pty. Ltd.
TEL +61-2-9417-9899
FAX +61-2-9417-5687
http://www.mcgraw-hill.com.au
books-it_sydney@mcgraw-hill.com

CANADA
McGraw-Hill Ryerson Ltd.
TEL +905-430-5000
FAX +905-430-5020
http://www.mcgrawhill.ca

**GREECE, MIDDLE EAST,
NORTHERN AFRICA**
McGraw-Hill Hellas
TEL +30-1-656-0990-3-4
FAX +30-1-654-5525

MEXICO (Also serving Latin America)
McGraw-Hill Interamericana Editores S.A. de C.V.
TEL +525-117-1583
FAX +525-117-1589
http://www.mcgraw-hill.com.mx
fernando_castellanos@mcgraw-hill.com

SINGAPORE (Serving Asia)
McGraw-Hill Book Company
TEL +65-863-1580
FAX +65-862-3354
http://www.mcgraw-hill.com.sg
mghasia@mcgraw-hill.com

SOUTH AFRICA
McGraw-Hill South Africa
TEL +27-11-622-7512
FAX +27-11-622-9045
robyn_swanepoel@mcgraw-hill.com

**UNITED KINGDOM & EUROPE
(Excluding Southern Europe)**
McGraw-Hill Education Europe
TEL +44-1-628-502500
FAX +44-1-628-770224
http://www.mcgraw-hill.co.uk
computing_neurope@mcgraw-hill.com

ALL OTHER INQUIRIES Contact:
Osborne/McGraw-Hill
TEL +1-510-549-6600
FAX +1-510-883-7600
http://www.osborne.com
omg_international@mcgraw-hill.com

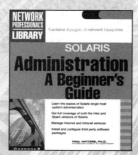

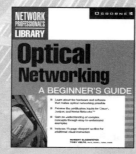